Digital Work in the Planetary Market

Digital Work in the Planetary Market

Edited by Mark Graham and Fabian Ferrari

The MIT Press
Cambridge, Massachusetts
London, England

International Development Research Centre
Ottawa • Amman • Dakar • Montevideo • Nairobi • New Delhi

Published by the MIT Press.

A copublication with
International Development Research Centre
PO Box 8500
Ottawa, ON K1G 3H9
Canada
www.idrc.ca/info@idrc.ca

The research presented in this publication was carried out with the financial assistance of Canada's International Development Research Centre. The views expressed herein do not necessarily represent those of IDRC or its Board of Governors.

The MIT Press would like to thank the anonymous peer reviewers who provided comments on drafts of this book. The generous work of academic experts is essential for establishing the authority and quality of our publications. We acknowledge with gratitude the contributions of these otherwise uncredited readers.

This book was set in Stone Serif and Stone Sans by Westchester Publishing Services. Printed and bound in the United States of America.

Library of Congress Cataloging-in-Publication Data

Names: Graham, Mark, 1980– editor. | Ferrari, Fabian, editor.
Title: Digital work in the planetary market / edited by Mark Graham and Fabian Ferrari.
Description: Cambridge, Massachusetts : The MIT Press, 2022. | Series: The MIT Press-International Development Research Centre series | Includes bibliographical references and index.
Identifiers: LCCN 2021037262 | ISBN 9780262543767 (paperback)
Subjects: LCSH: Employees—Effect of technological innovations on—Case studies. | Industrial productivity—Effect of technological innovations on—Case studies. | Electronic commerce—Case studies.
Classification: LCC HD6331 .D527 2022 | DDC 331.25—dc23/eng/20211208
LC record available at https://lccn.loc.gov/2021037262

10 9 8 7 6 5 4 3 2 1

Contents

Acknowledgments

The book has benefited from the conversations, debates, and political engagements that the authors have engaged in as part of the Fairwork and Geonet projects based at the Oxford Internet Institute, University of Oxford. Thank you very much to Daniel Abs, Iftikhar Ahmad, María Belen Albornoz, Moritz Altenried, Paula Alves, Branka Andjelkovic, Amir Anwar, Arturo Arriagada, Amri Asmara, Tat Chor Au-Yeung, Priashish Basak, Alessio Bertolini, Louise Bezuidenhout, Gautam Bhatia, Richard Boateng, Manuela Bojadzijev, Macarena Bonhomme, Maren Borkert, Fabian Brasemann, Rodrigo Carelli, Sonata Cepik, Chi Chan, Henry Chávez, Aradhana Cherupara Vadekkethil, Matthew Cole, Paska Darmawan, Stefano De Sabbata, Markieta Domecka, Veena Dubal, Darcy du Toit, Trevilliana Eka Putri, Chris Foster, Milena Franke, Sandra Fredman, Rafael Grohmann, Khadiga Hassan, Richard Heeks, Kelle Howson, Francisco Ibáñez, Svitlana Iukhymovych, Vladan Ivanovic, Tanja Jakobi, Athar Jameel, Hannah Johnston, Zoran Kalinic, Srujana Katta, Chris King, Maja Kovac, Martin Krzywdzinski, Larry Kwan, Jorge Leyton, Oscar Javier Maldonado, Shabana Malik, Claudia Marà, Évilin Matos, Paul Mungai, Tasnim Mustaque, Mounika Neerukonda, Sidra Nizamuddin, Sanna Ojanperä, Abigail Osiki, Amelinda Pandu, Balaji Parthasarathy, Leonhard Plank, Valeria Pulignano, Jack Qui, Ljubivoje Radonjić, Ananya Raihan, Pablo Aguera Reneses, Nagla Rizk, Nancy Salem, Julice Salvagni, Derly Yohanna Sánchez Vargas, Murali Shanmugavelan, Janaki Srinivasan, Fabian Stephany, Shelly Steward, Ralph Straumann, Sophie Sun, Pradyumna Taduri, Pitso Tsibolane, Anna Tsui, Funda Ustek-Spilda, Jean-Paul Van Belle, Michel Wahome, Jing Wang, Robbie Warin, Nadine Weheba, and Zermina.

The beginnings of this book emerged from an International Development Research Centre (IDRC)–supported research project ("Microwork and Virtual Production Networks in Sub-Saharan Africa and Southeast Asia") that took us to Malaysia, the Philippines, Vietnam, Ghana, Nigeria, and South Africa. In each of those six countries, we spoke with digital workers, managers of outsourcing companies, and policymakers.

Thank you to everyone who spoke with us, and thank you to IDRC for generously funding that research.

We were brilliantly assisted by the invaluable editing expertise of David Sutcliffe, and Christina Nichols. Thank you for so thoughtfully and thoroughly engaging with each text.

This book would not exist without Nola Haddadian and the team at IDRC. Nola—we acknowledge with gratitude the many ways you have offered encouragement, guidance, and support. Indeed, it is through IDRC's support that we are able to release this book under an open access license.

We also wish to thank the funders of our research for trusting us to tackle head-on pressing problems in the world of work and giving us the space and time to step back, reflect, think, and write. We acknowledge the Alan Turing Institute under the Engineering and Physical Sciences Research Council (EPSRC) grant EP/N510129/1, the German Federal Ministry for Economic Cooperation and Development (BMZ) and the Deutsche Gesellschaft für Internationale Zusammenarbeit (GIZ), the UK Economic and Social Research Council (ESRC) (ES/S00081X/1), the Leverhulme Trust (PLP-2016–155), the Ford Foundation, and the European Research Council (ERC-2013-StG335716-GeoNet). While working on this book, Fabian was supported by the ESRC under grant ES/P000649/1, studentship number 2094254, as part of the Grand Union Doctoral Training Partnership (DTP) and the University of Oxford (Scatcherd European Scholarship).

Both editors would like to thank the inspiring and encouraging students, staff members, and faculty at the Oxford Internet Institute and at Green Templeton College.

Mark would like to thank his parents, Jean and Hashem, for giving him a planetary perspective; David Keeling and Matt Zook for crucial inspiration on the journey that led here; and Kat for always inspiring the next steps.

Fabian would like to thank David Feeny for his invaluable advice. A special thanks goes to Gabrielle for her patience and support, and to Fabian's parents, Claudia and Hermann, for everything.

Finally, a thank-you to all of the book's authors. This book was written and edited during the COVID-19 pandemic, and we are immensely grateful to each of the authors for contributing under such difficult conditions.

1 Introduction

Mark Graham and Fabian Ferrari

In a rural Ugandan town, a day's drive from the nearest international airport, a few abandoned shipping containers sat beneath a communication mast. On one side of the mast was the main road linking the region to the rest of the country. You could almost miss the shipping containers from the road, hidden as they were behind a small kiosk selling snacks, sodas, and mobile phone credit. On the other side lay a dry playing field. A few boys kicked a ball around, and a hen and her chicks scurried to get out of the way.

This might seem an unlikely location for work that goes into developing the next generation of consumer-facing technologies. But that is exactly what was happening there. In 2012, a foreign-owned company put a few computers into shipping containers, powered them with generators, and connected them to the Internet wirelessly. Workers were then hired to train machine learning systems, run by companies in the Americas, Europe, and Asia, by classifying and annotating images and videos (Anwar and Graham 2020).

By 2017, when one of us visited, the demand for such work had increased so much that the work had been moved out of the shipping containers and into a much larger office space (see figure 1.1). Here, 300 people worked in shifts to classify data for foreign clients. On most of the workers' screens were street-level photographs of North American suburbs, and workers were carefully drawing the outlines of everything in the images in front of them: cars, pavement, buildings—even birds!

When asked to describe what they were doing, most workers responded—quite rightly—that they were annotating images. But when pressed for more detail, *why* the client wanted these images annotated or what they might be doing with them, the response was simply "They don't tell me; they just want lots of tagged images."

These are jobs that look as if they can be done from literally anywhere—in Antarctica or on a floating barge—apart from one key factor: the requirement for workers who are willing and able to carry out that labor. It is this tension that *Digital Work in the Planetary Market* explores. The digital revolution, coupled with widespread Internet

Figure 1.1
An AI training center in rural East Africa.
Source: Anwar and Graham (2020).

connectivity, means that work is becoming ever more connected, and the global production networks[1] that link workers and clients together are tapping into ever more
people, places, and processes worldwide. In this book, we have sought to bring together
a diverse range of perspectives in order to understand this process and what it means
for work and workers today.

Our entry point is the fact that an increasing amount of human activity, and with
it an increasing amount of work, is digitally mediated. Even the most intimate and
physically present of human exchanges—seeking medical advice, the dealing of drugs,
sexual intimacy—can generate all manner of digital data, faithfully captured by the
devices that are never far from us today. That data, then, becomes the raw material for
vast amounts and flows of human labor that transcend national boundaries—that have
apparently escaped the stickiness of geography, have become untethered from place.
From call center workers in Newcastle, to on-demand essay writers in Nairobi, to personal assistants in Nashville, to microworkers classifying images in New Delhi, workers
are increasingly enrolled into systems that analyze, transform, and build other services
and products with, and from, digital data.

Many of the world's most valuable companies rely on planetary networks of digital
work that underpin their products and services. These transnational connections can
lead to some unexpected outcomes. For example, third-party contractors around the
world transcribing audio for Apple to improve the automated speech assistant Siri have
overheard confidential medical information, drug deals, and recordings of American

couples having sex—all faithfully recorded by smart devices like the HomePod and Apple Watch (Hern 2019). Amazon's contractors in Costa Rica, India, and Romania are paid to structure, annotate, and organize conversations captured by Alexa to train Amazon's speech recognition systems (Day, Turner, and Drozdiak 2019). Google contractors label recordings of Google Assistant (Wong 2019), and Facebook uses Indian contractors to transcribe the private audio chats of users (Frier 2019). For some commentators, these revelations represent an extraordinary privacy scandal. However, these cases also neatly demonstrate that work and the networks that extract value from it are increasingly embedded into planetary systems. As ever more work is commodified and traded beyond local labor markets, we want to focus in this book on those systems of economic production and consumption that purport to transcend—or at least pay little attention to—the locations in which work is actually done.

For most of human history, economic production and transactions have required a certain amount of both synchronicity and proximity (Graham and Anwar 2018). Proximity afforded the synchronicity that was needed for the exchange of money; the exchange of goods; offers to buy and sell labor; and the exchange of both codified and tacit knowledge about the goods being exchanged, and the parties exchanging them (Fevre 1992). While labor markets did not necessarily require a *fixed* time and place for exchange, they did need *some sort of* time and place—if only because users of any market need to know when and where exchange can happen. But if work is now increasingly digital and transmittable across time and space, how does that affect the temporal and spatial nature of labor exchange?

As both transportation and communication technologies have advanced, technologies—and control of the infrastructures and systems that we build on top of them—have been used to command both time and space (Castells 2000; Harvey 2001). With each new technological revolution—from the steamship to the telegraph to the Internet—the world has shrunk. Fiber-optic cables now connect every major inhabited corner of the planet (Graham, Andersen, and Mann 2015). This command of space— through the vast infrastructures that have been overlaid onto all continents and seas (figure 1.2)—has also annihilated the temporal barriers to virtual exchange. With a few exceptions, those cables—and associated wireless networks—allow almost anyone anywhere to instantaneously connect to anyone else anywhere else to synchronously communicate via the exchange of files, data, video, and audio.

This apparent annihilation of time/space, of course, is not a new observation. In the 1990s, cyberutopians imagined that the Internet would bring into being a "cyberspace" that would allow humanity to coexist in virtual form. As John Perry Barlow famously announced at Davos in 1996, in his "Declaration of the Independence of Cyberspace":

Figure 1.2
Arrival of the first submarine fiber-optic cable into East Africa in the Kenyan coastal city of Mombasa on June 12, 2009. East Africa was the last major populated part of the planet to be connected to the planetary grid.
Source: Alamy.

"I come from Cyberspace, the new home of Mind. On behalf of the future, I ask you of the past to leave us alone. You are not welcome among us. You have no sovereignty where we gather." In this compelling vision, our material realities could be shed—simply left behind and transcended. By the first decade of the twenty-first century, however, a rather different vision of planetary unity was being advanced: not one in which everyone would be transported into the same "cyberspace," but rather one in which the world's spatial frictions would simply cease to be. Thomas L. Friedman's *The World Is Flat* (2005) perhaps best captured this imaginary of annihilated spatial frictions. Under this worldview, the planet becomes a truly level playing field in which anything can in theory be done from anywhere (Graham 2015).

What united both visions was an unrestricted extrapolation that turned a simple fact (i.e., that information and communication technologies afford widespread synchronous connectivity) into metaphors in order to make rather bombastic claims: of the death of distance, of a flat world, and of a utopian virtual cyberspace existing somewhere beyond the realm of the real. However, those visions—while obviously neat and compelling—belie the myriad ways that place, proximity, and positionality still matter.

Indeed, geographers responded to these claims with full force—producing article after article arguing that despite this wiring of the world, "geography still matters!" (Morgan 2004; Clare 2013). As often happens in the wake of these sorts of claims about technology when they suddenly chime with the public's imagination, the amount of energy taken to refute exaggerated claims about "the end of geography" was much greater than the energy taken to produce them. But even as scholars worked to critique and take apart overblown claims about the end of geography and the death of distance, the central ideas within those assertions were taken up even more broadly in talk of the "global." Whether it be "globalization," the "global market," or even the "global village," the *global* references something that is somewhere else from us but also nowhere in particular—a spaceless place that is at once everywhere and nowhere.

Our goal in bringing together this book—and the many different perspectives it contains—is to move beyond the "death of distance," the "world is flat," and the "geography still matters" propositions that have long shaped globalization discourses. We instead use the term *planetary* to return to a fundamentally different understanding of a worldwide market: a world of interconnections. Place, proximity, and positionalities will never be fully transcended—even digital data must be transmitted over physical infrastructure and will reside in a physical server, which will sit in a particular place and jurisdiction—but the planetary scale of connectivity means that they now matter in profoundly different ways. We wish to emphasize the globe-spanning nature of contemporary networks without resorting to an understanding of "the global" as a place beyond space. This framing forces us not to imagine away the always-existing economic geographies of work but to ask empirical, theoretical, and normative questions about how they will shape and be shaped by planetary-scale interactions and transactions.

From that starting point, this book ties together two core lines of inquiry. First, it attempts to understand how work itself is transforming within a planetary market, asking what it means to experience work in a digital production network, how artificial intelligence (AI) changes the spatial embeddedness of work processes, and what possibilities workers—when they sit in opaque networks of production—have to decommodify and improve the conditions under which they work. Second, the book seeks to understand and dissect the wider systems, networks, and processes that shape and give shape to digital work in the planetary market. It asks how transnational networks of machines and workers fuse together in value chains; how those networks and actors leverage, shape, and are shaped by economic geographies; how the relative materiality, immateriality, embeddedness, and disembeddedness of digital work influence actors who both extract value from it and perform it; and how the various forms of governance and unevenness within these planetary networks might be theorized.

Of course, to chase the history of planetary thinking in the social sciences is to chase a ghost. The very term *planetary thinking* is contested, ubiquitous, and difficult to grasp. In this chapter, it is therefore not our ambition to provide an etymological or intellectual history of planetary thinking in the social sciences. Rather we deploy the concept of the planetary market to shed light on networks of work that are characterized by planetary reach, by conjunctural geographies, by fragmentation and clustering, by platforms of commodification, and by planetary competition and resistance. We expand on each of these characteristics below.

Planetary Reach

At the time of writing in early 2021, over five billion people are connected to the Internet—almost two-thirds of the world's population.[2] Outside of North Korea, there are no cities or large towns in which it is difficult to obtain a high-speed Internet connection. In theory, one can connect from just about anywhere on Earth to the worldwide network. As a result, an increasing amount of the world's work is digitally transmitted over those cables; indeed, in many industries, production, coordination, and delivery can all be conducted digitally. Connectivity, for most uses, now potentially ceases to be a factor that determines the geography of production—nowhere is now off the map of connectivity.

From the 1980s onward, the liberalization of international trade and advances in international shipping and telecommunications networks ushered in an increasingly internationalized interconnectedness of economic activity, along with intensifying competition. The changes in the nature of global supply chains and employment that started during this time are still happening today. On a corporate level, firms began to restructure their activities, offshoring and outsourcing peripheral functions to take advantage of geographic variation in skills, costs, and institutional environments and increase flexibility and competitiveness. On a worldwide level, this corporate restructuring has led to the emergence of new international divisions of labor, in which not just certain industries but certain functions within industries have concentrated in specific locations. Perhaps most noticeably, lead firms in high-labor-cost countries have outsourced and offshored back-office work into massive service centers located in lower-labor-cost countries, including India and the Philippines (Peck 2017).

This book asks how today's digital geographies will shape the world of work to come, similarly to how the geography of connectivity in the 1980s and 1990s profoundly shaped the economic geographies of outsourcing and offshoring. For example, in chapter 7, Brett Neilson explores Chinese digital behemoth Alibaba's creation of a so-called Digital

Free Trade Zone in Malaysia. He argues that, far from being simple and deterministic, the relationship between geopolitical forces, warehousing practices, and labor control is complicated and contingent, defying simplistic explanations based in the China-US economic rivalry. In chapter 9, Hannah Johnston similarly argues that geopolitical ramifications—in particular, recent US sanctions against the Venezuelan state—have created a unique context for digital work. While digital labor platforms[3] have provided many Venezuelans with a lifeline during the country's ongoing economic collapse, Johnston underlines the ways in which crucial digital infrastructures like payment systems are disrupted by geopolitical conflicts. Venezuelans may be able to secure platform work to supplement their incomes, but whether they can successfully negotiate economic sanctions to get paid for that work is another matter entirely. In short, these chapters point to the importance of geopolitics, alongside simple connectivity and labor supply, in shaping digital work in the planetary market.

As ever more workers and more places get hooked into this market, capital finds ever more nodes through which to seek surplus value. This fact has two implications. First, digital and digitally mediated work can be done from an increasing number of places. That much digital work requires relatively little fixed capital and can be transmitted easily, creates the preconditions for a worldwide reconstruction of economic networks of production and consumption. Second, and relatedly, for most work that does not require the creation of a material product, physical distance can increase significantly between workers, bosses, and consumers. These features of the planetary market shape the transformation of work. In chapter 11, James Steinhoff considers the case of data science workers to argue that while the data science labor force is globally distributed, it is "predominantly tied to powerful firms concentrated in specific locales," most notably the US and China. Drawing on the concept of labor power, Steinhoff describes the proletarianization of data science work—that is, the reduction of its scarcity and the devaluation of its content—including the role of digital platforms in transforming tasks and networks.

That said, the almost-universal nature of potential connectivity by no means translates into actual affordances or practices. There are, and will always be, countless unconnected and uncommodified alternative economies (Gibson-Graham 2006; Graham 2019a). Yet as the reach of capital becomes increasingly untethered and globe spanning, it is clear that regulatory frameworks and supranational organizations must adapt to this new reality. Referring to the early origins of the International Labour Organization (ILO) as a system of international labor regulation, Janine Berg argues in chapter 16 that technological advances have "exposed the limits of labor regulation bounded by physical jurisdictions and conceived for the production of tangible products." As a result of the mismatch between newly unbounded networks of work and state-based regulatory structures, she makes the case for a new international governance system for digital work in the planetary market.

Conjunctural Geographies

There is a recent history of seeing digitally mediated work and production as existing in "the cloud." The flows of information within the cloud seem to be able to transcend physical laws, geographic constraints, and regulatory points of leverage (Hu 2015; Amoore 2020). Clouds normally float above our heads; they are intangible yet ubiquitous. The vision of clouds (or a "cyberspace") that is immaterial and disembedded from the "real world" or physical space has shaped much of today's digital imaginaries (Graham 2019b). The digital is seen and framed as being somewhere else. Peck and Phillips (2021, 82), for instance, in their dissection of how platform capitalism operates, note that "the matrix-like capacities of platforms mean that they can seem to be everywhere but at the same time remain placeless—their preferred address, appropriately enough, being 'the cloud.'"

Here we are inspired by the notion of "power-geometries" developed by Doreen Massey (1991; 2005). Specifically, this means not thinking about an online/offline dualism and not thinking of geography as something that can be flattened or shrunk. Space can be imagined instead as "articulated moments in networks of social relations and understandings, but where a large proportion of those relations, experiences and understandings are constructed on a far larger scale than what we happen to define for the moment as the place itself, whether that be a street, or a region or even a continent" (Massey 1991, 28). This notion of space scrutinizes how the relative mobility and connectivity of some people and places entrenches the marginalization of others. The planetary market is therefore not limited to a fixed point in the geometry of Euclidean space—the idea that space must be conceptualized in relation to discrete physical territories and geographic coordinates in which clearly identifiable positions can be mapped on a canvas. As Benjamin Bratton (2016, xvii) puts it, "Maps of horizontal global space can't account for all the overlapping layers that create a thickened vertical jurisdictional complexity, or how we already use them to design and govern our worlds." In other words, we need to come to grips with new ways of conceptualizing space, place, distance, proximity, and connectivity—taking into account that work can be transmitted over time and space in digitally mediated ways.

Several chapters of the book present and deploy novel ways of conceptualizing space, place, distance, proximity, and connectivity in the planetary market. In chapter 8,

Florian A. Schmidt sheds light on the relationship between the production of autonomous vehicles and the increasing demand for human-labeled training data for AI systems. Schmidt describes the specialized platforms that have emerged to fill the demand for training data processing, making use of spatially dispersed workforces of data annotators and "experimenting with various stacking orders of human labor—AI support and control systems, subautomation, and suboutsourcing." In chapter 15, Matthew Hockenberry focuses on the role of the mobile phone in contemporary logistical networks. Using the last-mile service Amazon Flex as a case study, he suggests that the mobile phone can be described as an interface between local sites of distribution and massive software systems of planetary production. This relationship, he shows, is key to understanding power relations in the gig economy and its modes of digitally mediated managerial control.

By thinking about connectivities as part of translocal power-geometries rather than disembedded online interactions, we would argue that the market through which labor power and services are traded is characterized by "conjunctural geographies" (Graham 2020)—that is, markets in which economic actors are simultaneously embedded into and disembedded from local contexts. Based on fieldwork in an e-commerce village in East China's Shandong Province, Lin Zhang shows in chapter 2 the distinct ways in which local handicraft-making traditions are intersecting with planetary systems of capitalist production—notably, Alibaba's e-commerce platform Taobao.com. Zhang develops the notion of "platformized family production" and examines its myriad contradictions in the Chinese countryside. In so doing, she "counterbalances digital labor studies' Western centrism by methodizing (rather than objectifying) China."

The digital, in each of these cases, is both there and not there, embedded and disembedded, material and immaterial. Far from being purely immaterial or virtual, the digital is constituted and sustained by human labor with respect to cables, pipelines, satellites, servers, the extraction of metals and minerals, maintenance, and more. In chapter 19, Joana Moll and Jara Rocha, using the everyday act of purchasing a book on Amazon as an example, argue that the implications of this process are far from mundane. Rather, a few clicks set in motion a massive and energetically costly machinery. Indeed, several chapters articulate how work and workers can be both empowered and disempowered by their reliance on firms, platforms, infrastructures, and border-crossing networks that are opaque, ephemeral, and transient and that allow for interactions at the speed of light but that constitute networks whose edges and nodes are placed *somewhere* and never nowhere. The ability to command and deploy those affordances is far from evenly distributed, and one of the primary contributions of this book will be to show how powerful actors used control over conjunctural geographies in order to further entrench their positions in the planetary market.

Fragmentation and Clustering

Even in a hyperconnected world dominated by platforms, economic geographies remain heterogeneous, clustered, and fragmented. Just because information-based work *can*, in theory, be requested and conducted from anywhere does not mean that it *will*. The planetary market facilitates a confluence that can transcend the spatial boundaries that have historically constrained both employers and workers, but the economic activities within it remain shaped and characterized by multiscalar and asymmetrical technological, political, social, cultural, and institutional factors. And the power to control, command, and obfuscate these inherently spatial infrastructures to annihilate time and space is unevenly distributed and experienced. While the planetary networks within which most digital work is embedded might seem opaque and unknowable to us, a key goal of bringing this book together is to provide a way in by giving an indication about key sites of both production and consumption.

In recent years, a number of scholars have highlighted that the interlaced processes of physical and cognitive human labor in various parts of the planet are key features of today's production networks, blurring the boundaries between digital, physical, and biological layers of extraction and exploitation (Mezzadra and Neilson 2017; Crawford 2021). Amazon's Echo smart speakers, for instance, require the extraction of rare earth minerals like neodymium. At the same time, the artificial neural networks of Amazon's virtual speech assistant, Alexa, rely on outsourced workers' cognitive labor in annotating large-scale training datasets.[4] These highly standardized and menial tasks are often performed by outsourced workers, as described by Paola Tubaro and Antonio Casilli in chapter 10. For Tubaro and Casilli, privacy violations and labor arbitrage are two sides of the same coin; they contend that the responsibilities of subcontracted workers who listen to recordings of such devices "include much more than just transcribing and annotating conversations to help automated speech algorithms 'self-learn.'"

There are various concepts we can use to make sense of the gaps between the metaphoric promotion of contemporary digital technologies as seamless or even magical entities, and the sobering reality of their reliance on the labor of distant workers. In chapter 13, Jathan Sadowski turns our attention to how, by mystifying the real operations of AI-powered technological systems, technology companies attempt to eradicate the role of the human labor that produces such systems. As he asserts, this sleight of hand dovetails with the fact that "the desire for AI in some places supplants the rights of humans in other places." In introducing the notion of "planetary Potemkin AI," Sadowski posits that prominent instances of AI are simply artificial displays of its future potential: a shiny facade of cultural hype allowing entrepreneurs to attract venture capital by masking the inputs of human labor.

Gray and Suri (2019, 1) have called this phenomenon "the paradox of automation's last mile." In other words, as AI systems advance, they rapidly create and dismantle temporary labor markets to support new, previously unneeded human-in-the-loop tasks. Inspired by critical political economy, Ekbia and Nardi (2017, 22) deploy a neologism, *heteromation*, to describe "the extraction of economic value from low-cost or free labour in computer-mediated networks," in which they see a "new logic of capital accumulation." By introducing the notion of "fauxtomation," Taylor (2018) posits that socialist feminism's myriad insights regarding the paradoxical relationship between domestic work and technology provide potent resources for debunking warnings about full automation. As Seaver (2018, 378) aptly puts it, "If you cannot see a human in the loop, you just need to look for a bigger loop." In other words, what is destructive about the planetary market is not so much that work happens *nowhere*; it is that it *does not matter where* it takes place. Why invest in local labor markets if the next human in the loop is just a click away?

The disciplines of geography and sociology offer a range of concepts to describe systems of production that link disparate places to exploit differences and, in so doing, create highly opaque networks: global commodity chains, global value chains, global production networks—all these approaches have been developed to study the heterogeneous relationships between spatially dispersed actors. However, with digitally mediated commodities and services—including social media platforms—it is difficult to gaze backward along the chain of production because these systems are often continually unfolding and rarely fixed in nature. In chapter 5, Sana Ahmad and Martin Krzywdzinski focus on an indispensable type of such work: content moderation. Despite having attracted considerable attention in this era of social media—and all the online hate and disinformation it supports and propagates—the value chain configurations of content moderation remain opaque. Drawing on fieldwork in India, Ahmad and Krzywdzinski seek to address this research gap, shedding light on the work and lives of content moderators. At the hidden nodes of even very fragmented digital production networks, there will always be real, human workers who are producing the outputs.

Platforms of Commodification

In his 1935 essay "The Work of Art in the Age of Mechanical Reproduction," German critical theorist Walter Benjamin famously points out that paradigmatic shifts in the ways in which art is reproduced have sweeping implications for its aesthetic, sociocultural, and political perception within society. The ritualized process of technical reproduction, Benjamin writes, diminishes the aura of an artwork by depriving it of its unique aesthetic authority—its one and only existence. As a consequence of the reproducibility of art across time and space, the mechanical destruction of authenticity causes a reconfiguration of the boundaries between private and public realms: it reshapes the flows of social life.

One does not have to sympathize with the cultural criticism of the Frankfurt School to acknowledge the relevance of Benjamin's insights for making sense of digital work in the planetary market. A key premise of this book is that many types of work have become commodified and easier to trade and govern. Ever more work is performed in and packaged into machine-readable units. The use around the world of standardized tools, files, processes, and protocols; the trading of work in the same systems, digital platforms, and networks; and the evaluation of work with common rating and reputation systems—all of this makes work identifiable, searchable, and tradable at a truly planetary scale. Fixed material infrastructures of computing, international standards, and global payment systems allow the integration into broader systems of production of work that is broken into commodifiable chunks. In a world of replicable digital infrastructures, there is no more *terra incognita*.

This is not an argument that geography no longer matters. Far from it. Digital networks of production settle precisely in the places with the most advantageous political economies. In chapter 14, Nick Srnicek addresses the question of whether AI is a centralizing technology that compounds the concentration of power and capital. He argues that "the emerging global value chain of AI is a profoundly unequal one" and, by scrutinizing the notion that data is the only major competitive advantage for a handful of Chinese and American platform companies, presents two other key drivers of monopolization: compute and labor. Srnicek's chapter usefully extends our theoretical and political horizons beyond a narrow focus on data and datafication. From this perspective, technology giants do not just *reflect* the structures of the planetary market; they *produce* the structures of this market. Given that some platform companies have reached such a gigantic scale that they now "seem to function as vital infrastructures in the world at large . . . such that living without them shackles social and cultural life" (Plantin and Punathambekar 2018, 2), it is crucial that we grasp and critically examine their political economy.

Digital production networks, through opaque and often untraceable connections, bring together workers and the objects and subjects of their work in ways that not only make proximity superfluous but also actively design against it. That said, several chapters in this book show that planetary systems work to conceal workers from each other and from other nodes in their production networks, as well as from their own local contexts. In chapter 6, Andreas Hackl addresses social enterprises that use digital labor platforms to provide work opportunities for refugees in the field of image annotation. Based on fieldwork with Syrian refugees in Lebanon, Hackl critically assesses the promise of digital inclusion in the light of a restrictive local labor market regime resulting from national policies of exclusion and control of immigrants.

We should add that the reach of commodification goes beyond the labor process itself. In fact, commodification can impact our closest social relations, for example with friends and family. Drawing on ethnographic fieldwork in Jakarta, Johan Lindquist focuses chapter 4 on the work of social media marketing services—that is, those involving the semiproduction and reselling of social media followers, likes, comments, views, and so on. At the heart of the digital production networks described in his chapter is "the combination of automation from below, shifting patron-client relations in the context of urbanization, and [entrepreneurial] aspiration." In describing how entrepreneurs in Jakarta recruit their friends, neighbors, and relatives to perform this type of illicit work in the shadows of (Western) social media platforms, Lindquist shows how work is grounded not only in distinct spatial and urban contexts but also in commodified social relations of production. To paraphrase Marx and Engels ([1848] 2008, 38), "The need of a constantly expanding market for its products chases [platform capitalists] over the entire surface of the globe. [Platforms] must nestle everywhere, settle everywhere, and establish connections everywhere."

Planetary Competition and Resistance

If the worldwide infrastructures, and the systems built on top of them, facilitate legibility of outputs and processes, the labor within those systems becomes a highly tradable commodity in a planetary system. And with a network linking together billions of people, most of whom live in low- and middle-income countries, we have a system of planetary competition. In a variety of ways, this book shows that the fact that capital and labor can operate out of and command different scales is a fundamental driver of exploitation.

In his study of the offshore outsourcing industry, Jamie Peck (2017, 10) notes that the logic of cutting and suppressing costs is the "elemental rationale" of the practice. Businesses can tap into workforces with ever-lower labor costs. At the same time, for almost all types of digital work, there are fewer digital jobs than there are workers able and willing to do them, creating an oversupply of labor that drives an international race to the bottom (Graham and Anwar 2019). Workers are naturally rooted to the places in which they live. "Labour power has to go home every night," as David Harvey (1990, 19) famously notes. However, while workers stay rooted and embedded in their local contexts, the lead firms that buy their labor do not have to be—they can search for the cheapest and most accommodating labor markets and regimes in any location across the whole surface of the globe.

Despite the intense competition arising between workers suddenly thrust into a planetary market, the chapters in this book show that there is no "global homogeneous workforce" that is alienated from the fruits of its labor in one, standard way. There are instead a range of factors, including racialized and gendered inequalities, that shape why particular workers in particular places are attracted to and enrolled into planetary networks. In chapter 18, Payal Arora and Usha Raman examine how the gendered nature of global value chains complicates the struggle for fairer supply chains. They specifically focus on the potential of digital storytelling campaigns to leverage the creative power of worker collectives, arguing that "we need to ask who and what determines how women workers are represented and reproduced on the Internet, how communities are formed and sustained, and whether and what kinds of change are possible." As they remind us, race, gender, cost, language, and culture all shape how people connect in the planetary market.

At first glance, the status quo of planetary competition between workers, coupled with unstable (or variable) labor demand, seems to create a structural precondition that inhibits any effective associational counterpower. But all is not hopeless for workers. The same networks that can produce a race to the bottom in terms of both pay and working conditions can be repurposed for new imaginings of solidarities and collective power. But can such solidarities arise *despite* and *across* racial and national differences? That is the key question of JS Tan and Moira Weigel, discussed in chapter 12. Focusing on the 996.ICU movement (i.e., protesting the "9:00 a.m. to 9:00 p.m., six days a week" working regime) initiated by software programmers in China in 2019, Weigel and Tan unveil the tensions between digitally mediated cognitive labor and transnational capital flows in shaping shared worker identities. They describe how workers repurpose transnational infrastructures of exploitation as infrastructures of collaboration (e.g., between Chinese and American software workers), thereby scrutinizing the supposedly frictionless nature of cognitive work. While workers today often lack effective bottlenecks or pressure points at which the collective withdrawal of their labor might prove effective, the very technology that fragments and commodifies their work simultaneously affords them the ability to coordinate at a scale previously unimaginable. It is from this foundation that we might imagine new ways of building worker power and networked forms of disruption.

However, the tensions between labor and capital do not play out in the same way across settings. Instead, the nature of such struggles is always shaped by contextual and geographical particularities. In chapter 3, Julie Chen and Cheryll Ruth Soriano advance our understanding of low-paid work in globalized platform capitalism. Juxtaposing the experiences of Filipino crowdworkers and Chinese workers in the ride-hailing and food-delivery sectors, Chen and Soriano pay particular attention to everyday resistance strategies on both individual and collective levels vis-à-vis modes of algorithmic management and control. While platforms and algorithms give rise to changing geographies of work, they also reconfigure the nature of labor contestation (see also Ferrari and Graham 2021).

These broader transformations affect not just the resistance strategies available to platform workers but also the organizational structure of unions. In chapter 17, Christina J. Colclough emphasizes workers' data rights and the key role of trade unions around the world in negotiating what she calls the "data life cycle at work." Unions, she asserts, should negotiate across the *entire* data life cycle at work/in production: from data collection to analysis, storage, and data off-boarding. It is therefore essential that we move beyond the individual rights stipulated in national data protection laws and consider data rights as collective rights—for example, by pushing for new ILO conventions that protect workers. Colclough's proposals include workers and places that are not connected to the planetary market. After all, she writes, "a globally established and enforceable set of rights will make sure that they too will be protected when that time comes."

Structure of the Book

As ever more work is commodified and traded beyond local labor markets, and as ever more workers continue to produce immaterial outputs, it is crucial to understand how these changes are affecting workers themselves and the wider transnational economic networks they are embedded in. We have therefore organized the book into four key sections:

1. Grounding planetary networks
2. Mapping planetary networks
3. Dissecting planetary networks
4. Reimagining planetary networks

The first section focuses on the experience of work in planetary systems, especially the conflicting dynamics of commodification and decommodification. These chapters point to the fact that labor remains geographically sticky and embedded in distinct contexts despite the fact that work is being embedded in planetary networks of production and consumption.

The second section highlights the different layers of digital production, the nodes in planetary networks, and how they relate to one another. While the first section provides case studies of the experience of work in planetary systems, this section addresses how these networks of work can be mapped and problematized in relation to questions of geopolitics and economic development.

The third section offers ways to dissect planetary networks of digital production. Our rationale for including this section is not simply to point to a few "appropriate" theoretical lenses or prisms but rather to highlight the productive multiplicity and interdisciplinarity of thinking about digital work and its networks in the contemporary historical moment.

The fourth and final section provides four imaginative chapters that not only challenge conventional wisdom but also provide constructive and practical suggestions to regulate digital work in the planetary market.

The Present and Future of the Planetary Market

In *Death of a Discipline*, Gayatri Chakravorty Spivak vividly outlines why she prefers the term *planet* over *globe*: "The globe is on our computers. No one lives there. It allows us to think that we can aim to control it. The planet is in the species of alterity, belonging to another system; and yet we inhabit it, on loan" (Spivak 2003, 72).

In this spirit, to speak of the planetary market is to posit instead a normative vision of an interconnected system that is aimed at fostering dignity, humility, empathy, mutual care, and worldwide solidarity. Wherever on the planet you may be and whenever you read these words, we hope that you find inspiration by studying the various chapters of this volume: Inspiration to appreciate and scrutinize the role of connectivity in today's world and the worlds to come. Inspiration to consider that nothing is inevitable about the globe-spanning systems and networks of computing that shape and are shaped by always-embedded social, cultural, and economic action and transactions. And, crucially, inspiration to reimagine and rebuild connectivities and connections in ways that center values that are both human and humane.

With more than five billion people connected to the Internet, and high-speed connections available everywhere—from Manhattan to Mozambique, from Antarctica to the International Space Station—this book explores how changing connectivities are transforming the networks of work and the experience of workers in these networks. It does so without resorting to restrictive imaginaries that either overemphasize the ways "geography still matters" or alternatively wish away the tethering of work to place. It does so to answer a combination of descriptive, theoretical, and normative questions that aim to both understand and reimagine the relative embedded and disembedded, material and immaterial, synchronous and asynchronous, and territorialized and deterritorialized natures of digital production today. The planetary market that we seek to understand, in other words, is one in which labor can be easily exchanged asynchronously and nonproximately but also one in which access, control, and power to negotiate the market are far from even. The market exists on a planetary scale, and—even though some of its features and participants can appear to seamlessly interact and transact in unbounded, friction-free, and transspatial ways—its participants are always firmly rooted in their own material geographies. And, as all the chapters of this book show, those geographies play a profound role in shaping the outcomes of the market for all its participants.

Notes

1. As Hess (2018, 2) puts it, a global production network can be defined as "the nexus of interconnected functions and operations through which goods and services are produced, distributed, and consumed."

2. See https://www.internetworldstats.com/stats.htm.

3. Digital labor platforms can be thought of as a set of digital infrastructures that mediate interactions between consumers and workers, bringing together the supply of and demand for labor. In most cases, a single company controls that infrastructure as a proprietary resource. However, there are also examples in which control is exerted by multiple economic actors. In this book, we therefore distinguish between two types of platforms: Geographically tethered platforms require that a job be done in a particular place (e.g., delivering food from a restaurant to an apartment or driving a person from one part of town to another). Cloud platforms, in contrast, manage work that can, in theory, be requested and conducted from anywhere. Requesters, or clients, in one country can use such platforms to find workers who may be located anywhere on Earth.

4. Artificial neural networks (ANNs) are computing systems that mimic the electrical operations of the brain's neuronal connections. Some ANNs apply deep learning techniques in that their hundreds of layers "are not designed by human engineers: they are learned from data" (LeCun, Bengio, and Hinton 2015, 436). Although the full history of ANNs goes back to the last century, the confluence since 2012 of three developments has been instrumental for them: the availability of large human-labeled training datasets, advanced algorithms to make sense of patterns, and immense computing power to perform the necessary modeling tasks.

References

Amoore, Louise. 2020. *Cloud Ethics: Algorithms and the Attributes of Ourselves and Others*. Durham, NC: Duke University Press.

Anwar, Mohammad Amir, and Mark Graham. 2020. "Digital Labour at Economic Margins: African Workers and the Global Information Economy." *Review of African Political Economy* 47 (163): 95–105.

Barlow, John Perry. 1996. "Declaration of the Independence of Cyberspace." *Electronic Frontier Foundation*, February 8. https://www.eff.org/cyberspace-independence.

Benjamin, Walter. 1935. "The Work of Art in the Age of Mechanical Reproduction." In *Illuminations*, edited by Hannah Arendt, translated by Harry Zohn (1969). New York: Schocken Books. https://web.mit.edu/allanmc/www/benjamin.pdf.

Bratton, Benjamin H. 2016. *The Stack: On Software and Sovereignty*. Cambridge, MA: MIT Press.

Castells, Manuel. 2000. *The Rise of the Network Society*. 2nd ed. Vol. 1 of *The Information Age: Economy, Society and Culture*. Cambridge, MA: Wiley-Blackwell.

Clare, Karenjit. 2013. "The Essential Role of Place within the Creative Industries: Boundaries, Networks and Play." *Cities* 34: 52–57.

Crawford, Kate. 2021. *Atlas of AI: Power, Politics, and the Planetary Costs of Artificial Intelligence*. New Haven, CT: Yale University Press.

Day, Matt, Giles Turner, and Natalia Drozdiak. 2019. "Amazon Workers Are Listening to What You Tell Alexa." *Bloomberg*, April 10.

Ekbia, Hamid R., and Bonnie A. Nardi. 2017. *Heteromation and Other Stories of Computing and Capitalism*. Cambridge, MA: MIT Press.

Ferrari, Fabian, and Mark Graham. 2021. "Fissures in Algorithmic Power: Platforms, Code, and Contestation." *Cultural Studies*.

Fevre, Ralph. 1992. *The Sociology of Labour Markets*. London: Harvester Wheatsheaf.

Friedman, Thomas L. 2005. *The World Is Flat: A Brief History of the Twenty-First Century*. New York: Farrar, Straus and Giroux.

Frier, Sarah. 2019. "Facebook Paid Contractors to Transcribe Users' Audio Chats." *Bloomberg*, August 13.

Gibson-Graham, J. K. 2006. *The End of Capitalism (As We Knew It): A Feminist Critique of Political Economy*. Minneapolis: University of Minnesota Press.

Graham, Mark. 2015. "Contradictory Connectivity: Spatial Imaginaries and Technomediated Positionalities in Kenya's Outsourcing Sector." *Environment and Planning A: Economy and Space* 47 (4): 867–883.

Graham, Mark, ed. 2019a. *Digital Economies at Global Margins*. Cambridge, MA/Ottawa: MIT Press/IDRC. https://www.idrc.ca/sites/default/files/sp/Images/idl-57429_2.pdf.

Graham, Mark. 2019b. "There Are No Rights 'in' Cyberspace." In *Research Handbook on Human Rights and Digital Technology: Global Politics, Law and International Relations*, edited by Ben Wagner, Matthias C. Kettemann, and Kilian Vieth, 24–32. Cheltenham: Edward Elgar.

Graham, Mark. 2020. "Regulate, Replicate, and Resist: The Conjunctural Geographies of Platform Urbanism." *Urban Geography* 41 (3): 453–457. https://doi.org/10.1080/02723638.2020.1717028.

Graham, Mark, Casper Andersen, and Laura Mann. 2015. "Geographical Imagination and Technological Connectivity in East Africa." *Transactions of the Institute of British Geographers* 40 (3): 334–349. https://doi.org/10.1111/tran.12076.

Graham, Mark, and Mohammad Amir Anwar. 2018. "Digital Labour." In *Digital Geographies*, edited by James Ash, Rob Kitchin, and Agnieszka Leszczynski, 177–187. London: SAGE.

Graham, Mark, and Mohammad Amir Anwar. 2019. "The Global Gig Economy: Towards a Planetary Labour Market?" *First Monday* 24 (4), April 1. https://doi.org/10.5210/fm.v24i4.9913.

Gray, Mary L., and Siddharth Suri. 2019. *Ghost Work: How to Stop Silicon Valley from Building a New Global Underclass*. Boston: Houghton Mifflin Harcourt.

Harvey, David. 1990. *The Condition of Postmodernity: An Enquiry into the Origins of Cultural Change*. Oxford: Wiley-Blackwell.

Harvey, David. 2001. "Globalization and the 'Spatial Fix.'" *Geographische Revue* 3 (2): 23–30.

Hern, Alex. 2019. "Apple Contractors 'Regularly Hear Confidential Details' on Siri Recordings." *Guardian*, July 26. https://www.theguardian.com/technology/2019/jul/26/apple-contractors-regularly-hear-confidential-details-on-siri-recordings.

Hess, Martin. 2018. "Global Production Networks." In *The International Encyclopedia of Geography: People, the Earth, Environment, and Technology*, edited by Douglas Richardson. Malden, MA/Oxford, UK: John Wiley & Sons. https://www.research.manchester.ac.uk/portal/files/70515260/wbieg0675.pdf.

Hu, Tung-Hui. 2015. *A Prehistory of the Cloud*. Cambridge, MA: MIT Press.

LeCun, Yann, Yoshua Bengio, and Geoffrey Hinton. 2015. "Deep Learning." *Nature* 7553 (521): 436–444.

Marx, Karl, and Friedrich Engels. (1848) 2008. *The Communist Manifesto*. London: Pluto Press.

Massey, Doreen. 1991. "A Global Sense of Place." *Marxism Today* (38): 24–29.

Massey, Doreen. 2005. *For Space*. London: SAGE.

Mezzadra, Sandro, and Brett Neilson. 2017. "On the Multiple Frontiers of Extraction: Excavating Contemporary Capitalism." *Cultural Studies* 31 (2–3): 185–204.

Morgan, Kevin. 2004. "The Exaggerated Death of Geography: Learning, Proximity and Territorial Innovation Systems." *Journal of Economic Geography* 4 (1): 3–21.

Peck, Jamie. 2017. *Offshore: Exploring the Worlds of Global Outsourcing*. Oxford: Oxford University Press.

Peck, Jamie, and Rachel Phillips. 2021. "The Platform Conjuncture." *Sociologica* 14 (3): 73–99.

Plantin, Jean-Christophe, and Aswin Punathambekar. 2018. "Digital Media Infrastructures: Pipes, Platforms, and Politics." *Media, Culture & Society* 41 (2): 163–174.

Seaver, Nick. 2018. "What Should an Anthropology of Algorithms Do?" *Cultural Anthropology* 33 (3): 375–385.

Spivak, Gayatri Chakravorty. 2003. *Death of a Discipline*. New York: Columbia University Press.

Taylor, Astra. 2018. "The Automation Charade." *Logic* 5: 149–163. https://logicmag.io/failure/the -automation-charade/.

Wong, Julia C. 2019. "'A White-Collar Sweatshop': Google Assistant Contractors Allege Wage Theft." *Guardian*, June 25. https://www.theguardian.com/technology/2019/may/28/a-white-collar -sweatshop-google-assistant-contractors-allege-wage-theft.

I Grounding Planetary Networks

2   Moving beyond Shanzhai? Contradictions of Platformized Family Production in the Planetary Network of E-Commerce Labor

Lin Zhang

One evening in 2016, I sat down with an e-commerce entrepreneur at a roadside barbecue stand in W village—a Taobao village in East China's Shandong Province specializing in the production and sales of handicrafts.[1] I became interested in rural e-commerce when I first visited W village in 2010. Over the past decade, I have witnessed the rapid expansion of e-commerce not only in W village but also across the country. By 2020, 1 percent of all villages in China (5,425) were branded as "Taobao Villages" by the e-commerce corporation Alibaba.[2] Despite the media hype about the "Taobao Village Phenomenon," my informant told me, "The golden days of rural e-commerce have passed," and a large number of entrepreneurs in W village are struggling to make enough money to support their families: "We are trying very hard to upgrade the industry and move beyond the *shanzhai* logic of production." He went on: "E-commerce has indeed made some of us rich, but vicious competition also threatened community solidarity and caused more interpersonal conflicts."

Shanzhai, literally meaning "mountain strongholds," initially appeared in ancient vernacular Chinese novels to describe the military fortresses created by Robinhood-like martial arts–practicing bandits in political exile from the imperial establishment. The contemporary usage of *shanzhai*, referring to manufacturing practices based on copying and accumulative minor modifications often in defiance of intellectual property rights, usually traced to the cottage industry of family-owned subcontracting manufacturing businesses prevalent in Hong Kong since the 1950s. These small businesses rode on innovations in a networked global division of labor while revitalizing traditional Chinese family production practices. This hybrid production system made Hong Kong, along with a few other countries and regions in East and Southeast Asia, a new frontier of global capitalist accumulation. Mainland China became a beneficiary of the system in the late 1970s, when it embarked on market reform, and emerged as a global manufacturing powerhouse in the 1990s.

However, it has been the southern coastal manufacturing hub Shenzhen's industrial ecosystem of shanzhai mobile phone production and sales that has garnered and sustained the most public attention (Ho 2010; Wallis and Qiu 2012; Zhang and Fung 2013; Chubb 2015; Lindtner 2020). This system has repurposed the informal and flexible but sophisticated networked division of labor, formed through export-driven manufacturing of global brands like Apple and Samsung, to create more affordable and versatile products for less affluent consumers in China and other developing countries. In the past decade or so, the system in South China has kept evolving—from manufacturing cheap global brand knockoffs for globally competitive Chinese indigenous brands like Huawei and Xiaomi, to forming a burgeoning incubating ecosystem for cutting-edge tech start-ups from around the world (Lindtner 2020).

In parallel to the development in Shenzhen, a new hybrid regime of what I call "platformed family production" emerged in rural China with the introduction of e-commerce. In turning peasants into e-commerce entrepreneurs and consumers and connecting rural manufacturing to e-commerce platforms, the hope is to upgrade Chinese manufacturing, transcending the existing regime of shanzhai to increase the value added in production through innovation and branding. The digital platform emerged, according to Nick Srnicek (2016, 4), in the aftermath of the 2008 global financial crisis as a "new business model" to revitalize a sluggish global capitalism. Platforms are two-sided markets that "bring together users, capture and monetize data" and "[need] to scale to be effective" (Woodcock and Graham 2020, 19). China, in particular, has embraced digital platforms in its effort to restructure an imbalanced economy. In the aftermath of the 2008 crisis, awakened to the unsustainability of and risk posed by an economy that was overreliant on low-value-added export-driven manufacture, the country embarked on a major national restructuring with the goal of transitioning into an economy propelled mainly by indigenous innovation, service industries, and domestic consumption. In a densely populated country with a huge rural population,[3] rural e-commerce carries the hope of forging an alternative path of rural development to unlock a more humane and sustainable model of development in China.

The new hybrid regime of platformized family production, in particular, is celebrated for its potential to reenergize the rural economy through a synthesis of existing rural manufacturing capacity; family-based organization of labor; and e-commerce's platform-mediated model of production, sales, and consumption. However, what is often missing from both the celebratory narrative of the platform economy and some critical research on digital labor is a reckoning with the escalating tensions between the distant nature and massive scale of e-commerce—which relies on and is embedded in the planetary networks of digital capitalism—and the local and material practices of village-based e-commerce production.

This chapter broadens the scope and meaning of the term *digital labor* to demystify the much-celebrated figure of the autonomous, individualized e-commerce entrepreneur in rural China by depicting the embeddedness of e-commerce work in a network of historically formed, gendered division of labor in the villages and in the collective social production on the Internet. As I will show, it is the articulation of and tensions between the individualized and intellectual property-conforming "immaterial labor" idealized by planetary networks of production, and the collective and hybrid (manual and intellectual) nature of productive and reproductive labor on the ground, that shape the experiences of digital work in the Chinese countryside (Hardt and Negri 2005).

The copresence of manufacturing and creative labor in W village allows us to scrutinize not only the blurring and imbricating of the two but also their intensifying tensions and how such tensions are manifested along gender, class, and generational lines. This positioning makes rural China a particularly interesting site to deconstruct the universality and novelty of technological entrepreneurialism and its empowering and democratic promises. In doing so, the chapter also counterbalances digital labor studies' Western centrism by methodizing (rather than objectifying) China—that is, acknowledging the West as a part of the formation of Chinese subjectivities that entered into Chinese history "in the form of fragmented pieces," but never in "a totalizing manner" (Chen 2010, 223).

Similar to platformized family production, shanzhai in W village is a product of the creative synthesis of a planetary system of capitalist production and local handicraft-making traditions. Public perceptions of shanzhai exist on a spectrum. At one extreme, we have outright condemnation and dismissal of shanzhai as mere counterfeiting and an obstacle to Chinese innovation.[4] Critics of shanzhai treat an idealized trajectory of capitalist development in Western societies as universal and subsume alternative experiences in non-Western or within Western societies as either a "lag" or a "lack." For them, the hybrid regime of shanzhai stands as a "transitional" stage to a more "developed" and "modernized" state of capitalism or, as Eckstein and Schwarz (2017, 7) put it with regard to mainstream perception of non-Western piracy practices, "as a crucial phase in the establishment of peripheral markets which will, if not criminalized and more fully 'developed,' naturally grow into the modern domain of copyright." At the other extreme, we hear enthusiastic celebration of shanzhai's limitless revolutionary potential as a more democratic, effective, creative, and competitive alternative to the innovation system of Silicon Valley, defying Silicon Valley's conformity to the global intellectual property rights (IPR) regime while seamlessly combining manufacturing labor with design and marketing.[5]

With regard to rural e-commerce, I identify more with the latter perception of shanzhai production as a culturally specific and historically contingent trajectory of capitalist development. But in taking seriously rural e-commerce entrepreneurs' struggles to move beyond shanzhai, I feel ambivalent about the celebratory narratives about shanzhai's boundary-crossing and dichotomy-defying potential in resisting Western hegemony. Instead, my observation in W and other Taobao villages informs me that, as a hybrid model and a result of China's negotiated integration into global capitalism, shanzhai is simultaneously productive and frustrating for its practitioners. As we will see, the rise of rural e-commerce and platformized family production, building on while trying to transcend the shanzhai logic of production, only heightened existing tensions between individualization/commercialization and collective organization of labor and community in rural China.

I argue that the platformization of handicraft production in rural China privileges the individualized e-commerce entrepreneur as its ideal subject, fetishizes and instrumentalizes innovation and creativity in conformity with the global IPR, and valorizes intellectual and digital labor disguised as information technology (IT) entrepreneurship. These tendencies not only contradict the reality of collective labor organization both on the e-commerce platforms and inside the villages, but also conflict with the indispensable role of gendered manual labor in the production process. These tensions, while immanent in the planetary networks of digital capitalism and thus not particular to W village or China, are being accentuated and complicated by the overt hybridity of platformized family production in the Chinese countryside. That hybridity is seen in the coexistence in the same geographical and temporal space of platform-mediated handicraft labor and e-commerce labor; village-based family production systems and networked e-commerce trading; and residual small peasant and socialist collective identifications and the individualizing forces of entrepreneurial economy. The primary goal of this chapter, then, is to analyze these contradictions in the specific context of e-commerce in W village.

In the following pages, I will show how the platformization of rural family production, despite the entrepreneurs' desire to transcend the shanzhai logic, both builds on shanzhai production and intensifies the contradiction between individual profiteering and collective production that is inherent to the shanzhai logic. I do so by telling ethnographic stories about the "winners" and "losers" of entrepreneurial reinvention as villagers were forced to compete on e-commerce platforms and learn to brand rural identities. My goal is to show how a new regime of value and valuation has taken shape in the process of platformization of village-based family production, which reinforces rather than overcoming inequalities and stratification in rural China. I tell these stories by drawing from data collected from several ethnographic trips (ranging from one to six months and conducted between 2010 and 2020) to a handicraft e-commerce village in Northeast China, as well as from archival research about the history of handicraft labor in the area and macropolitical economic data about rural e-commerce in China.

From Shanzhai to Platformized Family Production: Tensions in Planetary Networks of Labor

Surrounded by marshes and rivers that are a natural habitat for wild bulrush, and short of arable land, W and the adjacent 32 villages under the administration of B county boast thousands of years of history making handcrafts using bulrush. In the self-sufficient, small peasant economy, straw shoes, grass fans, and cushions were weaved mainly by women in the villages. The boundaries between innovation and copying and between mental and physical labor were blurred in this family-based and subsistence-driven village collective production system. Mothers passed weaving skills on to daughters, and villagers created new handicraft designs collectively through the natural process of diffusion.

This collective system of handicraft making was appropriated by the commune-based brigade enterprises in the early 1970s and then, when local (village and township) government became the organizer and coordinator of handicraft production, continued into the early reform years in the form of township and village enterprises (TVEs).[6] Since the late 1970s, an industrial chain for exporting handicrafts matured under the monopoly of the collective-owned No. 2 Handicraft Factory (hereafter No. 2). Older women weavers in the village recalled that most of their time during the agricultural slack season was spent weaving products, which they handed over on a weekly basis to village-based product collection centers; the products were then collected by No. 2. In the factory, the products were screened, packaged, and transported directly to the port city of Qingdao. From there, the handicrafts were shipped overseas to more than 20 countries in Asia and Europe, and to the United States. China's relative autonomy from the capitalist world system and its negotiated and gradual integration since the late 1970s had yet to generate a need for a capitalist IPR regime to ensure profit and incentivize innovation. This absence of a copyright/patent regime in cultural production under socialist state patronage reflected the broader national climate at the time (Han 2010). The incentive for creating new products, meanwhile, mainly came from the demand of the foreign businesses sourcing products from No. 2. By the late 1980s, weaving as a sideline production served the important functions of improving peasant family income and boosting B county's tax revenue.

Thus, in the absence of a copyright/patent system, the collective regime of handicraft production was formed initially under the small peasant economy based on the village lineage system, which, during the late socialist and TVE years, was repurposed to serve a state-commanded model of economy. This collective model became the foundation of the shanzhai production regime that emerged in the mid-1990s when handicraft production was privatized as part of a national trend following Deng Xiaoping's 1992 Southern Tour to advance China's economic reform.

Building on the handicraft subcontracting system established during the TVE era, the private export businesses boomed between 2001 and 2006. Growing overseas and domestic demand for woven products of all kinds prompted expanded production and diversified designs. New private handicraft factories and retail shops thrived in B County, keeping the female weavers busy at home while their husbands had to seek jobs in the cities due to the lack of work opportunities in the villages. Privatization and competition also created the issue of "piracy" by criminalizing "copying," which made village entrepreneurs aware of the need to protect intellectual property. The sharing and copying of designs, which used to be a benign community-building practice for thousands of years, and a nation-building practice in the socialist and early reform years, became counterfeiting and legal offenses when China became more integrated into the global capitalist division of labor as a manufacturer. Export business owners and villagers told me that during the boom years, it was a common practice for competitors to copy or appropriate each other's designs and sell the same and similar products at a lower price with impunity.

While the digitalization of handicraft sales through the mediation of the planetary production network carried with it promises to upgrade the industry beyond the export-oriented shanzhai model, the reality was more complicated. On the one hand, instead of competing with each other to manufacture for foreign brands like Walmart and Ikea and producing brandless high-quality products at a low cost, e-commerce entrepreneurs now competed with each other in innovation, branding, and pricing to tailor to the tastes and needs of a growing number of domestic e-commerce consumers. Technically, they had moved up the value chain to design, produce, and sell directly to customers. Intensified competition in the e-commerce marketplace and the open-sharing possibility of the Internet made it both more convenient and imperative for entrepreneurs to come up with new designs to distinguish themselves from their competitors in accordance with constantly shifting market trends and consumer preferences.

On the other hand, the search ranking-driven nature of Internet sales and the profit-maximizing algorithmic design of e-commerce platforms also discouraged rural entrepreneurs from investing their labor and time into designing and testing new products and improving the quality of existing products. One example of how Taobao's algorithm encourages shanzhai, or practices of copying, concerns how a *baokuan* (爆款)—that is, a best-selling product on Taobao—is created. A baokuan is born when a product, along with its many shanzhai variations, becomes so popular that it's used almost ubiquitously by consumers in different parts of the country and sold by numerous vendors on the Internet (and sometimes offline). Alibaba implicitly encourages the creation of baokuans by turning a blind eye on copying practices among listed e-sellers on its platforms because baokuan helps drive up search traffic and sales volume. Here the monopoly platform's overriding imperative of profit maximization, along with its nature as a digital landlord that profits by extracting rents from platform-based entrepreneurs, inhibits the entrepreneurs' innovative potential and perpetuates shanzhai production.

The phenomenon of baokuan reveals how platform-based sales encourage copying in production. The design of Taobao's complicated and frequently changing search-ranking algorithm and the availability of profit-maximizing paid marketing plug-ins like *Zhitongche* (直通车), however, work to discourage product innovation. Zhitongche is a paid search-ranking system that charges shop owners a per-click fee to help them improve their product-listing ranking on Taobao (Zhang 2020, 127). Village entrepreneurs told me that investing money and time into designing and prototyping a new handicraft design usually does not generate a commensurate reward for the innovators. Instead, it is much more profitable and cost efficient to copy or appropriate existing products, especially baokuan designs, while redirecting the capital saved into Taobao's paid marketing tools to bump up the product's search-result ranking. "People who invest into producing new designs often suffer," observed Lei, an art school graduate and urbanite who migrated to W village for e-commerce. He explained to me how e-commerce dampens the incentives for entrepreneurs to innovate and sometimes even hurts the quality of their products:

> People are constantly watching at each other's sales figures online. Once they notice a new product that actually sells well, they will ask around, locate the weavers, and ask them to supply the same products. Alternatively, they will show the weavers that they trust the picture of the new product and have them produce copies, sometimes with a little modification. For example, they might change the color of a futon's decorative cloth or add a cover to a storage basket. Then when they create a new listing on Taobao, they will label their "shanzhai product" with the same keywords as the original but sell at a much lower price. Sometimes the profit margin is so thin that they have to cut corners here and there to outcompete other sellers selling similar products. Why waste time designing and making new products when your efforts only enrich your competitors' pocket?

As a result, even when they have ideas for new designs, village entrepreneurs are reluctant to put more capital and resources into research and development for fear that imitators will steal their ideas and profits. The prevalence of design copying and appropriation in e-commerce at W village reflects the broader tension in the planetary network of digital labor. The Internet and other networked digital tools have energized both nonproprietary production and the practice of profiting from social production. Consequently, the distinctions between creativity and copying, and between individualistic profiteering and community-based collaboration, have become muddled (Jaszi 1991; Benkler 2006; Jenkins, Ford, and Green 2018).

The village-based family production network, meanwhile, further intensified the tensions between the embeddedness of labor and the planetary network's drive to extract profits. As we have already seen, the e-commerce in W village was built on the collective and open production network of village-based family handicraft making. That is, any e-commerce entrepreneur can choose to source a particular product from any weaver, though the relationships between e-commerce sellers and weavers are sometimes mediated by product collectors. According to Lei's account, this collective and open structure of production has made it easier to steal and copy one another's new designs. As Pei, another young e-commerce entrepreneur, explained to me, in the absence of a legally binding contractual relationship typical of formal business enterprises, the village production network overlaps with the informal lineage system of an agricultural society: "I can't keep my design away from my cousin, and he had to tell his wife about it. Then his wife's sister knows it too . . . and in no time, you see my design listed in every village shop's front page."[7] Platform-based market competition from other sellers, meanwhile, works to keep product unit price low, which results in the devaluation of handicraft-making labor. However, the platform itself benefits by pitting sellers against each other to offer high-quality products at a lower price to e-commerce consumers.

In fact, the tensions generated by the platformization of shanzhai production have been so thorny that they triggered a heated discussion at the 2013 inaugural Taobao Village Summit in Zhejiang Province. I participated in the Summit as part of my fieldwork. These tensions were the first topic brought up by Chen Liang, a senior researcher from Aliresearch, who chaired a panel discussion about the common issues facing Taobao villages. "Let's begin with the biggest challenge facing the upgrading of Taobao villages," he said: "How do we deal with *tongzhihua*?" (同质化, product homogenization). Then he invited the panelists to comment on the topic. One Taobao village entrepreneur confessed that shanzhai served a necessary function in platform-based and algorithm-mediated selling; he put it this way: "Taobao is a bottomless sea of commodities. If I am the only shop selling a specific product, few customers will notice me. Through copying and repeated sales of the same and similar products, we attract customer traffic towards these products, move up their platform ranking, and work together to create a baokuan." "However," he went on to say, "this would always lead to price wars and other forms of vicious competition." His comment generated much resonance with village entrepreneurs sitting in the audience. A few even jumped in to offer impassioned stories of vicious competition that had happened in their own villages. Nevertheless, the panelists were in consensus that shanzhai production is just an expediency, or a temporary and "immature" phase in the development of rural e-commerce, which will soon be transcended with the expansion and upgrading of industries.

What the panelists did not acknowledge is the contradiction between the individualizing logic of entrepreneurial competition and the collective nature of platform-mediated and village-based production. This contradiction, as I have shown, is inherent to the emerging planetary network of digital labor. In W village, only a few successful e-commerce entrepreneurs have been able to increase the value of their products through branding and self-branding, which has left other entrepreneurs feeling betrayed and marginalized. Rural e-commerce practitioners, as we will see, have to negotiate on a daily basis within the tensions resulting from the platformization of family and village-based production.

Branding Rural Identities: Going beyond Shanzhai?

Branding has been a crucial strategy for e-commerce businesses in W village to improve their products' value added, establish a loyal customer base, and stand out among the many competitors selling the same or similar products. For small, family-owned e-commerce businesses, the branding of their businesses has always been intertwined with the practice of self-branding or "the strategic creation of an identity to be promoted and sold to others" (Marwick 2015, 166). As Banet-Weiser (2012) has argued, branding is as much about culture as it is about economics, and it's inextricably linked to the process of identity formation in the planetary network of digital capitalism. Branding and self-branding, as I will show, became another site where the tension between individualization and the persistence of collective (and to a lesser extent, family) relations and identities played out as village entrepreneurs strove to upgrade their businesses beyond shanzhai.

The planetary market rewards those who are better at converting their rural identities into value to be added to the products sold. On the one hand, learning to brand one's e-commerce business is an individualizing process of locating and articulating one's niche and positioning in the market to distinguish one's business, or one's self as an "enterprise," from one's competitors. Critics of neoliberal market subjectivities have often linked contemporary branding and self-branding practices to the formation of individualized identities. For example, Alice Marwick (2015, 170) has shown how successful Silicon Valley self-branders presented their identities as "divorced from interpersonal and social ties," existing "in a competitive, insecure business environment" and acting "primarily through social media." Lily Chumley (2016, 125), in a different context, has described how art academy students in urban China learned to form brandable personal styles "through practices of self-narration and self-expression."

However, for the rural e-commerce entrepreneurs I encountered during my fieldwork, branding and self-branding were often informed by the collective residuals of locale-based community identities and were mutually constitutive with the emerging collective politics of platform-based rural development (backed by the corporate-state nexus) and that of "buy-rural" consumer citizenship among urban middle-class Chinese. This persistent relevance of collective identities and politics, and their subjugation by the logic of capital in branding, find echoes in Banet-Weiser's (2012) analysis of American commodity activism and Lilly Irani's (2019) study of the branding of handicrafts in rural India. Irani, in particular, when talking about how middle-class designers taught rural handicraft makers product branding in India, noted the tension within the call to innovate through branding, as peasants were instructed "to tweak symbolic forms and material cultures while remaining within elite understandings of community, culture, and authentic group difference" (Irani 2019, 199).

As I will show with the story of Pei and Ling in W village, it is often incumbent on the rural entrepreneurs themselves to live through, if not reconcile, this contradiction of the entrepreneurial labor of branding. For peasant e-commerce entrepreneurs, successful branding and self-branding not only require a certain level of cultural/linguistic literacy and technical competence (such as digital photography, graphics processing, and web design skills) but also demand a cosmopolitan sensibility regarding the demands of the planetary market (i.e., the taste of urban middle-class consumers), the corporate agenda of e-commerce platforms, and the political imperatives of the state. These deterritorialized values constitute a new regime of differentiation and governmentality, disciplining the rural entrepreneurs while also opening space for them to reinvent themselves and their businesses.

Pei and Ling's e-commerce business was deemed by many villagers the most successful in terms of branding. Having spent many years attending colleges and working white-collar jobs in a nearby city before returning to W village for e-commerce, they were more attuned to urban consumer tastes than other villagers, who had either stayed in the countryside their whole lives or only engaged in manual labor jobs in cities. The couple's sociable and expressive personalities also helped them better adapt to the planetary market's demands for personal expression, interactivity, and networking. After their return in 2008, they were the first in the village to register a trademark for their e-commerce business (in 2009) and the first to upgrade from Alibaba's customer-to-customer platform Taobao.com to its more advanced business-to-customer platform Tmall.com (in 2011).[8]

I first met the couple when I followed a team of visitors led by a group of county leaders on a "rural e-commerce village tour." People familiar with Chinese politics would recognize those tours as an appropriation of the working method of socialist mass line politics, a set of ideological commitment and praxis at the core of the Chinese Communist Party's social contract with the peasant and working-class citizens during the Maoist era. "The conditions in which the mass line had flourished are gone," argues political historian Lin Chun; its rhetoric and tactics, however, proliferated in contemporary Chinese political economy (Chun 2019). During communist mass mobilization campaigns, exemplary rural villages and urban work units would be selected and thrust by the powerful propaganda machine into the national limelight as "model villages" or "model *danwei*" for others to emulate. Those models would then serve as sites to propagate the central state's policy ideas and showcase local cadres' political achievement (*zhengji*, 政绩) and became places of political pilgrimage for leadership teams from other work units or villages (Diamond 1983; Meisner 2016).

As I have argued elsewhere, Alibaba appropriated this model of socialist mass mobilization campaign politics to form an alliance with governments in the construction and promotion of the "Taobao Village Phenomenon" (Zhang 2020). This hybrid version of collective politics has informed the branding strategies of many of the rural model e-commerce entrepreneurs. They have strategically crafted their brands and self-brands in accordance with the commercial and political demands of the corporate-state nexus in promoting rural e-commerce entrepreneurship. Pei and Ling's e-commerce business "*Mu Nuan*" was one of the most successful. The brand image of their business was meshed with Pei's self-brand as a socially responsible young entrepreneur of rural origin who had returned from the city to his home village to "modernize" and digitalize traditional handicraft culture.

Pei's rise started in mid-2013, when a journalist from the provincial TV station's agricultural channel came to W to report on the development of village e-commerce. Riding on a succession of commercial and political waves, Pei's career as a model e-commerce entrepreneur took off. In no time, his daily schedule filled with tasks like hosting guests on political pilgrimage to W, being interviewed by journalists from all over the world, and flying all over the country to attend award ceremonies, e-commerce workshops, and publicity events. This career culminated in the couple's workshop being visited by the governor of Shandong Province on his inspection tour of W village in the same year. Soon after the high-level inspection tour, Pei was awarded the prestigious title of "National Young Leader in Rural Development" by the Communist Youth League and the Ministry of Agriculture. Later in 2014, Pei was invited by Alibaba to serve as one of the eight bell ringers at the company's New York Stock Exchange initial public offering (IPO).[9]

One gets a glimpse of the couple's branding strategy, linking their personal entrepreneurial ambition with rural development and community empowerment, through the "brand story" told on the "About Us" page of their e-commerce shop. As shoppers click on the page, their attention is immediately caught by their brand logo, "Mu Nuan," juxtaposed with a close-up shot of a woman weaver's work-worn hands weaving a futon (see figure 2.1a). Mu Nuan's business goal, they find out, is to "rejuvenate rural handicraft industry, help absorb rural surplus labor, and promote rural economic development." As shoppers scroll down the page, they learn about the history of the local handicraft tradition and the steps involved in turning a wild bulrush plant into a finished futon. This storytelling about tradition serves as the backdrop framing Pei and Ling's entrepreneurial endeavor in digitalizing the age-old village industry and the public recognition that Pei and Ling and their shop have received over the years. In the middle of the page, shoppers are presented with three sets of photos and narratives showcasing the couple's achievements: hosting government officials such as the former governor of Shandong Province (see figure 2.1b), being interviewed by journalists from media outlets like the All-Russian State TV and China Central Television, and attending national political and commercial events.

Together, these visual and discursive branding materials tell a coherent story about both Mu Nuan and the peasant entrepreneurial couple. Through the story, the couple's personal identity as model peasant e-commerce entrepreneurs becomes thoroughly intertwined with Mu Nuan's brand image in giving social and cultural meaning to their labor. This "authentic" story evokes trust and respect from consumers searching for reliable sellers in a virtual shopping mall. By purchasing handicraft products from Mu Nuan, urban middle-class shoppers also derive virtuous satisfaction from supporting rural regeneration. Ultimately, Mu Nuan's brand story, like many other similar narratives about grassroots entrepreneurs on Alibaba's platforms, contributes to building the e-commerce giant's corporate image as a champion of grassroots empowerment and an ally of self-made entrepreneurs. This corporate brand image also aligns with the Chinese state's latest nation-building efforts in promoting rural economic and social restructuring through digitalization and microentrepreneurship. Here we see how an aspiration for personal entrepreneurial success and fulfillment becomes entangled with the corporate-state nexus's promotion of planetary market infrastructures in the practice of branding and self-branding.

However, while Mu Nuan's and Pei's brand images were built on the collective politics of corporate-state-nexus–backed digitalization of the rural economy, Pei had to

Figure 2.1
Branding material from Mu Nuan's e-commerce shop.
Source: Author.

carefully navigate the tensions between his individual achievement and his public role as a representative of collective politics. Pei's personal fame as a nationally recognized model entrepreneur not only connected him to elite political and commercial networks beyond the village but also made him an object of envy within the village. Some of the villagers I talked to questioned the authenticity of Pei's brand image and his motive in promoting village e-commerce. One villager confided: "I know it's a tough job being a representative of your village, not to mention being a national symbol for peasant entrepreneurship. They (the family) should get paid for the hard work. But it's problematic when you use your public image as a community representative for personal enrichment. What you do does not really benefit the community in any real sense. You are just a mouthpiece for the politicians and CEOs."

Later I learnt that this village entrepreneur was caught up in a price war with Pei over a new line of handicraft products sold on the Internet. He suspected that Pei had received preferential algorithmic treatment from the platform so that "he could live up to his role as a model entrepreneur." His suspicion was echoed by several other village entrepreneurs. Although such allegations could be groundless speculation motivated by jealousy and personal grudges, they spoke to the escalating interpersonal tensions within the community resulting from e-commerce. Other villagers questioned the logic of the new economy. They felt that it was unfair for the corporate-state nexus to promote a few individuals as model entrepreneurs, and then publicize their atypical experiences to hype up e-commerce. "I don't feel represented at all by the media propaganda," one villager shared: "All those publicities about e-commerce village did was to drive more people into an already overcompetitive market. My e-commerce business is suffering now because of competition, and no one wants to hear my story."

Herein lies the contradiction of the expansion of the planetary market in rural China. While it appropriates the village-based regime of handicraft production and the collective politics of mass line mobilization, by rendering rural development and peasant labor "entrepreneurial," the government has essentially aligned with digital platform monopolies in offloading responsibility for peasants and the countryside to individuals: "If your fellow villagers can do it, you can do it too!" The branding narratives, while tapping into the village handicraft tradition and community-based division of labor, celebrate personal empowerment and digital entrepreneurship, and romanticize the hard physical labor of weaving. From reading the media coverage and brand stories, we wouldn't know the personal contingency and corporate-state promotional efforts involved in cultivating a model entrepreneur, not to mention the sense of alienation that villagers have felt from this publicity. The entrepreneurial labor of branding in rural e-commerce, thus, is a practice of appropriating community-based rural identities and traditions to package and sell a niche product or an "authentic" self in a competitive market. In doing so, it has privileged "the individual, rather than the social, as a site for political action (or inaction) and cultural change (or merely exchange)" (Banet-Weiser 2012, 10).

The planetary market rewards those who are more adaptive to its logic of accumulation, which has constituted a new regime of subjectification and differentiation in shaping peasant identities. It has certainly opened up more opportunities for those villagers who are more outgoing, more expressive, better educated, and more "urban" and "middle-class." However, it also reinforces existing regimes of inequality along the lines of gender, age, education level, migration experiences, and economic standing. As I have shown elsewhere (Zhang 2017), the rise of e-commerce, coupled with the availability of more desirable alternative labor opportunities for younger women, the intergenerational power shift, and the rise of intravillage economic inequalities, has contributed to the devaluation of handicraft labor and the declining socioeconomic standing of women weavers relative to that of the e-commerce entrepreneurs. This depreciation of gendered handicraft labor, in turn, has deepened class and generational inequalities among women in the area. In contrast to the expanding army of e-commerce entrepreneurs and the celebration of Internet-based entrepreneurship, the number of handicraft makers has dwindled in the past decade.

Even within Pei's family, his self-brand as a young male entrepreneur overshadowed the contribution of other family members. When Pei was busy attending public events and socializing with political and corporate elites to maintain the visibility of his self-brand as a model entrepreneur, his wife and parents had to take full responsibility for the family business while taking care of his three young children. However, Pei had been the sole recipient of most of the political awards that the family business had garnered. In 2013 at the inaugural Taobao Village Summit, when I noticed that all of the rural e-commerce entrepreneur representatives invited to receive awards were males in their 20s or 30s, I realized that Pei's family dynamic reflects the broader inequalities in the rural entrepreneurial labor regime.

Conclusion

Through the case of the Chinese e-commerce village W, this chapter has traced the evolution of the hybrid regime of platformized family production in rural China and depicted the tensions produced when the individualizing drive of the planetary market to maximize profit contradicts the collective nature of platform-mediated and village-based practices of e-commerce labor. These tensions were already present in the shanzhai production regime long before the rise of digital platforms. Although plat-formized family production has been celebrated as an alternative model of rural develop-ment, shanzhai have received a mixed evaluation as either an impediment to China's modernization or a creative challenge to Western-dominated capitalism. By historicizing platformized family production and shanzhai, this chapter highlights the continuities of the emerging platform-based planetary production networks from the infrastructures and practices of older regimes of the global subcontracting system (Woodcock and Gra-ham 2020). It also maps the new tensions emerging between the embeddedness of digi-tal work and the reterritorializing drive of the planetary networks of digital capitalism.

While acknowledging shanzhai as a culturally specific and historically contingent material formation of global capitalist production and recognizing the achievement of digital platforms in lowering the threshold of business entry for peasant entrepreneurs, I question the celebratory narratives about shanzhai and platformized family production. The experiences of rural e-commerce practitioners in W village challenge the techno- and culturalist optimism about a hybrid capitalist production regime. The challenges that e-commerce entrepreneurs encounter in innovation and branding speak to an intensi-fied contradiction between individualizing entrepreneurialism and collective labor that is inherent to the new planetary system of digital production, which is itself accentuated in the overt hybridity of platformized family production in rural China. These hidden stories reveal the personal and collective challenges of and failures in entrepreneurial reinvention, which lay bare the limitations of IT-driven entrepreneurialization in resolv-ing the systematic problems at the core of contemporary global capitalism—namely, persistent inequality, structural labor shortages, and the unchecked power domination of political and economic elites. While the digital economy has made new winners, it has also facilitated the confluence of new and preexisting systems of differentiation and inequality in rural China. The varied experiences of W villagers in the new economy remind us of the culturally specific ways in which transformations in the global capital-ist labor regime are experienced by differently positioned subjects.

Notes

1. "Taobao villages" are named after Alibaba's customer-to-customer e-commerce platform Taobao .com. According to Alibaba, a Taobao village is a village that generates RMB 10 million or more in e-commerce sales annually and has 100 or more active online shops on Taobao operated by local residents.

2. See AliResearch, "China Taobao Village Report 2020," February 8, 2021, http://www.aliresearch .com/en/Reports/Reportsdetails?articleCode=167153834769125376.

3. In 2008, roughly 53 percent of the Chinese population was rural; by 2018, the percentage had decreased to 40 percent. See https://www.statista.com/statistics/278566/urban-and-rural-population-of-china/.

4. For example, see http://www.xinhuanet.com/2018-06/19/c_1123000916.htm.

5. This optimistic take on shanzhai is exemplified by *Wired* magazine's documentary about the shanzhai production system in Shenzhen. See https://www.wired.co.uk/video/shenzhen-full-documentary.

6. TVEs are market-oriented public enterprises under the purview of local governments. These enterprises emerged in the late 1970s and 1980s following China's economic reform. Many were established on the legacy of the commune and brigade enterprises founded during the Great Leap Forward and the later years of the Cultural Revolution.

7. For more information about the informal lineage system of the Chinese agricultural society, see the concept of "acquaintance society" (*shuren shehui*) in Fei, Hamilton, and Zheng 1992.

8. Tmall is Alibaba's upgraded e-commerce platform. Compared to its original Taobao platform, Tmall has a higher threshold of entry in terms of registration and maintenance fees.

9. Pei was not able to attend the IPO in the US because his visa was denied by the US immigration office.

References

Banet-Weiser, Sarah. 2012. *Authentic^{TM}: The Politics of Ambivalence in a Brand Culture*. New York: New York University Press.

Benkler, Yochai. 2006. *The Wealth of Networks: How Social Production Transforms Markets and Freedom*. New Haven, CT: Yale University Press.

Chen, Kuan-Hsing. 2010. *Asia as Method: Toward Deimperialization*. Durham, NC: Duke University Press.

Chubb, Andrew. 2015. "China's *Shanzhai* Culture: 'Grabism' and the Politics of Hybridity." *Journal of Contemporary China* 24 (92): 260–279.

Chumley, Lily. 2016. *Creativity Class: Art School and Culture Work in Postsocialist China*. Princeton, NJ: Princeton University Press.

Chun, Lin. 2019. "Mass Line." In *Afterlives of Chinese Communism: Political Concepts from Mao to Xi*, edited by Christian Sorace, Ivan Franceschini, and Nicholas Loubere, 121–126. Canberra: ANU Press.

Diamond, Norma. 1983. "Model Villages and Village Realities." *Modern China* 9 (2): 163–181.

Eckstein, Lars, and Anja Schwarz. 2017. *Postcolonial Piracy: Media Distribution and Cultural Production in the Global South*. London: Bloomsbury Academic.

Fei, Xiaotong, Gary G. Hamilton, and Wang Zheng. 1992. *From the Soil: The Foundations of Chinese Society*. Berkeley: University of California Press.

Han, Dong. 2010. "Can I Own My Writings and Sell Them Too? A Brief History of Copyright in China from the Late Qing Era to Mao's China." *Chinese Journal of Communication* 3 (3): 329–346.

Hardt, Michael, and Antonio Negri. 2005. *Multitude: War and Democracy in the Age of Empire*. Reprint. New York: Penguin Books.

Ho, Josephine. 2010. "ShanZhai: Economic/Cultural Production through the Cracks of Globalization." Paper presented at Crossroads: 2010 Cultural Studies Conference, Lingnan University, Hong Kong, June 17–21, 2010.

Irani, Lilly. 2019. *Chasing Innovation: Making Entrepreneurial Citizens in Modern India*. Princeton, NJ: Princeton University Press.

Jaszi, Peter. 1991. "On the Author Effect: Contemporary Copyright and Collective Creativity." *Cardozo Arts and Entertainment Law Journal* 10: 293.

Jenkins, Henry, Sam Ford, and Joshua Green. 2018. *Spreadable Media: Creating Value and Meaning in a Networked Culture*. Reprint. New York: New York University Press.

Lindtner, Silvia M. 2020. *Prototype Nation: China and the Contested Promise of Innovation*. Princeton, NJ: Princeton University Press.

Marwick, Alice E. 2015. *Status Update: Celebrity, Publicity, and Branding in the Social Media Age*. New Haven, CT: Yale University Press.

Meisner, Mitch. 2016. "Dazhai: The Mass Line in Practice." *Modern China* 4 (1): 27–62.

Srnicek, Nick. 2016. *Platform Capitalism*. Cambridge: Polity Press.

Wallis, Cara, and Jack Linchuan Qiu. 2012. "Shanzhaiji and the Transformation of the Local Mediascape in Shenzhen." In *Mapping Media in China*, edited by Wanning Sun and Jenny Chio, 127–143. London: Routledge.

Woodcock, Jamie, and Mark Graham. 2020. *The Gig Economy: A Critical Introduction*. Cambridge: Polity Press.

Zhang, Lin. 2017. "Entrepreneurial Labor: Digital Work and Subjectivities in China's New Economy." PhD thesis, University of Southern California.

Zhang, Lin. 2020. "When Platform Capitalism Meets Petty Capitalism in China: Alibaba and an Integrated Approach to Platformization." *International Journal of Communication* 14: 114–134.

Zhang, Lin, and Anthony Fung. 2013. "The Myth of 'Shanzhai' Culture and the Paradox of Digital Democracy in China." *Inter-Asia Cultural Studies* 14 (3): 401–416.

3 How Do Workers Survive and Thrive in the Platform Economy? Evidence from China and the Philippines

Julie Chen and Cheryll Ruth Soriano

Information and communication technology (ICT) has long been deployed to facilitate the acceleration of capital accumulation and precipitate a spatial reorganization of work on a global scale (Castells 2000; Tsing 2009). Business process outsourcing (BPO) and call centers are early examples of "virtual" workplaces that enable the mobility of labor across national borders without the traveling of immigrant workers (Aneesh 2006). The recent rise of digital labor platforms, particularly crowdwork sites such as Upwork, has led scholars to argue that a planetary labor market is emerging, further disempowering workers and exacerbating existing structural and geographical inequalities (Graham and Anwar 2019). How do platform workers in developing countries adapt to the global expansion of online gig work—work that is performed and paid via the mediation of digital platforms? How can their work strategies inform our understanding of the platformization of work on a global scale?

The chapter, which is based on our respective research projects about platform labor, one based in the Philippines and the other in China, explores these questions. Cheryll Ruth Soriano has spent four years conducting an ethnographic study of online freelance work and digital labor in the Philippines, and Julie Chen has studied drivers on the ride-hailing platforms and riders on the food-delivery platforms in China for four years using surveys, qualitative ethnographic observations, and interviews. Our shared interests in workers' lived experience led us to take a comparative perspective in exploring platform labor in the Philippines and China, two developing countries in Asia that are also major adopters of the platform economy.

This chapter focuses on the individual strategies and associational communities that workers establish in different spaces, virtually and physically, for their survival, development, and self-empowerment in a global context of platformization. Two arguments are advanced. First, the relationships embodied in the digital labor process demonstrate the interconnectedness between global capital and local labor (Kelly 2001). We demonstrate that local labor structures and conditions mediate the flow of global and state capital and the global rise of platform-based labor management to produce a local political economy of informal labor transactions and sensemaking. Second, we argue that these localized relationships often exist within the labor regimes permitted or even promoted by the national government through regulatory institutions and policies. This gives rise to diverse means of labor resistance strategies corresponding to workers' local culture of sensemaking, association, and informal organizing. Addressing the poor working conditions worldwide in the platform economy, some scholars have advocated new models for unionizing in digital workplaces (Wood, Lehdonvirta, and Graham 2018; Graham and Anwar 2019), but the challenge posed by planetary labor markets for meaningful collective arrangements is well recognized. The national labor regime provides a good context for understanding why it would be important to look beyond unionizing to examine initiatives emerging from workers to help them survive or even thrive in planetary labor markets.

We first discuss the roles played by state policy and regulations, local labor conditions, and digital platforms in shaping the labor regime for platform work in the Philippines and in China. We then demonstrate the various ways in which workers create informal associations and individual resistance strategies in the platform economy. We conclude with a discussion on the implications of the comparative study for our understanding of platform work in globalized platform capitalism.

Global Capital in Relation to State/National Labor Regimes

The Philippines

The growth and popularity of platform labor in the Philippines has to be understood in the context of the rise of BPO and a long tradition of the government pushing a strategy of labor export. Initially concentrated in metropolitan Manila, the government push for BPO growth as a job-generation strategy has allowed it to spread across the country. In the face of high unemployment rates, and with a significant English-speaking population, many Filipinos have taken on BPO work, most of which involves offshored call center or customer service support, data entry, technical support, or medical transcription work. BPO presents itself as a viable alternative to labor migration and offers many Filipinos a relatively secure tenure, which is not enjoyed by the local workforce in the manufacturing and agricultural sectors. However, the precarious conditions of BPO work are well documented, including long work hours and mental and emotional stress resulting from attending to irate customers on a daily basis, constant night shifts, mandatory overtime, and holiday work (EILER 2012; Fabros 2016). Platform labor, which allows workers to earn from home, thereby avoiding severe traffic conditions in the metropolis, emerged as a highly attractive alternative for many BPO workers who became discontent with the precarity and stress associated with BPO work.

To address the needs of the unemployed and marginalized groups, the Philippine government is now promoting platform labor, through its digitaljobsPH program, as a complement to BPO work, a catalyst for urban and rural development, and even an attractive option for fresh graduates. The labels of "modern heroes" and "world-class workers" that were previously attached to overseas Filipino workers and BPO employees are now being conferred on platform workers as well. The Philippines' Department of Information and Communications Technology (DICT)[1] estimated that at least two million Filipinos obtain gigs through online labor platforms, while Payoneer (2020) reported the Philippines to be sixth among the fastest-growing gig economies globally.

Despite the difficult conditions that platform workers face in the Philippines (Soriano and Cabañes 2019, 2020), including cases of exploitation and over work, it is undeniable that many Filipinos have found online freelance work to be highly fulfilling, allowing them to earn a good wage, raise their families comfortably, and even obtain a sense of self-worth. An important local context to be considered is the continuing expansion of the large informal economy and the continuing "flexibilization" of work that is driving the popularity of platform labor (Ofreneo 2013). The many Filipino professionals and casual employees who are moving into platform labor need to be considered in the context of the many others who belong to the informal economy—including food peddlers, mobile credit sellers, public transportation drivers, caregivers, domestic helpers, and student research assistants—who are also leaping eagerly at opportunities to obtain work on digital labor platforms. This explains why, despite critiques about poor security and the absence of long-term advancement, online labor platforms are often viewed locally as a viable employment option. The absence of adequate alternative job opportunities and the state's promotional attitude are what the Philippines and China have in common when it comes to the local development of a platform workforce.

China

The growth of the platform economy in China is phenomenal. In 2019, more than RMB 3.2 trillion (US$469 billion) worth of transactions took place in China's platform economy, involving 800 million Chinese, an 11.6 percent increase in the number of users from 2018 (SIC 2020). An estimated 78 million people have become service providers on these platforms, with about 12 million drivers working for the largest ride-hailing platform, Didi Chuxing (hereafter DiDi) (SIC 2020) and 2.7 million riders working for Meituan, a food-delivery platform that controls about 65 percent of the domestic market (SIC 2019).

Behind this exceptional growth is an influx of global and state capital, as well as institutional support from the central government. Chinese Internet companies Tencent and Alibaba are among the 10 largest tech companies in the world (Divine 2020), and they are aggressive investors in, and acquirers of, start-up companies. DiDi, which controls over 90 percent of the ride-hailing market in China, is one of the best-funded tech start-up companies, with $18.57 billion in funding, more than Uber before its initial public offering (CB Insights 2018). Among the top investors in DiDi are tech companies like Apple, SoftBank, Tencent, and Alibaba. In addition to private funds, DiDi has also attracted investment from prominent state-owned enterprises like China Life Insurance, the largest life insurer in China, and China Investment Corporation, a sovereign wealth fund that manages China's foreign exchange reserves and reports to the State Council (see Chen and Qiu 2019). The rapid development and adoption of mobile Internet is inseparable from the long-standing governmental investment in telecommunication infrastructure, including (more recently) artificial intelligence, big data, and cloud computing (W. Chen 2019).

Apart from offering policy support and investing directly in digital companies, the Chinese central government has also played a prominent role in restructuring the economy. Since the economic reform of the 1970s, the national government has orchestrated, via development strategies, a labor regime that reserves formal, well-protected employment to limited sectors while leaving informal labor practices to dominate manufacturing, construction, and now the urban service sector (Huang 2009; Lee and Kofman 2012). Since 2015, the national strategy to reduce industrial overcapacity in steel and coal has set in motion a new wave of precarious labor by state design (Lee and Kofman 2012), supplying abundant labor, including recently laid-off factory workers and migrant workers from rural areas (such as Hebei and Anhui Provinces) who face a shrinking labor market for manufacturing and construction jobs. Because of an economic slowdown, employment creation has become the top priority for the government to maintain economic and social stability.

The discourses of job creation and platform work as a new form of flexible employment with more autonomy are being promoted by leading platform companies in both the ride-hailing and food-delivery service sectors—as well as in national policies—to legitimate the economic and labor market restructuring (J. Y. Chen 2020). The discursive currency of official terminology such as "new forms of employment" accentuates the aspirations of working in the Chinese digital economy. Empirical studies, however, have found that the platform economy is dominated by informal workers who have little collective bargaining power and usually lack labor contracts or employment-related benefits (J. Y. Chen 2018; Sun 2019; Zhang 2019). Lax enforcement of existing labor law in China (Chan 2020) also contributes to the prevalence of precarious work conditions and the absence of social insurance among platform workers.

In short, while the Chinese government may appear to have played a more direct role than the Filipino government in fostering a platform economy through state capital investment, the cultural promotion of the platform economy as the national scheme to participate in global capitalism is no different. The divergent existing local labor regimes—that is, the preexisting BPO workforce and the information infrastructure in the Philippines, and the state-led shift in the labor market from manufacturing to service industry and a lack of an English-speaking workforce in China—have partially contributed to the booming of crowdwork in the Philippines and also the rapid development of a local-service platform economy in China. However, the economic pressure of global platform capitalism (Srnicek 2016), which has severely constrained the job opportunities available for workers globally, has also contributed to a deterioration of work conditions and labor rights in both developing countries.

Beyond Unionizing

Corresponding to the global spread of platform-mediated labor management catalyzed by the global flow of capital, platform workers across the world are fighting back through protests and strikes to unionize and enact an array of informal tactics of counteraction, and workers in the Philippines and China are no exception. However, their resistance strategies are constrained by local institutions and, at the same time, rooted in the local culture of informal association and workaround practices. There is no denying the importance of institutionalizing workers' right to unionize, but it is also important to explore the wide range of resistance strategies developed by platform workers in developing countries like the Philippines and China, where unionizing is ineffective or absent. In the Philippines, although wage workers have the right to self-organize and engage in collective bargaining, union membership continues to dwindle. Wage workers constitute 53 percent of the workforce in the Philippines, but less than 2 percent of that workforce (that is, less than 1 percent of the total workforce) is unionized, with annual strike numbers in the single digits (Ofreneo 2013; Serrano and Xhafa 2016). Scholars attribute this to the state's inability to properly protect workers and union members from employers' unfair labor practices (Serrano and Xhafa 2016).

In China, worker-initiated unionization is prohibited, and the state-sanctioned All-China Federation of Trade Unions (ACFTU) is the only legal trade union in the country. In the past few years, there have been scattered efforts to unionize platform workers at the municipal level (China Labour Bulletin 2018; Zhang 2019). The ACFTU campaigned in 2018 to mobilize various groups of workers, including drivers and couriers in the platform economy, to join the union.[2] But in practice, these newly established local unions for platform workers have been more interested in offering social support than in advocating for workers' collective bargaining rights (China Labour Bulletin 2019).

Therefore, it is worthwhile to examine ways other than formal unionizing in which workers organize in both countries. Specifically, we have observed that both Filipino workers on crowdwork platforms and Chinese workers on local-service platforms enact multiple "hidden resistance" strategies (Scott 1985) in their everyday working lives to circumvent the disciplinary controls embedded in platform labor arrangements.

Resistance Strategies in the Philippines: Enacting Imaginaries of Flexibility

Crowdwork platforms such as Upwork or Onlinejobs.ph impose control and extract value by acting as intermediary agents between workers (contractors) and clients; they also hold the power to determine the rules of interaction within their own digital ecosystems and facilitate conditions of work that they can update without consulting workers (Graham and Anwar 2019; McKenzie 2020). Labor platforms' affordances of search, matching, and datafication serving a large pool of clients (demand) and workers (supply) allow them to charge either the client or the worker (or both) for this service. Clients can explore the platform for workers or launch a competition for a job; at the same time, workers can vie for jobs by building a portfolio filled with personal information and their skills background.

However, we find that despite the disciplinary features of the platforms and clients, workers enact multiple strategies to circumvent and navigate platform and client controls. They engage in subtle forms of resistance and sensemaking (Shapiro 2018) through strategies such as "skills arbitrage," where they strategize in shifting between skills that can give them a better advantage (see Beerepoot and Lambregts 2014) or employ "platform diversification" by opening accounts across different platforms and maintaining as many networks and connections as possible within and outside these platforms. They also engage in temporal negotiation and reoutsourcing strategies that allow them to expand opportunities to take on larger pools of work against the controls of temporal arbitrage and the presumed limits of platform arrangements.

Strengthening the portfolio: Skills arbitrage and platform diversification   Portfolio construction is important in crowdwork because this determines a worker's likelihood of attracting a client amid increasing competition. Some workers strategically curate their portfolios, adding skills that they may not yet have mastered but that, when contracted, they then attempt to gain through intense consultation with peers, joining Facebook groups with free coaching advice, and watching training videos on YouTube.

Given the increasingly competitive environment, this "fake it till you make it" mantra is articulated by workers and coaches in freelancing training and meetup events. Curation of one's skills is related to skills diversification, in which workers learn multiple skills and shift from one to another depending on the circumstantial demands of the client. As one worker explained to us, "Although building expertise in, say, search engine optimization is important, we have to be flexible and learn as many different skills and tools as possible. If you don't keep up with what the platform demands, it will be hard to compete." It appears that skills diversification is part of the workers' imaginaries of flexibility that attract them to platform labor in the first place—some begin with basic skills like data entry but believe that the relative flexibility afforded by platform work will allow them to experiment with different projects and learn skills as they go. Thus, in the worker imaginary, their capacity to shift and expand from one skill to another (and also expand their project portfolio) is limited only by their entrepreneurialism, which primarily involves a mindset of persevering through, adapting to, and "rising above" the platform's conditions.

Related to skills diversification is platform diversification, in which workers learn how to flexibly shift from one platform to another (see Beerepoot and Lambregts 2014) to meet their own goals of earning a good wage and maintaining their competitiveness. Although the precarity embedded in the design of most labor platforms is well known, it is common practice for workers to diversify and create accounts in as many platforms as possible and expand their network to mitigate the challenges of labor seasonality and labor arbitrage. As an online freelancing coach explained to one of the authors, "Workers must learn how to explore as many platforms as possible. For if they stay in just one, like Upwork, they will be forced to take any project or rate offered to them by the platform."

Platforms have different focuses, features, and control mechanisms. As workers become familiar with them, they find it important to compare and make use of the respective advantages of each platform. Some, like Upwork, charge for fee cuts and "connects" (the number of projects a worker can bid on) that link them to a global pool of clients, for which Filipino workers must compete with aspirants from all over the world. However, Upwork also has a large number of clients and has institutionalized more safeguards against scams. On the other hand, Onlinejobs.ph, a foreign-owned platform that hires only Filipino workers, does not charge fee cuts for contracted projects. However, the rates can be lower, and the platform does not incorporate complaint mechanisms to protect workers from dishonest clients. There are also global platforms like 99Designs that attract those with specialized skills, and while they have relatively fewer jobs, the offered rates are higher, and there is a smaller pool of competitors. In sum, workers cushion against labor seasonality and precarity by selecting platforms that match their goals and capacities and by maintaining portfolios in diverse platforms.

Temporal negotiation Belying the imaginaries of flexibility, many workers also told us of the requirements to work within inflexible and predetermined schedules and to be constantly responsive to clients via email. Whereas "flexibility" and mobility have come to be important selling points of digital labor platforms, the professional habits that workers have created around these "always-on" and highly monitored work arrangements have forged new standards of professionalism that continue to be legitimized in platform work. This leads to an unspoken yet compulsory need for workers to assume the habit of constantly "performing presence" (Gregg 2013), which can lead to a "presence bleed," generating anxiety and compelling workers to develop an extra sensitive attunement to staying on top of their work, along with the ability to anticipate what needs to be done.

Filipino crowdworkers in our study describe the tension between flexibility and constraint in platform work, such that, although the work caters to their imaginaries of flexibility, some clients require them to install time-monitoring apps such as Hubstaff. In response, they may employ various strategies to fake working time, from having their partners move the mouse occasionally as they attend to their children's needs to having multiple screens that allow them to perform other jobs while showing the client that they are actively working. Some workers strategize by completing a task ahead of schedule but not immediately notifying the client about the completion. This allows them to take on other jobs or perform household chores while still being paid for the job. Thus, although they are bound by time-monitoring tools and controls, crowdworkers develop temporal negotiation strategies to regain some autonomy from the constraints on "flexibility" that platforms impose. Nonetheless, because of fears of labor seasonality, some Filipino crowdworkers take on more work than they can cope with when it is available or substantially extend their working hours, ending up feeling overworked but anticipating that they will reap future benefits such as client loyalty, good evaluation ratings, or higher rates.

Reoutsourcing Large-scale projects, which normally entail better payment, are valuable for crowdworkers to enhance their portfolios but difficult to obtain if one is new to the platform or works alone. Upwork, for example, charges a 20 percent cut of the first $500 a registered worker bills a client on the platform, but the rate drops to 5 percent for contract billings starting at $10,000 (Upwork 2020). In order to take on large and more profitable projects, some workers in our study became single "worker-agencies" who outsource projects or segments of their projects to other workers, including family members or neighbors. These agencies are able not only to command flexibility in choosing the scale of projects to bid on and navigating across platforms, clients, or projects but also to negotiate for higher rates. In so doing, they can improve their online portfolios while also increasing their influence and reputation among their local community of recruits and the online clients alike, from which they generate significant social and financial capital. The arrangement of worker-agencies can help mitigate the risks and precarity of labor seasonality because it enables relatively stable incoming work—the segments of a large project—for the recruited workers and allows worker-agencies to take on longer-term projects and establish trust with clients, which may lead to higher rates and noncash benefits some clients are willing to offer to "trusted contractors."

In sum, the strategies enacted by Filipino crowdworkers involve multiple negotiations of the controls enacted by labor platforms and clients, underscored by imaginaries of flexibility (Soriano and Cabañes 2019) that workers associate with platform labor. Skills and platform diversification, temporal negotiation, and reoutsourcing, are strategies developed by workers to negotiate vulnerability. In rural development theory, "livelihood diversification" has been a long-running strategy applied by peasants to allow them to manage the seasonality of farming (Ellis 2000, 1999). The theory argues that poverty reduction hinges on the capacity of precarious workers to combine different livelihood strategies and resources, reducing their vulnerability to shocks and risks. Similarly, diversifying skills and platforms allows digital workers to generate a cushion to not only manage the challenges of platform labor but thrive amid these controls. Scholars have also asserted that the dominant temporal order requires workers to synchronize (Snyder 2016) their time with employers or with other workers, and that this expectation also tends to be present in platform labor. The attempt—where workers have few mechanisms for formal negotiation due to labor arbitrage—to be in harmony with clients' expectations can also "destabilize workers' other social tempos" (Chen and Sun 2020, 1565). However, as we have shown in this chapter, negotiated temporality can be crucial for workers to circumvent the temporal arbitrage strategies embedded in the design of platform labor. The reoutsourcing of larger-scale projects is made possible through the informal self-organization of local workers. Within these local systems of exchange, workers are able to gain important bargaining capacity to transact with clients and at the same time obtain control in determining the price of labor for each worker under their agency.

Resistance Strategies: Building Vernacular Knowledge and Solidarity via Community of Practices

The resistance strategies deployed by Filipino platform workers are underscored by neoliberal ideologies of "individual entrepreneurial initiative" (Gandini 2016, 4; also see van Doorn 2017), which compels workers to circumvent the controls of traditional corporate institutions and the inefficiencies of local institutions to seize the imagined opportunities of economic gains. Social media groups, such as Facebook groups dedicated to online Filipino freelancing, play a crucial role in helping Filipino crowdworkers to learn through communities of practice. By sharing everyday experience and practical strategies (tips) to navigate the crowdwork platform system, Filipino workers build "entrepreneurial solidarities" (Soriano and Cabañes 2020).

Like Filipino crowdworkers, Chinese drivers and couriers also employ platform diversification (registering on multiple platforms to seek jobs) and temporal negotiations. For example, food-delivery riders engage in temporal negotiations by comparing orders at different apps and picking the ones with better payment (Chen and Sun 2020). Chen (2018) also documented that some drivers not only register multiple accounts on multiple ride-hailing apps but participate in "algorithmic activism"—using cheating apps or bots to manipulate the algorithms. Some bots enable drivers with lower ratings to circumvent the rating restriction so that they can be available for high-fare ride requests, and others allow drivers to reject as many requests as they like without risking their ratings.

Chinese platform workers develop their livelihood survival strategies to cope with fierce labor market competition catalyzed by the platform companies and by weak regulatory enforcement in the absence of institutional labor protection. In China, despite the legalization of ride-hailing platforms in 2016 and the passage of relevant local policies regarding the labor rights of drivers, the platform companies' blatant regulatory violations are rampant (Chen and Qiu 2019). The labor market for on-demand service platforms aggravates the existing informality, resulting in a proliferation of informal work. According to Chen, Sun, and Qiu (2020), the online ride-hailing market in China includes taxi drivers, private drivers (self-employed), drive-to-own drivers,[3] and full-time subcontracted drivers. There is also a small fraction of drivers who are formally employed by the platform companies with access to institutional labor protection.[4] Subcontracted drivers are hired and managed by fleet companies that affiliate with platform companies. Each group of drivers faces different levels of flexibility, labor protections, and income deductions by the platform or the employer company. Similarly, for the online food-delivery market, there are platform-hired riders, crowdsourced riders, subcontracted riders, and in-house riders. The number of platform-hired food-delivery riders has seen a sharp decline accompanied by the rapid growth of other types of workers since the online food-delivery market was consolidated in 2018 by the two market leaders in China—namely, Meituan and Ele.me (the latter is now part of Alibaba, the giant e-commerce company).

The categories and labels for different types of riders keep changing, suggesting the platform capital's response to market volatility. For example, the leading platform

Meituan started to call subcontracted, full-time food-delivery workers *Zhuansong* riders and created a new category called *Lepao* for the crowdsourced riders who are willing to work full-time or near full-time. Compared with ordinary crowdsourced (self-employed) riders, *Lepao* food-delivery riders face stricter labor controls with a required number of fulfilled orders, minimum online time of nine hours with four-hour covering the peak time, and limited right to reject assigned orders, but they are prioritized for job allocation on the platform. The discrepancy among the employment types illustrates varied levels of informality, labor protection, and schedule flexibility (table 3.1).

The proliferation of informal work in China's platform economy points to the measures platform capital has taken to enhance the flexibilization of production and services by pitting workers against each other—with the result of undermining labor unity in the respective sectors. Against the context of a deteriorating and volatile labor market in the Chinese platform economy, the online communities and the historical tactics of informal organizing contribute to a certain level of collective action among Chinese platform workers, albeit with limited scale and impact. Informally employed taxi drivers in China have tended to rely on their social networks to mitigate the vulnerabilities of their informal occupations (Ding 2014). The practices of forming virtual communities and using communication tools to maintain strong ties with coworkers (who may also be fellow villagers or relatives) are preserved when these workers migrate to ride-hailing apps. It is now common for private drivers on ride-hailing platforms to

Table 3.1

The labor rights of Chinese food-delivery riders

Rider type	Employer	Base salary	Institutional labor protection and social security	Flexible schedule
Platform-hired	Platform company	Yes	Yes	No
Crowdsourced	Self-employed	No	No	Yes
Subcontracted	Third-party labor agencies	Occasionally	Occasionally	No
In-house	Restaurant	Mostly no	Mostly no	Depending on the employer
Zhuansong (Meituan)	Third-party labor agencies	Yes	Partly	No
Lepao (Meituan)	Self-employed	No	No	Minimum online time

Source: Table modified and updated from Chen, Sun, and Qiu (2020).

join one or two social media groups at the national or local levels or both. There are also driver groups based on existing social networks.

Similar to crowdworkers in India (Gray et al. 2016) and the Philippines, drivers in China establish groups on social media to help build communities of practice (Wenger 2000), which allow drivers to disseminate information (Qiu 2016) and produce vernacular knowledge about how to survive and make a living in the platform-mediated work environment. Scott (1990) called this vernacular knowledge made visible and collective, produced, and articulated in a wide spectrum of activities "hidden transcripts" of resistance. For example, workers post daily performance and jokes, exchange tips and advice on how to handle unjustified customer complaints, develop quasi-open-access manuals for license tests, and sometimes share illegal tricks on how to get away with declining assigned jobs. Drivers rely on their digital literacy as well as on the collective wisdom of their extended social networks to cocultivate practices to navigate the ride-hailing platforms, which constantly change their algorithms, promotional schemes, and politics. Drivers also develop contingent tactics of resistance in those networks; a practice known among drivers as "pinning the driver (in the map)" (*zhazhen* in Chinese) is a case in point. "Pinning the driver" can mean two different resistance tactics.

One tactic is to cheat and game the system. In the intercapitalist competitions between rival ride-hailing platforms, one common strategy for platforms is to inject millions of dollars in the form of discounts for passengers and bonuses for drivers to retain both groups on their platform while driving their rivals out of cash or out of market. In the heyday of such price wars, as between DiDi and Kuaidi in 2014 and between then-merged DiDi-Kuaidi and Uber in early 2016, a driver would collude with friends to claim the cash bonus by asking the friends to send fake ride requests and pretending to have completed the ride without having driven to the destination. The driver and friends would split the bonus afterward.

Another way of "pinning the driver" turns the location-tracking algorithm on the ride-hailing platforms on its head. During planned strikes, some participant drivers would request ride service in order to identify nonparticipants, and then cancel the order or offer bad ratings and complaints to punish the strikebreaking drivers. The tactics of "pinning the driver" show how drivers can exploit circumstantial opportunities based on their knowledge about the platform.

Online communities of practice are also important for mobilizing (Qiu 2016). In 2019, a group of food-delivery workers for a platform called Shansong protested the company's move to subcontract temporary staffing agencies to expand the workforce, which would lead to a decline in their wages. After sharing their grievance in several WeChat groups and online forums, the workers mobilized around 300 experienced riders to stage a protest at Shansong's headquarters in the Haidian district of Beijing.[5] The potential threat to social stability induced a swift intervention by the local police and concerned authorities, who in turn pressured the platform company to satisfy some of the riders' demands.

Although platform-dependent drivers and food-delivery workers are reported to be one of the fastest growing groups of recalcitrant and protesting workers in China (China Labour Bulletin 2017), workers' informal organizing efforts have yet to translate into institutional changes or sector-wide solidarity. Indeed, individual or collective tactics to circumvent platform labor control are more often driven by hopes of immediate economic gains or by the threat of income decline. In both the Philippines and China, while workers' contingent and hidden strategies may allow them to survive, or even some to thrive, under precarious conditions, they neither challenge the structures of power underlying digital platform labor nor make demands on the state. Instead, they inadvertently function to justify platform labor arrangements and allow the state to evade responsibility.

Conclusions

This chapter has examined the experiences of Filipino crowdworkers and Chinese platform workers in the ride-hailing and food-delivery sectors. At first glance, one could categorize these into two distinct forms of platform work—namely crowdwork and "work on-demand via apps" (De Stefano 2016). But these two forms of platform work have much in common when it comes to local encounters with global platform capitalism and workers' resistance strategies to survive the platform economy in the long shadow of neoliberalism.

First, the global proliferation of digital platforms to mediate service provision, either through crowdwork platforms or through local job-match for transport or food-delivery services, is inseparable from the global dwindling of institutional labor protection in the past few decades of neoliberalism (Srnicek 2016). Both Filipino crowdworkers and Chinese platform workers face continued casualization and flexibilization of work in the prevailing informal labor market in their countries; these trends are aggravated both by platformization and also by the local government's development policies. These development policies, which resonate across many developing countries, help create symbolic value and discursive currency for platform work in the Philippines and China alike. The valorization of BPO work and the recognition by the state of Filipinos as distinct global knowledge service workers help explain why workers have positive imaginaries about platform work. Chinese development policy and state capital investment also help orient platform work toward an "aspirational labor" in the digital economy (Duffy 2016). This suggests that the global platformization of work cannot be attributed to the proliferation of digital platforms or capitalistic market forces alone. The proactive role local government plays in shaping and restructuring the workforce in the domestic and global platform economy, along with the limited or inadequate job opportunities in the country, contributes to workers' acceptance of platform work as a viable or even desirable alternative.

The second common trend revealed by Filipino crowdworkers and Chinese platform workers lies in their development of hidden resistance strategies. Filipino crowdworkers have initiated efforts to collectivize platform labor through social media groups (Soriano and Cabañes 2020), and Chinese platform workers use ICTs to inform and empower themselves (Qiu 2016) for economic gains.

Aligned with a historical orientation toward labor export and BPO work, Filipino workers contend with mostly global platforms engaging a foreign clientele. Given the difficulties of challenging global labor platforms and the lack of institutional support from local labor agencies to protect platform workers or to facilitate better alternatives for them, workers are compelled to strategize on their own while learning and exchanging these strategies through connective associations on social media. The geographic concentration of the Chinese platform workers in this study who engage with work-on demand via apps, on the other hand, has allowed them to actualize online mobilizations into physical protests (difficult for geographically dispersed online Filipino freelance workers), even as they also enact individual resistance strategies.

Yet both global platforms such as Upwork and local platforms like DiDi centralize power in designing and controlling labor arrangements that make it difficult for workers, even as a collective force, to negotiate changes on their own, especially when state governments either invest directly in the platforms or celebrate them as solutions to unemployment and are unable to meaningfully intervene. Therefore, everyday forms of resistance, deployed individually and often in covert ways, remain the most common survival skill for both groups of workers. The underlying neoliberal logic, as Brown (2015, 131) argues, "makes individual agency and self-reliance the site of survival and virtue," and this catalyzes workers to self-enterprise either individually or in communities of practice to capture contingent opportunities on their route to survival and success (or failure) in the platform economy. In this sense, even when some platform workers indeed thrive in both countries, they work to reinforce the global platform economy's oppressive conditions and further normalize the neoliberal worker subject.

This comparative study also reveals some unique resistance tactics enacted by Filipino crowdworkers and Chinese platform workers, which may inform future possibilities of worker empowerment and inspire further research. For example, Filipino crowdworkers' tactic of reoutsourcing large-scale projects is made possible through the informal self-organization and mobilization of a network of local workers. It remains to be seen whether platform workers in China and elsewhere in the world could develop similar worker-initiated informal collectives to engage in payment negotiation.

Notes

1. Emmy Lou Delfin, interview by Cheryll Ruth Soriano, February 5, 2020, DICT, Quezon City.

2. See http://politics.people.com.cn/n1/2018/0411/c1001-29917885.html [in Chinese].

3. After DiDi consolidated the domestic market in April 2016, it introduced a drive-to-own program to recruit drivers. Successful applicants only needed put down a RMB 20,000 ($3,060) deposit to get a free new car from a partner auto company that they would drive full-time for DiDi. For them to own the car, they had to join a revenue-sharing program and meet a certain number of fulfilled ride services in the next two to three years.

4. For example, Shouqi Yueche, a ride-hailing app introduced by the state-owned enterprise Shouqi Group in Beijing. Drivers on its platform are all formally employed by Shouqi Group.

5. Riders shared news and pictures of the protest and the workers' demands in an online forum called "Riders' Family," but the link was taken down quickly.

References

Aneesh, A. 2006. *Virtual Migration: The Programming of Globalization*. Durham, NC: Duke University Press.

Beerepoot, Niels, and Bart Lambregts. 2014. "Competition in Online Job Marketplaces: Towards a Global Labour Market for Outsourcing Services?" *Global Networks: A Journal of Transnational Affairs* 15 (2): 236–255.

Brown, Wendy. 2015. *Undoing the Demos: Neoliberalism's Stealth Revolution*. New York: Zone Books.

Castells, Manuel. 2000. *The Rise of the Network Society*. 2nd ed. Vol. 1 of *The Information Age: Economy, Society and Culture*. Cambridge, MA: Wiley-Blackwell.

CB Insights. 2018. "Didi Chuxing—CB Insights." September.

Chan, Jenny. 2020. "Employee Voice in China." In *Handbook of Research on Employee Voice*, edited by Adrian Wilkinson, Jimmy Donaghey, Tony Dundon, and Richard B. Freeman, 524–538. https://doi.org/10.4337/9781788971188.00039.

Chen, Julie Yujie. 2018. "Thrown under the Bus and Outrunning It! The Logic of Didi and Taxi Drivers' Labour and Activism in the On-Demand Economy." *New Media & Society* 20 (8): 2691–2711.

Chen, Julie Yujie. 2020. "The Mirage and Politics of Participation in China's Platform Economy." *Javnost—The Public* 27 (2): 154–170.

Chen, Julie Yujie, and Jack Linchuan Qiu. 2019. "Digital Utility: Datafication, Regulation, Labor, and DiDi's Platformization of Urban Transport in China." *Chinese Journal of Communication* 12 (3): 274–289.

Chen, Julie Yujie, and Ping Sun. 2020. "Temporal Arbitrage, the Fragmented Rush, and Opportunistic Behaviors: The Labor Politics of Time in the Platform Economy." *New Media & Society* 22 (9): 1561–1579.

Chen, Julie Yujie, Sophie Ping Sun, and Jack Linchuan Qiu. 2020. "Deliver on the Promise of the Platform Economy." Research Report, January. Bangalore: IT for Change.

Chen, Wenhong. 2019. "Now I Know My ABCs: U.S.-China Policy on AI, Big Data, and Cloud Computing." *Asia-Pacific Issues* no. 140 (September): 1–8. Washington, DC: East-West Center. https://www.eastwestcenter.org/publications/now-i-know-my-abcs-us-china-policy-ai-big-data -and-cloud-computing.

China Labour Bulletin. 2017. "New Normal? Strike Map Shows Steady Trends in Worker Actions in First Half of 2017." *China Labour Bulletin*, August 15. http://www.clb.org.hk/content/new -normal-strike-map-shows-steady-trends-worker-actions-first-half-2017.

China Labour Bulletin. 2018. "How Food Delivery Riders in Shanghai Got Their Own Trade Union." *China Labour Bulletin*, January 25. https://www.clb.org.hk/content/how-food-delivery-riders-shanghai -got-their-own-trade-union.

China Labour Bulletin. 2019. "All-China Federation of Trade Union Reform Observation Report." [In Chinese.] *China Labour Bulletin*. https://clb.org.hk/sites/default/files/%E4%B8%AD%E5%8D% 8E%E5%85%A8%E5%9B%BD%E6%80%BB%E5%B7%A5%E4%BC%9A%E6%94%B9%E9%9D%A 9%E8%A7%82%E5%AF%9F%E6%8A%A5%E5%91%8A202001.pdf.

De Stefano, Valerio. 2016. "The Rise of the 'Just-in-Time Workforce': On-Demand Work, Crowdwork, and Labor Protection in the 'Gig-Economy.'" *Comparative Labor Law & Policy Journal* 37: 461–471.

Ding, Wei. 2014. *Mobile Homelands*. Beijing: Social Sciences Academic Press.

Divine, John. 2020. "The 10 Most Valuable Tech Companies in the World." *US News & World Report*, September 17. https://money.usnews.com/investing/stock-market-news/slideshows/most -valuable-tech-companies-in-the-world/.

Duffy, Brooke Erin. 2016. "The Romance of Work: Gender and Aspirational Labour in the Digital Culture Industries." *International Journal of Cultural Studies* 19 (4): 441–457.

EILER (Ecumenical Institute for Labor Education and Research, Inc.). 2012. *Modern Day Sweatshops in the Service Sector: Business Process Outsourcing (BPO) in the Philippines*. Kowloon, Hong Kong: Asia Monitor Resource Centre. https://www.amrc.org.hk/sites/default/files/Business%20Process%20 Outsourcing%20in%20the%20Philippines.pdf.

Ellis, Frank. 2000. *Rural Livelihoods and Diversity in Developing Countries*. Oxford: Oxford University Press.

Fabros, Alinaya. 2016. *Outsourceable Selves: An Ethnography of Call Center Work in a Global Economy of Signs and Selves*. Quezon City: Ateneo de Manila University Press.

Gandini, Alessandro. 2016. *The Reputation Economy: Understanding Knowledge Work in the Digital Society*. New York: Palgrave Macmillan.

Graham, Mark, and Mohammad Amir Anwar. 2019. "The Global Gig Economy: Towards a Planetary Labour Market?" *First Monday* 24 (4), April 1. https://doi.org/10.5210/fm.v24i4.9913.

Gray, Mary L., Siddharth Suri, Syed Shoaib Ali, and Deepti Kulkarni. 2016. "The Crowd Is a Collaborative Network." In *CSCW '16 Proceedings of the 19th ACM Conference on Computer-Supported Cooperative Work & Social Computing*, 134–147. New York: ACM Press.

Gregg, Melissa. 2013. "Presence Bleed: Performing Professionalism Online." In *Theorizing Cultural Work*, edited by Mark Banks, Rosalind Gill, and Stephanie Taylor, 136–148. London: Routledge.

Huang, Philip C. C. 2009. "China's Neglected Informal Economy: Reality and Theory." *Modern China* 35 (4): 405–438.

Kelly, Philip F. 2001. "The Local Political Economy of Labor Control in the Philippines." *Economic Geography* 77 (1): 1–22.

Lee, Ching Kwan, and Yelizavetta Kofman. 2012. "The Politics of Precarity: Views beyond the United States." *Work and Occupations* 39 (4): 388–408.

McKenzie, Monique de Jong. 2020. "Micro-Assets and Portfolio Management in the New Platform Economy." *Distinktion: Journal of Social Theory*, 1–20.

Ofreneo, Rene E. 2013. "Precarious Philippines: Expanding Informal Sector, 'Flexibilizing' Labor Market." *American Behavioral Scientist* 57 (4): 420–443.

Payoneer. 2020. *Freelancing in 2020: An Abundance of Opportunities*. New York: Payoneer. https://pubs.payoneer.com/docs/2020-gig-economy-index.pdf.

Qiu, Jack Linchuan. 2016. "Social Media on the Picket Line." *Media, Culture & Society* 38 (4): 619–633.

Scott, James C. 1985. *Weapons of the Weak: Everyday Forms of Peasant Resistance*. New Haven, CT: Yale University Press.

Scott, James C. 1990. *Domination and the Arts of Resistance: Hidden Transcripts*. New Haven, CT: Yale University Press.

Serrano, Melisa R., and Edlira Xhafa. 2016. *From "Precarious Informal Employment" to "Protected Employment": The "Positive Transitioning Effect" of Trade Unions*. Geneva: International Labour Organization. http://www.global-labour-university.org/fileadmin/GLU_Working_Papers/GLU_WP_No.42.pdf.

Shapiro, Aaron. 2018. "Between Autonomy and Control: Strategies of Arbitrage in the 'On-Demand' Economy." *New Media & Society* 20 (8): 2954–2971.

SIC. 2019. *China's Sharing Economy Development Report 2019*. [In Chinese.] Beijing: State Information Center, Sharing Economy Research Center.

SIC. 2020. *China's Sharing Economy Development Report 2020*. [In Chinese.] Beijing: State Information Center.

Snyder, Benjamin H. 2016. *The Disrupted Workplace: Time and the Moral Order of Flexible Capitalism*. Oxford: Oxford University Press.

Soriano, Cheryll, and Jason Cabañes. 2019. "Between 'World Class Work' and 'Proletarianized Labor.'" In *The Routledge Companion to Media and Class*, edited by Erika Polson, Lynn Schofield Clark, and Radhika Gajjala, 213–226. London: Routledge Handbooks Online.

Soriano, Cheryll, and Jason Cabañes. 2020. "Entrepreneurial Solidarities: Social Media Collectives and Filipino Digital Platform Workers." *Social Media + Society* 6 (2): 1–11. https://doi.org/10.1177/2056305120926484.

Srnicek, Nick. 2016. *Platform Capitalism*. Cambridge: Polity Press.

Sun, Ping. 2019. "Your Order, Their Labor: An Exploration of Algorithms and Laboring on Food Delivery Platforms in China." *Chinese Journal of Communication* 12 (3): 308–323.

Tsing, Anna. 2009. "Supply Chains and the Human Condition." *Rethinking Marxism* 21 (2): 148–176.

Upwork. 2021. "Work the Way You Want." https://www.upwork.com/i/how-it-works/freelancer/.

van Doorn, Niels. 2017. "Platform Labor: On the Gendered and Racialized Exploitation of Low-Income Service Work in the 'On-Demand' Economy." *Information, Communication & Society* 20 (6): 898–914. https://doi.org/10.1080/1369118X.2017.1294194.

Wenger, Etienne. 2000. *Communities of Practice: Learning, Meaning, and Identity*. New ed. Cambridge: Cambridge University Press.

Wood, Alex, Villi Lehdonvirta, and Mark Graham. 2018. "Workers of the World Unite? Online Freelancer Organisation among Remote Gig Economy Workers in Six Asian and African Countries." *New Technology, Work and Employment* 33 (2): 95–112.

Zhang, Chenggang. 2019. *Employment Transformation: Digital Business Models and New Forms of Employment in China*. [In Chinese.] Beijing: China Workers Publishing House.

4 "Follower Factories" in Indonesia and Beyond: Automation and Labor in a Transnational Market

Johan Lindquist

In March 2019, in a quiet residential area of Bekasi, a commuter city in the eastern part of greater Jakarta, I watch Ibrahim finish up a FIFA soccer game on his PlayStation gaming system. Ibrahim produces and sells services such as the delivery of followers, likes, and comments on platforms like Instagram—what in the media has often been called "click farming"—but what I, in line with market terminology, will call "social media marketing services" (SMM services). If a customer wants to artificially increase the follower count on their Instagram account—for instance, as a basis for monetary gain through sponsored posts for companies or simply to appear more popular—they can contact Ibrahim, who can use the large number of accounts he controls or can access to add, say, 1,000 followers to the customer's account for a fee.[1] Ibrahim's monthly gross income was at the time, he claimed, around US$40,000 (although this fluctuated, often dramatically)—90 percent of which came from Instagram followers—which makes him one of the leading click farmers in Indonesia.

With his earnings, Ibrahim purchased a two-story house, in which he lives with his wife and daughter on the bottom floor while running his business on the second floor, where eight staff members work. In the room adjacent to the second-floor living room area where we are hanging out, three men in their early twenties are sitting at desks in front of laptop computers, packs of cigarettes and coffee at their sides, two floor fans keeping the humid heat at bay. Two are using WhatsApp for customer service—answering questions, copy-pasting price lists, and responding to problems—and a third, a programmer, is fixing bugs on the software application they base their business on, though he spends most of his time developing a new, improved system. Ibrahim's right-hand man, Hari, deals with the order list, for which they use Google Sheets, while his cousin and sister are in charge of administration and bookkeeping. In another room, a content writer is producing articles in Indonesian for Ibrahim's websites—so far around 120—that focus on keywords that aim to push them to the top of Google rankings. In other parts of the sprawling city, five YouTubers promote his websites on their channels as marketing affiliates. Ibrahim spends most of his time browsing the Internet, checking on competitors, looking for new ideas, and trying to figure out the next step forward for his business in the face of a fluctuating, cutthroat market.

In recent years, it has been widely publicized that the "like economy" (Gerlitz and Helmond 2013) or "influence economy" (Confessore et al. 2018) centered on social media has become compromised as the market for SMM services has grown. Beginning in 2014, countless accounts have been deleted in recurring Instagram purges to counter artificial inflation in follower counts, with many major celebrities losing a large proportion of their followers (Leaver, Highfield, and Abidin 2020, 137–138). A recent industry report suggests that more than half of all Instagram accounts worldwide have fake followers or comments, or use engagement bots, while the numbers for social media influencers are far higher (Hickman 2019). "Vanity metrics" (Rogers 2018) and "Insta fraud" (Ellis 2019), perpetrated when so-called social media influencers are paid to market products based on artificially inflated follower counts, appear to be prevalent.

With the growth of a broader Internet platform economy, the range of SMM services is expanding. These include the supply not only of Instagram followers but also of You-Tube subscribers, LinkedIn endorsements, IMDb views, TikTok likes, and Spotify premium plays, to name a few. This market, however, has been dominated over the past few years by Instagram, which has increasingly mediated the rise of social media influencers and the transformation of celebrity culture globally. In light of this, Alice Marwick (2015, 137) coined the term *Instafame*, or "the condition of having a relatively great number of followers on the app." In Indonesia, the supply of Instagram followers has commanded the SMM services market to such a degree that it is simply termed *jual* (sell) *followers*.

Little is known, however, about the actual organization of this market and the infrastructure and labor that underpin it. The "click farms" or "follower factories" that produce and sell SMM services via digital marketplaces have been considered key actors in this market, with both terms suggesting the existence of an industry based on digital sweatshop labor (see Tai and Hu [2018]). Beyond journalists' reports (e.g., Clark 2015; Confessore et al. 2018), however, there is no systematic description or analysis of these types of workspaces and their relationship to the broader market. This chapter fills this empirical gap by drawing on interviews with, and ethnographic observations of, 30 actors involved in SMM services in Indonesia between 2017 and 2019, as well as Skype interviews with 10 additional actors in Bangladesh, India, Egypt, Morocco, Russia, Serbia, Turkey, and the US undertaken in 2019. Based on this data, the chapter offers a description of a part of the market for SMM services based on websites such as the ones Ibrahim runs.

The chapter describes the labor that underpins this market in order to engage with broader scholarly discussions concerning digital labor. The representation of click farms as digital sweatshops is based on at least three premises: the SMM services market is organized according to a particular form of labor ("clicking"), there is a spatial concentration of labor ("farms"), and labor relations within this space are generally exploitative ("sweatshops"). My Indonesian interlocutors show that these are oversimplifications. Addressing these premises, the chapter will describe how the SMM services market is less concerned with "clicking" than with developing automation. In this process, diverse forms of labor such as customer service and marketing become critical as SMM services businesses scale up and reach a broader range of customers. This labor is dependent on translocal networked relations within Indonesia and across national borders, but also tends to be concentrated in particular spaces and organized by entrepreneurs like Ibrahim along the lines of kinship or friendship. This suggests that these forms of digital labor must be approached as much in terms of intimacy and even aspiration as in terms of inequality. In Indonesia, digital labor should be considered in the context of historically situated forms of labor organization based on patron-client relations characterized by both a degree of intimacy and inequality (Scott 1976). Historically, the power of the patron was centered on the control of material resources such as land, but in the digital economy the primary resource is knowledge, creating an increasing degree of instability as patron-client relationships can more easily be disturbed or upended (see Aspinall [2013]).

More generally, this perspective from the Global South allows for an engagement with current debates that take the Global North or North-South divides as a starting point for approaching digital labor. Much can be gained from considering the market for SMM services in particular, and the organization of planetary digital labor more generally, as culturally situated. The view from the SMM services market in Indonesia reveals, for instance, that the organization of planetary digital labor is shaped by language competence and that the global market as a whole remains largely obfuscated to even my most successful interlocutors. This perspective accords with recent calls for an attentiveness to "big data from the South," not least with respect to how theory often disregards "the specificities of distinct geographies, cultures, and communities" (Milan and Treré 2019, 320), while resonating with ongoing scholarly discussions about digital labor that aim to make "invisible productive activities visible" (Casilli 2017, 3947). Indeed, recent work on "commercial content moderators" (Roberts 2019), "ghost work" (Gray and Suri 2019), and the "remote gig economy" (Wood et al. 2019) has highlighted the importance of the concealed and precarious global labor force that works for tech giants like Amazon, Facebook, and Uber, as well as labor platforms such as Upwork (Irani 2015). Building on this emerging research field, which has focused on labor organization *through* corporate platforms, this chapter turns to labor taking shape *alongside* these platforms and highlights the specificities of these relationships in an uneven transnational market.

The Rise of Digital Indonesia

With more than 30 million people, Jakarta, the capital of Indonesia, is one of the largest urban agglomerations in the world; it is also characterized by an intense use of social media. In 2012, it was named the world's most active Twitter city (Lipman 2012). Five years later, it had the most location tags on Instagram Stories (Taylor 2017). Ride-hailing apps such as the Indonesian Gojek and Singaporean Grab have developed a wide range of services—from food delivery to cleaning services—that have transformed the urban landscape in Jakarta and other cities across the country (see, for example, Ford and Honan [2017]). Indonesians are also world leaders in time spent on the mobile Internet, around four hours per day, with nearly 85 percent of users accessing the Internet through a mobile device in 2015 (Google and Temasek 2017). For many people in Indonesia today, connecting to the Internet means using social media platforms. As Merlyna Lim (2018, 163) puts it, without a hint of irony, in Indonesia "Facebook, in fact, is more popular than the Internet."

Most of my interlocutors came of age in this rapidly expanding digital environment—the older ones in Indonesian-style Internet cafés (*warnet*), learning through collective browsing and inexpensive all-night sessions, the younger ones through individual smartphones (Lim 2018, 156). In this process, Internet cafés have been replaced by convenience stores such as 7-Eleven, which offer free Wi-Fi, thus becoming nodes in a "cyberurban" landscape where youth hang out (*nongkrong*), communicate, and share ideas (Lim 2018, 166). As a result, Internet cafés have increasingly been transformed into gaming centers that depend on high bandwidth. It is in these kinds of social spaces that my interlocutors have learned, through YouTube tutorials, Facebook groups, and Internet forums, how to make money with friends in the emerging digital economy. In these contexts, there is a pervasive discourse of being self-taught (*autodidakt*). As one of my interlocutors put it, he learned "along the way" (*dijalani* in Indonesian or *dilakoni* in Javanese). The key actors in this market are thus generally "geeks" who became experts through their own will rather than through formal training (Jones 2011, 19–20).

Although my interlocutors are geographically concentrated to a degree in the Jakarta region—particularly in Bekasi, Tangerang, and Bogor, major urban areas in the greater metropolitan region—many of them live in other major cities such as Bandung, Pekanbaru, and Yogyakarta. A few inhabit smaller cities. One of the key actors in the Indonesian market is even based in Amsterdam, where he had moved as a child with his parents from Indonesia. They are mainly young men, the majority in their late teens and early 20s, with the oldest in his early 30s. Most have a lower-middle-class to middle-class background—their parents are entrepreneurs, office workers, or teachers—and more than half have some college education. Their customers include web-based shops, companies, celebrities, politicians, and social media influencers. But they also include, for instance, nongovernmental organizations (NGOs), government agencies, provincial police officers, and, not least, high school students in search of Instafame.

Ibrahim entered the SMM services market in his teens, when he started playing the multiplayer role-playing game World of Warcraft and soon learned that it was possible to sell World of Warcraft accounts on digital marketplaces such as Kaskus (www.kaskus .co.id). When Twitter quickly became a public presence in Indonesia in 2012, Ibrahim's primary goal was to rise to the top of the rankings. He began to create Twitter accounts until he had around 100,000, which he eventually began selling on Kaskus, setting the stage for his business as it has developed until today. His story is familiar among my interlocutors, who often started out with gaming, hacking, or carding (i.e., credit card fraud)—not primarily in order to make money but to compete with peers.

While making money has certainly become their primary incentive, it is important to recognize the social element of play, and deception itself as a form of play, as a driving force for the evolution of the SMM services market since 2012. This is in line with scholarly writing that has highlighted the intimate links between play and labor (or "playbor") in emerging digital worlds (e.g., Scholz 2013; Postigo 2016). Regarding the Chinese game industry, Lin Zhang and Anthony Fung, in their article "Working as Playing? Consumer Labor, Guild and the Secondary Industry of Online Gaming in China" in the February 2014 issue of *New Media & Society*, have identified a "secondary industry" consisting of "gamer-initiated business and services that emerged to fill gaps in the chain of game production and consumption, which occupy a grey area that often merges consumption with production and play with profits" (quoted in Tai and Hu 2018, 2370–2371). It is in this gray area of gamers, hackers, and entrepreneurs—located alongside global platforms such as Instagram—that the Indonesian SMM services industry has taken shape.

The SMM Services Market

The market for SMM services is highly complex and characterized by a wide range of practices that often develop through experimentation. This chapter is concerned neither with comprehensively listing these practices nor with the impossible task of describing this market or the production of SMM services. Instead, the focus is on the forms of labor that underpin the reselling, or brokering, of these SMM services through websites. While my most successful interlocutors control a large number of Instagram accounts that they use when selling SMM services, they are not primarily concerned with mass-producing accounts. Instead, they generally run websites that focus on automated reselling, which has become an increasingly important part of the market around the world. This allows the significant scaling up of their businesses.

Sellers like Ibrahim need buyers to find the websites through which they sell their services. An Internet search for "buy follower" (*beli follower*), for instance, lists a wide range of websites where it is possible to purchase SMM services. Underpinning these websites are the so-called admin panels through which the website is managed, content is produced, and scripts are run that make the automated purchasing and selling of SMM services possible. These admin panels form the basis for a webshop. Some of the inter- locutors create panels themselves, but these are also increasingly available in a modular form for purchase or rent, a rudimentary version of services offered by the Canadian e-commerce giant Shopify.

Ibrahim has two primary websites at the top of Indonesian Google rankings, one for direct sales to clients and the other for resellers. The direct sales website offers more extensive individual customer support, while the reseller's website is largely automated and therefore cheaper. On the former website, a buyer—a social media influencer, for instance—contacts customer service and places a direct order. The buyer simply chooses the service they are interested in, say 1,000 Instagram followers, sends their Instagram user ID, and pays prior to transfer. On the latter website, it is necessary to register as a member. Members are able to log in, choose services from a menu, and after adding money to their account—usually through a bank transfer[2]—resell to their own customers in what is ideally a seamless process. In 2019, the reseller website had 6,000 registered resellers, of whom around 2,000 were highly active, which is in line with the most successful reseller sites in Indonesia.

For Instagram followers alone, depending on what services are currently available, customers can choose between dozens of types of accounts. Most notably, they vary in quality. The lowest-quality and cheapest accounts lack photos or posts and easily "drop" or are closed by Instagram. The higher-quality and more expensive accounts demand greater investment in terms of knowledge or labor—a photo, multiple posts, and some comments—and therefore have a higher chance of being identified as "authentic" by Instagram's algorithms. Ibrahim generally prioritizes the middle range but tests the accounts before reselling, as there is a balance between low prices and a good repu- tation for quality followers among the community of resellers that maximizes prof- its. There are also choices regarding speed of transfer—followers can be "injected" en masse into purchasing accounts or "dripped" in a gradual transfer so as not to awaken suspicion—and regarding the identity or geographical location of the followers: male or female, Brazilian or Indonesian, even from specific cities.

Application programming interfaces (APIs) facilitate data exchange between applications, allow for the creation of new applications, and form the foundation for the "web as platform." Critical to the evolution of digital platforms ranging from Facebook to Upwork (Helmond 2015; Gray and Suri 2019), APIs are also at the center of the SMM services market. Through a simple procedure that requires no programming skills—it can be learned from Internet forums or YouTube tutorials—Ibrahim can create a multi-sided interface between websites (usually located abroad) and his resellers in Indonesia, so that SMM services can be purchased and resold automatically. In other words, when his customer in Indonesia purchases 1,000 Instagram followers from his website, these are in fact automatically transferred from another seller—based in India, for instance—via API. This process is often disrupted during Instagram's security updates, however; the international market comes to a standstill, with an ensuing scramble to match new algorithms before businesses are able to run again.

Ibrahim's staff fills the orders for the direct sales website manually, which basically means copying and pasting the buyer's Instagram user ID and inserting within the software programs they are running the number of followers that will be purchased and in what time frame. The staff thus rarely engage in "clicking," more often "copy-pasting," *copas* for short. This is also the case with customer service, in which price lists and standard responses are copy-pasted, usually via WhatsApp.

Ibrahim focuses on the Indonesian market, not least due to his lack of English language skills. There is no Indonesian seller with a significant presence on the international market. In fact, most have limited knowledge of the broader international websites that they purchase from or the actual source of the services they purchase, guessing that they are also resellers and that the actual production of accounts takes place elsewhere—perhaps in India, Russia, or Turkey. Ibrahim is obsessed with figuring out the source of the production of accounts, so that he can offer competitive prices that would allow him to "go global." A common conspiracy theory among resellers is that Instagram itself is the source of the fake follower business and that the most successful players have help on the "inside."

Reorganizing Labor

The increasing use of admin panels within the SMM services market has brought about the combination of automated processes with new forms of labor organization. In this development, it is possible to see how many of the most successful SMM service businesses in Indonesia, and across the world, take a similar form: one key entrepreneur recruits a group of friends, relatives, or neighbors, who are paid a monthly salary and work in a shared physical space, usually in collaboration with others at a distance. The shift from play to labor is thus aligned with enduring social relationships.

Many of the most successful sellers often started out mass-producing accounts on their own—as Ibrahim did with Twitter—but later came to focus on reselling, thereby concentrating labor on marketing, customer service, and particularly Internet research, which leads to greater profit margins. For instance, Adi, my Indonesian interlocutor based in Amsterdam, who has been selling SMM services for nearly a decade, described a process whereby he had begun producing social media accounts through automated processes based on SIM-card verification. There were, however, frequent problems with automation, which made manual interventions necessary. He eventually realized that it was far easier and more profitable to turn over the production of accounts to digital labor platforms such as Fiverr. A market for admin panels has similarly developed centered on a small number of key developers. Well-functioning SMM service reseller websites have thus become widely available, increasing the incentive for entrepreneurs like Ibrahim and Adi to engage in arbitrage, while largely outsourcing technological innovation. As sales have scaled up and competition increased, Ibrahim and Adi have come to focus above all on reselling even though both have significant programming skills.

In particular, diverse forms of marketing strategies become critical. Sellers spam ads through accounts on Instagram and other social media platforms. For instance, Agus, based in Jakarta, had two staff designing ads for dozens of Instagram accounts that he used to market his own services. Over time, however, Ibrahim and others have shifted their strategy as Instagram increasingly closes down these types of accounts, engaged in what the platform terms "inauthentic activities,"[3] and ramps up security updates. Instead, Ibrahim primarily concentrates on pushing his own websites to the top of Google rankings through search engine optimization. He initially purchased Google ads but has more recently hired a university graduate as a full-time content writer to develop his blog, a strategy that appears to be both less expensive and more effective. To target potential resellers who lack previous experience and knowledge (i.e., entrants on the scene), he develops rankings with regard to basic keywords such as *jual follower* (sell follower)—terms that seasoned actors would never search for except to check the competition. Like Ibrahim, Adi paid a content writer to use specific keywords for titles, keywords, images, and hyperlinks based on research he conducted. Furthermore, Ibrahim and others also pay YouTube affiliates to market their services on their channels, particularly to recruit resellers.

Entrepreneurs like Ibrahim were constantly browsing the Internet and engaging in forums in order to learn more about developments in the market. Since being an early user of key terms is important for moving to the top of Google rankings, anticipating and describing how the market will develop appears to be critical. Adi, for instance, had his content writer blog about TikTok as it was becoming popular in anticipation that services would become available for purchase. Figuring out the best admin panels on the market and, above all, gaining an in-depth understanding of the differences in pricing and quality of the vast range of services available in Indonesia and around the world are absolutely critical.

Customer service is also important and should preferably be on call around the clock. As described in the opening vignette, Ibrahim had several staff dealing with customer service, responding to questions about and problems with services. Much of this work was done on laptops via WhatsApp or other platforms such as Line, but it is easily done on smartphones. During the time we spent together, Yohanes and Markus, who were based in Tangerang in Jakarta, were constantly in touch with customers on their phones, even while on the move. When they gave me a ride to the airport, Yohanes was texting in the driver's seat while Markus was steering with one hand on the wheel.

Spaces of Labor

Like Ibrahim, Agus—in his early 30s and one of the oldest and most experienced of my interlocutors—based his business out of a residential house he had purchased on the street where he had grown up in Tangerang in northwest Jakarta. In both cases, there was a clear spatial separation between family life and business. Unlike Ibrahim, Agus did not have a wife and children, but he kept the door to his bedroom, located behind the main office space, closed at all times. The public part of both houses had the feel of many small businesses or NGOs I had previously visited around the country, with desks and computers set up in offices in what would typically be a residential building. This is reminiscent of Chinese gold-farming "squads" who play online games in order to gather "virtual loot" that can be exchanged for "real-world currencies" (Tai and Hu 2018, 2371), much like Ibrahim did with World of Warcraft. These Chinese squads work in spaces that "look no different from a typical office arrangement" (Tai and Hu 2018, 2374). This setup contrasted with that of Yohanes, who moved to Tangerang from North Sulawesi with a group of three friends because the city has the best broadband in Indonesia and a well-known media college where they all study. He shared an apartment with his friends, but although they often worked on laptops there, they did not have defined workplaces. When we met at Starbucks, Yohanes pulled out his phone and told me, "This is where I work."

There was often a balance between the illicitness of the business and the allure of professionalism and legitimacy in the shaping of office spaces. While Yohanes and his friends, all in their early 20s, lived in a relatively anonymous apartment complex and couldn't have cared less about running a legitimate business, older interlocutors in residential areas were more concerned with how they were perceived and often attempted to hide their business from others. Neither Agus nor Ibrahim had signs in front of their houses to identify their business. Some neighbors wondered how they made money while working late at night indoors. It was considered *aneh* (strange), as one interlocutor put it, alluding to dark connections with the spirit world. In some cases, SMM services were the (more successful) back-office business of a business that ostensibly focused on website maintenance. Andreas, who for a time ran one of the best-known SMM services websites in Indonesia, rented an office in Jakarta's Central Business District in order to create a stronger impression on his customers and competitors. Indeed, even after his business had collapsed, a couple of Andreas's competitors believed he must be doing very well since he listed his office there. Similarly, most resellers created a distinctive logo and even staff uniforms. In some cases, they had office addresses that even appeared on Google Maps, but when I stopped by there was no such place.

Ibrahim's workspace is the closest to what might be termed a "digital sweatshop" that I have seen in Indonesia: one entrepreneur controls the business and the majority of the profits, while a group of workers gathered in one physical space are paid around $150 each month, with regular bonuses of around $100 per month. But the arrangement can hardly be understood in strictly exploitative terms—if anything, it is based on "lopsided friendships," kinship relations, or evolving patron-client relations (Wolf 2001). Acquaintances, friends, brothers, and cousins thus form the basis for the cheap labor that supplements automated processes from below. This type of arrangement offers critical insight not only into how planetary digital labor is taking shape in practice but also into how labor and commerce are organized in the cyberurban landscape (see Lim 2018, 166; Simone 2020). This reliance among small-scale entrepreneurs on intimate relations with workers accords with, but also moves us beyond, historical patterns of labor organization in Indonesia and across Asia. While patron-client relations have historically been based on material resources such as land and the importance of accessing seasonal labor, digital labor is primarily centered on knowledge. This fact can be considered in relation to an ongoing decentering of patron-client relations in the context of interrelated processes of political decentralization and digitalization in the post-Suharto era (Aspinall 2013). These types of labor relations are thus far more unstable; for instance, a few months of work for a business can easily form the basis for starting one's own independent business. Such instability leads to an upending or fragmentation of historical forms of patron-client relationships in the context of planetary urbanization (see Brenner and Schmid 2012).

The instability becomes evident in different ways. Agus, for instance, was constantly worried about his staff stealing the secrets that underpinned his business, and he offered several examples of former workers who had used his ideas to start up their own businesses. Andreas told me that it was difficult to collaborate with close friends or relatives because of the fluctuating nature of the market, which often made it difficult to offer a stable salary. This is consistent with the work of Janet Carsten (1997), who describes how the owners of Malay fishing boats avoided working with close kin because of the high-risk nature of the endeavor, as failure risked not only economic income but also, more seriously, kinship relations. Other Indonesian entrepreneurs, however, were more relaxed about these processes, as they recognized that ambitious workers, often friends, were bound to leave sooner or later. There was a general excitement among most of them that Indonesia was "going digital," thus shaping a broader sensibility centered on the "capacity to aspire" (Appadurai 2004).

To create a sustainable business, however, it is critical not only to retain staff but also to recruit a large group of resellers, who may be located anywhere in the country. Resellers can easily move between sellers such as Ibrahim and Agus, and create new automated connections through APIs. Agus called such resellers *copaser* (copy-pasters), with disdain, highlighting their lack of programming knowledge. Although it is possible to change connections, many do not, because they have established relations with the seller, receive good customer service, or are simply lazy. As Wayan, a Jakarta-based reseller, put it, "Malas ganti API, ikut teman" (I am too lazy to change the API, I just do what my friend does). In order to draw resellers into his fold, Ibrahim has developed an Android application for them and creates tutorials in which he offers tips on how to improve sales. As is typical across reseller sites, he offers likes and followers as bonuses based on monthly sales rankings. This is important in retaining a sense of community and ultimately their engaged membership. Although Ibrahim and other major sellers generally do not know their members, there is often interaction on WhatsApp groups and particularly on Facebook, where they brag about their economic success.

Generally, the SMM services market is thus dominated by cottage industries centered in particular places and on friendship, kinship, or neighborhood relationships. Labor does not necessarily take place in a well-defined space, as the term *cottage* suggests, but it is generally centered on a particular urban area, as in the case of Yohanes and his friends. To be successful, however, these cottage industries are highly dependent not only on networked connections with service providers and resellers but also, for instance, on You-Tubers who act as marketing affiliates. There is thus a continuum between concentrated and dispersed labor spaces.

Moving toward the Future

Many workers who engage with digital platform economies remain based in established employment structures—as is the case for Chinese taxi drivers who work across on-demand platforms like Didi Chuxing and with companies that control the traditional taxi industry (Chen 2018, 2694). This attentiveness to how platform economies coexist with established economies is critical when considering how both digital labor and general market engagement are shaped in cultural and economic contexts. My most successful interlocutors were highly cognizant of the fluctuations of the market for SMM services, recognizing that it could very well collapse within a few years as a result of security updates, increasing competition, or even the demise of the like economy. As a result, most were constantly looking for new opportunities. Arif, based in Jakarta, used his reseller business to boost his social media influencer account, which was his public persona and major source of income. Agus had developed a web-based travel agency that used advertising via several hundred Instagram accounts and fake ratings, together with collaborations with local tour guides, transport companies, and hotels, to develop a successful business focused on domestic tourism. Ahmad in Pekanbaru created a smartphone application for laundry pick-up and delivery and gamed the ratings for the app.

In particular, those who were older and more concerned with the near future—getting married and having children, for instance—attempted to develop business models that were more respectable and sustainable than selling SMM services. Hendro in Surabaya, for instance, was developing a soya milk business because he was betting on a general rise in lactose intolerance in the Indonesian population. Ana, one of a handful of women in the business, was a Balinese homemaker and former bank employee who had become a SMM services reseller when she had a baby. She spent a few hours a day selling on her laptop, but her long-term goal was to make enough money to set up a cookie and cake business out of her home. Some hoped to open their own offices focusing, for instance, on web design and social media management or to develop new ideas on Jakarta's media start-up scene. One invested in a 24/7 gaming center. Yohanes purchased a car that could be used as a taxi on ride-hailing platforms. Many, like Ibrahim, invested in a house as soon as possible, as well as secondary housing that could be subdivided into rental rooms (*kos*), or purchased land for long-term investment, while others focused on traditional offline businesses, such as laundry or shoe-cleaning services or shops that their parents or relatives could run. It is thus critical to consider how the SMM services market is considered temporary by most of my interlocutors, and often seen as a stepping-stone to what appear to be more sustainable types of businesses. More generally, this perspective allows us to decenter a planetary focus on digital labor and consider that labor is embedded in particular urban environments and commercial spaces.

Conclusion

Engaging with the SMM services market from the perspective of my Indonesian interlocutors allows for a degree of reconceptualization with regard to the particular biases that have come to shape representations of click farms and digital sweatshops. First, while there is a degree of spatial concentration in the organization of these forms of labor—based in urban areas, organized through cottage industries such as Ibrahim's, and nationalized with regard to language—this must be understood in tandem with, and not in contrast to, spatially distributed forms of labor. More specifically, the distribution and organization of labor should be considered along a continuum that ranges from programming to the production and selling of SMM services, which at times allows for, but does not necessarily depend upon, a particular form of spatial concentration. Although "geography has become less sticky" in this process, as "the ties between service work and particular places" have been severed (Graham and Anwar 2018, 3), it is important to specify that a degree of stickiness remains that is shaped in particular political and sociocultural environments. This stickiness remains evident even in the case of Adi, who works strictly on the Indonesian market despite the fact that he lives in Amsterdam, as the colonial historical connections between the Netherlands and Indonesia (previously the Dutch East Indies) shaped his migration.

Second, the labor that underpins click farming is centered not so much on "clicking" as on developing forms of automation from below that decrease the reliance on manual labor. Importantly, the basic forms of technological innovation that have shaped the evolution of platform economies, notably the use of APIs, are also critical to the shaping of secondary industries that are dependent on but relatively autonomous about these platforms. Manual labor, however, remains critical, primarily with regard to customer service, marketing, copy-pasting itself, and occasionally clicking when automation breaks down. In other words, automation and manual labor should be approached not as opposed but as integrated in a patchwork fashion as the labor of kin and friends becomes critical in keeping the system running.

Third, although these sites of spatial concentration, for instance Ibrahim's, may be very well be termed farms or factories of sorts, the Indonesian case suggests that the labor is not strictly exploitative or an end in itself for those involved but has more frequently evolved through play and tinkering, is organized along the lines of friendship or kinship, and is associated with broader aspirations. Although entrepreneurs such as Ibrahim keep the bulk of the profits, they often pay their workers relatively well. Rather than considering this as strictly a form of exploitation—a "sweatshop"—it is more productive to understand these as evolving but unstable forms of patron-client relationships that depend on certain forms of intimacy. However, these workplaces reveal as much about urbanization in cities like Jakarta, where kin and friends are drawn into new forms of economic engagement in an environment of precarity and experimentation, as they do about planetary digital labor (see Simone 2020). In other words, the combination of automation from below, shifting patron-client relations in the context of urbanization, and aspiration places us right in the middle of current debates about digital labor.

As Burrell (2012, 7) has noted in her ethnography of Internet cafés in Ghana, "Marginality can be defined as a position of relational disadvantage, of noncentrality but not absolute exclusion." This point allows us not only to nuance our understanding of click farming but also to move beyond "digital divide" as a defining concept for approaching the forms of labor, markets, and infrastructures that underpin contemporary forms of digital capitalism. More specifically, and in line with the theme of this book, an engagement with digital labor in a planetary market has much to gain by taking non-English-speaking communities in the urban Global South as an empirical starting point for analysis.

Acknowledgments

Thanks to Fabian Ferrari, Mark Graham, Doreen Lee, Daromir Rudnyckyj, and David Sutcliffe for helpful comments on an earlier version of this chapter. The research was funded by a Swedish Research Council grant (2017–02937).

Notes

1. Instagram is a social media platform founded in 2010 and owned by Facebook. It allows users to share "posts" (photos and videos with accompanying text), which are then seen by their "followers" (users who have chosen to be notified when a particular account posts new content). With more than one billion users, Instagram has become a major commercial force (Leaver et al, 2020).

2. Most Indonesians neither have credit cards nor are able to use PayPal, which keeps them from purchasing directly on the international market.

3. See https://instagram-press.com/blog/2018/11/19/reducing-inauthentic-activity-on-instagram/ and Petre, Duffy, and Hund (2019).

References

Appadurai, A. 2004. "The Capacity to Aspire: Culture and the Terms of Recognition." In *Culture and Public Action*, edited by Vijayendra Rao and Michael Walton, 59–84. Stanford, CA: Stanford University Press. https://gsdrc.org/document-library/the-capacity-to-aspire-culture-and-the-terms-of-recognition/.

Aspinall, Edward. 2013. "A Nation in Fragments." *Critical Asian Studies* 45 (1): 27–54.

Brenner, Neil, and Christian Schmid. 2012. "Planetary Urbanization." In *Urban Constellations*, edited by Matthew Gandy, 10–13. Berlin: Jovis.

Burrell, Jenna. 2012. *Invisible Users: Youth in the Internet Cafés of Urban Ghana*. Cambridge, MA: MIT Press.

Carsten, Janet. 1997. *The Heat of the Hearth: The Process of Kinship in a Malay Fishing Village*. Oxford: Clarendon Press.

Casilli, Antonio A. 2017. "Digital Labor Studies Go Global: Toward a Digital Decolonial Turn." *International Journal of Communication* 11: 3934–3954. https://ijoc.org/index.php/ijoc/article/viewFile/6349/2149.

Chen, Julie Yujie. 2018. "Thrown under the Bus and Outrunning It! The Logic of Didi and Taxi Drivers' Labour and Activism in the On-Demand Economy." *New Media & Society* 20 (8): 2691–2711.

Clark, Doug. 2015. "The Bot Bubble: How Click Farms Have Inflated Social Media Currency." *New Republic*, April 21. https://newrepublic.com/article/121551/bot-bubble-click-farms-have-inflated-social-media-currency.

Confessore, Nicolas, Gabriel J. X. Dance, Richard Harris, and Mark Hansen. 2018. "The Follower Factory." *The New York Times*, January 27.

Ellis, Emma Grey. 2019. "Fighting Instagram's $1.3 Billion Problem—Fake Followers." *Wired*, September 10. https://www.wired.com/story/instagram-fake followers/.

Ford, Michele, and Vivian Honan. 2017. "The Go-Jek Effect." In *Digital Indonesia: Connectivity and Divergence*, edited by E. Jurriëns and R. Tapsell, 275–288. Singapore: ISEAS.

Gerlitz, Carolin, and Anne Helmond. 2013. "The Like Economy: Social Buttons and the Data-Intensive Web." *New Media & Society* 15 (8): 1348–1365.

Google and Temasek. 2017. *e-Conomy SEA Spotlight 2017: Unprecedented Growth for Southeast Asia's $50B Internet Economy*. Singapore: Temasek. https://www.blog.google/documents/16/Google-Temasek_e-Conomy_SEA_Spotlight_2017.pdf.

Graham, Mark, and Mohammad Amir Anwar. 2018. "Two Models for a Fairer Sharing Economy." In *The Cambridge Handbook of the Law of the Sharing Economy*, edited by Nestor M. Davidson, Michèle Finck, and John J. Infranca, 328–340. Cambridge: Cambridge University Press. https:// papers.ssrn.com/sol3/papers.cfm?abstract_id=3325820.

Gray, Mary L., and Siddharth Suri. 2019. *Ghost Work: How to Stop Silicon Valley from Building a New Global Underclass*. Boston: Houghton Mifflin Harcourt.

Helmond, Anne. 2015. "The Platformization of the Web: Making Web Data Platform Ready." *Social Media + Society* 1 (1): 1–11. https://doi.org/10.1177/2056305115603080.

Hickman, Arvind. 2019. "Majority of UK Instagram Influencers Engage in Fakery—Landmark New Study." *PR Week*, July 9. https://www.prweek.com/article/1590362/majority-uk-instagram -influencers-engage-fakery-landmark-new-study.

Irani, Lilly. 2015. "Difference and Dependence among Digital Workers: The Case of Amazon Mechanical Turk." *South Atlantic Quarterly* 114 (1): 225–234.

Jones, Graham. 2011. *Trade of the Tricks: Inside the Magician's Craft*. Berkeley: University of California Press.

Leaver, Tama, Tim Highfield, and Crystal Abidin. 2020. *Instagram: Visual Social Media Cultures*. Cambridge: Polity Press.

Lim, Merlyna. 2018. "Dis/Connection: The Co-evolution of Socio-cultural and Material Infrastructures of the Internet in Indonesia." *Indonesia* 105: 155–172.

Lipman, Victor. 2012. "The World's Most Active Twitter City? You Won't Guess It." *Forbes*, December 30. https://www.forbes.com/sites/victorlipman/2012/12/30/the-worlds-most-active-twitter -city-you-wont-guess-it/.

Marwick, Alice E. 2015. "Instafame: Luxury Selfies in the Attention Economy." *Public Culture* 27 (1): 137–160.

Milan, Stefania, and Emiliano Treré. 2019. "Big Data from the South(s): Beyond Data Universalism." *Television & New Media* 20 (4): 319–335. https://doi.org/10.1177/1527476419837739.

Petre, Caitlin, Brooke Erin Duffy, and Emily Hund. 2019. "'Gaming the System': Platform Paternalism and the Politics of Algorithmic Visibility." *Social Media + Society* 19 (4): 1–12. https://doi .org/10.1177/2056305119879995.

Postigo, Hector. 2016. "The Socio-technical Architecture of Digital Labor: Converting Play into YouTube Money." *New Media & Society* 18 (2): 332–349.

Roberts, Sarah T. 2019. *Behind the Screen: Content Moderation in the Shadows of Social Media*. New Haven, CT: Yale University Press.

Rogers, R. 2018. "Otherwise Engaged: Social Media from Vanity Metrics to Critical Analytics." *International Journal of Communication* 12: 450–472.

Scholz, Trebor. 2013. *Digital Labor: The Internet as Playground and Factory*. New York: Routledge.

Scott, James C. 1976. *The Moral Economy of the Peasant: Rebellion and Subsistence in Southeast Asia*. Princeton, NJ: Princeton University Press.

Simone, AbdouMaliq. 2020. "To Extend: Temporariness in a World of Itineraries." *Urban Studies* 57 (6): 1127–1142.

Tai, Zixue, and Fengbin Hu. 2018. "Play between Love and Labor: The Practice of Gold Farming in China." *New Media & Society* 20 (7): 2370–2390.

Taylor, Elise. 2017. "The Most Geo-Tagged City on Instagram Stories May Surprise You." *Vogue*, August 2. https://www.vogue.com/article/jakarta-indonesia-instagram-stories.

Wolf, Eric. 2001. *Pathways of Power: Building an Anthropology of the Modern World*. Berkeley: University of California Press.

Wood, Alex J., Mark Graham, Vili Lehdonvirta, and Isis Hjorth. 2019. "Good Gig, Bad Gig: Autonomy and Algorithmic Control in the Global Gig Economy." *Work, Employment and Society* 33 (1): 56–75.

5   Moderating in Obscurity: How Indian Content Moderators Work in Global Content Moderation Value Chains

Sana Ahmad and Martin Krzywdzinski

Cairncross's (2001) observation that "companies will locate any screen-based activity anywhere on earth, wherever they can find the best bargain of skills and productivity" has often been cited to illustrate the reach of offshoring and international outsourcing. Content moderation is an important part of this global "outsourcing complex" (Peck 2017) that exemplifies its dynamic structures in terms of creation of new digitally mediated economic geographies and continual changes to the contours of the planetary labor market.

As Roberts (2019) and Gillespie (2018a) emphasize, content moderation is a core process for maintaining the social media platforms that have become a central element of contemporary social exchange and global public communication. Despite the enormous social and political importance of the practice, relatively little is known about content moderation. The available bits of public information about it are hidden within the self-declared statements and transparency reports from the social media firms. Content moderation has often been understood in the public discourse as an automated task; the importance of human content moderation has been highlighted by scholars and journalists only recently.

The increasing interest in content moderation has been driven by scholars arguing that social media are part of the public sphere, and therefore the rules governing them should not be set by firms following narrow economic interests (Klonick 2017; Gillespie 2018b). However, the focus of this chapter is not consider in detail whether the onus of user content management should be put on social media firms (Shepherd et al. 2015). The focus is rather to take a step further to untangle cryptic clues about actual outsourcing practices.

Trying to understand why social media firms outsource content moderation service work, to whom they outsource it, and how they find their outsourced contractors is as complicated as unpacking the technological tools and software that are used for moderating content. In this chapter, we analyze the relations between social media firms and their suppliers in India based on the global value chain (GVC) approach (Gereffi,

Humphrey, and Sturgeon 2005; Ponte and Sturgeon 2014). Following an analysis of content moderation value chains, we consider the content moderation labor process and analyze the attendant working conditions.

This chapter focuses on India, which—along with the Philippines—has become a core destination of content moderation outsourcing, according to various investigative scholarly works (Ahmad 2019) and articles in the media.[1] These are the main questions guiding the analysis:

1. What are the value chain configurations through which global social media firms and suppliers in India coordinate content moderation services?
2. How is the labor process of content moderation organized and controlled within these value chain configurations?

First, we define content moderation and place its importance for social media firms. We then outline our motivations for using GVC theory and the labor process approach to analyze the outsourcing of content moderation to India. After providing an overview of how the empirical research was conducted, we develop our analysis of content moderation value chain configurations, with a focus on economic upgrading possibilities for the suppliers in India. We then describe the content moderation labor process with special attention to the working conditions and mobilities of Indian content moderators. In the conclusion, we revisit our main arguments and recommend the role of public and private policies in regulating outsourced content moderation practices.

Defining Content Moderation

According to Sarah T. Roberts (2017, 1), "Content moderation is the organized practice of screening user-generated content posted to Internet sites, social media, and other online outlets, in order to determine the appropriateness of the content for a given site, locality, or jurisdiction." The global content moderation market is segmented into different moderation types, primarily *proactive* moderation (before the content is published on the site) and *reactive* moderation (after the content is published on the site) (Grimmelmann 2015). Moderating content has transitioned from open and voluntary moderation of text-based social communities (Usenet groups, Wikipedia, etc.), to the deployment by media firms of word filter technologies along with human skills for comment moderation, to contemporary large-scale moderation practices that use professional moderators and basic algorithms (Roberts 2017).

Roberts (2019) notes that content moderation is a crucial aspect of protecting corporate identity, maintaining the operational laws of platforms, and sustaining as well as driving an increase in the number of users and their activity on the platforms. Gillespie (2018a) goes a step further in stating that moderation is an "essential, constitutional and definitional" aspect of what platforms do, adding that this content moderation work is hard because it is "resource intensive and relentless."

On the one hand, content moderation is a tremendously sensitive practice that lies at the core of the activities of social media platforms like Facebook and YouTube. On the other hand, as Sam Levin writes in the *Guardian*, "Silicon Valley has stuck to its foundational belief that tech firms are ultimately not accountable for the content on their platforms."[2] Indeed, the Silicon Valley–based social media giants have since their inception enjoyed nonliability through Section 230 of the Communications Decency Act in the United States. This regulation has offered these platforms and other websites a "safe harbor" from liability because the third-party postings or content generated by users on these platforms is not their responsibility. For some, Section 230 has also meant a "marketplace orientation" where these platforms can take advantage of the free speech paradigm because "suppression of speech can be anathema to the marketplace theory" (Medeiros 2017, 2).

However, international scrutiny of social media platforms' moderation policies has increased as a result of many legal regulations, notably Germany's Network Enforcement Act (*Netzwerkdurchsetzungsgesetz*), India's intermediary liability regulations, and Iran's demand that the messaging platform Telegram relocate its distribution networks in the country. In a similar vein, a number of governments, including those of India and Indonesia, have increasingly pressured the Chinese social media firm ByteDance to set up domestic content moderation units in compliance with local regulations. Analyst Kalev Leetaru has gone a step further and likened social media platforms to "opaque black boxes into which we have absolutely no insight or voice."[3] Such statements, however, reduce users, content moderators, and other engaged participants to powerless positions while ignoring the economic incentives, audience interests, and wider political movements that influence these platforms (Gillespie 2018a).

Global Value Chains and the Labor Process Approach

Adopting a Global Value Chain Approach

The outsourcing policies of social media firms have created global content moderation value chains as a part of the planetary labor market (Graham and Anwar 2019). In these value chains, we can distinguish three major actor types: social media firms, multinational enterprises (MNEs), and content moderation suppliers (figure 5.1).

The lead actors are the social media firms (e.g., Facebook, Google)—mainly based in the US but also in Europe and China—that control social media platforms and the

Figure 5.1
Idealized content moderation value chain.
Source: Authors.

standards and software infrastructures that guide the work of content moderators. In some cases, these firms cooperate with MNEs that provide IT solutions and business process outsourcing (BPO) services. MNEs (e.g., Genpact, Accenture) usually have their headquarters in the Global North and subsidiaries in the Global South. There are also, however, Indian firms providing BPO services related to content moderation (e.g., Foiwe Info Global Solutions). The MNEs provide content moderation services themselves and also outsource it to domestic content moderation suppliers in India or other countries like the Philippines. In some cases, social media firms engage directly with Indian (or Philippine) content moderation suppliers.

India is one of the main destinations of content moderation outsourcing, accounting for over a tenth of moderation workers worldwide.[4] In addition to this outsourcing of content moderation for markets in the Global North, there is an expanding content moderation market in India itself. Indeed, a greater expansion of the mobile phone user base in rural and non-English-speaking regions of India (Tenhunen 2018), together with cheap mobile Internet packages, has sparked growth in content in vernacular languages.

Content moderation GVCs are characterized by high power asymmetries between the lead social media firms in the Global North and the content moderation suppliers in the Global South; these asymmetries influence employment and working conditions. A recent contribution to GVC theory (Ponte and Sturgeon 2014) argues that these power asymmetries are based on a number of factors. From the supplier perspective, one factor is related to technological and organizational capabilities. Most content moderation suppliers do not have technological capabilities and depend completely on software infrastructures provided by the lead firms. But even in cases of more capable suppliers, the monopolistic or oligopolistic structure of lead firms, combined with the low costs for the firms of switching between suppliers (in the case of highly codified and standardized transactions), leads to huge power asymmetries between lead firms and suppliers (Ponte and Sturgeon 2014).

With content moderation practices treated as industrial secrets, there is a lack of scholarship about the structure of content moderation value chains. Social media clients declare several reasons for this secrecy, such as protecting the identities of workers (Gillespie 2018b), preventing users from "gaming the rules" when posting illicit content on social media platforms (Roberts 2016), and safeguarding their proprietary technology. We can, however, build on existing research about the position of Indian firms in value chains shaped by IT BPO, which includes call center firms and others (Noronha and D'Cruz 2020).[5]

The GVC literature has developed a complex classification of value chain structures (Gereffi, Humphrey, and Sturgeon 2005). In the case of BPO-based value chains, two types are of particular relevance. Value chains with low supplier capabilities, a high codification of transactions, and strong direct control of suppliers by lead firms are characterized as "captive." They do not leave space for the upgrading of the suppliers' capabilities and are often associated with low-road approaches regarding wages and working conditions (Schrage and Gilbert 2019, 206). Value chains with a high codification of transactions but rather arm's-length relations between lead firms and suppliers, low direct control, and low switching costs are characterized as "market-based."[6] Some authors (Lakhani, Kuruvilla, and Avgar 2013, 453) argue that market-based value chains are associated with employment systems relying on "moderately skilled workers" and providing better working conditions than captive ones. Ponte and Sturgeon (2014) emphasize, however, that low switching costs between suppliers can constitute the basis for high power asymmetries between lead firms and suppliers, leading to high price competition, low wages, and bad working conditions.

Working Conditions in the Indian IT Sector: A Labor Process Perspective

A key argument of our chapter is that the opacity of the content moderation industry affects the working conditions of content moderators. There is a lack of systematic studies on the topic that draw on established sociological concepts such as labor process theory. Only media reports about the great psychological stress caused by this form of work have drawn public attention to this area of employment.[7]

We do, however, have a longer history of research into the broader Indian IT BPO sector. Labor process analyses of India's call center firms have provided useful insights into the work organization and management strategies of these firms and the country's position in the (then) new international division of labor (Batt et al. 2005; Noronha and D'Cruz 2006). In their discussion on the characteristics of labor processes in call center firms, Batt et al. (2005) emphasized the vulnerability of the workforce due to the subordinate position of Indian firms in GVCs. As Taylor and Bain (2005) have pointed out, standardized, simple, and tightly scripted tasks have been outsourced to India, and case studies have described tight technological control of the labor process leading to increased work pressure and stress (Taylor and Bain 2005; Noronha and D'Cruz 2006).

Shehzad Nadeem's (2011) ethnographic study of the Indian call center industry looks at the proletarianization of white-collar workers who are engaged in rote customer service work. The 24-hour work cycle encourages long working hours and night shifts, leading to workers' estrangement from social ties and the normal rhythms of life. Nadeem's study not only captures workers' frustrations and their exploitation but also tries to grapple with the dialectic of outsourcing in India. For him, the "concrete realities of a particular place" in India have been transformed into a space of capital accumulation (Nadeem 2011). The creation of spaces such as India's special economic zones is designed to obfuscate the workers both from their counterparts in outsourcing nations and from consumers.

At the same time, existing studies on the Indian IT sector confirm a central argument of labor process analysis: that even highly standardized and technically controlled work processes still require the agency of the workers—that is, their problem-solving ability and participation in coping with the innumerable situations in which standards and technical controls are insufficient (Smith and Thompson 1998; Thompson 2003). Research on call centers has particularly highlighted the emotional work of Indian call center agents in managing stress and unforeseen difficulties in communicating with customers (D'Cruz and Noronha 2008; Remesh 2008). On this basis, Indian workers are trying to work out a path toward professionalization (D'Cruz and Noronha 2013), but this remains difficult given the market-based and captive value chains in the Indian IT sector (Taylor and Bain 2005; Upadhya 2010). We expect to encounter similar developments in Indian content moderation companies.

Data and Methods

This study is based on 35 interviews with content moderators, representatives from suppliers located in India, domestic social media firms, Indian trade unions, and civil society organizations.[8] In order to understand the position of Indian firms within GVCs, we started our empirical analysis with interviews with management representatives from social media firms and Indian content moderation suppliers. We conducted interviews with two domestic social media firms. DSM-01 is a medium-sized firm (50–249 employees) that currently handles over 150 million user accounts, and DSM-02 is a small firm (10–49 employees) that went out of business in 2019. In addition, we elicited data through an email exchange with the policy communications manager of an American conglomerate (GSM-01), which owns the biggest social media platform worldwide, with currently over 2 billion user accounts.

Interviews were conducted with representatives of six suppliers in India (SU-01 to SU-06): four chief executive officers, one operations manager, and one team leader. The six suppliers included two small domestic start-ups, three medium-sized domestic firms, and one medium-sized subsidiary of an MNE. Five of the firms are based in India, and one is located in the United States.

Our analysis of the content moderation labor process combines information from the management interviews with information from interviews with content moderators. In total, we interviewed nine content moderators (CM-01 to CM-09), all having permanent employment status for this study. CMs 05 to 08 were employed by a supplier firm but worked directly at the Indian subsidiary of an American video-sharing social media platform (GSM-02). In addition, we interviewed three content operators, two of whom worked at a domestic social media firm and one at a Chinese social media firm (CO-01 to CO-03). *Content operator* is a designation specific to domestic and regional social media firms; the job profile of a content operator extends beyond content moderation to other content-related tasks.

We faced several difficulties in accessing the target participants. We approached all of the workers on a popular professional networking website. We sent hundreds of workers a connection request, but only a few responded. Of these, a smaller number agreed to be interviewed. We applied a snowball sampling technique to contact further interviewees.

We conducted supplementary interviews with representatives of seven trade unions engaged in organizing IT workers. In order to understand how social media firms establish their content moderation policies, we also interviewed representatives from eight civil society organizations focusing on freedom of speech and online governance mechanisms in India.

The Position of Indian Firms in Content Moderation Value Chains

Content moderation value chains are controlled by social media firms, mainly located in the Global North. These firms argue that they select their suppliers carefully, but they also emphasize the need for flexibility and the ability to quickly expand (but also contract) the volume of their outsourced content moderation business. The policy communications manager of a global social media company described the company's approach to choosing its outsourcing locations and partners as follows: "We work with a global network of partners, so we can quickly adjust the focus of our workforce as needed. For example, it gives us the ability to make sure we have the right language expertise—and can quickly hire in different time zones—as new needs arise or when a situation around the world warrants it. These partners are carefully selected and reputable" (GSM-01).

Interviews with Indian suppliers show, however, the major role of price competition in the relations between social media firms and suppliers. The service level agreements of social media firms with their Indian suppliers are mostly price-based and project-oriented. Further, the two parties agree upon an overhead count (number of workers) before the onset of the project, and workers are employed by the contracted supply firms (SU-02, SU-04, SU-05). In part, Indian first-tier suppliers outsource certain projects to Indian second-tier suppliers, according to the managers of two small Indian companies (SU-05, SU-06).[9] The extent of such domestic outsourcing is unknown, however, as other managers of medium-sized content moderation firms stated that this would not be cost-effective (SU-02, SU-04, SU-05). Nevertheless, the manager of one supplier firm stated that freelance content moderators for its moderation projects are also sourced from external databases of Indian recruitment companies (SU-02).

There is a clear division of labor between social media firms and their content moderation suppliers. All product-oriented aspects such as training, moderation policies, and moderation software systems are managed by the social media firms. The human resources–related aspects such as wages, leave of absence, employment benefits, and other administrative tasks are managed by the supplier firms. Regarding recruitment and performance control, social media firms oscillate between the roles of supervision and direct intervention.[10]

Using the governance typology developed by Gereffi, Humphrey, and Sturgeon (2005), we can characterize the relationships between content moderation suppliers and social media firms in some cases as market-based and in other cases as captive. The social media firms exercise a high degree of power by dictating stringent standards in terms of technology and tools to be used for moderating content.

All content moderation suppliers interviewed for this study were very clear that there was no way of expanding their services or moving up the value chain. Certain possibilities for strengthening the position of Indian content moderation suppliers arise from the growing competition between the social media firms and from their interest in the Indian consumer market. The Indian social media landscape also benefits from growth of content in local languages. These developments have benefited both domestic and regional social media platforms, which primarily cater to consumers generating content in Indian vernacular languages.

The broadening of client firms through the inclusion of Chinese and domestic social media firms also presents opportunities to Indian content moderation firms, as it could create a potential overlap of "multiple production networks" (Horner and Nadvi 2018) and reduce dependence on customers from North America and Europe.[11] India remains an important location for the Chinese technology company ByteDance, which owns both the video-sharing platform TikTok and the social networking platform Helo. However, a recent decision by the Union Government in India to ban 59 Chinese applications, including TikTok, in order to protect the country's "national security and sovereignty" could limit these opportunities.[12]

The Content Moderation Labor Process

The high power asymmetries between the lead firms and suppliers in content moderation GVCs strongly influence the labor process. In this section, we analyze the recruitment processes, work organization, and working conditions in this labor process. We also discuss the content moderators' mobilities within and across moderation value chains, with a focus on their individual strategies for better working conditions and wages.

Recruitment Process

From the outset, it is useful to iterate that content moderation is not a standard business terminology similar to other job designations for consumer services in the IT sector. Instead, a careful analysis of advertisements for this work shows a diverse range of job titles, such as "system analyst," "website administrator," "process associate," and "process executive." The use of such generic terms can be attributed to several factors, including the diversity of firms offering content moderation services, the required skills, and the differing demands of global clients. These "multitudinous" job titles, as Roberts (2019) puts it, further obscure the landscape of content moderation from public visibility.

Mostly freshly graduated, the moderators we interviewed had all been encouraged by friends to apply for moderation jobs, often without knowing exactly what the work would entail. Those applying for work that included projects for global social media firms stated that it did not matter if the "job entailed BPO-styled working conditions" as long as the brands were well known in the employment market (CM-03, CM-06, CM-07, CM-08). However, agreements between the social media firms and suppliers require moderators to sign nondisclosure agreements, often even during the recruitment process. Along with working in opacity, moderators offer their labor in exchange for a mostly stagnant salary and few benefits under pressure of rising unemployment in the country.

The recruitment process is generally lengthy, with several rounds of interviews and assessments that aim to check the workers' cognitive capacities and grasp of the required language for moderating content. In some cases (GSM-02), the social media firms directly intervene in the process by conducting the final interview. In other cases, the suppliers undertake the complete recruitment process, with no participation by social media firms.

An important factor in the acceptance of relatively low wages and difficult working conditions is the composition of the content moderation workforce. The workers we interviewed for this study were young, below the age of 35 years, mostly male (75 percent of the sample), and unmarried. They held different educational qualifications such as engineering and technology, computer applications, management studies, media and communications, and education sciences. While we lack empirical data on where they undertook their higher studies, the workers came from both urban and rural regions of India. In many cases, content moderation was their first job, which they considered an entry point into the IT sector and a means of acquiring work experience.

Work Organization
Moderation can start before user content is published on social media platforms (proactive filtering, which takes place in real time), or it may take place after it is uploaded (reactive filtering). Reactive filtering is often applicable in high-volume platforms such as those owned by social media firms GSM-01 and GSM-02 and depends on complaints made by external parties or users, who can flag or prompt review of content on the platform. In reactive filtering, two processes are involved: automated and manual moderation. Automated moderation entails automatic detection of user content matching the unique codes or hashes or digital fingerprints, resulting in deletion or approval of the content in compliance with the platform's policies. Child sexual abuse, revenge porn, and so forth are examples of content that are typically moderated via automated filters (e.g., Microsoft PhotoDNA). Usually, such content does not go into the manual queues.

However, a large amount of other content ends up in the queues of the moderators. Across all our cases, every moderator is assigned to a particular content queue, such as hate speech, copyright, or spam. The specific tasks of the content moderators depend on the policies of their customers. In most cases, the content moderators review massive amounts of user-generated content and make decisions to allow "flagged content" (i.e., content marked by users as offensive or unacceptable) on the platform, delete the content, or even ban the user. These decisions must be delivered at high speed and require intimate familiarity with the respective platform's policy guidelines. In some of the companies, there is a second layer of moderation, the quality analysis team, which checks the decisions of content moderators. In other cases, senior moderators may perform quality control.

In certain cases (CM-03, CM-04, CM-09), the content moderators were only tagging the content, since the policies of the social media platform they were working for did not require the active deletion of content. Instead, they were required to tag the problematic content so that it became invisible to either the user or the country where this type of content was not allowed.

Through our analysis, we can observe that the content moderation process displays a strict work hierarchy, with moderators assigned to different levels based on their performance. The moderators are generally evaluated monthly against how many pieces of content they moderated and how many pieces they routed to colleagues in the other levels when they found it too difficult to decide themselves. In one of our cases, the moderator target (i.e., amount of content to be moderated) ranges from 2,500 to 5,000 pieces of content every month (CM-05, CM-06, CM-07, CM-08). The targets might differ in other cases, depending on the kind of content (video targets tend to be smaller), the size of the moderation workforce, and the demands placed by the social media firms.

We encountered diverging points of view regarding the automation of content moderation. On the one hand, several suppliers we interviewed were investing in automation of the labor process. Our research shows that they implement basic filters or more advanced automated technology for content moderation, depending on the requirements of the social media firms (SU-01, SU-04, SU-06). On the other hand, moderators working in two supplier firms that had already implemented the content moderation software provided by social media firms were vocal about the errors made by these tools (CM-03, CM-09). Rather than fearing replacement by automated moderation systems, they seemed more concerned about the low accuracy and extra work these tools create for them, such as correcting the automated suspension of genuine profiles of social media users (CM-03). A moderator working at a direct subsidiary of another social media firm (GSM-02) noted that while they have not encountered such problems, they have to ensure that such automation-generated errors are quickly resolved so as not to lose user trust in the social media platform (CM-08).

Working Conditions

The most distressing element of content moderation work is the nature of the content that falls into the queues of the workers. Almost all workers recounted experiences of watching content involving pornography, assault, animal abuse, and live suicide. As we have described above, content moderators work in different content queues. Depending on the content queue (such as hate speech, nudity, self-harm, etc.) the frequency of the psychologically distressing content may be higher. In some content queues, such as news articles, the prevalence of distressing content is rare. Independent of the length of the training that they were given at the onset of their work, all moderators admitted that watching such disturbing content distressed them.[13] However, they believed that one had to learn to adapt to such things. Bad management practices, long working hours, and lack of growth opportunities were cited instead as the main sources of their dissatisfaction with content moderation work. One moderator (CM-01), employed at the supplier firm SU-01, noted that he was not prepared to watch such content. SU-01 provided only one to two days of training to its employees at the outset of any content moderation project. An excerpt from the interview with CM-01 highlights their working conditions:

> Sometimes I worked for 16 hours a day. After completing my shift, I used to go back home with an alcohol bottle and sleep. I tried also going with my friends to movies. I managed somehow. I had to look for better opportunities. I didn't have a laptop so I would borrow one from my friends, browse, try to learn something. From Coursera, I started learning neural networking. I had to ask Coursera to let me attend the course for free. I told them that I work for a small company. They accepted my request. It kept me busy and distracted.

Content moderators are cognizant of the multidimensional psychological impact of moderation on them, which extends beyond watching the distressing content. Their work is strictly timed and monitored through targets and "time punching." Failure to complete their tasks leads to disciplinary measures such as being issued statutory warnings, then being shifted to relatively easier (in terms of content complexity) work levels or even to another project, and eventually being "put on the bench," as content moderators described serving the notice period before their termination (CM-01, CM-06, CM-07, CM-08).

While conflict with management could range over several issues, such as work shifts, salary, or working hours, it also arose from lack of growth opportunities for moderators. Low wages, lack of skill development, and lack of promotion opportunities are the main reasons for the high attrition rate in this business. The suppliers note that high attrition rates are definitive of the IT sector in India and allow content moderators to participate in an expanding content moderation service market in the country (SU-01, SU-03, SU-04, SU-05). They affirm that constant recruitment drives nevertheless keep the turnover rate of workers high.

Climbing the Ladder or Creating Their Own Staircase: Workers' Strategies for Change

Content moderators are, however, not passive and defenseless. Roberts's (2019) argument that content moderators use their "high level cognitive functions" and "cultural competencies" is right. Moderators exercise agency using their cognition and cultural knowledge, albeit within a standardized and controlled labor process. Moderators are vocal about why they think global social media firms outsource moderation work to

India. Apart from the cost-effectiveness, they note that these firms need "localization experts" (CO–03, CM-06, CM-08). An anecdote from CM-06 who quit moderating for a global social media firm (GSM-02) after three years can be understood within this context: "I can tell you that these companies also outsource because they need the localization experts, because they are trying to capture the Indian social media market. If you look at this Chinese social media firm, they are hiring in India every day. You see, if you are good with the content, you know the local language, and you have the X factor in operations, you will get the job." While a considerable level of cultural knowledge and understanding is necessary in all content moderation work, two factors are associated with an even higher demand for this knowledge.

The first factor is the type of projects and markets the Indian suppliers are serving. As we have already mentioned, the number of social media platforms in India has greatly increased. Expansion of regional and domestic social media platforms in the Indian market has created jobs for experienced moderators who are employed as content operators. Catering primarily to the Indian users who generate content in non-English and vernacular languages, the work of content operators constitutes a range of operations-related tasks such as user acquisition, user engagement, and developing content moderation policies, in addition to checking the quality of work by external moderators.

Content operators are employed directly at the regional and domestic offices of the lead firms' offshoring units in India. "At least we are paid better here," commented CM-08, who resigned from working as a content moderator in an Indian supplier firm and found new opportunities as a content operator working directly for a social media company. Better wages, however, do not always mean better work quality, as the content operators interviewed for our study decried the lack of training and growth opportunities (CM-06, CM-08).

The second important factor is the level of involvement of moderators in improving the social media firms' content moderation policies. These policies are guarded by social media firms as "trade secrets" and function to "protect the client brand" (Roberts 2019). Soon after their recruitment, moderators at small- and medium-sized suppliers are trained for a few days, whereas large supplier firms organize training periods ranging from one to three months. The training provided by firms mostly focuses on formal content moderation policies. This policy training is mandatory in every service agreement between social media firms and suppliers and varies according to the needs of the clients and the capacities of the suppliers.

Content moderators note, however, that the rules and policies taught during the training are not all encompassing. Lack of clear policies on "edgy content" (CM-07), "newsworthy content" (CM-08), or even foreign language content (CM-05) make the work difficult. Added to this are ambiguous policies regarding politicians and celebrities. In cases where there are no clear policies, moderators must create their own workflows, made up of a sequential set of steps in the work process. Giving an example of judging the intent of a user who posted a hacking video, CM-08, employed at a supplier working for a large social media firm (GSM-02), provides a glimpse into his new workflow:

> This hacking video which once came in my queue was complicated. There were no clear rules on it. Therefore, I had to judge the intent of the user. The first thing I did was to check if it is a hacking tutorial or not. If it is a tutorial, then the policy requires me to allow it, but if the video is promoting hacking then I must delete it. Now how do you assess all this? I check the video title, the description, the video tags used, the user's channel, other videos posted by this user, and the nature of those videos. This is the way to make a new workflow. Takes a long time sometimes. No policy tells us how to check the intent of the user on the video.

Content moderators working directly for an Indian subsidiary of a social media firm (GSM-02) reported that they can influence the policy documents through what they call "ideation"—that is, providing ideas to make the policies better (CM-05, CM-08). This requires the moderators to record new solutions they create in the policy documents. Afterward, they make a presentation to their managers and demonstrate how such a policy change can be beneficial to the social media firm and its consumers. By playing a role in improving the policy documents, which are updated every few months, the content moderators can develop and demonstrate their expertise. We found this close involvement of content moderators in improving the moderation policies in only one case. In the other cases, the large distance between the social media firm and the supplier, as well as the high standardization of work processes, excluded this type of job enrichment.

In the absence of internal interest representation and career opportunities, moderators make use of the growing reliance of social media firms on the Indian labor market and construct their own "career staircases" (James and Vira 2012) across the different global, regional, and domestic firms engaged in the content moderation sector in India. At the same time, the Indian IT sector offers us concrete examples of collective struggles, especially concerning unpaid wages and layoffs. Interviews with trade unions show that following the 2008 global financial crisis, the effects on IT workers' job security started becoming noticeable. Both the Union for ITeS Professional (UNITES) and the Forum for IT Employees (FITE) were formed primarily in response to increasing layoffs at Indian IT firms (Noronha and D'Cruz 2020). However, there remains a lack of research about the struggles to unionize workers engaged in the content moderation value chains.

Conclusion

The starting point of our analysis was the outsourcing of content moderation under-taken by global social media firms. These practices have largely remained hidden and continue to veil the relationships with suppliers and the working conditions of offshored content moderators.

The outsourcing of content moderation has created GVCs and global economic geog-raphies characterized by strong power asymmetries. Located mainly in North America and Europe, the social media firms (i.e., the lead firms in the value chain) control the technological infrastructure as well as the rules and standards of the content modera-tion process, leaving very little room for upgrading on the side of Indian suppliers. Some cases can be described as captive value chain configurations, with the social media firms exerting tight control over all internal processes in the supplier firms. In other cases in our study, suppliers enjoyed a little more autonomy, and the value chain configurations could be described as market based. Even in these cases, the high standardization and codification of tasks as well as price competition limited the scope for supplier upgrading.

Understanding the important role of content moderation in the business model of social media firms enables us to situate the labor of content moderators, which is often contracted and located in internationally outsourced and offshored regions of the world. We have shown how opacity influences their labor process: applicants mostly apply for work having no information about the tasks they will have to per-form, and they are strictly discouraged from talking about their work. At the same time, they work with very stressful content, in a strictly standardized workflow, and under enormous time pressure. It is not surprising that this labor model is characterized by a very high attrition rate and repeated reporting of health (psychological) damage.

Our analysis also shows that the knowledge and experience of workers remains important, despite the high standardization and technological control of the labor process. This was clear in one of our cases, where moderators had the possibility to influence the moderation policies developed by the social media firm. In most cases, however, content moderators have limited opportunities for skill development and growth. Moreover, integration within these GVCs does not lead to enhanced social protection and labor rights. Facilitated neither by the suppliers nor by the social media firms, content moderators must create their own paths for mobility and growth. Given the growing importance of social media markets in the Global South, Chinese and Indian social media firms are expanding and creating new employment opportunities for moderators. North American and European firms also increasingly need content moderators as localization experts. This is a source of labor power that can be used at the individual level as well as a basis for organizing professional groups. Finally, firms and regulators have a responsibility to improve the conditions of this work, which is so critical for the functioning of social media platforms and for sustaining public discussion.

Notes

1. See, for example, http://gawker.com/5885714/inside-facebooks-outsourced-anti-porn-and-gore-brigade-where-camel-toes-are-more-offensive-than-crushed-heads; https://www.telegraphindia.com/7-days/guardians-of-the-internet/cid/1669422; and https://tech.economictimes.indiatimes.com/news/internet/meet-the-indian-warriors-who-watchhours-of-beheadings-murders-gory-content-to-clean-the-internet/58901110?redirect=1.

2. See http://www.theguardian.com/technology/2017/dec/05/youtube-offensive-videos-journalists-moderators.

3. See https://www.forbes.com/sites/kalevleetaru/2018/09/08/is-social-media-content-moderation-an-impossible-task/.

4. See https://www.telegraphindia.com/7-days/guardians-of-the-internet/cid/1669422.

5. The IT BPO sector in India includes a broad range of services supplied to different industries, such as health, finance, law, and technology.

6. These characteristics of market-based chains have also been observed by the GVC scholars in "modular" value chains, although the two differ regarding the complexity of transactions. We do not engage in a discussion on modular chains in the chapter because it is not relevant to our cases.

7. See, for example, https://www.nytimes.com/2010/07/19/technology/19screen.html; https://www.wired.com/2014/10/content-moderation/; https://www.theatlantic.com/technology/archive/2019/06/facebook-and-youtubes-platform-excuse-dying/591466/; https://sz-magazin.sueddeutsche.de/internet/three-months-in-hell-84381; https://economictimes.indiatimes.com/tech/internet/indias-graduates-line-up-to-rid-facebook-of-inappropriate-content/articleshow/65676967.cms?from=mdr; and https://www.theverge.com/2019/2/25/18229714/cognizant-facebook-content-moderator-interviews-trauma-working-conditions-arizona.

8. In the interest of protecting the anonymity of our target participants, we identify them by codes. DSM refers to domestic social media firm, SU refers to supplier, CM refers to content moderator, CO refers to content operator, and GSM refers to global social media firm.

9. First-tier suppliers provide their services directly to social media firms, and the second tier supplies these services to the first tier.

10. For some social media firms, direct intervention includes taking part in the recruitment process.

11. Interviews with content operators employed at domestic and Chinese social media firms in India show that these firms outsource moderation work to external suppliers in India. Having no direct communication with the external content moderators, our interviewees had no knowledge about who the moderators are and where they work. Therefore, the future potential of this outsourcing can only be estimated.

12. See https://www.thehindu.com/news/national/govt-bans-59-apps-including-tiktok-wechat /article31947445.ece.

13. The training provided by the companies focuses on formal content moderation policies and instructions on using the content moderation software. These trainings aim at instructing moderators on how to review content and make decisions regarding it. At the end of the training, the moderators must take a test, and, based on their results, they either are sent to different difficulty levels or retake the training.

References

Ahmad, Sabrina. 2019. "'It's Just the Job': Investigating the Influence of Culture in India's Commercial Content Moderation Industry." Master's thesis, University of Oxford. Preprint, submitted in July. https://doi.org/10.31235/osf.io/hjcv2.

Batt, Rosemary, Virginia Doellgast, Hyunji Kwon, Mudit Nopany, Priti Nopany, and Anil da Costa. 2005. "The Indian Call Centre Industry: National Benchmarking Report Strategy, HR Practices, & Performance." CAHRS Working Paper 05–07. Ithaca, NY: Cornell University, School of Industrial and Labor Relations, Center for Advanced Human Resource Studies.

Cairncross, Frances. 2001. *The Death of Distance: How the Communications Revolution Will Change Our Lives*. London: Orion.

D'Cruz, Premilla, and Ernesto Noronha. 2008. "Doing Emotional Labour: The Experiences of Indian Call Centre Agents." *Global Business Review* 9 (1): 131–147.

D'Cruz, Premilla, and Ernesto Noronha. 2013. "Hope to Despair: The Experience of Organizing Indian Call Centre Employees." *Indian Journal of Industrial Relations* 48 (3): 471–486.

Gereffi, Gary, John Humphrey, and Timothy Sturgeon. 2005. "The Governance of Global Value Chains." *Review of International Political Economy* 12 (1): 78–104.

Gillespie, Tarleton. 2018a. *Custodians of the Internet: Platforms, Content Moderation, and the Hidden Decisions That Shape Social Media*. New Haven, CT: Yale University Press.

Gillespie, Tarleton. 2018b. "Regulation of and by Platforms." In *The SAGE Handbook of Social Media*, edited by Jean Burgess, Alice Marwick, and Thomas Poell, 254–278. London: SAGE.

Graham, Mark, and Mohammad A. Anwar. 2019. "The Global Gig Economy: Towards a Planetary Labour Market." *First Monday* 24 (4), April 1. https://doi.org/10.5210/fm.v24i4.9913.

Grimmelmann, James. 2015. "The Virtues of Moderation." *Yale Journal of Law and Technology* 17 (1): 42–109. https://digitalcommons.law.yale.edu/yjolt/vol17/iss1/2/.

Horner, Rory, and Khalid Nadvi. 2018. "Global Value Chains and the Rise of the Global South: Unpacking Twenty-First Century Polycentric Trade." *Global Networks* 18 (2): 207–237. https://doi .org/10.1111/glob.12180.

James, Al, and Bhaskar Vira. 2012. "Labour Geographies of India's New Service Economy." *Journal of Economic Geography* 12 (4): 841–875.

Klonick, Kate. 2017. "The New Governors: The People, Rules, and Processes Governing Online Speech." *Harvard Law Review* 131 (6): 1599–1670. https://harvardlawreview.org/wp-content/uploads/2018/04/1598-1670_Online.pdf.

Lakhani, Tashlin, Sarosh Kuruvilla, and Ariel Avgar. 2013. "From the Firm to the Network: Global Value Chains and Employment Relations Theory." *British Journal of Industrial Relations* 51 (3): 440–472.

Medeiros, Ben. 2017. "Platform (Non-)Intervention and the 'Marketplace' Paradigm for Speech Regulation." *Social Media + Society* 3 (1): 1–10. https://doi.org/10.1177/2056305117691997.

Nadeem, Shehzad. 2011. *Dead Ringers: How Outsourcing Is Changing the Way Indians Understand Themselves*. Princeton, NJ: Princeton University Press.

Noronha, Ernesto, and Premilla D'Cruz. 2006. "Organising Call Centre Agents: Emerging Issues." *Economic and Political Weekly* 41 (21): 2115–2121.

Noronha, Ernesto, and Premilla D'Cruz. 2020. "The Indian IT Industry: A Global Production Network Perspective." Working Paper no. 134. Berlin: Berlin Institute for International Political Economy, Hochschule für Wirtschaft und Recht Berlin. https://www.ipe-berlin.org/fileadmin/institut-ipe/Dokumente/Working_Papers/ipe_working_paper_134.pdf.

Peck, Jamie. 2017. *Offshore: Exploring the Worlds of Global Outsourcing*. Oxford: Oxford University Press.

Ponte, Stefano, and Timothy Sturgeon. 2014. "Explaining Governance in Global Value Chains: A Modular Theory-Building Effort." *Review of International Political Economy* 21 (1): 195–223.

Remesh, Babu. 2008. "Work Organisation, Control and 'Empowerment': Managing the Contradictions of Call Centre Work." In *In an Outpost of the Global Economy: Work and Workers in India's Information Technology Industry*, edited by Carol Upadhya and A. R. Vasavi, 235–262. New Delhi: Routledge.

Roberts, Sarah T. 2016. "Digital Refuse: Canadian Garbage, Commercial Content Moderation and the Global Circulation of Social Media's Waste." *Wi: Journal of Mobile Media* 10 (1): 1–18.

Roberts, Sarah T. 2017. *Content Moderation*. In *Encyclopedia of Big Data*, edited by Laurie A. Schintler and Connie L. McNeely, C: 1–4. Cham, Switzerland: Springer International.

Roberts, Sarah T. 2019. *Behind the Screen: Content Moderation in the Shadows of Social Media*. New Haven, CT: Yale University Press.

Schrage, Stephanie, and Dirk Ulrich Gilbert. 2019. "Addressing Governance Gaps in Global Value Chains: Introducing a Systematic Typology." *Journal of Business Ethics* (January): 1–16.

Shepherd, Tamara, Alison Harvey, Tim Jordan, Sam Srauy, and Kate Miltner. 2015. "Histories of Hating." *Social Media + Society* 1 (2): 1–10. https://doi.org/10.1177/2056305115603997.

Smith, Chris, and Paul Thompson. 1998. "Re-Evaluating the Labour Process Debate." *Economic and Industrial Democracy* 19 (4): 551–577.

Taylor, Phil, and Peter Bain. 2005. "'India Calling to the Far Away Towns': The Call Centre Labour Process and Globalization." *Work, Employment and Society* 19 (2): 261–282.

Tenhunen, Sirpa. 2018. *A Village Goes Mobile: Telephony, Mediation, and Social Change in Rural India*. New York: Oxford University Press.

Thompson, Paul. 2003. "Fantasy Island: A Labour Process Critique of the 'Age of Surveillance.'" *Surveillance & Society* 1 (2): 138–151.

Upadhya, Carol. 2010. "Taking the High Road? Labour in the Indian Software Outsourcing Industry." In *Labour in Global Production Networks in India*, edited by Anne Posthuma and Dev Nathan, 300–320. New Delhi: Oxford University Press.

6 Digital Livelihoods in Exile: Refugee Work and the Planetary Digital Labor Market

Andreas Hackl

The seemingly inclusive and accessible characteristics of digital platform work have inspired a new generation of social enterprises and international development initiatives that see it as a promising contribution to refugees' livelihoods. These initiatives include social enterprises that connect refugee workers to jobs through digital platforms, including in fields of work such as image annotation and language services. On a basic level, platform work can be seen as a form of self-employment that uses an online platform to match digital workers with buyers of work, thereby connecting supply and demand (de Groen et al. 2018). Such platforms have supplied transnational labor markets with individual workers who are excluded from formal employment and face unstable working conditions (Gregg and Andrijasevic 2019). There are now a growing number of work platforms and initiatives that focus on connecting some of the world's most marginalized populations, such as refugees, with an increasingly planetary-scale digital economy. As these efforts often need to circumvent barriers to digital access, they highlight important opportunities for inclusion in a digitized future of work. At the same time, this chapter will demonstrate forcibly displaced persons' ambivalent experience with platform work provides a unique perspective on the practical limitations of the idea that the digital economy is inclusive and a potentially powerful tool for economic development.

The emergence of a planetary digital labor market has been discussed as a possible contributor to economic development in marginalized regions of the world through providing access to work opportunities and alternative sources of income (Graham, Hjorth, and Lehdonvirta 2017). However, workers in developing countries are most affected by uneven Internet connectivity, time zone differences, language problems, a lack of security, and inadequate pay mechanisms (Robinson et al. 2020). In addition, the digital economy has further widened regional and gender divides, while digital labor platforms trigger fears of "nineteenth-century working practices and future generations of 'digital day labourers'" (ILO 2019, 18). As digital inequalities become more ingrained and insidious, they threaten to leave those without resources ever further behind (Robinson et al. 2020). For example, digital economies have exacerbated economic divides and social inequality in Africa (Karar 2019). Some usage of digital technology, therefore, perpetuates a capitalist system that builds on alienated and exploited labor (Bilić, Primorac, and Valtýsson 2018).

This critique stands vis-à-vis evidence that digitalization has allowed many workers to access new labor markets, while also facilitating new kinds of access to their local market through digital media or platforms. Indeed, platform labor is often simultaneously a site of degradation and one of opportunity for those who have few viable alternatives (van Doorn, Ferrari, and Graham 2020). In supportive economic and policy environments where refugees have the right to work, such as in Germany, digital skills training programs have advanced their economic integration and social mobility, if only for a limited number of motivated individuals (Mason 2018). Digital labor platforms in developing countries are often highlighted positively as well because they provide an alternative source of livelihood amid a scarcity of other opportunities (Heeks 2017).

These benefits have engendered widespread hopes that *digital livelihoods*—including skills training and opportunities for digital work and entrepreneurship—will become a force of economic development among marginalized populations. As the image of digitally connected refugees captures the public imagination, Internet connectivity and mobile devices have become a focal point of refugee support (Latonero, Poole, and Berens 2018). The United Nations High Commissioner for Refugees (UNHCR) sees mobile and Internet technologies as potentially transforming the lives of refugees by improving security, protection, information access, and health services (Vernon, Deriche, and Eisenhauer 2016). Behind some of the expectations that digital inclusion can trigger social and economic change stand powerful assumptions and ideas promoted by a variety of actors in the private sector, in politics, and in international development practice. One of these ideas is that the Internet can benefit the world's poor "by removing frictions, barriers, and intermediaries that stand between producers of goods and services in the Global South and consumers of those things in the Global North" (Graham 2019, 267). Moreover, widespread techno-optimism suggests that the Internet allows anyone to work from practically anywhere, as long as they learn the skills and have a computer and an Internet connection (Kaurin 2020).

However, the Internet and its economic dimensions do not merely remove frictions but also contribute to new divides and forms of exclusion. Refugee status often comes with a lack of bank accounts and financial access, which is confounding at a time when electronic payments have replaced the cash transactions that long defined informal refugee economies. Moreover, poor refugees often struggle to afford data plans, purchase hardware, or establish a safe place from which to work. Although digital economies undoubtedly have a connective quality that crosses boundaries, they have failed to fundamentally transform refugees' marginalized positions as underpaid informal workers with ambiguous legal statuses who struggle to make ends meet.

Digital Work and Migration

The study of digital platform work has not devoted much attention to the role of migrants or refugees, although migrant workers provide much of the labor power behind gig economy services (van Doorn, Ferrari, and Graham 2020, 2). Migrants tend to inhabit particular margins in formal and informal national economies. Platform labor often promises easy access and has therefore been popular among low-wage migrant workers, who have traditionally been excluded from standard employment relations. Van Doorn, Ferrari, and Graham (2020, 4–5) identify why this is the case, arguing that the onboarding process for work platforms is low-threshold and often resembles how many migrants have already experienced informal work. Digital platforms are further seen as lax with respect to their enforcement of formal requirements such as background checks or business licenses of freelancers. Moreover, the ability to work through platforms in English offers an additional inclusive potential, while some app-based platforms allow workers flexibility on cashing out money and offer them a degree of autonomy in deciding when to work or not. However, the inclusiveness of these jobs comes with a widespread reclassification of work as self-employment, which degrades labor standards.

We will see that the particular experiences of refugees mirror some of these aspects while contrasting others. The problems refugees encounter in trying to access platform work are well illustrated by a question the user Hussein posted in the community forum of Upwork, one of the world's largest freelancing platforms: "Hello, I'm a Syrian but I live in Lebanon, currently I'm trying to verify my account and I have 2 issues: Syria is not listed in the dropdown menu when I try to select the ID issue country. There is only one accepted, the passport, but I don't have that, I have a birth certificate paper, I can't get the passport because of the war there. I hope you consider my situation, thank you."[1]

This comment encapsulates some of the key challenges that refugees face in accessing platform work independently. More generally, it suggests that there is something distinctive about the relationship between the digital economy and the condition of being forcibly displaced from one's home country. I therefore ask: How does someone's exile from a homeland determine their marginal position vis-à-vis the planetary digital economy, and how does inclusion in this economy impact the experience of exile?

What does the case of digital refugee workers tell us about the materiality and embeddedness of digital work in the concrete social, economic, and political conditions that frame its production?

This chapter will answer these questions from the perspective of refugees working through three social impact work platforms that hire refugees. These platforms have the specific aim of supporting refugees in two types of digitally mediated home-based work—namely, remote language training and image annotations for datasets used in the training of artificial intelligence (AI). After a note on methods, I will provide a brief overview of the refugee workers' characteristics and the impact of the COVID-19 pandemic on their work. The subsequent sections will summarize the findings on barriers to digital access; on refugees' work experience on the three platforms; and on the wider conditions of their work, including payment levels, as well as the perceived benefits of online work. This is followed by a discussion of the mediating role of these social impact platforms between a planetary-scale labor market and marginalized refugee populations. The concluding section will return to the above conceptual questions about the relationship between the digital economy and the experienced condition of forced displacement.

Methods

This research is rooted in a two-year project on digital refugee livelihoods at the School of Social and Political Science, University of Edinburgh.[2] The methods included ethnographic research and on-site interviews among refugees in Lebanon and Germany. A second phase, conducted mostly digitally and remotely amid the COVID-19 pandemic, included remote interviews and surveys with refugees from a variety of countries and locations. These focused on refugee freelancers who worked from home for one of three social enterprises through digital platforms. The total number of surveyed freelancers in diverse locations[3] was 131.

The first surveyed social impact platform is NaTakallam (Arabic for "We Speak"), a US-registered social enterprise that has matched some 200 displaced persons with over 10,000 clients across some 100 countries for online language sessions by 2021. Students and their refugee conversation partners are linked by an online system for booking and payments, as well as by the software used for the video sessions. Humans in the Loop is a provider of digitally mediated work that is specifically dedicated to refugees and people in conflict-affected countries. It primarily sources work in image annotation for the training of AI datasets. Initially launched in Sofia, Bulgaria, to source work for the local refugee population, it has since expanded into Turkey, Iraq, Syria, and other locations in collaboration with local partner organizations. They have provided income opportunities for some 459 digital workers through 362 projects sourced from 61 different clients. Some 100 individuals were actively working on projects in the first quarter of 2021. Finally, TaQadam (Arabic for "Progress") is a US-based enterprise for image annotation and crowdsourced geospatial imagery analysis that has outsourced work through its own platform primarily to a small crowd of Syrian refugees in Lebanon, alongside a pool of Lebanese citizens. Similar to those working for Humans in the Loop, freelancers working for TaQadam classify and annotate aspects of images to train algorithms, classify objects, and build visual datasets.

Due to the relatively small size of the cohorts that worked through the digital platforms of the three social enterprises, the results gained from the surveys and interviews are only representative of this specific kind of refugee platform work. Because these three platforms specifically aim to support refugees while mediating between freelancers and the planetary market, the experience of refugees who work on the free market through larger work platforms without such support may diverge in significant ways.

Introducing the Refugee Platform Workers

Sitting in a café in the Beirut district of Bourj Hammoud, a Syrian woman we will call Haneen[4] opened her laptop and pointed out an image annotation tool on her screen, which showed a satellite image of buildings surrounded by fields. She demonstrated how she usually searched for names of companies and annotated whether it was a sale location, a warehouse, or another type of building. This work is a human-powered task that trains AI software, thereby improving its vision and classification of images. For a while, the family had access to only one laptop, which Haneen shared with her brother. Soon her younger sister, who was 16 years old, also got involved, and sometimes even the younger ones at ages 10 and 9 contributed a few clicks. With some of the money, they eventually bought a second laptop. Their digital work was crucial for their household's economic survival.

Bashir was 25 years old when I met him at his Beirut home, two years after he arrived in Lebanon. Asked about his work as a conversation partner with NaTakallam, he pointed to the corner of his living room, where his laptop sat on a table, and said: "It's great working from here." He didn't need to beat Beirut's chaotic traffic to meet students on the other side of town. When he was still in Syria, Bashir studied English literature at Damascus University and worked for a company that repaired and sold laptops and mobile phones. When he arrived in Lebanon, he struggled to find work amid labor market restrictions and systematic discrimination. Syrian refugees in Lebanon are officially allowed to work in only three sectors of the economy: construction, cleaning, and agriculture. Eventually, he managed to secure a scholarship for a course at a Lebanese university and began giving Arabic lessons to foreigners. This is when Bashir learned about NaTakallam, and he soon became one of its most active freelancers, teaching students and building relationships with people from the United States, Europe, and other places.

The fields of image annotation and language training are similar in the sense that refugees did the work from home, often without alternative sources of income, while facing difficulties in getting paid without holding bank accounts. Language service providers like NaTakallam function as a digital platform that link students from potentially anywhere on the planet with refugee conversation partners who can also be located anywhere, as long as they pass the interview process and have Internet access. Image annotation work is often repetitive, and larger projects are usually broken up into sets of microtasks that are distributed among a pool of prescreened and trained workers.

The freelancers across the three platforms shared a number of characteristics. For example, they were predominantly well educated. This high level of education somewhat mirrors the educational levels in the platform economy (Berg et al. 2018). At NaTakallam, 95 percent of surveyed language trainers had a background in higher education and had attended college or completed a bachelor's degree. A similar picture emerges from the two image annotation platforms. At Humans in the Loop, 14 of the 17 interviewed freelancers had attended some university.[5] At TaQadam, 84 percent of the Syrian and Lebanese freelancers surveyed held a degree. The educational backgrounds were extremely diverse and included a variety of academic disciplines, ranging from computer science or engineering to various fields of the humanities and social sciences. Some of them entered the digital labor market because their host country did not accredit their preexisting qualifications and did not allow them to practice the professions in which they were trained.

The age of surveyed freelancers varied between the three employers, although most were relatively young. At NaTakallam, 54 percent were between 26 and 35 years old and 37 percent between 36 and 45. At TaQadam, which included nonrefugee freelancers from the Lebanese host community, the average age was 23 years. As mentioned above, the freelancers' much younger siblings also often got involved in image annotation work.

Impact of the COVID-19 Pandemic

In 2020, the COVID-19 pandemic gave home-based digital work renewed significance. Asked specifically about changes in their experience of online work during the pandemic, nearly half (45 percent) of surveyed freelancers at NaTakallam stated that their income had increased since the outbreak. Their customers, who are mostly located in the Global North, suddenly had time to fill with language learning while sitting at home. A little over half agreed that without online work, they would not have been able to pay their rent or to buy food or basic services. Bashir, the freelancer working with NaTakallam, said he registered "maybe 30 percent more demand" than usual during the pandemic, adding: "When the quarantine started, I felt lucky that I had work with NaTakallam and my work was already online."

Growing dependency on home-based platform work emerged alongside the economic hardship that intensified for many refugee families during the pandemic. They were often the first to lose their jobs, while falling through the gaps of social safety nets, experiencing xenophobia, and coping with increased precarity (Dempster et al. 2020). Many freelancers reported that other members of their household had lost their job, or that they had lost their own jobs, had to sell personal items, or borrow money.

Barriers to Accessing Digital Work

The marginalized position of refugees in relation to the planetary digital labor market is exemplified by the barriers to access they face. In the surveys and interviews, the freelancers highlighted the lack of a reliable Internet connection and a convenient place to work from as major problems. This combined with a lack of good hardware and regular electricity cuts to undermine their ability to work efficiently.

As Hussam, a 32-year-old Syrian freelancer who was internally displaced to the city of Azaz, put it: "The difficulties here in Syria are the Internet problems . . . [S]ometimes they don't deliver electricity for days, maybe four days without it." An unreliable Internet connection paired with recurring electricity cuts meant that NaTakallam's language sessions were often interrupted or had to be rescheduled. Some 34 percent of surveyed freelancers at NaTakallam stated that they had difficulties working on the Internet due to a slow Internet connection.

Problems with obtaining adequate hardware posed another barrier. A 25-year-old Syrian woman in Lebanon who worked in image annotation wrote in her survey response: "[This work] is not permanent and I can only work on phone-based projects because I cannot buy a computer." In a similar vein, a 20-year-old Syrian in Azaz who worked in image annotation said: "The major difficulties I faced in work [are that] my computer is very, very weak. I don't have money to get a better one."

Problems with getting paid electronically have posed a major challenge for refugees' access to digital work; 26 percent of NaTakallam's freelancers had "no access to bank accounts or bank cards," and 32 percent stated that they faced difficulties getting paid. The banking and payment problems can often single-handedly cause a job opportunity to go wasted (Bayram 2019). Money transfer services like Western Union are widespread, but they incur fees and don't always work well for remote employers. Mobile wallets theoretically allow receiving payments from abroad, but without a local bank account, users cannot easily cash out their digital money.[6] Yet another barrier to accessing digital work in a sustainable way is the refugees' housing situation. Although most research participants had access to a private room, some stated that they didn't have a private room to work from. None of the respondents reported access to any kind of formal office space.

These barriers are paralleled by a frequent mismatch between the demands of the digital labor market and many refugees' digital literacy and skill levels, as well as English language skills. This hints at an important limitation of this analysis: in focusing on the experiences of workers with relatively high education levels who are already included on digital work platforms, it does not capture the challenges of refugees who would not be able to earn an income on such platforms without prior intensive training (Hackl 2021).

Working Conditions and Payment Levels

The freelancers across the three social impact platforms shared the position of marginality in the local labor markets and in relation to the planetary market. Moreover, the very confinement of situations of displacement that restricted their digital access became one of the reasons they became viable digital laborers: they needed money to support themselves and their families while coping with the challenges of forced displacement, which often involves exclusion from formal labor markets. The social enterprises responded by offering digital work opportunities that are tailored to this need, which can in turn create economic dependency on this ongoing support.

Refugee workers in image annotation often depended on this work as their only source of labor-based income. Few had other local jobs, and some had income from family members as an additional contribution to the household. Among the 17 workers interviewed at Humans in the Loop, only two had another job. In Lebanon, online work through TaQadam and its partner platform was the only source of income for 24 out of 31 respondents (77 percent). More than two-thirds considered their work "extremely important" for their economic survival, while the rest saw it at least as "very important." The overall impression is therefore that this digital work represents the main pillar of their livelihood for a strong majority of the respondents despite it not being designed as a secure and sustainable form of work.

This dependency and lack of alternatives mean that they are more likely to accept unfavorable conditions. Freelancers who label data and train algorithms that power AI technology do so mostly without access to a fair wage or basic benefits (Sinders

2020). Although the social enterprises aim to offer fair wages and good working conditions, they also depend on clients who expect competitive prices. Calculating average monthly income for this fluctuating kind of microwork in image annotation is extremely difficult, as the amount of work constantly changes, while some months do not offer employment at all. At one of the surveyed platforms, the average monthly salary that respondents estimated for themselves was around $270 for an average estimated 35 hours of digital work per week or 140 hours a month.

The freelancers' experience was made difficult by the fluctuating nature of microwork in image annotation and the tight deadlines of project submission. As one Syrian freelancer in Azaz, northern Syria, said: "On a long project . . . it was huge. A lot of work, we maybe worked up to 15 hours a day, but at least 10 hours on average, and a minimum of 8 hours a day, over a period of two months. . . . The pay was little, maybe 1,400 Turkish lira, or around $200, for two months of work. That's very little, but unfortunately there is no alternative. It's the work I have." The irregularity of the workload meant that freelancers often had weeks without work but also months where they worked at least eight or more hours per day. More than two-thirds of freelancers at Humans in the Loop were looking for other job opportunities because of the instability of annotation jobs.

Under the difficult circumstances of deadlines and urgent project submissions, fatigue posed another problem. Projects had to be delivered on time and at prices that were based on numbers of annotations rather than hourly rates. If annotators made mistakes and submitted low-quality work, they had to correct it without extra pay. A 50-year-old Iraqi annotator based in Bulgaria who had a background as a dental technician, said in an interview: "The difficulty, sometimes when they [the clients] need the work in three or four days—it's not easy, it needs from you to be very careful. And when you start to work, you try to deliver it on time, you get very tired. . . . We are refugees, a lot of people take advantage that we are weak. They work on our head, [demand the] maximum, whatever they can take from us. They are treating us like slaves."

Well aware that her direct employer, a social enterprise dedicated to supporting refugees, was doing its best to get work to them, the Iraqi annotator put the blame on the corporate clients. The mediating role of the platforms meant that refugee workers often had no direct contact with the buyers of their work. This relationship was very different from that experienced by language conversation partners, whose contact with the buyers of their work—the language students—was often very close and sometimes led to friendships. Yet this work also involved a range of unfavorable conditions—32 percent of freelancers working as language conversation partners reported that preparation time was not paid, while a quarter found that digital work does not provide security. Another quarter complained that their work often takes place at inconvenient times due to time differences between their location and that of students, who are often based in North America or another distant location.

Of the $15 fee the conversation partners earned per hour of Skype conversation, $10 went to them and $5 flowed back into NaTakallam.[7] Payment levels varied significantly from tutor to tutor. Bashir, who was based in Lebanon, made about $400 a month on average by teaching Arabic online. In a very good month, he made up to $800. The platform became Bashir's primary source of income and remained crucial for his economic survival and his ability to continue his studies. The freelancer Osama made only around $40 when he started out teaching Arabic over the Internet but soon managed to increase his monthly income to around $250. Finding an appropriate job in the local labor market in Lebanon was an ongoing challenge for him: "In general, when they see you are Syrian on your CV, employers don't usually hire you here."

Among the 82 freelancers surveyed at NaTakallam, 35 percent earned less than $200 a month, 44 percent earned between $200 and $400, and 21 percent earned between $400 and $600 or more. Although this work constituted between 75 and 100 percent of total income for about a quarter of the freelancers, 30 percent said it was less than 25 percent of their total income, and another 30 percent that it was between 25 and 50 percent. Another job (46 percent) and support from family members (15 percent) were the most common sources of additional income, alongside money from aid organizations and other freelancing work. Their income from NaTakallam was nonetheless crucial for the economic survival of their households, as some 63 percent stated that they supported between two and four people through their work and a quarter of respondents supported more than four people; the rest supported only themselves.

Flexible and Safe: Perceived Benefits of Home-Based Work

Working from home was highlighted as a particularly welcome alternative to the challenges of the local labor market in many places. More than two-thirds of language conversation partners at NaTakallam saw the ability to work from home and use their time flexibly as a positive feature of their work. In a similar vein, a 20-year-old Syrian image annotator in Turkey explained: "I like online work more because it can happen from the house. I don't feel the tiredness so much [working at home] as I do when I work outside the house, in Istanbul." Working from home further provided refugees with a sense of security in areas where commuting to work poses a considerable challenge.

Due to social and cultural factors, home-based work in the gig economy is seen as an attractive option for many Syrian women refugees (Hunt, Samman, and Mansour-Ille 2017). This highlights how platform work continues long-standing features of women's work in domestic and market economies, including the celebration of worker flexibility, which often results in a combination of taken-for-granted care work and housework with paid digital labor (Gregg and Andrijasevic 2019). Among the surveyed refugees, women especially considered the ability to work from home to be beneficial for their family life and other responsibilities. As a 32-year-old Afghan woman who worked for Humans in the Loop from Bulgaria said: "I am a single mother, and I live here with my two kids. I am the one who works. I don't have any family in Bulgaria. . . . I prefer online work because my son needs constant care." Another refugee woman in Lebanon highlighted the importance of home-based freelancing for "earning more money to live with the economic difficulties that we are facing in Lebanon, especially that I am a divorced mom."

Somewhat counterintuitively, working from home was further associated with increased international connections from within a situation of confinement. As one survey respondent working with NaTakallam put it: "I love working from home, it costs less and saves time and effort. In the time of the corona[virus pandemic], I was able to get to know a lot of new people through NaTakallam despite the fact that others suffered from loneliness." Some interpreted this as a source of increased (digital) mobility within a situation of confinement, with one respondent saying: "It lets me travel every day to a different country by thoughts without any passport or visa, and I got new friends compensating me of my friends who I lost during the conflict. NaTakallam is my family." In a similar vein, one refugee woman in Lebanon wrote in her survey response: "I most like about my work with NaTakallam that I am a part of and that I am in contact with new people from different countries around the world." Especially in a situation of exclusion, as it often affects refugees in their respective locations, home-based freelancing in language training carried with it the ambivalent experience of enjoying meeting new people but also feeling isolated working from home. Indeed, 43 percent of the surveyed freelancers at NaTakallam stated that working from home is socially isolating.

The positive evaluation of home-based platform work was also partly determined by the lack of alternatives: Syrian survey respondents in Lebanon stated that working over the Internet was simply the only option because they were not legally allowed to work elsewhere in their field and that it also allowed them to avoid local discrimination. Indeed, as one respondent in the survey stated, "When I started [with NaTakallam] in Lebanon, it was a way to escape from racism."

Incubation and Mediation: Connecting Refugees with the Digital Labor Market

The three social enterprises connect refugees to remote work opportunities on their digital platforms with the help of two main interventions: mediation and incubation.

Mediation refers to their inclusive intervention into an otherwise exclusive relationship between individual refugees and digitally mediated work. These interventions include bargaining with clients to ensure favorable working conditions for freelancers, supporting freelancers with training, and making sure that payments reach them even in the absence of bank accounts. *Incubation* refers to the fact that these platforms create a closed labor market of a few dozen, or at a maximum a little more than 100 freelancers, thereby shielding them from direct competition in the planetary market. Rather than investing large amounts of unpaid work time into searching for gigs, as is common on microwork and freelancing platforms, refugees working for the three social enterprises are offered work as projects or individual jobs become available. To be sure, some level of competition remains within this "incubator," primarily because including more freelancers sometimes means that each of them gets a smaller slice of the pie.

That the social enterprises aim to support refugees through platform work does not necessarily mean that they manage to realize all their aims. Bound by market rules and competitive pricing, the social impact platforms in image annotation struggled to attract clients who were prepared to pay more than the low prices of the global market. The planetary competition that pits workers around the world against each other contributes to a race to the bottom (Graham and Anwar 2019). Humans in the Loop's struggle with this dynamic started with their initial aim to fix hourly minimum prices. They soon discovered that clients found this unpredictable and demanded fixed pricing per annotation or per image instead. This forced the conditions of work away from guaranteed hourly wages. The clients in this field know little about the microworkers that train AI, who are in turn often unaware of the purposes of their tasks. This labor and its working conditions are intentionally kept hidden by key industry actors (Tubaro, Casilli, and Coville 2020).

Social enterprises like Humans in the Loop and TaQadam stand in an ambivalent space between worker and client, helping refugees to support their livelihoods by mediating between the digital marketplace and the workers. This role involves tensions, as the demands of the market don't always fit their expectations. The standard pricing most clients expect in data training for a so-called bounding box annotation is around $0.05, and between $0.08 and $0.10 for a polygon. At Humans in the Loop, only half of this amount goes straight to the annotator. These are challenging preconditions for anyone hoping to achieve decent working conditions.

Annotators feel fatigue and frustration when the pricing set at the initial agreement does not match the effort the project takes. This is why Humans in the Loop has been trialing each project with a sample to determine how unit pricing will translate into hourly payments before the price is fixed. This is to meet their goal of a minimum wage of €3 per hour across all projects. Yet their power to change the underlying conditions is sometimes limited.

Iva Gumnishka, the founder of Humans in the Loop, recalls the problems that led to a recent project experience that many of her annotators struggled with:

> We ask for estimates from the clients, so they price a project in the fairest way, but sometimes these estimates clients give us, or their samples, are not accurate. Recently, a client had sent us one sample and it turned out that the project was actually more difficult. If in the trial it took us one minute per image, in the actual project it took four or five minutes per image—the difference was huge. We tried to bring this up later and the client simply said, "We are a big company and you have to calculate in contingency."

Such experiences show the social enterprises' determination to negotiate more favorable conditions for their freelancers but hint at their limited power as mediators. The fear of losing a good client through demands that are too high is always present, as clients can easily move elsewhere and hire workers in India, China, the Philippines, or Pakistan. Among the conversation partners in NaTakallam's remote language training, the mediation is done by the social enterprise's digital booking system and staff, who connect freelancers to clients looking for language practice or translation services. To a certain extent, it is then up to the freelancers how they cultivate their clients and whether they manage to build a cohort of regular students.

Mediation regarding payment is crucial for including refugees in digital platform work. With varying degrees of success, the social enterprises channel the money clients pay into their accounts to individual refugees without bank accounts, often in remote locations. Getting cash to freelancers involves partnering up with local nongovernmental organizations, who distribute the money as cash or a check. Sometimes the only option is to bring cash into a country in person and distribute it on the ground. Without this mediation, most refugee freelancers would simply not be able to receive payment for platform work. At the same time, social impact platforms effectively charge refugee workers a substantial commission of up to 50 percent to cover running costs and other expenses. As refugee labor thereby funds part of the enterprises' expenses and helps ensure its financial sustainability, these social impart platforms come to resemble private employment agencies in a digital world of work.

Career Progression and Uncertain Futures

Building on important support mechanisms, the social enterprises aim to extend into a pathway toward career progression. One of the key challenges remains how to turn refugees' digital livelihoods into social mobility and increased access to decent work.

The platforms in image annotation held short training sessions before individual projects. In collaboration with partner organizations, some platforms offered longer, three-month training sessions in web design or other digital skills, alongside English language training. Humans in the Loop, for example, held 12-week courses of 16 hours per week in computer skills and English literacy, alongside shorter trainings in Excel and graphic design. These skills could be transferable into other forms of employment, and social enterprises like Humans in the Loop encourage and support students in these courses to move on to decent, sustainable work. However, refugees in many locations faced severe restrictions to their economic activity and to the kind of work they could access even if their digital skills were well developed. This is, in part, why many remain dependent on platform work and freelancing as a source of income.

Asked about their plans for their professional futures, a little more than half of the image annotators surveyed in Lebanon stated that they wanted to become successful online freelancers. Other career aims expressed by image annotators were continuing university studies or learning a new profession, as well as using training in digital skills to find secure employment at a local workplace. Although image annotation is a highly specific and often repetitive work, some freelancers managed to use their income to open small enterprises. The 22-year-old Syrian Shyar, who lived in an Iraqi refugee camp, opened a mobile repair shop within the camp using the money he saved from freelancing with Humans in the Loop.

Among freelancers involved in language training, 84 percent agreed that this work has given them "new professional goals" or built their existing skills, including in translation and intercultural communication, and 85 percent agreed that working online has improved their English language skills. The majority felt that working with NaTakallam improved their understanding of people from different cultural backgrounds; this included meeting people from elsewhere and making new friends.

Conclusion: The Displaced Marginality of Refugee Platform Work

The enduring impact of forced displacement determines refugees' marginal position vis-à-vis the planetary digital labor market. This marginality stems from barriers to digital access that are specific to the circumstances that surround many refugees, including political and economic exclusion, unreliable infrastructures (especially Internet and electricity), exclusion from bank accounts and digital payment mechanisms, and a lack of globally competitive digital skills and English language abilities. At the same time, it is precisely this marginality that makes refugees a valuable source of digital labor for the clients looking to train AI data cheaply and readily available providers of language conversation sessions for paying students in varying time zones around the world who require flexibility. Refugees' difficulties in finding adequate work in the restrictive labor markets of host countries, alongside experiences with discrimination, determine their position vis-à-vis the planetary market as a readily available cheap labor force in need of an alternative source of livelihood.

The case of refugees in the digital labor market underlines that the materiality of their displaced condition defines the products of their work and thereby becomes implicated in the planetary geography of production. Freelancers in image annotation must compete with pricing for workers in low-income countries despite often residing in middle- and upper-income countries. Their experience of the planetary digital market is deeply embedded in the specific experience and circumstances of the displaced condition and the national context they find themselves in. At the same time, refugees' inclusion in this market also results in a partial disembedding of the value of their labor from the national context into the international level of competition. Inclusion in the digital labor market displaces them once more.

How does this precarious inclusion of refugees in digital labor markets impact their experience of living in exile? Refugees are exiles and economic outcasts in a world that is spanned by the planetary digital market; their inclusion in this market leads to forms of self-employment that largely mirror the piecemeal work refugees have long done in informal economies. Still, home-based platform labor offers an important source of livelihoods that support the economic survival of displaced individuals, families, and households. The sometimes-unfavorable conditions of this low-paid, insecure work highlight that inclusion of refugees in digital markets reproduces the very marginality that pushed them to get involved in the first place. Rather than becoming self-reliant employees with transferable skills, they often remain dependent on the ongoing mediation and support of the platforms, with limited possibilities for career progression. Without the continuing mediation and incubation of the social enterprises that are dedicated to supporting them, many would not be able to compete or receive payment on the global market and often would not even be able to afford a computer.

To be sure, the two fields of refugee platform work discussed are notably different in experience and nature of work. Seen together, they nevertheless highlight the limits of the digital economy's inclusive role for people at the world's margins. In order to realize the potential for economic inclusion and development that digital livelihoods are sometimes associated with, there is a need for ambitious, long-term policies that frame the further development of digital platform work in AI and other fields "by taking into account the concrete conditions of its production" (Tubaro, Casilli, and Coville 2020, 11). In the case of refugees, this includes the need for improved financial and digital access, better working conditions, and a revision of restrictive national refugee policies that impede people's access to distant jobs and platform work. This effort should support and build on the important pioneering work social impact platforms for refugees have done thus far by strengthening their capacity to mediate effectively between the planetary digital market and the people at the world's economic margins.

Notes

1. Upwork community forum at https://community.upwork.com/t5/Admin-Support-Specialists /ID-verification-Syria-is-not-listed/m-p/549134.

2. The research project was funded by the Economic and Social Research Council (ESRC), UK.

3. At NaTakallam (https://natakallam.com), 82 freelancers responded to the survey; most of them were forcibly displaced persons from various countries including Syria, Lebanon, Iraq, Burundi, Afghanistan, Palestine, and Venezuela. The research with Humans in the Loop (https:// humansintheloop.org) was a collaborative effort with their annual impact assessment in 2020 and involved structured remote interviews with 17 freelancers located in Iraq, Syria, Turkey, and Bulgaria. At TaQadam (https://taqadam.io), 32 Lebanese and Syrian freelancers, all based in Lebanon, responded to the online survey in July 2020.

4. All names of refugee platform workers in this chapter are pseudonyms and have been anonymized to protect the privacy of research participants.

5. The overall educational levels of freelancers at Humans in the Loop may differ from this snapshot of 17 interviewees, who only make up a small share of the total workforce.

6. Mobile money transfer and mobile wallet systems are designed to avoid bank fees and restrictions by allowing consumers to transfer money, purchase products, and use alternative currencies at virtually no cost. Without a bank card and an account to cash out digitally stored money, however, refugees can make little use of these systems. Moreover, prominent services such as PayPal are banned in some locations, including Lebanon.

7. NaTakallam announced an increase of their prices in October 2020, from the previous $15 per hourly conversation session to $25. These increases were meant to ensure the sustainability of the social enterprise while further improving its impact on the lives of refugees and their host communities.

References

Bayram, Ahmad Sufian. 2019. *A World of Limited Possibilities: Refugee Youth and Job Opportunities within the Lebanese Law and Market*. Beirut: SPARK. https://www.ahmadsb.com/research/Refugee -Job-Opportunities-in-Lebanese.pdf.

Berg, Janine, Marianne Furrer, Ellie Harmon, Uma Rani, and M. Six Silberman. 2018. *Digital Labour Platforms and the Future of Work: Towards Decent Work in the Online World*. Geneva: International

Labour Organization. https://www.ilo.org/global/publications/books/WCMS_645337/lang--en/index.htm.

Bilić, Paško, Jaka Primorac, and Bjarki Valtýsson. 2018. "Technology, Labour and Politics in the 21st Century: Old Struggles in New Clothing." In *Technologies of Labour and the Politics of Contradiction*, edited by Paško Bilić, Jaka Primorac, and Bjarki Valtýsson, 1–16. Cham, Switzerland: Palgrave Macmillan.

de Groen, Willem Pieter, Zachary Kilhoffer, Karolien Lenaerts, and Irene Mandl. 2018. "Employment and Working Conditions of Selected Types of Platform Work." Luxembourg: Publications Office of the European Union.

Dempster, Helen, Thomas Ginn, Jimmy Graham, Martha Guerrero Ble, Daphne Jayasinghe, and Barri Shorey. 2020. "Locked Down and Left Behind: The Impact of COVID-19 on Refugees' Economic Inclusion." Washington, DC: Center for Global Development. https://www.cgdev.org/publication/locked-down-and-left-behind-impact-covid-19-refugees-economic-inclusion.

Graham, Mark. 2019. "The Internet at the Global Economic Margins." In *Society and the Internet*, edited by Mark Graham and William H. Dutton, 255–278. Oxford: Oxford University Press.

Graham, Mark, and Mohammad Anwar. 2019. "The Global Gig Economy: Towards a Planetary Labour Market?" *First Monday* 24 (4), April 1. https://doi.org/10.5210/fm.v24i4.9913.

Graham, Mark, Isis Hjorth, and Vili Lehdonvirta. 2017. "Digital Labour and Development: Impacts of Global Digital Labour Platforms and the Gig Economy on Worker Livelihoods." *Transfer: European Review of Labour and Research* 23 (2): 135–162.

Gregg, Melissa, and Rutvica Andrijasevic. 2019. "Virtually Absent: The Gendered Histories and Economies of Digital Labour." *Feminist Review* 123 (1): 1–7. https://doi.org/10.1177/0141778919878929.

Hackl, Andreas. 2021. *Digital Refugee Livelihoods and Decent Work: Towards Inclusion in a Fairer Digital Economy*. Geneva: International Labour Organization. https://www.ilo.org/wcmsp5/groups/public/---dgreports/---ddg_p/documents/publication/wcms_780060.pdf.

Heeks, Richard. 2017. "Decent Work and the Digital Gig Economy: A Developing Country Perspective on Employment Impacts and Standards in Online Outsourcing, Crowdwork, Etc." Working Paper 71. Manchester: Centre for Development Economics. http://hummedia.manchester.ac.uk/institutes/gdi/publications/workingpapers/di/di_wp71.pdf.

Hunt, Abigail, Emma Samman, and Dina Mansour-Ille. 2017. "Syrian Women Refugees in Jordan: Opportunity in the Gig Economy?" London: Overseas Development Institute. https://odi.org/en/publications/syrian-women-refugees-opportunity-in-the-gig-economy/.

ILO. 2019. "Work for a Brighter Future: Global Commission on the Future of Work." Geneva: International Labour Organization. https://www.ilo.org/wcmsp5/groups/public/---dgreports/---cabinet/documents/publication/wcms_662410.pdf.

Karar, Haytham. 2019. "Algorithmic Capitalism and the Digital Divide in Sub-Saharan Africa." *Journal of Developing Societies* 35 (4): 514–537.

Kaurin, Dragana. 2020. *Space and Imagination: Rethinking Refugees' Digital Access*. Geneva: UNHCR Innovation Service. https://www.unhcr.org/innovation/wp-content/uploads/2020/04/Space-and -imagination-rethinking-refugees-digital-access_WEB042020.pdf.

Latonero, Mark, Danielle Poole, and Jos Berens. 2018. *Refugee Connectivity: A Survey of Mobile Phones, Mental Health, and Privacy at a Syrian Refugee Camp in Greece*. Cambridge, MA: Harvard Humanitarian Initiative. https://hhi.harvard.edu/publications/refugee-connectivity-survey-mobile-phones-mental -health-and.

Mason, Ben. 2018. *Tech Jobs for Refugees: Assessing the Potential of Coding Schools for Refugee Integration in Germany*. Brussels: Migration Policy Institute Europe. https://www.migrationpolicy.org /sites/default/files/publications/TechJobsRefugees_Final.pdf.

Robinson, Laura, Jeremy Schulz, Hopeton S. Dunn, Antonio A. Casilli, Paola Tubaro, Rod Carveth, Wenhong Chen, Julie B. Wiest, Matías Dodel, Michael J. Stern, Christopher Ball, Kuo-Ting Huang, Grant Blank, Massimo Ragnedda, Hiroshi Ono, Bernie Hogan, Gustavo Mesch, Shelia R. Cotten, Susan B. Kretchmer, Timothy M. Hale, Tomasz Drabowicz, Pu Yan, Barry Wellman, Molly-Gloria Harper, Anabel Quan-Haase, and Aneka Khilnani. 2020. "Digital Inequalities 3.0: Emergent Inequalities in the Information Age." *First Monday* 25 (7), July 6.

Sinders, Caroline. 2020. "Examining the Human Labor behind AI." Mozilla Foundation, May 14. https://foundation.mozilla.org/en/blog/examining-human-labor-behind-ai/.

Tubaro, Paola, Antonio A. Casilli, and Marion Coville. 2020. "The Trainer, the Verifier, the Imitator: Three Ways in Which Human Platform Workers Support Artificial Intelligence." *Big Data & Society* 7 (1): 1–12. https://doi.org/10.1177/2053951720919776.

van Doorn, Niels, Fabian Ferrari, and Mark Graham. 2020. "Migration and Migrant Labour in the Gig Economy: An Intervention." *SSRN*, July 1. Available at https://ssrn.com/abstract_id=3622589.

Vernon, Alan, Kamel Deriche, and Samantha Eisenhauer. 2016. *Connecting Refugees: How Internet and Mobile Connectivity Can Improve Refugee Well-Being and Transform Humanitarian Action*. Geneva: UNHCR. https://www.unhcr.org/en-us/publications/operations/5770d43c4/connecting -refugees.html.

II   Mapping Planetary Networks

7 Working the Digital Silk Road: Alibaba's Digital Free Trade Zone in Malaysia

Brett Neilson

A warehouse is a lot like a computer, according to Zhu Lijun, leader of the algorithm team at Cainiao network, the logistics arm of China's e-commerce giant the Alibaba Group. The "common reliance on storage, extraction, and processing lends the two some striking operational and structural parallels," the engineer told an audience at the 2018 Global Smart Logistics Summit in Hangzhou (Alibaba Tech 2018). What are we to make of this comparison, given the increased presence of automated technologies in warehouses and the debate concerning their implications for workers (Delfanti and Frey 2020; Beverungen 2021)? To understand the warehouse as a computer with the spatial qualities of an industrial facility is to bring the question of digital work into settings that are at once technical and physical, software-driven, and primed for hard labor.

This chapter explores how the nexus of computing and warehousing inflects the geopolitical shifts surrounding Alibaba's development of the Digital Free Trade Zone (DFTZ) on the fringes of Kuala Lumpur International Airport (KLIA). Launched in 2017 as part of Alibaba's Electronic World Trade Platform (eWTP), the DFTZ is funded by a state-private partnership involving government-linked corporation Malaysian Airports Holdings Berhad (MAHB), Pos Malaysia, Cainiao, and Lazada, Alibaba's Southeast Asian retail platform. Although the DFTZ is incomplete, presenting difficulties for the study of the labor regimes that it will support, an investigation of the technical, institutional, geopolitical, and economic arrangements surrounding the project sheds light on the conditions that shape digital work in a planetary environment marked by the increasing presence of Chinese commerce. This chapter contends that the modes of power that propel China's digital expansion reduce to neither state prerogatives nor capital operations. Crucial to these modes of power are practices of data extraction, analysis, and intervention that transmute relations among geopolitical strategies, commercial activities, infrastructural installations, and labor force control.

Zhu Lijun's trio of storage, extraction, and processing provocatively, although surely not deliberately, echoes Friedrich Kittler's (1997) well-known typology of media functions: storage, transmission, and processing. And Lijun's emphasis on extraction in a presentation that drew parallels between warehouses and computers is telling. If transmission describes the channeling of messages as signals and the capacity of media to overcome spatial distances, extraction refers to the removal of value or information from objects or messages undergoing storage, transmission, or processing. That an engineer engaged in warehouse design should be attuned to such dynamics is unsurprising, given that data extraction is central to the business models of e-commerce companies and other digital platforms. Writing with Sandro Mezzadra, I have argued that data extraction opens "new frontiers for the expansion of logics of property" and blurs "borders between processes of governance and dynamics of capitalist valorization" (Mezzadra and Neilson 2017, 195). Exploring these processes of opening and blurring in the operations of platform companies such as Alibaba is a crucial step toward understanding the expanding role of extraction in the global economy.

Platform businesses pursue a mode of "dual value production" by which "the monetary value produced by the service provided is augmented by the use *and* speculative value of the data produced before, during, and after service provision" (van Doorn and Badger 2020, 1476). The e-commerce warehouse, for instance, houses inventory whose storage, processing, and sale generate revenue. At the same time, the warehouse is a site for the extraction of data that not only feeds back into operations but also constitutes an asset class in its own right. This extractive function of the warehouse has become one of its primary economic rationales, situating it front stage of logistical transformations and struggles in which automation is at stake. In her history of US foreign trade zones, Dara Orenstein (2019) argues that the distinction of processing from manufacturing was a primary point of contention in the twentieth-century warehouse.[1] Today, anxieties circulate less around the concern that the warehouse might position itself as a factory and more around the relation among extractive modes of data capture and exploitative modes of labor control.

A large body of publications documenting urban activism and labor struggles against the warehousing practices of Seattle-based e-commerce giant Amazon has emerged in recent years (see, for instance, Ruckus 2016; Boewe and Schulten 2017; Geissler 2018; Apicella and Hildebrandt 2019; Bad Barcode 2019; Flaming and Burns 2019; Graham et al. 2019; Transnational Social Strike Platform 2019; Alimahomed-Wilson and Reese 2020; and Berlin vs. Amazon 2021). Researchers know less about the logistical operations and labor deployment of warehouses run by Alibaba, Amazon's main Chinese rival. Although Amazon closed its domestic e-commerce business in China in 2019, it continues to compete with Alibaba on a global scale, especially in Southeast Asia, where it has entered into an agreement with the Vietnam E-Commerce Association and opened its Prime platform in Singapore.

Alibaba's decision to invest in Malaysia's DFTZ occurs in the context of this mounting competition. The DFTZ is part of an Alibaba initiative known as the eWTP, which has also begun projects in Rwanda, Belgium, and Ethiopia. The eWTP seeks to shape global trade in ways that express the growing influence of Chinese Internet firms in consonance with the Digital Silk Road components of China's Belt and Road Initiative (BRI). As Maximiliano Facundo Vila Seoane (2019, 2) explains, the eWTP "attempts to globalize a China-centered and privately-led global digital trade order to challenge the previous wave of US-led globalization and its infrastructure." The questions that inform my analysis are how much this geopolitical drive shapes operational processes or vice versa, and to what extent, in turn, the nexus of geopolitics and warehouse operations influences labor relations and processes in the DFTZ. This chapter grapples with these issues by interrogating the institutional, economic, and technical factors that converge in the formation of the DFTZ and, in particular, their relevance for understanding transformations to digital work wrought by automation.

In the first section, I turn my attention to the institutional architectures that contribute to the making of the DFTZ, considering the extent to which Alibaba's involvement in this zoning project aligns with the Digital Silk Road components of China's BRI. In particular, I critically assess the claim that Alibaba's expansive activity promotes an "inclusive globalization" that contrasts with the global dominance of US technology firms by offering opportunities for small and medium-sized enterprises (SMEs) to access consumer markets in China. The second section of the chapter examines the labor regimes surrounding the DFTZ and how they are shaped by matters of infrastructure, data management, and automation. My focus is on demonstrating that the digital work practices sustained by the DFTZ cannot be fully explained as the result of the importation of a Chinese labor model but must account for multiple factors, including platform dynamics and Malaysian government digital economy policies. In this way, I dissect the geopolitical, technological, and infrastructural elements of DFTZ operations with a view to showing how the e-commerce warehouse mobilizes multiple forms of power and extraction.

Institutional Architectures of the Digital Free Trade Zone

"Our responsibility today is not to reverse globalization but to improve it" (Ma 2018, para. 7). These words, written by Jack Ma, Alibaba's founder and former executive chairman, capture much of the rhetorical energy surrounding the making of the DFTZ. Ma also pronounces his opposition to the "trade war sparked by the United States" (Ma 2018, para. 15), but the discourses supporting the eWTP advocate a China-centered and privately led global digital trade regime that supposedly contrasts to the predominantly US-led wave of globalization dating from the 1990s. Vila Seoane (2019, 6) outlines several aspects of this discursive strategy: First, US-led globalization has benefited a few large corporations, whereas the eWTP seeks to offer opportunities to SMEs that have previously experienced difficulty accessing global circuits, an approach that will allegedly assist the economic advancement of women and young people. Second, Ma's own business history illustrates a path to success for these parties. Third, whereas container trade fueled US-led globalization, Alibaba aims to spearhead international trade reliant on the circulation of small packages. Fourth, digital infrastructures can speed up trade and turnover times in ways that demonstrate why entrepreneurial activity should lead state digital strategies. Fifth, the eWTP spreads along the Digital Silk Road and accords with BRI prerogatives, providing opportunities for partner countries to partake in China's economic rise.

Together, these discursive overtures amount to a claim for facilitating an "inclusive globalization" based on collaboration and partnership with SMEs and BRI-participating countries. As Hong Shen (2018, 2685) outlines, such advocacy of inclusive globalization is an important element of China's Digital Silk Road policy vision, alongside cutting industrial overcapacity, enabling corporate China's global expansion, supporting the internationalization of the renminbi, and constructing a China-centered transnational network infrastructure. Alibaba's DFTZ activities are thus discursively positioned to bolster BRI Digital Silk Road ambitions even as their entanglement with trade and investment liberalization opens potential tensions with China's state-centric Internet governance model.

Notwithstanding this emphasis on alignment with the BRI, Alibaba's involvement with the DFTZ stems not so much from the governmental cues of the Chinese state as much as from an invitation from Malaysia's government to assist with the development of infrastructure, skills, and knowledge relevant to e-commerce expansion. In November 2016, the administration of Prime Minister Najib Razak engaged Jack Ma as an advisor, an appointment that catalyzed the official launch of the DFTZ in November 2017. Gomez et al. (2020) classify the DFTZ as a state-private venture, as it involves collaboration among Malaysian government–linked corporation MAHB, formerly government-linked corporation Pos Malaysia, and Alibaba majority–owned companies Lazada and Cainiao. The initiative has three stages.

The first is already operative. It comprises an e-fulfillment hub run by Pos Aviation, a branch of formerly government-linked corporation Pos Malaysia, and Lazada, a Southeast Asian e-commerce platform that Alibaba has owned 83 percent of since 2017 (after an initial acquisition of 51 percent in 2016) and that is operative across Malaysia, Indonesia, the Philippines, Vietnam, Thailand, and Singapore. Significantly, the capital for the establishment of this e-fulfillment hub, which occupies KLIA's former low-cost-carrier terminal, was provided not by Alibaba's Lazada but by Malaysia's Pos Aviation, reversing "the traditional foreign direct investment (FDI) model where the foreign technology partner usually provides some or all of the capital" (Tham 2018, 3).

In stage two, Cainiao (cofounded by Alibaba in 2013 and currently majority-owned by Alibaba at 63 percent) partnered with MAHB to build an Association of Southeast Asian Nations (ASEAN) e-commerce hub consisting of a cargo terminal, sorting centers, warehouses, and fulfillment centers, which are essential logistics facilities for supporting regional e-commerce activities. Operative at the end of 2020, the ASEAN hub is bankrolled by a joint venture owned at 70 percent by Cainiao and 30 percent by MAHB. The third stage of the DFTZ is an expansion into KLIA Aeropolis,[2] featuring warehouses, a multimodal transport hub, a regional distribution center, and light industry. This phased development positions the DFTZ as a site where infrastructural installations merge with institutional design to facilitate modes of trade and governance that augment capitalist accumulation and shift geopolitical relations in ways that foreground the power of technological systems as much as they do nation-state prerogatives.

As Gomez et al. (2020, 79) explain, the role of the Malaysian enterprises in the DFTZ is primarily "to get land and approval from local authorities, as well as access to state incentives." By contrast, Alibaba provides critical expertise and technical infrastructure, and promises "to create demand for the facilities at the e-commerce hub, via its business and corporate partners" (79). In this sense, Alibaba reaches beyond bricks and mortar investment to position itself as "the key enabler of Malaysia's digitalization strategy" (Vila Seoane 2019, 9). Crucial here is the deployment of Alibaba Cloud data technologies to reduce trade turnover and customs clearance times and connect Malaysian consumers and SMEs with their counterparts in China. Alibaba Cloud established a Kuala Lumpur data center in late 2017 (Cheh 2017). The collaboration of Malaysian financial services corporations Maybank, Public Bank, and CIMB Group with the Alibaba affiliate Ant Group to establish the Alipay mobile payment system in Malaysia is another part of the picture (Chew, Shen, and Ansell 2020). In short, the willingness of Malaysia to open its territory, population, and business environments to the deployment of Alibaba's data ecosystem (see also Naughton [2020] on Alibaba's implementation of its City Brain program in Malaysia) brings with it hopes of bootstrapping its digital economy, not least through the operations of physical e-commerce infrastructures in the DFTZ.

Although SME export opportunities are a key part of Alibaba's eWTP rhetoric and Malaysian government motives, such advancement matters little for a partner like MAHB, whose primary interest lies in increased air cargo and freight traffic. In any case, the extent to which DFTZ operations will benefit Malaysian SMEs remains unknown.

Alibaba clearly seeks to encourage SMEs to list on its platforms, but the company also has interests in using the DFTZ to advance its global trading and logistics businesses, especially in the Southeast Asian region. As many commentators point out (Tham and Kam 2019; Vila Seoane 2019; Gomez et al. 2020), the DFTZ also provides a technologically efficient and low-tariff environment for the import of Chinese goods into Malaysia, creating domestic competition for Malaysian SMEs. Certainly, Malaysian SMEs can benefit from streamlined export processes, but their ability to do so rests on the development of viable products as well as the acquisition of business digitalization skills, which Alibaba and other providers offer only through training that comes at a price. Insofar as access to the Chinese market goes, Malaysian SMEs will have to compete with their Chinese counterparts on Alibaba's domestic e-commerce platforms. Additionally, they will have to negotiate customs procedures for importing goods into China or other countries, which the DFTZ will not harmonize. There are thus significant barriers to the realization of the inclusive globalization vision that animates the eWTP.

Beyond these barriers, Alibaba's inclusive globalization rhetoric obscures further elements of the company's operations, including questions of labor deployment in the DFTZ, data extraction, and the possibility of forcing partner countries into new forms of digital dependency (Vila Seoane 2019). Nonetheless, the discourse of inclusive globalization emerges in a planetary environment in which US technological firms have entrenched dominance. In signaling alignment with the BRI and contrasting its activities with a supposedly exclusive US-led globalization, Alibaba attempts to suggest that its business models and processes are more attentive to the needs and desires of partner nations and enterprises than those of its North American competitors. Unsurprisingly, much criticism of Alibaba's activities in Malaysia echoes more general concerns about the BRI. For instance, US army officer Hugh Harsono (2020, paras. 10 and 11) links the DFTZ not only to considerations of digital dependency but also to anxieties of "debt-trap diplomacy" and scenarios of Chinese geopolitical control of the Strait of Malacca. Even academic studies, which are generally more circumspect than articles penned by military personnel, adopt the concept of "digital empire" to analyze Alibaba's expansionary activities and describe e-commerce in Southeast Asia as a "key battlefield" upon which the company competes with Amazon (e.g., Keane and Yu 2019, 4634).

I do not seek here to disavow this language of imperialism and conflict, which registers the geopolitical dimensions of the DFTZ and echoes more sophisticated analyses of "data colonialism" (Couldry and Mejias 2019). Rather, the goal is to understand how the extractive dynamics of the digital economy intersect its institutional and technological aspects. With respect to institutional conditions of e-commerce in Southeast Asia, the international business literature is revealing. Writing with Xinyi Wu, global value chain scholar Gary Gereffi positions the Internet governance environments in China and the US as key to understanding the differing business models and internationalization strategies of Alibaba and Amazon (Wu and Gereffi 2018). Noting that both companies have expanded their businesses beyond e-commerce, these authors challenge the notion that digital economy firms are asset light. In particular, they note Amazon's tendency toward vertical integration of its business operations and contrast its ownership of assets along its supply chain (from inventory to warehouses, logistical networks, data centers, computing applications, and cloud computing services) to Alibaba's preference to partner with local companies in its internationalization efforts. While Amazon's asset-heavy supply chain introduces last-mile delivery problems in environments such as Southeast Asia, Alibaba has to negotiate difficulties introduced by China's tight Internet governance model. At stake is not only the prospect that Chinese government requests to access data or information held by the company might damage its reputation or services—although Alibaba warns about this possibility in its annual reports—but also the challenges of operating beyond a domestic environment in which state restrictions on foreign investment in the e-commerce sector have contributed to the firm's growth.

Although the Alibaba Group has been listed on the New York Stock Exchange since 2014 and the company's board is highly internationally networked (De Graaff 2020), the firm benefits from Chinese state support in the form of government-generated rents and strategic public policies (Gomez et al. 2020, 4). Lin Zhang (2020) demonstrates how Alibaba's relationship with the state has evolved over time. For her, the role of Chinese petty capitalist entrepreneurs who utilized Alibaba's domestic e-commerce platforms was crucial in transforming the company's relationship with the state, which became more symbiotic following the 2008 global financial crisis. Because the firm was able to marry platform dynamics with small capitalist activity and venture capital investment in ways that rivalled the state's historical monopoly over "'pillar industries' and the construction and management of infrastructures," the "post-2008 Chinese state reacted by working more closely with Alibaba in promoting its own economic and social reform agenda" (Zhang 2020, 131). However, in the case of Alibaba, as in that of other large Chinese privately owned enterprises, it is difficult to ascertain exactly how party-state-business relationships resolve themselves. Consequently, while Alibaba develops its international business strategies within broad guidelines set by the state, the forms of power it exercises through expansion activities such as those realized in the DFTZ cannot be immediately equated with the expression of Chinese party-state sovereign power.

At stake is rather a technologically mediated form of power that combines digital platform operations, data extraction, labor exploitation, state dynamics, and spatial

strategies in ways that both accentuate and diminish the national denomination of capital. Again, it is significant that Alibaba initiated its involvement in the DFTZ at Malaysia's
behest. The company continues to work in partnership with Malaysian privately owned
and government-linked corporations. Alibaba plans and operates in the DFTZ with the
assistance of multiple Malaysian government agencies, including the Malaysian Digital
Economy Corporation (MDEC), the Ministry of Communications and Multimedia, the
Ministry of Transport, the Ministry of International Trade and Industry, and the Malaysian Investment Development Authority. The DFTZ is as much a product of Malaysia's
National Policy on Industry 4.0 (Industry4WRD)—which aims to transform the nation's
economy through the deployment of automation and data technologies—as it is of
China's Digital Silk Road initiative.

   Certainly, the zoning strategies involved resonate heavily with long-established spatial economic practices in Malaysia and other Southeast Asian countries that Aihwa Ong
has for over two decades analyzed by deploying the concept of *graduated sovereignty*. For
Ong (1999, 217), graduated sovereignty describes a situation "whereby even as the state
maintains control over its territory, it is also willing in some cases to let corporate entities set the terms for constituting and regulating some domains." At stake are "de facto
or practical adjustments and compromises in national sovereignty" that mobilize "foreign investment, technology transfers, and international expertise to specific zones" (Ong
2006, 78). That the DFTZ opens a space for investments, technologies, and expertise that
travel from Alibaba's headquarters in China's Zhejiang Province contrasts with Ong's later
assessment of Kuala Lumpur as seeming like "a cultural and economic extension of California" (2006, 82). In investigating the labor regimes that emerge in this zone, it is also
necessary to account for how the computational, commercial, and discursive workings
of platforms have transformed the digital economy in the past 15 years. Doing so, however, requires an engagement with questions of infrastructure, data management, and
automation that extends beyond an analysis of the DFTZ's institutional architectures.

Working the Digital Free Trade Zone

There at least four groups of workers associated with the DFTZ. Gomez et al. (2020,
45) report that the Cainiao-MAHB joint venture will support a division of labor "estimated to be 37% of skilled workers (operations manager, facilities technicians, logistics planner, etc.) and 52% semi-skilled (equipment operators, assemblers, service and
sales workers, etc.)." To these two groups, we must add the petty entrepreneurs whose
SME activities the eWTP will supposedly enable. A further group of workers provides
technical support for Alibaba's platform and logistics operations from China. Of these

groups, the last two are the easiest on which to obtain information about labor condi-tions and processes. There are multiple challenges in understanding the labor regimes that apply for skilled and semiskilled workers who staff and manage DFTZ facilities. For a start, the ASEAN e-commerce hub to be operated by Cainiao and MAHB has only recently begun operations (Alibaba Group 2020a). Although some knowledge can be gleaned from recruitment advertisements, conjecture based on Cainiao's warehousing and logistics activities in other locations is necessary. The Lazada–Pos Aviation venture deploys sophisticated handling systems such as automated guided vehicles (AGVs) but also maintains a flexible labor force to smooth out operations during peak periods. I will discuss these employee groups, and the techniques and technologies that shape the labor regimes under which they work, in this order: Chinese tech workers, Malay-sian petty entrepreneurs, and skilled and semiskilled workers in DFTZ facilities.

If the warehousing facilities in the DFTZ function like computers, as Zhu Lijun sug-gests (Alibaba Tech 2018), then these computers are programmed at a place called Xixi. Located in the Chinese city of Hangzhou, Xixi is Alibaba's main headquarters, where over 20,000 of its 100,000 employees work. A technology park surrounded by start-up enter-prises, the campus boasts features such as facial recognition technologies, autonomous vehicles, cashless payment for food, and a hotel with robot room service delivery (Saiidi 2019). Here, Alibaba maintains its corporate office as well as the headquarters of its main e-commerce brands, including Taobao, AliExpress, Tmall, and Tmall Global, the platform on which Malaysian SMEs will be able to market their products to Chinese consumers. Cainiao and Ant Group also locate their main offices at the Xixi campus. In December 2019, Alibaba established the secretariat of the eWTP in the adjacent Xixi Wetlands Park to manage the trade platform's "daily operations, international cooperation, training and exchange programs, achievement displays, and the release of rules and models" (eWTP 2019, para. 1). As the March 2019 visit to the Alibaba campus by a 30-member Malay-sian delegation from 19 government departments and agencies (Digital News Asia 2019) attests, Xixi is a site intensely connected to the administration and operations of the DFTZ and, in particular, to the control of flows of information and finance associated with it.

Alibaba promotes Xixi, like its other China-based offices, as a dynamic, youthful, and future-oriented workplace. However, the campus has also gained a reputation as a site of overtime work culture, stagnant salary and benefit growth, and health damage caused by demanding management. Extended work hours without overtime pay are a feature of tech industries worldwide, but the prominence of such "hustle culture" in the Chinese tech sector became conspicuous in early 2019 when workers began to rebel through a social media campaign (Li 2019). The 996.ICU movement started in March 2019 with an anonymous upload to the GitHub code-sharing platform complaining that the labor expectations of Chinese tech entrepreneurs risked sending employees to the intensive care unit (ICU). The number 996 refers to 12-hour days, 9:00 a.m. to 9:00 p.m., six days a week (see also chapter 12). The movement gathered pace on social media, attracting letters of solidarity from US tech workers and even denouncements of labor law violation in Chinese state media (Xingfa 2019). Many stories about the protest led with images of the Xixi campus (see, for example, Lin and Zhong 2019; Yang 2019). Alibaba's founder, Jack Ma, exacerbated the situation by declaring: "To be able to work 996 is a huge bliss. If you want to join Alibaba, you need to be prepared to work 12 hours a day, otherwise why even bother joining?" (Chen 2019).

As Xiaotan Li (2019) explains, the 996.ICU labor protest emerged when layoffs and hiring freezes stirred dissatisfaction among college-educated tech workers who could no longer hold on to the "big firm dream" that sustained their commitment to long work hours. According to Kevin Lin (2020, 52), the 996.ICU campaign signaled "the potential of a new type of labor organizing in China." On the one hand, the movement was able to escape state repression due to its decentralized networked operation. The protesters also succeeded in publicly damaging the reputation of large tech companies. On the other hand, the campaign never involved stoppages and was ultimately unable to force workplace changes. With respect to Alibaba's DFTZ activities, the 996.ICU protest shows how the informational labor that supports the development and operation of the platforms and logistical routines essential to the zone's functioning rests in the extraction of time and life from young Chinese tech workers. The question is whether this work culture extends to Malaysia and will somehow be imported into the zone with Alibaba's infrastructure investments and associated practices of technology transfer.

In a blog post, a young entrepreneur called Jason Low, who participated in Alibaba's Netpreneur Training program, an eWTP initiative that sends Malaysian business practitioners to Hangzhou for training, reports on his interactions with Alibaba tech workers. Low (2019, para. 10) emphasizes that Alibaba "has never enforced the 996-work schedule to any of its employees. Most of their staff's [sic] who work a 996 schedule, are people who believe that they have a mission to fulfill, therefore putting their best into achieving results for the company, and their clients." He goes on to state that his own work hours "are within the vicinity of 166. 16 Hours a Day, 6 Days a Week" (para. 13) and to suggest that those who hate their 996 jobs ought to quit. Low's account presents only a single opinion, but it does register the extent to which a culture of work sacrifice can take grip within the second group of workers I have mentioned, the Malaysian petty entrepreneurs who seek to sell products into the Chinese market using the eWTP. I have already outlined the institutional and technical hurdles faced by these entrepreneurs in comparison to their Chinese counterparts using the DFTZ facilities to import goods into

Malaysia. However, Alibaba has an established record of successfully recruiting small entrepreneurs as sellers on its e-commerce platforms and extracting the surplus value generated by these subjects' labor through datafication and selection mechanisms.

Zhang (2020, 130) details how Alibaba's growth into a monopoly platform in China was embedded "in China's petty capitalist tradition and the changing political economic configuration of the contemporary Chinese society." Although the company adopted strategies similar to those of large Western platforms to "encourage user participation, drive commodification, achieve datafication, and promote market expansion," the grafting of these platform mechanisms onto Chinese petty capitalist labor practices and tensions with state-tributary modes of production was crucial to its expansion. Aside from constructing "a network of governmental, media, and scholarly agents to motivate user participation and canvass political support," Alibaba attracted sellers to its platforms by picking model entrepreneurs to create "success stories" (see chapter 2). This frequently involved channeling traffic to bump up product listing rankings for chosen entrepreneurs, offering them opportunities to participate in promotional activities, and spreading media publicity about their "success" for others to emulate. A similar strategy can be observed in building the eWTP. For instance, a promotional video (Alibaba Group 2020b) touts the story of DESA, an initiative designed by alumni of Alibaba's Netpreneur Training Program to market fresh produce grown by Rwandan rural communities to Chinese consumers. MDEC, one of the main governmental backers of the DFTZ, is also active in promoting such "success stories," featuring on a YouTube playlist (MDEC 2020) over 60 interviews with petty e-commerce entrepreneurs selling goods as diverse as cosmetics, hardware, traditional medicines, detergents, and baby products. In line with the eWTP rhetoric of inclusive globalization, many of these stories feature the upward business activity of women and young people.

These promotional efforts ignore the fact that many businesses that market goods on e-commerce platforms are run by "individual or households who employ a small number of workers but who are themselves involved in the labor process," according to Alan and Jean Smart's 2005 book *Petty Capitalists and Globalization* (quoted in Zhang 2020). Notwithstanding the possibility that petty capitalist entrepreneurs may exploit workers within their business units, they are themselves exploited by the platform through their participation in the labor process. That platform companies extract rent for each transaction they orchestrate is a known feature of their business models. In the case of Alibaba, Zhang (2020, 131) explains that "unequal profit-driven and algorithm-mediated distribution of resources" as well as the "deployment of user data and manipulation of rankings" have swung in favor of bigger sellers and corporate expansion since the company gained monopoly status in the Chinese market. The anti-Taobao movement of 2011, which involved frustrated small-sized Chinese entrepreneurs placing a large number of orders with big sellers, leaving negative comments, and refusing to finalize payments, registers the extent of dissatisfaction that can develop. The question is whether similar discontent will emerge among Malaysian petty entrepreneurs who encounter difficulties selling into the Chinese market and face increasing competition from Chinese SMEs using the eWTP to import products into Malaysia. As Vila Seoane (2019, 3) writes, "It is unclear to what extent the eWTP will really be inclusive or, instead, just another way of enlarging social differences in favor of transnational capital."

The implications of this situation for workers on the ground in the DFTZ is another matter. In the case of the Lazada–Pos Aviation venture, there is clear investment from management in promoting their DFTZ facility as a highly automated environment. A site visit report from the Selangor Information Technology and E-Commerce Council (Kong 2017), currently Sidec (Selangor Information Technology & Digital Economy Corporation), and an MDEC (2018) promotional video document the presence of AGVs in the distribution center at KLIA Air Cargo Terminal 1. Manufactured by Quicktron in Shanghai, these AGVs are identical to those deployed by Cainiao in mainland Chinese warehouses and bear a strong resemblance to the robotic vehicles, originally developed by Kiva Systems (now Amazon Robotics), used in many Amazon fulfillment centers. Equipped with sensors that allow them to communicate with each other as well as with sensors embedded in the warehouse floor, the AGVs are able to lift shelves and drive them to where a product is needed. The system reputedly increases productivity by eliminating the long march of workers known as pickers to retrieve items from shelves and by mobilizing artificial intelligence to remap and optimize the use of warehouse space.

However, despite the prevalence of this technology in promotional materials associated with the Lazada–Pos Aviation facility, there were only 10 AGVs deployed at the site during the pilot phase in 2017 (Kong 2017, para. 21), compared, for instance, with the presence of 700 such vehicles in the smart warehouse at Cainiao's Wuxi Future Park in China's Jiangsu Province (Laubscher 2020, para. 12). Pos Aviation's website features images that attest the continued use of more traditional warehouse picking and packing labor at the facility (Pos Aviation 2017a). The same website provides visual evidence of workers undertaking heavy handling activities such as handover, break bulk, and sorting (Pos Aviation 2017b), which makes sense given that the installation doubles as an air cargo terminal. All of this points to the maintenance of a labor-intensive work regime at KLIA Air Cargo Terminal 1 despite management's emphasis on the introduction of more efficient border clearance and fulfillment processes. Employee reviews for Lazada on websites such as Indeed (2020) and Jobstreet (2020) present a mixed picture, with warehouse workers often commenting positively on the company's dynamic ethos but complaining about the fast pace, steep key performance indicators (KPIs), long hours, inability to take breaks, lack of benefits, and casual hiring practices. An advertisement for part-time pickers and packers at Lazada placed on the website Profdir Malaysia (2019) by the labor agency Manpower Group Solutions details 12-hour shifts at a rate of MYR 100 (approximately US$25) per day. Another issue raised by workers is "pressure with foreigners" (Indeed 2017), a comment that confirms reports that "Lazada executives from China have often been quick to impose what has worked for the mainland Chinese market with little regard to local needs or sensitivities in Southeast Asia's fragmented markets" (Zhai and Potkin 2020, para. 23).

A company report for Pos Malaysia by AmInvestment Bank (2019) details slow progress in the DFTZ. According to this market analysis, since "commencing operations in October 2017, Pos shared that the utilization of Kuala Lumpur International Airport Air Cargo Terminal 1 by industry players is still below expectations, with a view that in order for the project to take off, there is a need for other countries in the region to set up similar distribution centers to facilitate cross-border e-commerce trade" (para. 9). It is thus unsurprising that the opening of the Cainiao MAHB hub is likely to pose further challenges for Lazada's logistical operations and employment regimes. At this stage, it is difficult to assess to what extent the promise to make "constant improvements" to supply chain services through "automation, robotics and artificial intelligence and big data" (Alibaba Group 2020a, para. 6) will be fulfilled in the Cainiao facility. Nonetheless, informed speculation is possible since Cainiao utilizes the same warehouse management system across the many installations it runs, often in partnership with third-party operators. Such conjecture is risky, given that labor process studies have shown that production regimes can vary significantly across warehouses run by the same company (Dörflinger, Pulignano, and Vallas 2020). In the case of Cainiao, however, the commitment of software engineers such as the previously mentioned Zhu Lijun (see Gu 2017) to work on the development of particular algorithmic routines in warehouse management allows insight into the modality of worker interactions with automated technologies that are liable to play out in the DFTZ.

One such routine draws on research concerning the bin packing problem—an algorithmic conundrum with many logistical applications, from truck loading to choosing the most efficiently sized boxes into which to pack items being shipped from a warehouse. A variation of the so-called P versus NP problem, an unsolved dilemma in computer science, bin-stacking algorithms have been a focus of Cainiao engineers and their collaborators in recent years.[3] Interestingly, the approach these researchers take is not one of deploying automation to replace human workers or to trace and track them in ways that force their compliance with KPIs and standard operating procedures. Rather, in order to assign the best-sized boxes for item packing, this research seeks to generate knowledge about human deviation and to use the resulting data to optimize algorithmic prescriptions.

It is well known that warehouse workers may deviate from algorithmically assigned work tasks to realize efficiencies and take advantage of information that the algorithmic design does not incorporate (see, for instance, Loewen 2010, 709–710). Less explored are deviations that derive from a user's aversion, inability, or discretion when it comes to implementing algorithmic prescriptions rather than from a lack of objective information in the algorithm. Jiankun Sun et al. (2020) conducted an experiment for two weeks across four Cainiao warehouses to gather data about such deviations, particularly with regard to workers' decisions to use larger boxes than those prescribed by the standard Alibaba bin-packing algorithm to pack items. They then "proposed a method to revise the algorithm design by building a machine learning model to predict humans' non-conforming behavior and using the predictions to adjust the algorithmic prescriptions" (30). Such an exercise in "human-centric" automation definitely belongs to the class of algorithmic adjustment that draws on data generated by labor processes to feed back into and "improve" operations. Although this kind of fine tuning is by no means unique to Cainiao warehouses, it does give some insight into the kind of algorithmic regulation likely to take shape alongside other labor control processes linked to hiring, surveillance, and employment conditions in the DFTZ. In particular, it suggests a mode of automation that accommodates and exploits human deviations by funneling them into efficiency-building operations rather than allowing them to assume the form of sabotage, stoppage, or subversion.

Aside from the hype about AGVs and other technologies, the DFTZ presents a scenario where labor exploitation and data extraction link to long-standing warehouse employment practices that have undergone transformation with the rise of e-commerce. The question of how these practices articulate to the rhetoric of "inclusive globalization" surrounding the eWTP and China's Digital Silk Road initiative remains open. The result is rather a peculiar interaction among globally diffused technology company work cultures, petty capitalist labor regimes, the expansionary drive of private Chinese digital enterprise in its complex interactions with the party-state, Malaysian government efforts to adapt to the demands and opportunities of capital accumulation through zoning strategies and digital economy initiatives, and the platformization of logistical processes through modes of data extraction that not only feed back into operations but also fuel new horizons of capitalist speculation and valorization. Taken together, these factors make the DFTZ a unique zoning experiment that articulates to the other global sites of the eWTP but also remains embedded in local business practices and labor arrangements.

Conclusion

In November 2020, the Chinese government blocked the initial public offering (IPO) of Ant Group, a financial services company specializing in digital payment systems and majority-owned by Jack Ma. Widely seen as evidence of the Chinese state cracking down on private technology firms, the IPO suspension can more appropriately be understood as a peculiarly Chinese reaction to the more global governmental dilemma of whether fintech enterprises should be regulated as financial companies or as technology companies (Broby 2020). Viewed in the longer run of platform-state relations, the cancellation is another move in a complex series of moves that have led both to "deepened collaboration between Alibaba and the various levels of government in China" and to a "more interventionist stance" from the central government (Zhang 2020, 124). To some extent, the blockage of the IPO marks a limit at which the institutional apparatus of the state encounters the infrastructural power exercised by technology firms. However, to understand this regulatory intervention as a definitive assertion of the former over the latter is perhaps to overinvest in the indisputability of centralized control exerted by the Chinese Communist Party and to downplay the entanglement of institutional and infrastructural power in the operations of both state agencies and platform companies. The efforts of Alibaba to promote its eWTP activities in Malaysia and elsewhere as part of a program of inclusive globalization that reflects Digital Silk Road priorities also partake in these dynamics. There are dangers in seeing the emergence of the DFTZ either as the expression of Chinese grand strategy driven through the BRI or as the result of freewheeling technology company platformization that draws opportunistically on state rhetoric to justify its expansionism. Most glaringly, these perspectives fail to account for Malaysian government and commercial interests that have been pivotal in establishing the DFTZ.

That a logistics park and warehousing facility should become so crucial to digital trade developments and regional business dynamics registers the importance of infrastructures of circulation and storage to contemporary modes of capitalist expansion. The emergence of the DFTZ within the growing competition between Chinese and US firms for Southeast Asian e-commerce markets suggests that its economic purposes cannot be separated from geopolitical imperatives. However, it is a long stretch to join these geopolitical forces, which manifest in narratives of China-US technological decoupling, to operational conditions—as if one mandated the other. Ultimately, the presence of different business models and institutional architectures may not shape operations in the DFTZ in ways that have determinate outcomes for labor regimes. The question of infrastructural and technological forms becomes more relevant for charting the variations of digital work that accompany the spread of Chinese digital commerce. If an analytical emphasis on extraction highlights the data economies and labor dynamics that accompany the transformation of storage and processing in the warehousing industries, attention to geopolitics suggests the difficulty of separating institutional from infrastructural dynamics in the making of planetary markets. It is at this intersection of social form and technological materiality that the logistical installations appearing in the DFTZ are likely to shift digital work practices in ways unforeseeable by familiar scripts of national regulation and international rivalry.

Notes

1. Orenstein (2019, 169–177) recounts how the US Foreign Trade Zones Act, from the time of its implementation in 1934 to its amendment in 1950, imposed a ban on manufacturing. This prohibition meant that warehouse operators in such zones continually pressed the limits of what counted as manufacturing as opposed to processing, handling, manipulation, refinement, and so forth.

2. See http://www.kliaaeropolis.com/.

3. Hardesty (2009) offers a simple explanation of the P versus NP problem as being about the most efficient way to execute a given algorithm relative to the number of elements the algorithm has to manipulate.

References

Alibaba Group. 2020a. "Malaysia Airports and Alibaba Announce Operation Commencement of Cainiao Aeropolis eWTP Hub, Malaysia." Press Release, November 3. https://www.alibabagroup.com/en/news/article?news=p201103.

Alibaba Group. 2020b. "What Is the eWTP?" YouTube video, 1:53. May 14. https://www.youtube.com/watch?v=QSQwzCFu4_M.

Alibaba Tech. 2018. "AI Acrobatics: Cainiao's Flexible Automated Warehouse." *Hacker Noon*, July 3. https://hackernoon.com/ai-acrobatics-cainiaos-flexible-automated-warehouse-47e865f53e5f.

Alimahomed-Wilson, Jake, and Ellen Reese, eds. 2020. *The Cost of Free Shipping: Amazon in the Global Economy*. London: Pluto Press.

AmInvestment Bank. 2019. "Pos Malaysia: Company Report." May 6. http://www.bursamarketplace.com/mkt/tools/research/ch=research&pg=research&ac=715485&bb=728975.

Apicella, Sabrina, and Helmut Hildebrandt. 2019. "Divided We Stand: Reasons for and against Strike Participation in Amazon's German Distribution Centres." *Work Organisation, Labour & Globalisation* 13 (1): 172–189.

Bad Barcode. 2019. *NYC Cultural Workers against Amazon.* January. https://drive.google.com/file /d/1IhEUibOma3E4xPD2x-WrIkwTzScX1OVN/view.

Berlin vs. Amazon. 2021. *Ein Anti-Amazon-Fightblatt.* Accessed January 23, 2021. https://berlin vsamazon.com/.

Beverungen, Armin. 2021. "Remote Control: Algorithmic Management of Circulation at Amazon." In *Explorations in Digital Cultures*, edited by Marcus Burkhardt, Mary Shnayien, and Katja Grashöfer. Lüneburg: Meson Press.

Boewe, Jörn, and Johannes Schulten. 2017. *The Long Struggle of the Amazon Employees—Laboratory of Resistance:* Interim Assessment and Prospects for *Union Organising* at the Global *E-Commerce* Leader in Germany and Europe. Brussels: Rosa Luxemburg Stiftung.

Broby, Daniel. 2020. "Ant Group: Jack Ma's Biggest Market Debut Suspended amid Fears over Regulation." *The Conversation*, November 5. https://theconversation.com/ant-group-jack-mas -biggest-market-debut-suspended-amid-fears-over-regulation-149475.

Cheh, Samantha. 2017. "Malaysia Gets First Global Data Center, Thanks to Alibaba Cloud." *Techwire Asia*, October 30. https://techwireasia.com/2017/10/malaysia-gets-first-global-data-center -thanks-alibaba-cloud/.

Chen, Lulu Yilun. 2019. "Jack Ma Draws Controversy by Lauding Overtime Work Culture." *Bloomberg*, April 12. https://www.bloomberg.com/news/articles/2019-04-12/jack-ma-draws-controversy-by -lauding-overtime-work-culture.

Chew, Boon Cheong, Xiaobai Shen, and Jake Ansell. 2020. "Alipay Entered Malaysia: A Closer Look at the New Market Entry Strategy Driven by Chinese Tourists." *Qualitative Research in Financial Markets*, July 15. https://doi.org/10.1108/QRFM-06-2019-0069.

Couldry, Nick, and Ulises A. Mejias. 2019. *The Costs of Connection: How Data Is Colonizing Human Life and Appropriating It for Capitalism.* Stanford, CA: Stanford University Press.

De Graaff, Nana. 2020. "China, Inc. Goes Global: Transnational and National Networks of China's Globalizing Business Elite." *Review of International Political Economy* 27 (2): 208–233. https:// www.tandfonline.com/doi/full/10.1080/09692290.2019.1675741.

Delfanti, Alessandro, and Bronwyn Frey. 2020. "Humanly Extended Automation or the Future of Work Seen through Amazon Patents." *Science, Technology, and Human Values.*

Digital News Asia. 2019. "Malaysia Participates at New Economy Workshop at Alibaba Business School." March 11. https://www.digitalnewsasia.com/digital-economy/malaysia-participates-new -economy-workshop-alibaba-business-school.

Dörflinger, Nadja, Valeria Pulignano, and Steven Vallas. 2020. "Production Regimes and Class Compromise among European Warehouse Workers." *Work and Occupations*, July 20.

Electronic World Trade Platform (eWTP). 2019. "eWTP Sets Up Secretariat in Hangzhou." Accessed October 29, 2020. https://www.ewtp.org/article.html?id=Secretariat-in-Hangzhou.

Flaming, Daniel, and Patrick Burns. 2019. *Too Big to Govern: Public Balance Sheet for the World's Largest Store*. Los Angeles: Los Angeles County Federation of Labor. https://economicrt.org/publication/too-big-to-govern/.

Geissler, Heike. 2018. *Seasonal Associate*. Los Angeles: Semiotext(e).

Gomez, Edmund Terence, Siew Yean Tham, Ran Li, and Kee Cheok Cheong. 2020. *China in Malaysia: State-Business Relations and the New Order of Investment Flows*. Singapore: Palgrave Macmillan.

Graham, Mark, Rob Kitchin, Shannon Mattern, and Joe Shaw, eds. 2019. *How to Run a City like Amazon, and Other Fables*. London: Meatspace Press.

Gu, Lei. 2017. "专访菜鸟网络高级算法专家朱礼君：算法优化能为智能物流带来什么?" [Interview with Zhu Lijun, a Senior Algorithm Expert on Cainiao Network: What Can Algorithm Optimization Bring to Intelligent Logistics?]. *Lei Phone*, July 1. https://www.leiphone.com/news/201706/xBpbhuSWw424iTjD.html.

Hardesty, Larry. 2009. "Explained: P vs. NP." *MIT News*, October 29. https://news.mit.edu/2009/explainer-pnp.

Harsono, Hugh. 2020. "The China-Malaysia Digital Free Trade Zone: National Security Considerations." *The Diplomat*, July 25. https://thediplomat.com/2020/07/the-china-malaysia-digital-free-trade-zone-national-security-considerations/.

Indeed. 2017. "Lazada Employee Review. Inbound Assitant." https://malaysia.indeed.com/cmp/Lazada/reviews/inbound-assitant?id=d18f6d58103c8a6c.

Indeed. n.d. "Lazada Employee Reviews for Warehouse Worker." Accessed November 16, 2020. https://malaysia.indeed.com/cmp/Lazada/reviews?fjobtitle=Warehouse+Worker&fcountry=MY.

Jobstreet. 2021. "Lazada Malaysia." https://www.jobstreet.com.my/en/companies/462498-lazada-malaysia/reviews?mode=sentiment_reviews&sentiment_name=workload&sentiment_type=negative.

Keane, Michael, and Haiqing Yu. 2019. "A Digital Empire in the Making: China's Outbound Digital Platforms." *International Journal of Communication* 13: 4624–4641. https://ijoc.org/index.php/ijoc/article/view/10995.

Kittler, Friedrich. 1997. *Literature, Media, Information Systems: Essays*, edited by John Johnston. London: Routledge.

Kong, Xavier. 2017. "[Exclusive Report] Pos Malaysia Stepping Up to Meet E-Commerce Demands." Selangor Information Technology and E-Commerce Council (SITEC). November 7. https://www.sidec.com.my/exclusive-report-pos-malaysia-stepping-up-to-meet-e-commerce-demands/.

Laubscher, Henrik. 2020. "Logistics—The Secret Ingredient in China's E-Commerce: How Alibaba and JD.com Accelerate Logistics Innovation." *TechNode*, August 19. https://technode.com/2020/08/19/logistics-the-secret-ingredient-in-chinas-e-commerce/.

Li, Xiaotan. 2019. "The 996.ICU Movement in China: Changing Employment Relation and Labour Agency in the Tech Industry." *Made in China Journal*, June 18. https://madeinchinajournal

.com/2019/06/18/the-996-icu-movement-in-china-changing-employment-relations-and-labour
-agency-in-the-tech-industry/.

Lin, Kevin. 2020. "Tech Worker Organizing in China: A New Model for Workers Battling a Repressive State." *New Labor Forum* 29 (2): 52–59.

Lin, Qiqing, and Raymond Zhong. 2019. "'996' Is China's Version of Hustle Culture. Tech Workers Are Sick of It." *New York Times*, April 29. https://www.nytimes.com/2019/04/29/technology/china-996-jack-ma.html.

Loewen, Kyle. 2018. "Reproducing Disposability: Unsettled Labor Strategies in the Construction of E-Commerce Markets." *Environment and Planning D: Society and Space* 36 (4): 701–718.

Low, Jason. 2019. "The 996 Work Culture in China: A 1st Hand Experience." *Jason Low* (blog), April 21. https://www.linkedin.com/pulse/996-work-culture-china-1st-hand-experience-jason-low-/.

Ma, Jack. 2018. "Opinion: How Does Globalization Evolve with E-Commerce." *CGTN*, October 3. https://news.cgtn.com/news/3d3d774e33456a4e7a457a6333566d54/share_p.html.

MDEC (Malaysia Digital Economy Corporation). 2018. "DFTZ AGV." YouTube video, 3:29. June 17. https://www.youtube.com/watch?v=s-kGZ-D-PbM.

MDEC. 2020. "#eCommerce." YouTube playlist, 63 videos. September 4. https://www.youtube.com/playlist?list=PL1L7ne3V2SBC7N8Yrl0kp6dTQ_smCmyAX.

Mezzadra, Sandro, and Brett Neilson. 2017. "On the Multiple Frontiers of Extraction: Excavating Contemporary Capitalism." *Cultural Studies* 31 (2–3): 185–204.

Naughton, Barry. 2020. "Chinese Industrial Policy and the Digital Silk Road: The Case of Alibaba in Malaysia." *Asia Policy* 15 (1): 23–39.

Ong, Aihwa. 1999. *Flexible Citizenship: The Cultural Logics of Transnationality*. Durham, NC: Duke University Press.

Ong, Aihwa. 2006. *Neoliberalism as Exception: Mutations in Sovereignty and Citizenship*. Durham, NC: Duke University Press.

Orenstein, Dara. 2019. *Out of Stock: The Warehouse in the History of Capitalism*. Chicago: University of Chicago Press.

Pos Aviation. 2017a. "E-Fullfilment." https://www.posaviation.com.my/services/e-commerce-solutions/e-fullfilment/.

Pos Aviation. 2017b. "Cross Dock." https://www.posaviation.com.my/services/e-commerce-solutions/cross-dock/.

Profdir Malaysia. n.d. "Part Time Picker and Packer—Lazada." Accessed November 16, 2020. https://my.profdir.com/jobs-for-part-time-picker-&-packer-lazada-shah-alam-kuala-lumpur-cdga.

Ruckus, Ralf. 2016. "Confronting Amazon." *Jacobin*, March 31. https://www.jacobinmag.com/2016/03/amazon-poland-poznan-strikes-workers/.

Saiidi, Uptin. 2019. "We Went Inside Alibaba's Global Headquarters: Here's What We Saw." *CNBC*, September 10. https://www.cnbc.com/2019/09/11/we-went-inside-alibabas-global-headquarters-heres -what-we-saw.html.

Shen, Hong. 2018. "Building a Digital Silk Road? Situating the Internet in China's Belt and Road Initiative." *International Journal of Communication* 12: 2683–2701. https://ijoc.org/index.php/ijoc /article/viewFile/8405/2386.

Sun, Jiankun, Dennis J. Zhang, Haoyuan Hu, and Jan A. Van Mieghem. 2020. "Predicting Human Discretion to Adjust Algorithmic Prescription: A Large-Scale Field Experiment in Warehouse Operations." *SSRN*, July 14. https://doi.org/10.2139/ssrn.3355114.

Tham, Siew Yean. 2018. "The Digital Free Trade Zone: Putting Malaysia's SMEs onto the Digital Silk Road." *Perspective: Researchers at ISEAS-Yusof Ishak Institute Analyse Current Events* 2008 (17). https://www.iseas.edu.sg/images/pdf/ISEAS_Perspective_2018_17@50.pdf.

Tham, Siew Yean, and Andrew Kam Jia Yi. 2019. "Exploring the Trade Potential of the DFTZ for Malaysian SMEs." *Trends in Southeast Asia* 2019 (3), January 29. Singapore: ISEAS.

Transnational Social Strike Platform. 2019. *Strike the Giant! Transnational Organization against Amazon*. https://www.transnational-strike.info/app/uploads/2019/11/Strike-the-Giant_TSS-Journal.pdf.

van Doorn, Niels, and Adam Badger. 2020. "Platform Capitalism's Hidden Abode: Producing Data Assets in the Gig Economy." *Antipode: A Journal of Radical Geography* 52 (5): 1475–1495. https:// doi.org/10.1111/anti.12641.

Vila Seoane, Maximiliano Facundo. 2019. "Alibaba's Discourse for the Digital Silk Road: The Electronic World Trade Platform and 'Inclusive Globalization.'" *Chinese Journal of Communication* 13 (1): 68–83.

Wu, Xinyi, and Gary Gereffi. 2018. "Amazon and Alibaba: Internet Governance, Business Models, and Internationalization Strategies." In *International Business in the Information and Digital Age (Progress in International Business Research, Vol. 13)*, edited by Rob van Tulder, Alain Verbeke, and Lucia Piscitello, 327–356. Bingley, UK: Emerald.

Xingfa, Gao. 2019. "'996' Schedule Must Not Be Imposed on Workers." *China Daily*, April 15. https:// global.chinadaily.com.cn/a/201904/15/WS5cb411e2a3104842260b63fc.html.

Yang, Yuan. 2019. "China Tech Worker Protest against Long Working Hours Goes Viral." *Financial Times*, April 3.

Zhai, Keith, and Fanny Potkin. 2020. "Alibaba Suffers Culture Conflicts." *Japan Times*, March 27. https://www.japantimes.co.jp/news/2020/03/27/business/alibaba-suffers-culture-conflicts/.

Zhang, Lin. 2020. "When Platform Capitalism Meets Petty Capitalism in China: Alibaba and an Integrated Approach to Platformization." *International Journal of Communication* 14: 114–134.

8   The Planetary Stacking Order of Multilayered Crowd-AI Systems

Florian A. Schmidt

What is the impact of the high demand for artificial intelligence (AI) training data for autonomous vehicles on the working conditions of crowdworkers? This chapter will put an emphasis on the planetary dimensions of this particular outsourcing stack, its structural aspects, its layered and siloed qualities, its fractal and redundant features, as well as its fragilities and uncertainties for the different stakeholders.

The analysis focuses on the intersection of four interdependent developments that culminated in 2018: First of all, there was the race of several dozen very well financed automotive and technology companies to be the first to bring self-driving cars onto the streets. Second came the ensuing unprecedented demand for vast amounts of highly accurate training data necessary to teach the cars how to navigate traffic based on vision. Third, there was the restructuring of large crowdsourcing platforms in order to cater to the specific needs of the automotive industry and orchestrate the required workforce for them. And finally came the crash of the Venezuelan economy, because of which Venezuelans inadvertently ended up providing the brunt of the work for this mammoth task of manual image labeling in the service of AI development.

The main argument of this chapter is that this interplay of planetary economic forces and events that unfolded in 2018—their synchronicity—was not merely a freak occurrence but instead refined and laid bare the mechanics of how capital can conjure up, train, and dismiss hundreds of thousands or even millions of digital workers as needed—much more rapidly than would be possible with production sites bound to a physical location.

As the chapter will show, the long-existing infrastructure of crowdsourcing platforms underwent a significant update through this succession of events and has since become much more capable through its adaptation to very demanding and deep-pocketed clients from the automotive industry. Future spikes in demand for digital labor may have nothing to do with self-driving cars, and next time it probably will not be Venezuela that happens to have the cheapest workforce on offer globally. But the development of the structures described here demonstrates how to match excess capital with an oversupply of labor just in time, to high standards, and without having to commit to brick-and-mortar factories and local workers on the ground—let alone national labor laws and regulations. Thus, labor has become *almost* as liquid as capital. I write "almost" because, as I will also show, the same economic desperation that can make labor matchlessly cheap and flexible on the planetary digital market can also eventually inhibit the free flow of labor by preventing access to said market through crumbling infrastructure, blackouts, and embargos.

First, I will briefly show why the push for full automation, self-driving cars, and self-learning algorithms has somewhat counterintuitively led to a surge in the demand for manual labor, mostly in the form of crowdsourced image annotation. Then I will explain how the degree of accuracy necessary for this type of work has forced the crowdsourcing industry to fundamentally restructure its processes—from a very direct, or flat, model that provided clients with little more than direct access to a crowd available for completing general tasks to a model in which the platform orchestrates every detail of a highly complex and multilayered process while the client buys the end results without ever coming into contact with the crowd. Here, the focus is on making visible how this shift from *general-purpose crowdwork* to what I will call a *specialized, full-service crowd-AI stack* has wide implications for the legal classification of workers as independent contractors and for the working conditions on these platforms.

This new generation of platforms is experimenting with various stacking orders of human labor—AI support and control systems, subautomation, and suboutsourcing. The crowdworkers both train AI systems and are trained by AI systems, with humans and machines working together in ever-more-complex structures. The chapter will conclude with a description of the turbulent working conditions that Venezuelan crowdworkers had to endure in 2018 and 2019 in order to show that high demand for digital labor and a well-designed digital workplace are not enough to ensure a reliable work environment. Unfortunately, it appears that the only constant in this highly dynamic planetary outsourcing stack is the continued precarity of the working conditions.

Speaking of the planetary dimensions of this phenomenon, however, it must be mentioned that this chapter is only able to look at publicly crowdsourced labor. This is the more visible side of training data production commissioned by clients based in the Global North, done mostly by workers in the Global South, especially in Venezuela now. The Chinese stack for the production of training data unfortunately remains entirely in the dark, as does any work not done on publicly advertised platforms that are open to crowdworkers. A clear view of the developments sketched out in this chapter is further obstructed by the secrecy of the industry, which is concerned about preserving both its technological trade secrets and its competitive advantage gained through circumventing national labor laws and regulations via global outsourcing.

The research in this chapter is based on interviews conducted in 2018 and 2019 with CEOs of training data producers (Mighty AI, Hive, understand.ai, Clickworker, Playment, and Crowd Guru) and crowdworkers (mostly from Mighty AI and mainly from Venezuela).[1] Other crucial sources have been my direct observation of the platforms over the years; the platforms' communication with workers and clients through forums, advertising, and press releases; and experience of using their annotation tools, partly by logging on as a crowdworker myself (Schmidt 2016, 2019). From the photos I annotated in that role in 2018, it became apparent that the German car industry was among the most important clients of the platforms at that time. But client companies could not be confirmed officially due to the nondisclosure agreements preventing the platforms from disclosing the names of their clients.

Why Manually Annotated Images Continue to Be in Such High Demand

The question of whether the ambitious goal of bringing fully autonomous vehicles onto regular urban streets will be achieved in the foreseeable future remains open. Although impressive progress has been made, various difficult problems have emerged that have dampened the optimism of the engineers working on this challenge. The euphoria over the promise of *fully* automated vehicles (defined by the Society of Automotive Engineers as SAE Level 5) may have been overly optimistic, but semiautonomous vehicles (SAE Level 4) too need millions of labeled images as ground-truth data to model and predict what is happening around them in traffic. By 2018, 55 companies had secured licenses to test autonomous vehicles in California, while others were operating cars on the streets of Arizona (DMV CA, Department of Motor Vehicles California n.d.).

Traditional auto manufacturers' fear of being left on the sidelines by Google's Waymo or by Tesla has triggered what might turn out to be an investment bubble or at least a risky gamble on whether this technology will ever actually become viable. Billions of dollars keep being invested in the development of autonomous vehicles, and hundreds of millions of those dollars trickle down the supply chain into the crowdsourced production of AI training data. Market leader Waymo was able to raise $3 billion in two venture capital rounds within just a month in 2020 (Etherington 2020). Volkswagen, having already invested $2.6 billion in the autonomous vehicle company Argo AI in June 2020, announced the expenditure of another $91 billion on the development of electric autonomous vehicles in its new unit the Volkswagen Autonomy GmbH through 2025. In the meantime, Scale AI became the first training-data provider to reach a valuation of over $1 billion in August 2019, turning it into a so-called unicorn. In April 2021, it reached a valuation of $7.3 billion, after it had raised a total of $600 million in venture capital (Kahn 2021).

Not all production of training data revolves around image annotation for autonomous vehicles, but at least for the time being this is where the money is for the crowdsourcing platforms. Typically, the images are stills taken from videos shot in traffic, which are then manually annotated so that a machine can recognize every object within the frame. Humans have to, for example, draw two-dimensional bounding boxes around cars, draw three-dimensional cuboids to orient cars in space, or assign descriptive labels such as "truck," "tree," "school bus," "bicycle," and so forth to every pixel in a video frame. This so-called full semantic segmentation is currently the most common and most time-consuming of the various forms of image labeling: unassisted by automation, a worker may take up to two hours to complete a full semantic segmentation of a traffic scene.

At first glance, one is tempted to assume that the manual annotation of training data is a transitory phenomenon, a job that will soon be either finished or entirely automated. How hard can it be? But one crucial factor behind the sheer amount of work is that it is being done in a highly redundant fashion. The various clients need very similar sets of annotated images; it would be much more efficient for the automotive companies to draw their training data from a collectively produced pool of annotated images (different stakeholders now increasingly pay lip service to this idea). However, because of the competitiveness of the market, such sharing currently seems out of the question in most cases.

One interrelated consequence that has not yet been taken sufficiently into consideration in the debate around the public safety of self-driving vehicles is that by training cars based on these siloed datasets and opaque procedures, the manufacturers will end up with vehicles that react differently in extreme situations, or so-called edge cases. From the perspective of other participants in traffic, or regulators, for that matter, such an outcome cannot be tolerated. It therefore seems plausible, though speculative at this point, that manufacturers will eventually be obliged to all use the same training datasets or even the same algorithmic models as a common standard for the critical decisions that their vehicles constantly have to make in traffic. If this is going to be the case, it truly becomes a winner-take-all game for the car manufacturers to compete to be the one to set this standard. The fact that the quality of these algorithmic models is highly dependent on the quality of the training data gives all the more reason why so much money is being invested in the type of outsourcing system described here.

Moreover, while the training data itself could to some extent indeed be shared, the more important market, according to the CEOs interviewed for this study, is or will be the one for validation data, in which human cognition is needed to evaluate retroactively the decisions that the autonomous systems have already made in traffic. This, of course, is highly case-specific, legally delicate, and confidential information—data that cannot be shared with competitors.

Last but not least, human labor continues to be in high demand because of how messy reality turns out to actually be. The systems need to be constantly retrained on ever-evolving traffic scenarios. One example would be the sudden large-scale rollout of commercial e-scooters (driven, just like the development of autonomous vehicles, by venture capital speculation) in 2017 (Hawkins 2018). Not only did this rollout lead to emergent behavior patterns in traffic—new silhouettes crossing the streets at unexpected speeds—but the scooters also fall under equally emergent legal restrictions, which are different and subject to change in every European metropolis.

Another vivid edge case example that illustrates geographic variety is that autonomous vehicles have difficulties processing jumping kangaroos (Ackerman 2017). As Mark Mengler, CEO of understand.ai, described in an interview for this study, it is quite likely that autonomous vehicles will have to be geofenced, meaning that they will not be able to cross invisible digital boundaries, such as between countries. Before being allowed to cross into another geographic zone, they will have to download extensive updates. Since the peculiarities even of neighboring countries are so data-intensive, it would not be possible or practical to have them all preinstalled onboard. As the next section shows, more and more annotation tasks can be done automatically, but it seems likely that the machines will have to be continuously trained by humans in the loop, especially for new tasks, new edge cases, and retroactive data validation.

From Legacy, General-Purpose Crowdwork to Specialized Full-Service Crowd-AI Stacks

Even before the first pedestrian was killed by a self-driving car in 2018, it was clear that in contrast to accuracy in annotating images of cats or food via crowdsourcing, accuracy in the production of ground-truth data for autonomous vehicles is a matter of life and death.[2] The clients buying this data demand an accuracy of at least 99 percent, to be guaranteed by the producer of the training data; the need to match that goal is the single most important reason for a cascade of structural shifts in how crowdsourcing platforms operate. It has led both to the emergence of new and specialized full-service producers of training data, organized as layered crowd-AI stacks designed to cater exclusively to clients at the intersection of the automotive industry and AI research, and to the transformation of older, hitherto flatter general-purpose crowdsourcing platforms toward that end.

For the purposes of contrast, it is best to look back briefly at Amazon Mechanical Turk (MTurk), the oldest and most prototypical crowdsourcing platform for microtasks. Founded in 2005, with a workforce of about half a million people, mostly from India and the US, MTurk is the prime example of what new competitors such as Playment (founded in 2015 in Bangalore, with around 300,000 workers) have started to refer to as "legacy crowdsourcing platforms" (Magistretti 2017). MTurk is a generalist platform with an application programming interface that allows paying customers to give "human intelligence tasks" directly to a distributed crowd by addressing them like a general-purpose computer. It is flat in the sense that the client gets its results directly from the crowd, without any hidden processing or quality management layers.

While Amazon does exert some influence on the organization of the work, it frames itself as a marketplace, or infrastructure provider, that can be held accountable for neither the quality of the results nor the working conditions on the platform. The client customers of MTurk select, train, and pay the individual crowdworkers; they are also responsible for the description of tasks, the development of specialized tools, and the quality control of the results. In this legacy form of crowdwork, the platform manages to externalize most risks and responsibilities to the other two parties involved—that is, the clients and the workers.

The clients from the automotive industry reversed this logic and externalized the burden (and potentially the legal liabilities) of quality control to the training data providers. Because the new specialist companies that have emerged maintain an internal crowdsourcing platform, they can now offer fully managed data labeling or end-to-end project management. Nothing is done by the client, they promise.

The following are the most prominent examples among a dozen of these companies (data regarding investments via https://www.crunchbase.com/). The Seattle-based Mighty AI, founded as Spare5 (app.spare5.com) in 2014 and backed by $27.3 million in venture capital, was acquired by Uber for an undisclosed sum in 2019. In 2018, it had a workforce of about half a million people, three quarters of whom lived in Venezuela at the time. The San Francisco–based company Hive (thehive.ai, hivemicro.com), founded in 2013 and backed by $20 million in venture capital, had a workforce of over a million people from supposedly 150 different nations (though between 60 and 75 percent lived in Venezuela in 2020; more on the origin of the workers below). The above-mentioned Scale AI (scale .com), founded in San Francisco in 2016 and backed by $118 million in venture capital (a lot, by comparison), had a workforce of 30,000 people in 2018 (small, by comparison).

These training data producers operate as multilayered, full-service black boxes without direct contact between their clients and the crowdworkers (see also Tubaro and Casilli 2019). This new and much deeper structure of partly hidden image-processing layers involving both human labor and AI automation constitutes a consequential departure from the MTurk model of legacy crowdsourcing for all three parties involved. The clients no longer have to develop their own tools for data annotation, train the crowd, or sort and evaluate the results provided. For this convenience, they have to pay substantially higher prices (which is why some experienced clients continue to use MTurk and do the quality control themselves).

For the workers, this shift means that they have to learn new software tools less often; that the tools are more reliable, more convenient to use, and constantly developed as proprietary assets of the platform; and also that the task descriptions are less faulty and easier to understand. There is a lock-in effect here: switching platforms means not only losing one's reputation and qualifications but also the accumulated skill of handling proprietary tools, at least to some extent (after all, the tasks are very similar). Still, for the workers, it is much safer and more reliable to deal only with platform providers instead of having to adapt to ever-changing clients—especially when it comes to getting paid reliably at the end of each week instead of having to fear late payments, disputes about inferior results due to faulty tools and descriptions, or even wage theft (all of which have been grievances for workers on MTurk for years).

For the platform providers, however, the shift to full-service solutions not only means much higher investments, it also entails the looming legal risk of getting sued for the potential misclassification of their workers as independent contractors rather than employees of the platform, as happened to CrowdFlower (*Otey v. CrowdFlower*, class action lawsuit filed in 2012, settled in 2015).[3] More rudimentary legacy platforms like MTurk, which is notoriously unresponsive to the grievances of its workforce, can very plausibly argue that their workers are merely freelancers or hobbyists whom the platform helps by connecting them to external clients via a marketplace. But full-service stacks, in which workers have no direct contact with clients, will find it much more difficult to defend the current classification of their workers as independent contractors. Although the new system is in certain ways more reliable for the workers, the entire business model is built on shaky ground as regards their legal status. In the following section, I will show in what other ways these full-service crowd-AI stacks have changed how work is being orchestrated, and how this is the result of having to deliver high volumes of training data with guaranteed high accuracy.

Platforms Investing in Tailor-Made AI Tools and Handpicked Crowds

Scale AI used to offer a price calculator on its website. In mid-2018, the price for just nine annotations in a single image was $1.00—provided the client bought 10,000 images.

The price for the much more complex semantic segmentation of an entire image, with a guaranteed accuracy of 99.2 percent, was $6.40; if the client opted for "express urgency," the same service cost $16.00 per image. Given how many well-funded automotive companies desperately need millions of this type of annotated images, it is not surprising that training data providers have become so attractive to venture capital.

An individual human without AI assistance would need up to two hours to process an image that costs $6.40 retail. Thus, the platforms could not be profitable if they paid their workers a minimum wage at the standard of Western industrial nations. To be able to deliver high-quality service at speed, volume, and a competitive price, they have therefore developed a number of instruments and strategies:

1. Invest in custom-made, AI-enhanced, semiautomatic production tools that heuristically do the semantic segmentation in advance and then guide the attention of the crowdworkers to areas where the system is less certain about what it has recognized in an image.

2. Invest in quality management through process optimization regarding how granular the jobs become when split up into microtasks and how they are best reassembled afterward, with successive layers of quality control (monitoring both the workforce itself and the results) done alternately by humans and AI.

3. Invest at the same time in automated training of the workforce and gamification mechanisms to incentivize the ambition, focus, and skills of workers as well as in labor-intensive human community management.

4. Invest in access to a cheaper workforce either by offering task descriptions, automated training tutorials, and human community management in languages spoken in low-wage regions of the planetary market for digital labor; or by suboutsourcing part of the labor to business process outsourcing (BPO) firms that have a local workforce on site in developing countries and that can make the work accessible to people with language skills not supported at scale by the platform itself.

Together, these decisions on investments shape what I think is best described as a crowd-AI stack, a complex proprietary solution with alternating layers of human management, algorithmic management, AI automation, and manual human labor. The competing producers of training data try to gain a competitive edge by favoring different stacking orders of these data annotation and quality control layers. While some, like understand.ai, a training data company based in Karlsruhe, Germany, are investing heavily in new AI tools in order to reduce the number of workers necessary; others, like Playment in Bangalore, prioritize access to a cheap workforce and, as the company name suggests, gamification mechanisms to keep that workforce focused and motivated. Both use workers from India, but for understand.ai this is a BPO layer alternating with local student temp workers in Germany and involving as much automation as possible.

The fact that the producers of training data do not merely supply AI development services but are also developing and employing their own AI technology to streamline processes leads to an interesting paradox: the growth of AI increases both the demand for manual labor and the demand for AI automation. The goal of the hard-to-automate manual labor is the training of AI models, while, at the same time, AI automation is used to train and support the manual labor that makes it more reliable and cost effi-cient. In short, humans and AI train each other.

Although they are reliant on crowdworkers, the training data providers market themselves as AI companies, while the term *crowd* is pushed into the background— possibly due to its negative connotations of cheap labor and low-quality results or maybe simply because it is yesterday's buzzword. This development is reflected in the fact that some of the specialist platforms have a client-facing company name, web-site, and appearance that emphasizes AI, along with an entirely different crowd-facing name, platform, and appearance promising prospective workers that they can make money quickly through microtasks. Mighty AI's crowd platform is Spare5, Hive's plat-form is Hive Work (the worker platform of thehive.ai is also known as Hive Micro), and Scale AI's platform is Remotasks.

But even with this two-faced approach, the new specialists must convey to their clients a seemingly contradictory message that advertises both a high degree of auto-mation from quasimagical AI as well as human precision from well-trained and hand-picked crowdworkers. On their respective websites, these specialist platforms advertise the shift away from rudimentary crowdsourcing as "trained crowd labor," "known crowds," "curated crowds," or "crowd qualification." The message for clients is that the work is given not to a random, anonymous, and potentially incompetent mass but to handpicked groups of experts who are trained and monitored constantly.

Workers on the new platforms must go through a longer training phase, in which they specialize in certain types of tasks and, as in a computer game, level up to qualify for more sophisticated, better-paying tasks. This specialization, however, negatively affects which tasks they can see in the future (a serious source of stress for the workers, discussed below). The accuracy of the individual workers is tracked constantly, and they get qualitative and quantitative feedback on how well they do, partly automati-cally and partly from management.

As Daryn Nakhuda, cofounder and former CEO of Mighty AI, explained to me, the platform funnels incoming tasks in bulk to preselected subgroups to train them more quickly and efficiently. Thus, the workers are not an open and unstructured crowd that self-selects incoming tasks freely. Instead, they are subject to various degrees of hierarchy, specialization, and orchestration conducted by the platform providers. For example, normal workers are called "Fives," but there are also "SuperFives" with access to better-paying tasks, more direct rapport with community management, and the privilege to beta-test new tools early.

If a worker gains access to tasks, the payment is generally more reliable than on legacy crowdwork platforms, though not necessarily higher. In interviews I conducted in 2018, the workers on Spare5 felt much better treated than on legacy crowdwork platforms, mostly because they had reliable human interaction with the platform staff in the form of good community management and direct, immediate, and personal responses to their questions. They were proud to be part of the company. This positive view changed, however, after Uber acquired the platform in 2019.

Fluctuations in Labor Demand and Migrant Crowdworkers

A crucial function of crowdwork is to provide employers with a buffer for rapid fluctuations in labor demand. In this, the platforms resemble temporary staffing agencies, only the frequency and volume with which they can mobilize and dismiss workers is orders of magnitude greater. For the car companies, which need waves of data annotation labor rather than a constant amount, it would, in most cases, make no sense to build up a workforce in-house. By serving multiple clients, the platforms should theoretically be able to level out the waves of demand into a constant stream, but this is often not the case. And even though the demand for manual image annotation has risen substantially since 2017, we still see a constant oversupply of labor (as became apparent in the various interviews I conducted with workers in 2018 and 2019; see also below). The platforms discussed here attract, train, and put on hold—in other words produce—far more workers than they regularly need, and yet this oversupply of labor is necessary to swiftly cope with peaks in demand. It is not a bug but a feature. The problem is well known in other areas of the gig economy, where it is managed through strategies like Uber's "surge pricing," a technique that Hive and others have started to use as well.

The oversupply of labor is a constant source of stress for the workforce. "Why don't I see any tasks?" was the most common concern in forums and conversations among workers in 2018. For the workers, it is especially irritating when colleagues are shown tasks when they are not, and the lack of transparency regarding the distribution of tasks leads to a lot of second-guessing about potential correlations with one's work history, performance, levels of accuracy, or experience points. What is causing the stress is not only the volatility of the total amount of work available, but that the workers, being very well connected via external forums and social media, do know of collogues who have access to tasks while they themselves don't. The workers do not know whether they are not receiving tasks due to a decision by human management or by algorithm.

Most importantly, the constant oversupply of labor (see figure 8.1) erodes any negotiating power for better pay because for every task there is already a long line of people willing to do it for less money. On top of this, the oversupply leads to an indirect deterioration of average hourly earnings due to the unpaid downtime of waiting and searching for tasks across platforms—time spent desperately hitting the refresh button in the hope for more work. As in the rest of the gig economy, there is little flexibility or autonomy left if you have to jump at any opportunity to do a gig or tasks before someone else scores, and this competition is much more extreme if the work is not location-based, like food delivery or chauffeur rides, but can be done from anywhere in the world.

Where the producers of training data operate in the form of BPO firms, we can still see a slower, more conventional model of taking advantage of different prices for labor on a global market because the employers open shop locally (e.g., in Kenya or Nepal), where labor happens to be cheap. For crowdsourced microtasks, however, the disenfranchised workforce has begun to virtually roam the globe in search of tasks—almost like migrant agricultural workers.

What we see unfolding in the realm of manual data annotation is a truly planetary market for digital labor in which the tasks dynamically flow to those people who are willing to accept the lowest remuneration at any given point in time. As in a system of communicating vessels, the average hourly wage paid out by the platforms for relatively unskilled labor seems to level out globally. In 2018, experienced data annotators earned between $1 and $2 per hour (an estimate based on my interviews with CEOs and crowdworkers, and on forum debates among workers). As this is piecework, inexperienced workers of course earn much less. A large quantitative study from 2018 found that workers on MTurk, too, earned about $2 per hour on average (Hara et al. 2018).

As explained above, Hive, Mighty AI, and Scale AI have separate websites for their clients and their workforce; because the workers enter the virtual factory through a separate entrance, it is easy to follow their ebbs and flows, and also their countries of origin, simply by using Amazon's web traffic analysis tool, found at alexa.com/siteinfo. That is, one can use the web traffic of the crowdwork platform as an approximate measure of worker supply. I followed this data in 2018 and 2019, triangulating it with various interviews with crowdworkers. The two most important findings were that, in those two years, several hundred thousand workers were moving back and forth between platforms (especially between Mighty AI and Hive) desperately looking for tasks—and that up to three-quarters of them were based in Venezuela.

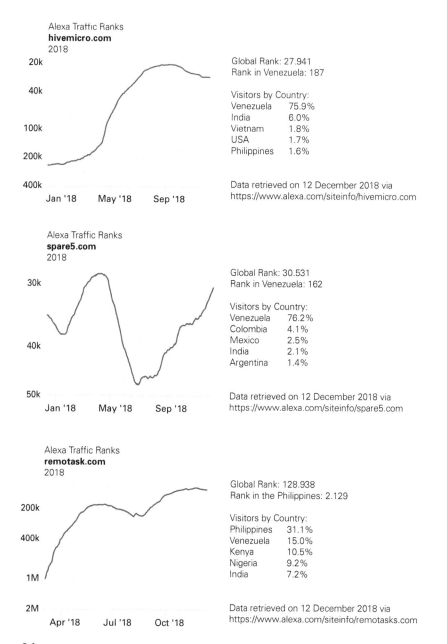

Alexa Traffic Ranks
hivemicro.com
2018

Global Rank: 27.941
Rank in Venezuela: 187

Visitors by Country:
Venezuela   75.9%
India   6.0%
Vietnam   1.8%
USA   1.7%
Philippines   1.6%

Data retrieved on 12 December 2018 via
https://www.alexa.com/siteinfo/hivemicro.com

Alexa Traffic Ranks
spare5.com
2018

Global Rank: 30.531
Rank in Venezuela: 162

Visitors by Country:
Venezuela   76.2%
Colombia   4.1%
Mexico   2.5%
India   2.1%
Argentina   1.4%

Data retrieved on 12 December 2018 via
https://www.alexa.com/siteinfo/spare5.com

Alexa Traffic Ranks
remotask.com
2018

Global Rank: 128.938
Rank in the Philippines: 2.129

Visitors by Country:
Philippines 31.1%
Venezuela   15.0%
Kenya   10.5%
Nigeria   9.2%
India   7.2%

Data retrieved on 12 December 2018 via
https://www.alexa.com/siteinfo/remotasks.com

Figure 8.1
Graphs showing the fluctuations in web traffic on the crowdwork platforms belonging to Hive, Mighty AI, and Scale AI in 2018.
Source: alexa.com/siteinfo.

At the end of 2018, Hive Work was ranked #187 of the most frequented websites in Venezuela (up to #123 in October 2020), and Spare5 (Mighty AI's work platform) was ranked #162 (down to #333 in October 2020). The country supplied around 75 percent of the workforce of Spare5 throughout 2018. At Hive Work, this percentage rose from 55 to 75 percent over the course of 2018 (and back down to 55 percent in late 2020). As I learned in my interview with Kevin Guo, CEO of Hive, the first half of 2018 saw the number of workers on his platform grow from 100,000 to 300,000, at a speed of up to 3,000 new registrations per day (at the end of 2020 it stood at more than a million workers). Considering the parallel rapid growth on Spare5, at least 200,000 people from Venezuela must have been searching for work at the time on these two platforms alone. In the first half of 2018, Scale's Remotasks predominantly attracted English-speaking workers from the Philippines and India, with 31 percent of the workers coming from each (at the end of 2020, its workers mainly came from Venezuela, the Philippines, and Kenya, which provided 36, 22, and 11 percent of the workforce, respectively). Playment drew its workforce of 300,000 people entirely from India, and continues to be entirely focused on this country.

For the image annotation platforms to stay competitive, it matters where the workers live, in regard to how expensive the labor is, but for older companies, it is not easy to adapt. Crowd Guru, founded 2008 in Berlin, is a platform with an almost entirely German-speaking workforce. When it comes to microtasks that can be done by anyone anywhere, it is impossible for a company like Crowd Guru to compete with platforms that can mobilize workers from the Global South for a tenth of the cost. In 2018, the CEO of Crowd Guru, Hans Speidel, told to me in an interview for the original report (Schmidt 2019) that from time to time he was approached by small BPO firms who offered him their workforces as a form of suboutsourcing. However, as Speidel explained, the inclusion of a cheaper external workforce would alienate or antagonize the German workforce, which had developed over time a sense of community important for social cohesion and loyalty to the platform.

The situation is completely different for platforms like Appen (appen.com), founded 1998 in Australia and with a current workforce of over a million, and Clickworker (clickworker.com), founded 2005 in Germany and with a current workforce of over two million, who produce a large quantity of training data for voice assistants. Since this type of work entails teaching the machines to understand various dialects, a culturally diverse workforce is key. Most audio tasks are distributed to regions where consumers have great purchasing power. It can be lucrative if the AI voice assistant understands, say, a thick Bavarian accent to ensure a smooth purchase via voice control. These tasks are much better paid, but because they are spread widely among people with various dialects, the demand is too sporadic for those individuals to make a living from it. Here, we indeed find the hobbyist crowdworkers who only work on occasion without getting exploited.

Learning from the Venezuelan Workers

In 2018, Venezuela inadvertently became the key supplier of cheap digital labor in the field of data annotation for the automotive industry. For this it was advantageous that the country has a well-connected, well-educated middle class and a reasonably good technical infrastructure—remnants of more fortunate times. The socioeconomic collapse of Venezuela had been a decade in the making, but hyperinflation and mass starvation became particularly acute between 2017 and 2019. During this period of collective hardship, crowdwork became a lifeline for hundreds of thousands of Venezuelans. It is not that the crowdsourcing platforms discussed in this chapter deliberately decided to go to Venezuela. They merely decided to offer the work in Spanish, and Venezuelans, in search of a means to make money online, found the work through Google, YouTube, Reddit forums, and word of mouth.

The average hourly earnings of $1.50–$2.00 paid out by Spare5 at the time were perceived as a pittance by crowdworkers from the Global North, but for the Venezuelan workers, such an income meant the difference between starving and being able to provide for a family. Those who worked for Spare5 were perceived by their neighbors as relatively affluent and quickly recruited more friends and family. One Venezuelan engineering student explained to me that some of his colleagues wanted to keep "the goose that lays the golden eggs" a secret but that he felt morally obliged to tell many others.

The Venezuelan workers from Spare5 that I interviewed in 2018 were very satisfied with the platform, especially in comparison with other providers of microtasking crowdwork. They felt they were dealing with a trustworthy company that treated them with respect. They valued the user-friendly interface and tools and most importantly the reliable weekly payments via PayPal. They experienced the work as intrinsically rewarding, were proud of the quantified and gamified feedback they received in the form of experience points and special ranks, and were proud to be part of the company. This is important because it shows that doing this type of work can actually be quite a positive experience in and of itself—if it weren't for the extreme precarity.

As explained above, the unpredictable availability of tasks had been a systemic source of stress for workers within the Spare5 platform. However, their uncertainty reached new heights in June 2019, when Uber ATG (Advanced Technology Group, Uber's branch specialized on autonomous vehicles) acquired Mighty AI and shortly thereafter informed the Venezuelan workers, via a popup window on Spare5, that their lifeline had been suspended. As Andrea, a longtime SuperFive—one of the few hundred most productive and accurate workers—and hitherto always in close contact with management, recalled: "When we realized that us losing access was not a technical error, but an intentional action to leave us on the sidelines for an indefinite time, it was as if the floor under our feet disappeared." The SuperFives in particular, who strongly identified with their special role and with the company, were deeply disappointed by how they were treated.

It seems that Uber's sudden exclusion of Venezuelan workers was due to US sanctions against Maduro. Around the same time, Adobe discontinued access to its cloud service for Venezuelan users, directly referencing compliance with an executive order of the US against Venezuela as the reason (Lee 2019). The Spare5 workers eventually got paid three weeks later, after having to sign a statement confirming that they were not affiliated with the government. Finally, Uber also restored access to their workplace while, curiously, applying a new geoblocking strategy—now excluding workers from regions such as Europe. By October 2020, as inferred from the Alexa web traffic tool, the share of Venezuelan workers on Spare5 had risen to over 88 percent (with India following at 4.4 percent), but the overall volume of traffic had dropped.

Before the Uber acquisition, Mighty AI was an outsourcing service popular with various automotive companies, among them some large German car manufacturers. Afterward, Uber discontinued the client-facing brand, Mighty AI, while its crowd platform, Spare5, now serves only its internal program of developing autonomous vehicles, which of course makes the pool of tasks available to the workers much smaller.[4]

The Venezuelan workers have developed several strategies to survive the extreme volatility of their digital workplace. In addition to switching back and forth between various platforms, they are also renting out valuable, leveled-up accounts with access to good tasks to others while they are not using them. They are doing this either locally with friends and neighbors or via members-only Discord groups where renters have to pay a monthly fee to get access. As a result, and ironically, the far ends of the tenuous suboutsourcing stack are effectively unknowable to each other. Just as the workers can never be quite sure which car company currently employs them, the employers cannot be sure who is actually doing the work.

While the Venezuelan workers are hyperconnected via Slack and Discord, they are often physically stuck in abject poverty with outdated computing equipment. Their livelihood is threatened by blackouts, corruption, organized crime, and food shortages on their side of the screen and by the capriciousness of algorithmic management, venture capital, and political sanctions on the other.

Douglas, a 21-year-old engineering student from Venezuela, explained: "The situation is better than five years ago, mainly because—this may sound crazy to you—most of the criminals have fled the country. The crime rate is still really high, but it is more secure now to go outside without getting robbed. But there is not much for me out there anyway, because I do almost everything here on the computer." However, staying at home did not protect Douglas from being robbed: "During one of the blackouts, people climbed into my courtyard, where, right under my window I keep some livestock for extra food. They took a few chickens and climbed back. Behind my house, there is a kind of wasteland with improvised settlements, and from there people must have observed that I have chickens here."

The example of Venezuela might seem extreme, a freak occurrence in how its crash coincided with the hype around autonomous vehicles. But then again, as an ever-larger percentage of the world's population goes online while at the same time geopolitical constellations are becoming less stable, many other countries could potentially be the next Venezuela for digital labor in the years to come.

Conclusion

Returning to the initial question of this chapter, what is the impact of the high demand for AI training data for autonomous vehicles on the working conditions of crowdworkers?

On the one hand, this demand has improved the working conditions of the crowd significantly, at least in some respects, over those of flat, general-purpose, legacy crowdwork platforms (like MTurk). The workers deep within the training-data crowd-AI stack can follow a career path by gaining specialized skills; their progress within the system is tracked and documented, and they can reach more senior roles and enjoy a sense of mastery over professional tools and skills. More experienced workers benefit from training and become less exchangeable and more valuable to their employers, and the workers welcome constructive feedback and support from a responsive and human community management that treats them with respect and replies to their concerns quickly. Most importantly, the workers can rely on getting paid weekly by the platforms and do not have to deal with unpredictable payment practices of ever-changing clients treating them merely as interchangeable subhuman machine parts.

On the other hand, even though in the best-case scenario outlined here, the work experience has improved as a result of the shift toward specialized AI training-data platforms, a set of interconnected, fundamental, and potentially unsolvable problems remain for workers in the global crowdwork market: the race to the bottom in terms of wages and, maybe even worse, the constant insecurity or precarity regarding the question of whether there will be enough work the next day. What the labor is worth in monetary terms is negatively affected not only by the drive toward ever more automation but also by the fact that the work can be funneled almost instantaneously to an even cheaper workforce across the globe. Even if the platforms do their best to design a virtual workplace that treats the individual crowdworkers with respect and pays them reliably for their work, there is no guarantee that tomorrow the tasks a worker has just specialized in will not be automated or performed by someone even more desperate.

Probably the most important lesson from studying the crowdsourced production of AI training data is that in the relatively short time between mid-2017 and the end of 2018, the automotive industry, through a supply chain of venture capital–funded platforms, was able to access—or rather create—hundreds of thousands of workers. In other words, capital conjured up a massive, globally distributed workforce almost overnight.

A crowd is a mass phenomenon in which the individual human is by definition replaceable. The crowdworkers become the equivalent of the seemingly endless mass of repetitive and interchangeable microtasks. As long as it is easy to produce workers in an instant—workers who recruit themselves and can be trained and managed automatically—the workforce has hardly any negotiating power to improve its wages or working conditions. That is to say, the problem of the crowd remains the crowd.

Finally, I want to point to the fascinating self-similarity (see figure 8.2) between the layered structure of the crowd-AI stacks described here and the layered structure of

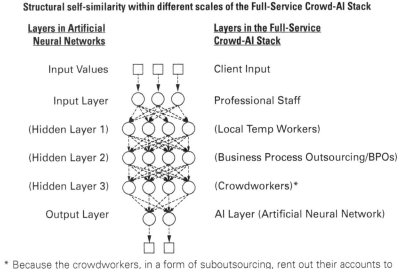

Structural self-similarity within different scales of the Full-Service Crowd-AI Stack

<u>Layers in Artificial Neural Networks</u>	<u>Layers in the Full-Service Crowd-AI Stack</u>
Input Values	Client Input
Input Layer	Professional Staff
(Hidden Layer 1)	(Local Temp Workers)
(Hidden Layer 2)	(Business Process Outsourcing/BPOs)
(Hidden Layer 3)	(Crowdworkers)*
Output Layer	AI Layer (Artificial Neural Network)

* Because the crowdworkers, in a form of suboutsourcing, rent out their accounts to others, they, too, become a hidden layer or black box, not just for the clients, but effectively also for the platform providers.

Figure 8.2
Structural self-similarity within different scales of the image processing stack.
Source: Author.

the artificial neural networks for image recognition used within those larger planetary outsourcing structures. On both the micro and the macro level, these systems are characterized by hidden processing layers—black boxes within black boxes. Although the accuracy of the end results is being guaranteed, nobody really knows in its entirety how these results, for which the crowds are providing training data, come about.

Notes

1. The project was funded by the German Hans Böckler Foundation. References within this chapter to interviews with platform CEOs are based on work published in the longer German version of the report (Schmidt 2019).

2. In June 2016, the driver of a Tesla died in a car crash in Florida while using the "autopilot" mode of the vehicle. The first pedestrian fatality happened in March 2018, when a woman was killed by an Uber test vehicle in Arizona (Schmelzer 2019).

3. "In 2014, workers sued CrowdFlower under the Fair Labor Standards Act ('FLSA') and Oregon's minimum wage law for failure to pay adequate wages. In response, CrowdFlower argued that the microtask workers were independent contractors, based on the terms in the EULA, and thus the minimum wage laws would not apply. The employee status question, however, was foreclosed by settlement before it could be decided by the court" (Cherry 2017, 1823).

4. Remarkably, Uber sold its ATG branch to the start-up Aurora in December 2020, apparently either externalizing or potentially giving up entirely on its endeavor to produce self-driving cars.

References

Ackerman, Evan. 2017. "Autonomous Vehicles vs. Kangaroos: The Long Furry Tail of Unlikely Events." *IEE Spectrum*, July 5. https://spectrum.ieee.org/cars-that-think/transportation/self-driving /autonomous-cars-vs-kangaroos-the-long-furry-tail-of-unlikely-events.amp.html.

Cherry, Miriam A. 2017. "The Sharing Economy and the Edges of Contract Law: Comparing U.S. and U.K. Approaches." *George Washington Law Review* 85 (6): 1804–1845. https://www.gwlr.org /wp-content/uploads/2018/03/85-Geo.-Wash.-L.-Rev.-1804.pdf.

DMV CA (Department of Motor Vehicles, State of California). n.d. "Autonomous Vehicle Testing Permit Holders." Accessed September 6, 2021. https://www.dmv.ca.gov/portal/vehicle-industry -services/autonomous-vehicles/autonomous-vehicle-testing-permit-holders/.

Etherington, Darell. 2020. "Waymo Expands First External Investment Round to $3 Billion." *TechCrunch*, May 12. https://techcrunch.com/2020/05/12/waymo-expands-first-external-investment -round-to-3-billion/.

Hara, Kotaro, Abigail Adams, Kristy Milland, Saiph Savage, Chris Callison-Burch, and Jeffrey P. Bigham. 2018. "A Data-Driven Analysis of Workers' Earnings on Amazon Mechanical Turk." *Proceedings of the*

2018 CHI Conference on Human Factors in Computing Systems 449: 1–13. New York: Association for Computing Machinery.

Hawkins, Andrew J. 2018. "The Electric Scooter Craze Is Officially One Year Old—What's Next?" *The Verge*, September 20. https://www.theverge.com/2018/9/20/17878676/electric-scooter-bird -lime-uber-lyft.

Kahn, Jeremy. 2021. "Data-labeling Company Scale AI Valued at $7.3 Billion with New Funding." *Fortune*, April 13.

Lee, Dami. 2019. "Adobe Is Cutting Off Users in Venezuela Due to US Sanctions." *The Verge*, October 7. https://www.theverge.com/2019/10/7/20904030/adobe-venezuela-photoshop-behance-us -sanctions.

Magistretti, Bérénice. 2017. "Playment Raises $1.6 Million to Improve AI Training through Crowd-sourced Data Tagging." *VentureBeat*, November 21. https://venturebeat.com/2017/11/21/playment -raises-1-6-million-to-improve-ai-training-through-crowdsourced-data-tagging/.

Schmelzer, Ron. 2019. "What Happens When Self-driving Cars Kill People?" *Forbes*, September 26. https://www.forbes.com/sites/cognitiveworld/2019/09/26/what-happens-with-self-driving-cars-kill -people/.

Schmidt, Florian A. 2017. *Digital Labour Markets in the Platform Economy: Mapping the Political Challenges of Crowd Work and Gig Work*. Bonn: Friedrich-Ebert-Stiftung. https://library.fes.de/pdf-files/wiso /13164.pdf.

Schmidt, Florian A. 2019. *Crowdproduktion von Trainingsdaten* [Crowd production of training data]. HBS Study no. 417, February. Düsseldorf: Hans-Böckler-Stiftung. https://www.boeckler.de/pdf /p_study_hbs_417.pdf.

Tubaro, Paola, and Antonio Casilli. 2019. "Micro-work, Artificial Intelligence and the Automotive Industry." *Journal of Industrial and Business Economics* 46 (3): 1–13. https://hal.archives-ouvertes.fr/hal -02148979/document.

9   In Search of Stability at a Time of Upheaval: Digital Freelancing in Venezuela

Hannah Johnston

"You know, I want to make a suggestion," Enrique said at the end of our interview. As an Argentine national and aspiring platform worker who had relocated to Uruguay earlier in 2020 in search of greater economic stability, Enrique told me that many of his clients were also from Argentina. They paid him in Argentine pesos, but he needed and preferred clients who paid in dollars; the relative stability of the US dollar—especially compared with Argentina's currency, which had an inflation rate of over 53 percent in 2019 (Mander 2020)—made it easier to save money for the medium and long term.

Enrique continued: "If you can interview some people of Venezuela, maybe? They have many more issues than people in Argentina and their rates are very, very low. . . . I think they have really a lot of issues, you know? I always wonder how things are going over there because they have a very difficult situation, you know, in the market. Even here on Workana, you know? If I take this job for $10, they can maybe do it for $1."

As it happened, I had already observed the phenomenon Enrique mentioned: the growing number of Venezuelan workers on digital labor platforms who were willing to work for very low wages. In fact, I had begun a small research project to determine whether the number of Venezuelan platform workers was indeed increasing and, if so, to better understand why this influx was taking place. Specifically, I was interested in whether and how planetary labor markets were helping individuals to navigate the collapse of the domestic economy and the corresponding hyperinflation of the bolívar, Venezuela's national currency. My findings from this project suggested that a growing number of Venezuelans are on digital labor platforms and, drawing on a series of qualitative interviews, that platforms are being used as a survival strategy by individuals seeking to weather the country's economic instability.

I began conducting interviews in 2019 with workers throughout Latin America to better understand their experiences of working remotely. Research conducted in Eastern Europe suggests that although cloud workers are technically capable of working for a global clientele in planetary labor markets, regional markets are known to develop, particularly when there are distinct linguistic needs (Aleksynska, Bastrakova, and Kharchenko 2018). This sparked my curiosity about Spanish-language platforms and the experiences of Spanish speakers on global platforms. Over the course of interviewing workers like Enrique, I learned of other labor market dynamics that impacted workers from the region: I was repeatedly told of increased competition among Spanish-speaking workers due to an influx of Venezuelans on a variety of digital platforms. In the words of Martin, a voice-over actor from Mexico, "It is sad because you can observe the other applicants when you are applying for a job offer and 50 percent of them are Venezuelans. And that 50 percent of Venezuelans ask [for] 10 times less money in order to get the job." Comments like these propelled me to learn more about the specific experiences of Venezuelans working on digital labor platforms. Why were they turning to digital platforms? What unique challenges and opportunities do these types of jobs present to them? And how do such experiences complement or contrast with the lives and careers they had envisioned for themselves?

Following the economic collapse of the country and hyperinflation that has affected the country since 2016 (Graham-Harrison, Torres, and Daniels 2019), a growing number of Venezuelans have turned to the planetary labor market to meet their material needs. Digital labor platforms are frequently associated with disruptions because of their capacity to reshape local industries, but within the Venezuelan context it is the disruption of local economic production that has pushed workers online. Platforms have provided stability for individuals amid the economic collapse; as their proponents have argued, digital labor platforms have provided Venezuelan workers with new income streams, flexible work arrangements, and opportunities for entrepreneurship (Manyika et al. 2016). At the same time, however, the relative success of Venezuelans stems from the decline of economic and employment opportunities available in the territory they inhabit.

Drawing on 12 qualitative interviews with Venezuelan platform workers, this chapter examines how digital platforms (such as Workana and Upwork), also referred to as profession-based freelancing platforms (Howcroft and Bergvall-Kåreborn 2018), are being used as a lifeline for workers in a time of economic turmoil. The chapter reveals a harsh irony about the role that such platforms play: They provide people with a means to meet their financial obligations and to put food on the table, and are thus viewed favorably by their users. However, the gravitation of users to this method of working is driven not by individuals' desire to pursue online entrepreneurship opportunities, flexibility, or any of the narratives typically espoused by promoters of platform work but by the absence of viable employment alternatives and the failure of the Venezuelan state to mitigate the economic crisis and hyperinflation.

Global Trends and the Rise of Platform Work in Venezuela

Anyone interested in the growth of digital labor platforms is aware of the dearth of reliable or comparable data on the number of platform workers and their general demographic and economic characteristics (O'Farrell and Montagnier 2020). While the digital nature of labor platforms would make it relatively easy for platform firms to produce these types of statistics, they have been reticent in doing so. Market share has a direct impact on a platform's ability to realize network effects (i.e., its ability to meet and match the needs of customers) and thus on its overall valuation (Bergvall-Kåreborn and Howcroft 2014; Srnicek 2016). Revealing information about rates of use could therefore place a platform at a competitive disadvantage. Absent data derived from the platforms themselves, researchers and governments have turned to other mechanisms to obtain this information.

Governments and researchers have sought firstly to collect information about platform labor market participation from workers directly. In a limited number of countries, questions have been introduced on labor force surveys (O'Farrell and Montagnier 2020; Piasna 2020). More often, independent researchers have administered their own surveys by recruiting workers on or off digital labor platforms. While it is impossible to obtain a representative sample with this approach (because of the absence of general population statistics), such efforts can shed light on overall online labor market trends, particularly when studies are repeated at regular intervals. An additional approach, scraping digital labor platform websites for data with the purpose of counting the number of workers and tasks available, has also been used (Kässi and Lehdonvirta 2018). Overall, most of these independent studies have been conducted in the Global North or have focused on English-language platforms. This suggests that the data is unlikely to capture the breadth of activity in Latin America, West Africa, or Asia. Even so, research that has been global in scope points to a sharp rise in the number of Venezuelan platform workers in recent years.

One key indicator that points to a dramatic rise in the number of Venezuelan platform workers is provided by the Online Labour Index (OLI), a project of the Oxford Internet Institute, which scrapes data from a selection of major English-language platforms globally. The project's worker data is derived daily from Guru, Fiverr, Freelancer .com, and PeoplePerHour, with the dataset going back to June 2017 (Kässi and Lehdonvirta 2018). Data on available jobs is then aggregated and classified thematically by the type of task (for example, creative and multimedia or writing and translation). The number of workers on the platforms is also captured, as is information about their country of residence and skill set. Although an imperfect proxy (the data does not include, for example, time worked on the platform), the project has documented increases in the number of people working on these platforms since it began in 2017 (Stephany et al. 2020). While the project probably undercounts Venezuelan platform workers because it does not include any Spanish-speaking platforms, it nonetheless documents a significant increase in the number of workers from Venezuela. While there is an overall upward trend in Venezuelan workers since the project began in 2017, this increase is most apparent in late 2019 and 2020 (figure 9.1).

Other studies have also reported a growing number of Venezuelan workers engaged in cloud work. For example, the International Labour Organization's (ILO's) global microworker survey (which predates the OLI and has been conducted twice, first in 2015 and then in 2017) also notes an increase in the number of Venezuelans active on select platforms, though their dataset is significantly smaller (Berg et al. 2018).

Florian Schmidt, in a study about generating training data for self-driving cars, found a remarkable incidence of Venezuelans working online in 2018. Focusing on a subset of platforms that specialize in artificial intelligence (AI) training data, he reports that these platforms now amass workforces of hundreds of thousands and that on some the workforce is nearly 75 percent Venezuelan (Schmidt 2019; see also chapter 8 in this volume). Compared to the platforms included in the OLI or surveyed by the ILO, which predominantly facilitate direct client-worker relationships, the specialized AI

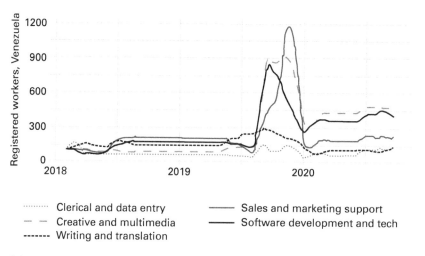

Figure 9.1
Venezuelan platform workers, 30-day moving average. Note: Replication of methods and modification of code reported in Stephany et al. (2020).
Source: Derived from Online Labour Index (ilabour.oii.ox.ac.uk).

training-data platforms examined by Schmidt provide much greater oversight of the workforce. He remarks that these platforms must "invest in new, often AI-enhanced, custom-made production tools that both automatically support and control the workforce, [and] invest in the pre-selection and training of crowdworkers" because of their commitment to providing high levels of data accuracy to clients on an ongoing basis (Schmidt 2019, 4). In other words, for these platforms to maintain their relationships with clients, managing the crowd becomes an integral part of their quality control process. Such jobs may be more stable than those on typical digital work platforms (i.e., those where the platform does not guarantee work quality), which are commonly criticized for their lack of reliable earnings and tasks (De Stefano 2015).

Schmidt's study is an interesting point of contrast for the information presented and discussed in the remainder of this chapter. Schmidt writes that AI firms with high levels of oversight were engaged in developing the necessary infrastructure to accommodate and onboard an inexpensive workforce. AI platforms gained popularity in Venezuela around 2018, a time of economic collapse when the reserve wage for Venezuelan labor was in decline. AI platforms saw these workers, and their corresponding low wages, as an opportunity to capture greater profits. They thus sought to develop and invest in this workforce by creating the necessary infrastructure and supports to be fully functional in countries like Venezuela, which offered an inexpensive workforce. This included, for example, increasing the linguistic capacity of their platforms by "translating the tasks, the training, and the community management into the language of low wage regions on the global market for digital labour" (Schmidt 2019, 14), all of which allowed them to establish a known and reliable workforce.

Unlike the highly standardized data-generative work performed on AI platforms like those studied by Schmidt, digital platforms like Workana, Upwork, and Freelancer.com are less involved in the labor process, and tasks tend to be unique and varied in their requirements and expectations. The work is less repetitive, and the evaluations of work quality tend to be more subjective—particularly for fields like design, a popular specialization of workers in Venezuela. Job terms and evaluation are also determined between the worker and client directly—which is different from Schmidt's finding of AI data-training platforms that intermediate this process and actively manage their crowds.

Because global freelance platforms seek to recruit a global workforce, they may be unwilling or unable to offer translation or customer service support in all of the countries where they are used. Indeed, this is the case in Venezuela. The workers I interviewed had to figure out independently how to navigate job and payment systems on platforms, and they were not offered support or guidance on how to handle the unique geopolitical challenges that they faced as participants in a planetary labor market. The geopolitical conditions in Venezuela both pushed them to participate in digital labor platforms and created unique barriers to accessing some elements of platform infrastructure. This has caused particular challenges for workers' ability to receive payment following US sanctions against the Venezuelan state.

Hyperinflation and Digital Work

Historically, the Venezuelan economy has been underpinned by rents derived from the country's large oil reserves; however, this reliance on resource extraction has left the economy susceptible to commodity price vulnerabilities. When the economy has flourished, improving the economic well-being of individual Venezuelans, it has done so by redistributing rents obtained from resource extraction activities (Rosales 2016). Yet this resource-based approach to industrialization and development never translated to a diversification of domestic economic activity. Instead, the state remained extremely dependent on a growth strategy underpinned exclusively by extractive industries (Auty 1986). As a result, the country came to rely on imports for a range of basic and necessary goods from food to medicine (Burki 2017; Purcell 2017). While this posed no issue when crude prices boomed, as such imports could be easily afforded (Bridge 2008), the 2014 collapse of oil prices coupled with recent economic sanctions, including economic sanctions imposed by the US in 2019, have propelled the Venezuelan economy to the brink of collapse.

For decades, and even during times of relative prosperity, Venezuela has struggled to maintain the stability of its currency (Gallegos 2016). While inflation has been a long-standing concern, it reached new heights with the collapse of oil prices. During this time, the government attempted to maintain "unsustainable market controls that . . . include a strict exchange control that eroded the value of the legal tender, the *bolívar*, while driving the country to hyperinflation" (Rosales 2019). One such control is the government-backed, artificially high exchange rate that exists in parallel with the rapidly devalued black-market rate for bolívars (Kiguel, Lizondo, and O'Connell 1997; Di John 2005). While stores of foreign currency held by the Central Bank of Venezuela were initially used to delay the impact felt by a country highly dependent on imports of basic goods (Gallegos 2016), and regular banking transactions in US dollars were previously prohibited, such controls have now largely been dismantled. By 2019, government coffers were so low, the country turned toward de facto dollarization (Bull and Rosales 2020).

Indeed, the collapse of the bolívar spurred vast emigration to other countries that boast more stable economies (Castillo Crasto and Reguant Álvarez 2017). Conditions have become difficult throughout the country for those who remain, including those who previously lived middle-class or even upper-middle-class lives. Devaluation of the currency has happened at such a rapid rate that holding bolívars for any period of time has become a risky proposition. Money is better spent immediately on any material good because, unlike the bolívar, such goods are more apt to retain their value—even within the short term.

For example, Emilia, a Caracas-based labor lawyer now working at Upwork whom I interviewed in the course of this research, explained that she felt hyperinflation most acutely with the items she purchased regularly; it was with these items that she would be able to see the vast changes in the number of bolívars that she was charged. She stated, "You have to be ahead of what is coming, and you have to be prepared if you want to maintain some sort of living. . . . I spent two or three years giving up things that I like, like going to the movies or eating outside, or meeting with friends in a restaurant or a café or something like that, because you have to keep your money for the really important things. So that was a huge change for me and for many of us that live here." Emilia explained that the cost of both discretionary and routine purchases changed with every trip to the store. This was not the case for rent, mortgages, and, importantly, Emilia's salary, which remained relatively static, leaving her increasingly unable to meet the market price for food and medications.

So while the bolívar has become tremendously devalued, wages have tended to stagnate. As such, even the jobs held by professionals—like lawyers, doctors, and geographers, occupations held by those interviewed as part of this research—no longer provide enough income to put food on the table, let alone to support the standard of living that workers enjoyed a decade ago. For those who have Internet access and computers, obtaining foreign currency has become a key strategy to secure some semblance of security. Some have bought Bitcoin (Cifuentes 2019; Rosales 2019; Bull and Rosales 2020). Others have turned to digital labor markets as a strategy to obtain foreign currency and reduce their exposure to hyperinflation.

The rapid and extreme increase in the number of Venezuelan workers active on platforms during the second half of 2019 (shown in figure 9.1) corresponds with the introduction of expanded US sanctions targeting Venezuela, under Executive Orders 13850 and 13884 (and perhaps others).[1] Among other things, the introduction of these sanctions has made international banking transfers to Venezuela more difficult for those who rely on financial support from abroad in the form of remittances.

While Venezuela has experienced little relief since 2019, the sharp increase in the number of registered platform users in the final quarter of 2019 did decrease in December before beginning to rise steadily again in 2020. One possible explanation could be the annual trends in digital labor markets, which have been shown to wane during the holiday season (Stephany et al. 2020). Alternatively, the decrease could also be explained by phenomena such as platform upkeep and the removal of worker accounts. It may also reveal logistical difficulties that the sanctions posed to the ability of digital workers to fully participate in these labor markets, as discussed in the next section.

Motivations, Payment Regulations, and Obstacles

The strategy of using digital labor platforms to withstand Venezuela's economic turmoil is—despite the desperation and difficulty of the lives of many with whom I spoke—a privilege. In order to make their way online, workers must have some basic infrastructure—that is, a computer and reliable Internet access. On platforms like Upwork, Workana, and Freelancer.com (the sites where the interviewees for this chapter were recruited), workers frequently have a marketable skill set, including knowledge of English and high levels of computer literacy, that appeals to international purchasers of their services. In my purposive sampling of respondents, which sought to recruit respondents of various experience levels who were providing diverse services such as translation, design, and professional services, all were well educated, having received or being on course to receive at least a bachelor's degree, and more than half had master's or professional degrees.

Nearly all were attracted to digital labor platforms after hearing through their informal networks about online earning opportunities. Most had a friend or a family member who had suggested that such platforms could provide a viable source of income in dollars. For respondents, the decision to enter these labor markets was uniformly and merely a matter of survival. The need for foreign currency had become a frank reality for maintaining stability at a time of economic and political upheaval. When asked why he started working on the platform, Hugo, who was trained as a lawyer and lives in a city two hours west of Caracas, described the situation frankly: "I had been working [locally] but the devaluation [of the bolívar] was so huge that I told myself 'I need to make income in a foreign currency.'" Samuel, a medical doctor from Porlamar, a small city on an island off Venezuela's northern coast, felt similarly. Hyperinflation had eroded his doctor's salary so significantly that at the time of our interview, he was paid the equivalent of US$2 every 15 days. He continued to work as a doctor as his main job but was also working as a freelance medical writer for US-based clients, where he could make upward of an additional $200 a week. His medical job seemed to provide him with a sense of purpose; his platform work, meanwhile, gave him the financial means necessary to continue to provide medical care within his local economy.

Multiple respondents were still engaged in academic study, even though they were unlikely to find jobs in the near future that would compensate them at the levels they were earning online. Isidro, a civil engineering student, was in the tenth year of a degree that, he noted, typically takes five years to complete. His studies, he explained, were delayed by depression and other personal issues but also by constitutional reforms and job actions that had shut down the university. Working online as an administrative assistant and content moderator helped to cover his tuition and living costs while he worked to complete his academic program. "Imagine this," Isidro explained from his apartment in Caracas, "I make $50 a week. And now imagine a professor that has many years of experience and that dedicates many hours more than what I dedicate to work, that earns $3 a month." Meanwhile, Lucia, who lives in the northwestern state of Zulia and was midway through earning a third master's degree in petroleum geology, started managing social media accounts for foreign companies because she simply did not have enough money to survive. Her credentials had landed her a once-comfortable public sector job supervising drilling engineers in the country's then-booming oil sector. But although she continued to hold this position, she explained, "We haven't gone to the office in the last two years because, due to the sanctions, we don't have any work to do, so we are staying at home and they haven't paid us since." Nonetheless, she continued to pursue ongoing education in her professional field. This differed from Beltran, a medical doctor from San Cristobal near the Colombian border. Beltran was soft-spoken for most of the interview but stressed just before we hung up the call, "What I can earn in one month working on Upwork is more than what my parents can earn [locally] together in Venezuela throughout the whole year. You can make that part of your report because that . . . that is Venezuela." Beltran had abandoned working as a doctor altogether to help support his parents and other dependents.

When it comes to emerging economies, there is a growing debate about the costs and benefits that platforms present vis-à-vis job quality and skills development. There is also significant speculation about how labor platforms might be used in shaping, for better or worse, development agendas. The political and economic situation in Venezuela, as a driver of platform participation, further complicates this debate. Critics frequently take a long view, arguing that digital labor platforms, and particularly microtasking work, can deskill workers or otherwise contribute to underemployment (Berg et al. 2018). Researchers have scrutinized, for example, the unequal access to and distribution of platform work that commonly results in university graduates from the Global South providing low-skilled content moderation services for Western countries, effectively cleaning up the digital trash and cloud waste produced by developed economies (see, for example, Gray and Suri 2019). Such positions, they argue, have limited opportunity for career advancement, skills acquisition, or upward mobility. Similar analyses demand an accounting of the true cost of Western students' hiring university graduates from developing nations to write their university papers and artificially inflate their grades (Lancaster 2016). While these examples raise important moral questions about the job quality, labor market fairness, and prospects of online work, Heeks et al. (2020) note that digital platforms can also fill labor market voids by providing new, and in some ways, better jobs. This latter optimism may be more aligned with the current role that platforms play for workers in Venezuela: they can provide stability in the presence of market collapse and the tools required to withstand periods of domestic economic turmoil. Nonetheless, these current opportunities lack the career potential that, for many, their previous employment provided.

Yet even in Venezuela, there have been instances, like those observed by Schmidt (2019),[2] where platforms have worked to build infrastructure to onboard Venezuelans to capitalize on workers' desperation and need for income. In such cases, corporate profit motives may create incentives to keep wages low and lead to longer-term underdevelopment. But the short-term changes in the Venezuelan economy have been so extreme that workers have nevertheless been compelled to navigate these systems in whatever manner makes it easiest for them to participate. In doing so, they are attempting to take advantage of the benefits of working online that are otherwise unavailable locally—notably, a stable currency.

There are, however, unique challenges for platform workers in Venezuela. The first is the material challenge of working from a region with an unstable Internet connection and an unreliable energy grid. While energy costs are generally considered affordable, in large part due to government subsidies,[3] there are frequent interruptions to service. The instability of these connections was acutely apparent during interviews with many of the respondents; for example, in the process of coordinating interviews, I was asked about the possibility of conducting midnight Skype meetings or WhatsApp conversations because Internet connections and energy grids were less taxed at these antisocial hours. Uneven access to information and communications services also made large cities like Caracas more reliable than less densely populated regions. Isidro, the civil engineering student, mentioned that one reason he continued to rent an apartment in Caracas rather than living with his family outside of the city was that the Internet connection was more reliable for his online work.

The second principle challenge that Venezuelan platform workers face relates to the ways that geopolitics and international regulations shape workers' everyday experiences of the labor market. US sanctions placed against the Venezuelan government have had consequences for individual workers, constraining their ability to access the money they earn online. The sanctions, as written, are intended to deprive the Maduro regime and its supporters of financial support from abroad. However, payment processors—firms like the US-based PayPal that are used by international platforms like

Upwork and Freelancer.com—are realistically unable to distinguish between supporters of the regime and ordinary citizens. As a result, it has become standard practice at many firms to cease to provide services to subscribers from sanctioned countries. As a result, though Venezuelans remain technically able to access the work opportunities that digital labor platforms provide, it is difficult for them to be paid for their work. In other words, although the planetary labor market is global in scope and participation, the lived experiences of workers in this labor market can differ according to their location. Venezuelans must overcome the additional barriers these sanctions create in order to participate.

Workers have developed a variety of workarounds to address the complications that US sanctions have introduced. The educational levels and occupational histories of some respondents were accomplished enough that they had traveled abroad prior to the current period of hyperinflation and been able to set up overseas bank accounts. Ariel is a trained cartographer who now does design work on Upwork and Fiverr and has a complex business that allows him to sell T-shirts to US consumers using third-party printing services and the Etsy platform—all from his home in Caracas. He explained that he had acquired a foreign bank account during travel to the United States in 2012, when his wages as a geographic information systems specialist were sufficient to fund an international trip. "This account," Ariel explained, "has helped me a lot. It has opened the door to these platforms. It has helped me to charge for my work." A US-based bank account has made it easy for Ariel to obtain a PayPal account that could be verified by a US financial institution; in this way, he was able to avoid being removed from the PayPal platform. He figured that he slipped between the cracks because his bank was based in the US.

For people like Susana from Caracas who do not have foreign accounts, sometimes using the accounts of friends located elsewhere is a feasible solution. Susana had been working on platforms for several years, but, because of the sanctions, she had to devise a new way to access the money she was making. She asked a friend living abroad for assistance. "I asked him a favor, 'Could you open a PayPal account for me?' because in Venezuela they're blocked. He was happy about it so he always receives my money. Actually, the account is more mine than his because he never uses it. . . . He only opened it for me." Susana's system had worked for some time, but she explained that she was now in the middle of a dispute with Upwork, the main platform she works on. Upwork had recently flagged her account because the contact details of her worker profile on the platform differed from the contact information on the PayPal account, which, indeed, was in the name of her friend. At the time of the interview, she was under a two-day suspension and was in communication with the platform to try to figure out the best way forward. As a top-rated worker, she wanted to maintain her profile and account—but also wanted to be paid for the work she completed. She was not quite sure what to do.

For those who earn and keep most of their earnings outside the country, the second challenge comes with transferring currency into the country. With increased dollarization, this is becoming less of an issue. Isidro, the civil engineering student, told me: "Five years ago, the word *dollar* was like a taboo . . . something mystical. Like, you said, 'I have $5' and people used to get scared. Right? That was because the change to dollars wasn't [embraced by the Venezuelan government until recently]. Now, the government is taking measures to make sure that everyone is paying taxes in dollars. . . . Now, businesses are charging you in dollars directly." While none of the respondents I interviewed paid taxes on the income they earned on platforms, the increased use of dollars has made it easier to spend the money they make online. However, such purchases are typically made on the black or gray market, in the form of direct financial transfers between individuals. These remain completely outside of the view of the state and are nearly always digital.

Additionally, and nonetheless, there are still some items that people will purchase in the national currency, and for which they will sometimes need to convert dollars to bolívars. Emilia, the labor lawyer, explained that when she started working online, she was able to set up a Payoneer account.[4] Two months later, sanctions were introduced and she lost her ability to use this account. She was hesitant to share the full details of how she ultimately managed to secure access to a PayPal account but said that she prefers to keep all her money in the United States. When Emilia needs bolívars, she explained, "I do a transfer to someone that has a PayPal account but has the bolívars here." She can then collect the bolívars through this informal transfer network without ever having to deal with a Venezuelan financial institution.

Long-standing parallel official and unofficial exchange rates have fostered these types of informal financial arrangements for years (Gallegos 2016). Indeed, Emilia and others noted that such arrangements are commonplace. Now, even though the government has embraced dollarization, US policy still makes international transfers difficult (Kurmanaev and Herrera 2020). Emilia told me, "We can't [go to a bank and ask for US dollars to be exchanged] because there's some executive order from the US government. Before the sanctions, there was a possibility to do the transfer directly from your Payoneer account to your bank account here in Venezuela, so it was easier, but right now, we can't do that." Instead, she goes to her friend—a reliable one she trusts—but she still spends the money quickly. "It is a matter of hours that you have because you can't afford to keep the bolívars in your bank account. They lose value in a matter of minutes sometimes. It's a little traumatic [and has been] for the past three or four years."

Conclusion

In Venezuela, digital platforms can offer some workers—notably those with the resources, skills, and capital to effectively market themselves—an avenue to withstand the economic disruptions that have plagued the country. The growth of platform work in Venezuela highlights two important takeaways for the study of platform work: First, it serves as an example of the uneven geographic distribution of cloud work in the planetary labor market and lays bare some of the ways in which planetary labor markets are entwined with local economies. In this case, the influx of Venezuelan platform workers began because of a faltering national economy and the decline of viable local employment options; such trends continue. Second, this case highlights how even workers in a global labor market—who can, in theory, work from anywhere—still encounter obstacles that constrain their ability to fully participate. Venezuelan workers' challenges derive from cross-jurisdictional regulation and geopolitics, particularly US sanctions against the Maduro regime. Indeed, workers experience planetary labor markets differently depending on their location, and workers in Venezuela face unique challenges.

Although digital freelancing appears to be disembedded from any singular economy, it informs and is informed by the regions where the work is performed. It is only because of the Venezuelan economic collapse, which pulled an increasing number of workers to sign up as a survival strategy, that digital labor platform work has grown there so dramatically in recent years. What is more, the collapse of the domestic currency has made Venezuelans a comparatively cheap workforce relative to others who might be working in the planetary market; this is particularly true in the context of Latin America.

While global cloud work platforms like Upwork, Workana, and Freelancer.com have provided many Venezuelan workers with a lifeline, the largest global platforms are neither built for nor designed to accommodate any particular workforce—especially not to accommodate one affected by a series of complex US sanctions levied against the Maduro regime. Amid international rules and regulations prohibiting US persons from engaging in transactions with and supporting the Maduro government, many individuals working from Venezuela are encountering obstacles in their attempts to receive payment for their online work. They have thus had to develop alternative and informal financial workarounds to access their platform earnings. While digital labor platforms are often accused of circumventing established laws and regulations—a trend that is most frequently cited with regard to labor and employment law (see, for example, Cherry 2015; Rogers 2016)—in this case it is individual workers who are evading established rules. Whether workers have US bank accounts or navigate informal transfers on the black market through social networks, in this context their actions are better understood as an example of "reworking." Re-working, as an expression of worker agency, comprises efforts to redistribute resources to improve workers' material conditions and in some cases, as in Venezuela's, to pursue survival (Anwar and Graham 2019).

At the same time, the very existence of rules and regulations prohibiting financial transfers to Venezuela suggests that there are avenues for regulating the platform economy that have not yet been explored. This is notable because the vast majority of transactions and exchanges that take place on digital labor platforms remain wholly unregulated and, in the eyes of some, unregulatable (Johnston and Land-Kazlauskas 2018). Indeed, the cross-jurisdictional nature of online labor platforms has raised questions about how regulatory enforcement would take place; many of these work transactions occur between actors operating in different countries with distinct legal frameworks. While this case shows that individual workers have developed workarounds to the regulation brought on by sanctions (in this case, workarounds including gray-market financial transfers), the process through which the sanctions have been operationalized suggests that it may be possible to use payment processors as a site for regulatory intervention and enforcement. With sufficient political will, payment processing could, for example, be reserved for platforms that promote equitable working conditions such as minimum wage payments or dispute resolution mechanisms; such an intervention could thus be used to improve working conditions on platforms more generally.

Notes

1. In 2014 and 2015, Venezuela experienced a significant bout of political turmoil as thousands took to the street in anti-government protests. The Venezuelan government, led by Nicolás Maduro, responded forcefully to this unrest. This, in turn, triggered US sanctions (asset blocking and visa restrictions) of select Venezuelan nationals who were accused of human rights violations, antidemocratic actions, and corruption. The Maduro regime has remained in power but has since become the target of a much broader array of sanctions that have targeted the economy more generally (Congressional Research Service 2020).

2. Notably, even platforms discussed by Schmidt (2019), which sought to onboard Venezuelan workers specifically, have more recently faced challenges related to US-imposed sanctions, discussed in the following paragraphs. See also chapter 8 in this volume.

3. Interestingly, these subsidies have also helped to make Bitcoin mining more accessible (Cifuentes 2019).

4. Payoneer, like PayPal, is an international digital financial services company that is frequently used by platform workers. Often, it is an intermediary step as workers seek to move money they have made from their platform worker account to their domestic bank account, although money can also be retained within a Payoneer account.

References

Aleksynska, Mariya, Anastasia Bastrakova, and Natalia Kharchenko. 2018. *Work on Digital Labour Platforms in Ukraine: Issues and Policy Perspectives*. Geneva: International Labour Organization. https://www.ilo.org/travail/WCMS_635370/lang--en/index.htm.

Anwar, Mohammad Amir, and Mark Graham. 2020. "Hidden Transcripts of the Gig Economy: Labour Agency and the New Art of Resistance among African Gig Workers." *Environment and Planning A: Economy and Space* 52 (7): 1269–1291. https://doi.org/10.1177/0308518X19894584.

Auty, Richard M. 1986. "Resource-Based Industrialization and Country Size: Venezuela and Trinidad and Tobago." *Geoforum* 17 (3–4): 325–338.

Berg, Janine, Marianne Furrer, Ellie Harmon, Uma Rani, and M. Six Silberman. 2018. *Digital Labour Platforms and the Future of Work: Towards Decent Work in the Online World*. Geneva: International Labour Organization. https://www.ilo.org/global/publications/books/WCMS_645337/lang--en/index.htm.

Bergvall-Kåreborn, Birgitta, and Debra Howcroft. 2014. "Amazon Mechanical Turk and the Commodification of Labour." *New Technology, Work and Employment* 29 (3): 213–223.

Bridge, Gavin. 2008. "Global Production Networks and the Extractive Sector: Governing Resource-Based Development." *Journal of Economic Geography* 8 (3): 389–419.

Bull, Benedicte, and Antulio Rosales. 2020. "Into the Shadows: Sanctions, Rentierism, and Economic Informalization in Venezuela." *European Review of Latin American and Caribbean Studies* 109: 107–133. https://www.jstor.org/stable/pdf/26936905.pdf.

Burki, Talha Khan. 2017. "Ongoing Drugs Shortage in Venezuela and Effects on Cancer Care." *The Lancet Oncology* 18 (5): 578.

Castillo Crasto, Tomás Elías, and Mercedes Reguant Álvarez. 2017. "*Percepciones sobre la migración venezolana: causas, España como destino, expectativas de retorno*" [Perceptions of Venezuelan Migration: Causes, Spain as Destination, Return Expectations]. *Migraciones* 41: 133–163.

Cherry, Miriam A. 2015. "Beyond Misclassification: The Digital Transformation of Work." *Comparative Labor Law & Policy Journal* 37: 577.

Cifuentes, Andres F. 2019. "Bitcoin in Troubled Economies: The Potential of Cryptocurrencies in Argentina and Venezuela." *Latin American Law Review* 3: 99–116. https://doi.org/10.29263/lar03.2019.05.

Congressional Research Service. 2020. "Venezuela: Overview of U.S. Sanctions." Washington, DC: Library of Congress. *In Focus*, October 30. https://fas.org/sgp/crs/row/IF10715.pdf.

De Stefano, Valerio. 2015. *The Rise of the "Just-in-Time Workforce": On-Demand Work, Crowdwork, and Labor Protection in the "Gig-Economy."* Conditions of Work and Employment Series no. 71. Geneva: International Labour Organization. https://www.ilo.org/wcmsp5/groups/public/---ed_protect/---protrav/---travail/documents/publication/wcms_443267.pdf.

Di John, Jonathan. 2005. "Economic Liberalization, Political Instability, and State Capacity in Venezuela." *International Political Science Review* 26 (1): 107–124.

Gallegos, Raul. 2016. *Crude Nation: How Oil Riches Ruined Venezuela.* Lincoln: University of Nebraska Press.

Graham-Harrison, Emma, Patricia Torres, and Joe Parkin Daniels. 2019. "Barter and Dollars the New Reality as Venezuela Battles Hyperinflation." *The Guardian*, March 14. https://www.theguardian.com /world/2019/mar/13/venezuela-hyperinflation-bolivar-banknotes-dollars.

Gray, Mary L., and Siddharth Suri. 2019. *Ghost Work: How to Stop Silicon Valley from Building a New Global Underclass.* Boston: Houghton Mifflin Harcourt.

Heeks, Richard, Karsten Eskelund, Juan Erasmo Gomez-Morantes, Fareesa Malik, and Brian Nicholson. 2020. "Digital Labour Platforms in the Global South: Filling or Creating Institutional Voids?" Digital Development Working Paper Series Paper no. 86. Center for Digital Development, University of Manchester. http://hummedia.manchester.ac.uk/institutes/gdi/publications/workingpapers /di/dd_wp86.pdf.

Howcroft, Debra, and Birgitta Bergvall-Kåreborn. 2018. "A Typology of Crowdwork Platforms." *Work, Employment and Society* 33 (1): 21–38. https://doi.org/10.1177/0950017018760136.

Johnson, Jackie. 2019. "Bitcoin and Venezuela's Unofficial Exchange Rate." *Ledger* 4: 108–120. https://doi.org/10.5195/ledger.2019.170.

Johnston, Hannah, and Chris Land-Kazlauskas. 2018. *Organizing On-Demand: Representation, Voice, and Collective Bargaining in the Gig Economy.* Conditions of Work and Employment Series no. 94. Geneva: International Labour Organization. https://www.ilo.org/wcmsp5/groups/public/---ed_pro tect/---protrav/---travail/documents/publication/wcms_624286.pdf.

Kässi, Otto, and Vili Lehdonvirta. 2018. "Online Labour Index: Measuring the Online Gig Economy for Policy and Research." *Technological Forecasting and Social Change* 137: 241–248.

Kiguel, Miguel A., J. Saul Lizondo, and Stephen A. O'Connell. 1997. *Parallel Exchange Rates in Developing Countries.* London: Macmillan Press.

Kurmanaev, Anatoly, and Isayen Herrera. 2020. "Venezuela's Capital Is Booming: Is This the End of the Revolution?" *New York Times*, February 18. https://www.nytimes.com/2020/02/01/world /americas/Venezuela-economy-dollars.html.

Lancaster, Thomas. 2016. "'It's Not a Victimless Crime'—the Murky Business of Buying Academic Essays." *The Guardian*, October 19. https://www.theguardian.com/higher-education-network/2016 /oct/19/its-not-a-victimless-the-murky-business-of-buying-academic-essays.

Mander, Benedict. 2020. "Argentina's Inflation Nears Highest Level in Three Decades." *Financial Times*, online edition, January 15. https://www.ft.com/content/e6f5c436-37d2-11ea-a6d3 -9a26f8c3cba4.

Manyika, James, Susan Lund, Jacques Bughin, Kelsey Robinson, Jan Mischke, and Deepa Mahajan. 2016. "Independent Work: Choice, Necessity, and the Gig Economy." McKinsey Global

Institute Report, October 10. http://www.mckinsey.com/global-themes/employment-and-growth/independent-work-choice-necessity-and-the-gig-economy.

O'Farrell, Rory, and Pierre Montagnier. 2020. "Measuring Digital Platform-mediated Workers." *New Technology, Work and Employment* 35 (1): 130–144.

Piasna, Agnieszka. 2020. "Counting Gigs: How Can We Measure the Scale of Online Platform Work?" Working Paper 2020.06. Brussels: European Trade Union Institute. https://www.etui.org/sites/default/files/2020-09/Counting%20gigs_2020_web.pdf.

Purcell, Thomas F. 2017. "The Political Economy of Rentier Capitalism and the Limits to Agrarian Transformation in Venezuela." *Journal of Agrarian Change* 17 (2): 296–312.

Rogers, Brishen. 2016. "Employment Rights in the Platform Economy: Getting Back to Basics." *Harvard Law & Policy Review* 10 (2): 479–520.

Rosales, Antulio. 2016. "Deepening Extractivism and Rentierism: China's Role in Venezuela's Bolivarian Developmental Model." *Canadian Journal of Development Studies/Revue Canadienne d'études du développement* 37 (4): 560–577.

Rosales, Antulio. 2019. "Radical Rentierism: Gold Mining, Cryptocurrency and Commodity Collateralization in Venezuela." *Review of International Political Economy* 26 (6): 1311–1332.

Schmidt, Florian Alexander. 2019. "Crowdsourced Production of AI Training Data: How Human Workers Teach Self-Driving Cars How to See." Working Paper Forschungsförderung no. 155, August. Düsseldorf: Hans-Böckler-Stiftung. https://www.boeckler.de/pdf/p_fofoe_WP_155_2019.pdf.

Srnicek, Nick. 2016. *Platform Capitalism*. Cambridge: Polity Press.

Stephany, Fabian, Michael Dunn, Steven Sawyer, and Vili Lehdonvirta. 2020. "Distancing Bonus or Downscaling Loss? The Changing Livelihood of US Online Workers in Times of COVID-19." *Journal of Economic and Human Geography* 111 (3): 561–573. https:///doi.org/10.1111/tesg.12455.

10 Human Listeners and Virtual Assistants: Privacy and Labor Arbitrage in the Production of Smart Technologies

Paola Tubaro and Antonio A. Casilli

In spring 2019, public outcry followed media revelations that major producers of allegedly automated voice-activated devices recruit human operators to listen to, transcribe, and label users' conversations. These high-profile news stories originated in journalistic and scholarly investigations, and in the voluntary disclosures of whistleblowers. The scandal started with a *Bloomberg* report on April 10, 2019, disclosing that thousands of Amazon workers listen to the private conversations of users of the smart speaker Echo. Workers include both employees and subcontractors of Amazon, located in the US and in India. A company spokesperson claimed that these privacy violations concerned "an extremely small number" of the 100 million–strong Echo user base (Day, Turner, and Drozdiak 2019).

A few months later, the Flemish Radio and Television Broadcasting Organization (VRT) revealed that third-party outside contractors were eavesdropping on audio recordings of users of Google Home smart speakers and smartphone apps. The practice was not characterized as an exception; Google subcontractors were said to "systematically" listen after logging into a secure platform. Some of the conversations they accessed contained sensitive information, such as private arguments, confidential business conversations, and the whereabouts of children (Verheyden et al. 2019). Even more intimate details were said to reach Apple. According to a whistleblower who used to work for a subcontracting company, these included "confidential medical information, drug deals, and recordings of couples having sex." This data was collected via the company's voice assistant, Siri, which is included in most of its devices from iPhones to HomePod smart speakers and Apple Watches. As Amazon had done earlier, an Apple spokesperson claimed that this concerned "a very small random subset, less than one percent of daily Siri activations" (Hern 2019).

Following these revelations, which brought to the fore whistleblowers from within tech companies, other news stories followed at rapid pace. In August 2019, Microsoft and Facebook were exposed in the international press for subcontracting providers in the Philippines, Bulgaria, and Mexico to listen to personal conversations on Skype (Cox 2019) and for recording and transcribing Messenger voice chats (Frier 2019). But even following this steady drip of news reports, tech companies have yet to demonstrate that they have built the necessary safeguards into their devices and software. Since 2019, very few of these companies have paused their eavesdropping programs or enhanced their privacy controls. The most common corporate responses have been limited to tweaking privacy policies and/or internalizing these processes, entrusting them to on-site employees who are submitted to more stringent nondisclosure agreements (NDAs) (Carr et al. 2019).

News reports of these egregious cases of privacy erosion display a remarkable common feature: they traditionally adopt the viewpoint of consumers worried about intrusions in their daily lives and intimate spheres, and about potential ensuing security issues. There is a tension between these recent privacy concerns and companies' need to collect the data necessary to the operation of the artificial intelligence (AI) systems that run smart speakers, smartphones, and mobile applications. Workers who remotely listen to consumers' conversations, called "data associates," "raters," or "reviewers," provide indispensable quality controls to improve automated processes such as voice-activated virtual-assistant software, machine translation, and speech-recognition systems. While the terms of use of most devices do inform users that personal data is used to train and test AI systems, they do not always explicitly state that human teams listen to recordings. Even when they do, they minimize the impact of their intervention, as, for example, Amazon for which it is "an industry-standard practice where humans review an extremely small sample of requests to help Alexa understand the correct interpretation of a request and provide the appropriate response in the future" (Amazon n.d.). Importantly, by characterizing these activities as AI training, to improve the tools, companies reinforce the belief—which, as we will see, is rather a misconception— that privacy violation is limited to a transitory period and that it will stop as soon as full-fledged machine learning kicks in. Moreover, the attempt to reassure consumers that this process "includes multiple safeguards to protect customer privacy" (Amazon n.d.) rarely provides further details.

In this chapter, we show that the job descriptions of these third-party workers include much more than just transcribing and annotating conversations to help automated speech algorithms "self-learn." These workers often verify the results of the software's calculations, fix errors, and compare automated transcriptions to human-made ones. In some instances, workers' tasks even consist of directly executing speech commands that the AI systems are unable to interpret, thus "impersonating" virtual assistants by completing the very same tasks they are supposed to perform automatically. These multitudes of contributors work in the shadows because their very existence—as humans who listen to other humans—is embarrassing for the companies that sell alleg-edly automated voice-activated solutions. Indeed, admitting their role in developing smart technologies would be at odds with the common marketing claim that these technologies can become deeply integrated into our lives, precisely because they are activated by simple voice command (see, for example, Martinez and Cameron n.d.). Advertising campaigns have created the expectation that smart technologies effort-lessly interpret and act upon these commands. If the recent scandals plainly exposed the unrealistic nature of these claims, they have not stopped the recruitment of human "remote listeners." It turns out, as we will discuss in more detail, that their function remains crucial and cannot be automated. Ironically, voice assistants need humans but obfuscate their contribution.

We argue that privacy issues related to the development of voice assistants are not isolated offenses. Rather, they are intrinsically related to the labor-intensive nature of today's models of automation, which are based on machine learning and fueled by human-produced data. The production systems underpinning these models cross bor-ders, procuring workers in (mostly) low-wage countries to listen to the voice recordings of consumers in (primarily) Western Europe, North America, and other higher-income parts of the world. Indeed, digital technologies enable workers' outputs to be immedi-ately transferred to any place, reducing the need for physical proximity. Companies' efforts to minimize labor costs are limited only by the need to match the language competencies of consumers and workers. The result is a complex geography that largely reproduces linguistic proximities inherited from the colonial past.

The conditions of labor and the remuneration of these remote listeners lie at the heart of the problem. Even less-intrusive computing techniques that mitigate privacy issues on the consumer side—primarily in the Global North—do not eliminate the need for humans in the loop in the Global South. In the remainder of this chapter, we describe the extent and relevance of this human contribution, and the harsh condi-tions under which it is obtained—including low salaries, precarity, and lack of social protection. We conclude that privacy issues are only one side of a more complex, mul-tifaceted problem that cannot be solved without also addressing the working condi-tions and remuneration of the people who toil behind the production of purportedly automated voice assistants.

To support our argument, we use interviews that we conducted in 2018–2019 with start-ups specializing in automation and particularly voice technologies, as well as with a small number of whistleblowers who had formerly worked as remote listeners for international platforms and for subcontractors of major multinational technology companies. To reach out to them, we engaged in a broad effort to publicize our study through social media, inviting participation widely; we also used snowballing and leveraged personal contacts with digital rights associations. Moreover, we rely on an extensive, two-year observation of platform websites, press releases, publications, and other public documentation. To a lesser extent, we also use some data from a questionnaire that we distributed to over 900 online workers on the platform then called Foule Factory (now Wirk.io) in France in 2018 (Casilli et al. 2019).

The Real Humans behind "Automated" Voice Assistants

Voice-activated assistants were among the first products of AI to be widely marketed worldwide. From general-purpose assistants such as Amazon's Alexa, Apple's Siri, and Microsoft's Cortana to more specialized products for connected objects such as voice-activated coffee machines (and other home- or car-automation devices), their use has become ubiquitous in the last few years. The current capacities of these smart solutions are the result of major advances in natural language processing and speech-recognition research. Answering even a mundane question about the weather at a certain location or the recipe for a home-cooked dish requires realizing a sequence of operations, each of which can be challenging for a machine. Before an actual answer can be provided, a question uttered by the user needs to be transcribed, analyzed for semantic and syntactic features, and adjudicated against a database of facts and preanswered questions. The computational solution to these problems relies on machine learning, a technique that "teaches" computers to find solutions from data without having to rely on explicitly programmed rules at each step of the process. Machine learning is the technique that has fueled the current AI boom. Given sufficiently large sets of examples, machine learning models can detect regularities and patterns in the data, which they then use as a basis to make predictions or decisions. Better-quality and larger datasets allow progressive refinement of results. Put differently, data is as necessary an input to AI as the algorithms (or computer programs) that handle it.

To illustrate the functioning of voice assistants more concretely, let us go back to the example of a question about the weather. First, an algorithm must be "trained" with sample data, which in this case will be audio recordings of people asking for the weather. Large numbers of such recordings are needed so that the algorithm can learn that they all mean the same thing despite differences in timbre, type and tone of voice, regional accents, and background noise level. But initial training is only one step toward the production of a functioning AI solution, as subsequently the algorithm needs to be tested and may undergo other phases of training to improve its performance. Some of these steps may include direct human interventions, whereby an operator takes over to

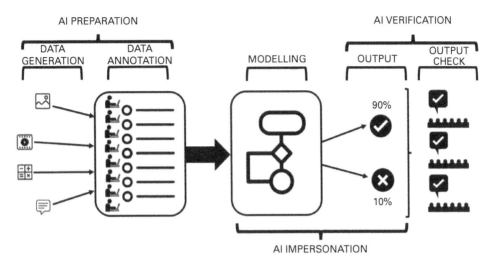

Figure 10.1
Platform-mediated human labor in three phases of the development of machine learning–based voice assistants. Note: Data is generated, then annotated, filtered, and enriched (AI preparation). It is subsequently used to train a machine learning model, which produces outputs verified by workers (AI verification). In some cases, workers replace automated processes in real time to complete training datasets or to correct mistaken outputs (AI impersonation).
Source: Tubaro, Casilli, and Coville (2020).

perform the tasks that the AI system is unable to execute due to lack of data, defective parameters, or flaws in the code. Later updates may be needed if, for example, new words emerge to describe known phenomena (like the annually updated names of tropical storms and hurricanes) or the very phenomena change (due to unusual weather activity or climate change, for example). In the following subsections, we show that these solutions require, at the same time, large amounts of personal data and large amounts of human work to make this data suitable for use in machine learning. It is from this mix of factors that the recent scandals originate, and as we will see, they present only the tip of the iceberg. Platform-mediated labor is required for each phase of the production of an AI system: preparation, verification, and impersonation (figure 10.1).

AI Preparation

We refer to the tasks needed for data generation (voice recordings) and for data enrichment or, more technically, data annotation (transcriptions, classifications) as "AI preparation" (Tubaro, Casilli, and Coville 2020). Often referred to as "AI training" in the industry, this is an early phase that occurs at input level, starting before a voice assistant is marketed. At this stage, paid workers include not only listeners who take other people's recorded voices as inputs, but also speakers—workers who get remunerated to record their voices before listeners can start their operations.

In the preparation phase, companies use specialized digital platforms to recruit on-demand workers to generate the recordings needed to train algorithms before they are brought to market. These platforms (Casilli and Posada 2019) allow client companies to fragment large data projects into small tasks and allocate them to masses of anonymous providers, each of whom executes a tiny part of the whole. Tasks may consist of reading aloud and audio recording a few short sentences. One in five respondents to our French questionnaire reported that this was the latest task they had done. Some mentioned variants such as recording five different ways to ask the same question and reading aloud (and recording) a story for children. These tasks receive a fixed, usually low price. For example, on Atexto, a specialized platform that offers voice-related tasks exclusively, the recording of 10 sentences in Spanish was paid $0.50 in winter 2020 and was expected to take only a couple of minutes. Rates are similar (though slightly more variable depending on customers) on Clickworker, a larger platform with a significant presence throughout Europe and North America, which says on its blog that "voice recording is one of the most popular job types on our platform" (Bayhan 2019). On Upwork, an international freelancing platform, remunerations are higher (between $10 and $20) but for larger batches of 140–300 sentences taking up to 75 minutes.

These platforms also offer other tasks that serve to enrich the "raw" data obtained through recordings. Some of our questionnaire respondents said that they did tasks that entailed checking the quality of the audio recordings made by other workers (curiously enough, one of them reported that she once recognized her own voice). Other common enrichment tasks are transcriptions and classifications of audio datasets. Human-made transcriptions provide examples of how to associate sounds to words—a necessary step before giving them meaning. Classifications serve to add metadata—for example on the emotional state of the speaker—with the ultimate purpose of fine-tuning the voice assistant's understanding and nudging it toward more suitable responses. Depending on the platform, pay rates range from $0.085 to $1 per audio minute (an expression that denotes the length of the audio file to be transcribed, not the time spent working on the transcription).

Despite the media revelations that we presented at the beginning of this chapter, the large amount of personal data that is collected, stored, and handled at this stage has attracted relatively little attention so far. Voice is one of several features unique to the physical and physiological identity of a person and is therefore considered personal data—protected in the European Union under the General Data Protection Regulation

(GDPR). In this sense, even the recording of a paid worker reading aloud a standard, client-provided sentence raises potential privacy issues. In a not-too-distant future, potential advances in voice recognition may make individual reidentification increasingly easy. While workers are asked for their consent when they accept these tasks, compliance with the GDPR requires further provisions such as the right to opt out later on—provisions that require coordination between platforms and final clients and are thus difficult to implement.

AI Verification

We alluded earlier to the common claim that AI training may be transitory and disappear as the technology matures. Indeed, one may speculate that future progress might reduce the data needs of machine learning. The potential development of "unsupervised" algorithms that are able to find patterns in data without any need for enrichment (such as classifications) may lower the demand for third-party labor for preparation tasks. But even under this scenario, there will still be a need for human work at output level, to review and, if necessary, to correct the results of the algorithm. This is what Tubaro, Casilli, and Coville (2020) call "AI verification." Once a voice assistant has been developed and brought to market, its functioning needs to be continuously checked for accuracy: Does it provide the correct answer when people ask a question about (to stick to the same example) the weather? If not, what may have gone wrong? What needs to be added or changed? This is precisely the work of the human remote listeners highlighted in the 2019 press stories and explains why there is a need not only for standardized examples created in the production phase but also for real-world voices of actual consumers in everyday settings—despite the ensuing privacy violation issues.

In the course of our fieldwork, we realized that verification tasks for voice assistants are not generally offered on generalist platforms, where anyone may register, because of the sensitive information they involve. They are more commonly outsourced through what Casilli et al. (2019) call "deep labor" platforms, such as Appen and Pactera Edge. These platforms often require an entry qualification test for new workers and usually pay by the hour rather than by piecework (see also chapter 8 in this volume). One of our interviewees, committing to work for a fixed number of hours every week, received $10 per hour—although after a few months, the number of assignments dropped significantly, reducing the hours and, consequently, the earnings. These platforms are usually tightly managed by a network of subcontractors, with a division of labor in which each of them deals with one aspect (contracting, day-to-day operations, payments, technical infrastructure, etc.). The complexity of the system does not facilitate tight control of privacy protection; this particular interviewee was never asked to sign any confidentiality agreement regarding handling personal data (whether it included consumers' own voices or personal details about their lives).

When the voice assistant producer is a major multinational company and the amount of data to be processed is consistently large, verification tasks may be outsourced to salaried workers recruited by a subcontractor as part of a business process outsourcing (BPO) value chain. These are repetitive jobs often paid at minimum wage, but with the safeguards and protections associated with salaried employment, these workers at least enjoy more predictable flows of assignments and income. Workers usually must sign strong NDAs, and, according to our interviewees, they are not even allowed to share work-related information with their office mates. As discussed later, these jobs do not offer workers adequate protection against the psychosocial risks induced by the nature of their work. Both the problematic (and sometimes distressing) nature of the real-life content they listen to and the obligation to keep the information confidential constitute a burden that these human remote listeners are often left alone to handle.

AI Impersonation

According to Tubaro, Casilli, and Coville (2020), "AI impersonation" occurs when human paid labor does not support the processes of data production or algorithmic quality assurance but replaces them when they fail. Nontransparent use of low-paid humans instead of algorithms may seem deceptive to consumers and the general public. However, "faking" AI is sometimes done for legitimate reasons, such as to understand the production process of some functionality before actually designing an algorithm to automate it. In the field of AI, this "Wizard of Oz" technique dates back to the second half of the twentieth century. Initially designed for natural language processing, it consists of setting up an experiment where a hidden human (the "wizard") simulates the behavior of a smart computer application to test how users react to a system that they believe to be autonomous (Kelley 1983). In this sense, AI impersonation can be close to AI preparation, and dissimulation of the presence of human listeners may be justified by corporate officials as a way of "faking it until you make it." According to the founder of an AI start-up whom we interviewed in 2018, "What people don't realize is that the vast majority of B2B start-ups we know of are human-based." This is not fraud or deception but rather "a gamble on the future. They have to create their own data . . . and then, on that basis, develop machine learning models *hoping that one day* the process will be automated" (Casilli et al. 2019, emphasis added).

Sometimes, impersonation also verges on AI verification, when correction of algorithmic failures requires real-time human intervention. The development of Google Duplex, an early-stage AI-based voice assistant to make restaurant reservations by phone on behalf of clients, illustrates both cases. Asked to comment on this in 2019, the company itself admitted that about 25 percent of calls placed through Duplex started with a human, and about 15 percent of those that began with an automated system had a human intervene at some point (Chen and Metz 2019). The human impersonator can be seen as preparing AI in the former case and verifying/correcting it in the latter.

Generally speaking, impersonation happens when humans outperform computers in terms of either efficacy or cost. The idea that prompted Amazon to launch its pioneering platform Mechanical Turk in 2006 was to integrate humans (amusingly termed "artificial artificial intelligence") directly into software programming. According to Irani (2015, 225), this platform was "born out of the failures of artificial intelligence to meet the needs of Internet companies." Ekbia, Nardi, and Šabanović (2015) further stretch this idea by suggesting that failures are actually constitutive aspects of AI production. When new technological solutions are introduced, they promise to automate some process and to be labor saving. But whenever technical limitations threaten delivery on this promise, "human beings are brought into the fold" (7). Cheap labor is one of the tools available to AI producers to compensate for the shortcomings of their technologies. This is an instance of the tension, illustrated by Sadowski (see chapter 13), between technology companies' promises and the masked inputs of human labor they nevertheless need.

Local and Remote AI-Oriented Labor

In virtually all fields of AI, cost efficiency factors in the decision to bring human workers into the loop. In principle, AI preparation, AI verification, and AI impersonation tasks are not geographically bound to any place and can be performed from anywhere, provided there is a computer (or even just a tablet or a smartphone) with broadband. When it comes to voice-activated solutions, linguistic factors largely determine the trade-off between recruitment of local and remote listeners. If a company wants to market a voice assistant to a new country, it needs to ensure its algorithm is trained in the languages spoken in that country. Data preparation and verification in particular often require perfect language fluency and sometimes a more fine-grained knowledge of regional dialects, idiomatic expressions, or domain-specific vocabulary. Therefore, these tasks will be primarily directed at native speakers, sometimes targeting specific countries: on platforms, it is not uncommon to see voice-recording tasks directed exclusively to, say, "Mexican Spanish speakers" or open only to residents of Mexico, while enrichment tasks are more often open to any native speakers of Spanish.

This poses additional constraints on speech recognition models compared to other fields of AI. Data annotation for computer vision algorithms is customarily outsourced on behalf of European or North American companies to foreign workers wherever labor costs are low (Schmidt 2019; see also chapter 8 in this volume). Instead, we have encountered several instances of voice-related tasks performed within Europe—in Bulgaria, France, Ireland, and Spain. Linguistic needs are likely to keep at least some of these activities within the same countries where the final consumers are located. Nevertheless, recruiting local listeners does not necessarily mean that labor is negotiated locally. Deep labor platforms, for instance, put in place complex outsourcing networks that span national boundaries to enable cost optimization. Some of our interviewees identify as native speakers of French, live in France, and were paid to listen to recordings of French users. But they were contracted by international platforms on behalf of foreign clients, and their day-to-day managers, technical support officers, and other interlocutors were spread throughout Europe (figure 10.2).

Additionally, some degree of offshoring still takes place, at least among countries sharing a common language. This mirrors complex historical interdependencies, so that,

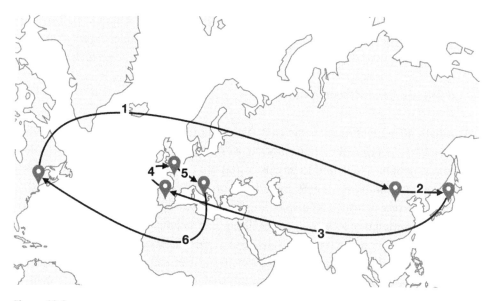

Figure 10.2
The circuitous supply chain of data produced by platform workers to train voice assistants. Note: The data produced by platform workers to train voice assistants establishes a circuitous supply chain spanning across several countries. In one case, AI verification is handled by a Chinese platform (1) that relies on a Japanese online service (2) and its Spanish subsidiary (3) to recruit workers in France (4). Workers are supervised by an Italian company (5) and use a technical infrastructure directly controlled by the final client, a producer of smart speakers located in the US (6).
Source: Authors' elaboration.

for example, a lot of French-language work goes to French-speaking African countries. It is for this reason that, while offshoring is possible only to a limited extent in the specific case of voice assistants, the companies targeted by the media revelations that opened this chapter rely heavily on data associates and raters located in low- and medium-income countries, especially in Southeast Asia. As attested in the literature about platform-based outsourcing, these flows of labor follow existing paths of economic, cultural, linguistic, and political dependency (Fuchs 2016; Casilli 2017; Graham, Hjorth, and Lehdonvirta 2017; Couldry and Mejias 2019). Major platforms and platform-based BPO vendors are located in countries or zones that offer particular legal and economic advantages, and they manage their international workforce from there. For tech companies, platformization represents a way to circumvent fiscal, privacy, and labor regulations, by arrogating to themselves a problematic double freedom of movement—both of labor and of data, at planetary scale. In the platform economy, the workforce is geographically dispersed and distributed along constantly reconfiguring supply chains. Digital intermediation services act as "techno-immigration systems" (Aytes 2012) that allow remote access to foreign workers without importing labor through immigration and even without offshoring via direct foreign investment.

In sum, each phase of the production of AI leverages a planetary labor arbitrage by coordinating local workers (both employees and local contractors of tech companies) and remote third-party workers. Overall, the production and development of voice assistants displays a complex geography, intertwining national and international dimensions, and organized along linguistic lines. This two-level labor arbitrage goes hand in hand with an equally complex privacy arbitrage, whereby clients and platforms seek to simultaneously lower labor costs and channel data to countries where privacy and data protection laws provide uneven levels of safeguard.

Consumers and Workers: A Dual Set of Privacy Risks

Due to the very nature of the technology underpinning them, voice assistants entail risks for all the humans involved—both consumers and workers. The presence of the latter engenders risks for the former: when producers of smart devices conceal the role of flesh-and-blood workers behind automation, consumers underestimate the likelihood and magnitude of potential privacy violations; the broader implications of consenting to terms of use are unclear. Consumers may not know that the assistant records not only bland questions such as "What is the weather like today?" but also their requests for, say, a certain type of porn videos or a prescription drug needed for a condition they are otherwise unwilling to disclose.

Our interviews with former remote listeners point to further risks largely obfuscated from view. Consumers are unlikely to realize that individual reidentification is difficult but not impossible. In principle, recordings are anonymized and fragmented into small bits of a few seconds before reaching human remote listeners, but they may occasionally include mentions of names, addresses, or even social security numbers. Consumers also dictate text to their voice assistants—personal and professional messages and documents that may include sensitive or identifying information. Additionally, remote listeners told us that they might come across several pieces of the same conversation in the same series of transcriptions, enough to draw up a basic profile of the user or their mood at the moment. An even more widespread problem is that a voice assistant may switch on inadvertently and record conversations that were not intended for it, including, for example, interactions with children. This occurs because the algorithms for detection of "wake words" (that is, the special words or phrases that are meant to activate voice assistants, like "Siri" and "OK Google") are still largely imperfect (Coucke et al. 2019).

Another set of risks emerges when we shift our attention from AI consumers to the invisibilized workers that make AI possible. Workers do not only analyze and transcribe consumers' data; they also produce data themselves, especially in the AI preparation phase. While the short recording of a standard sentence is generally harmless (for example, pronouncing the name "Alexa"), multiple recordings of information about the worker (such as their location, skills, preferences, etc.) may be matched with other data or metadata (type of device used, time to perform a task, platform logs, etc.) to produce identifying information.

Casilli et al. (2019) also identify four main categories of psychosocial risk for all these workers—whether they be primarily speakers or listeners. The first risk is losing sight of the objective of their work: especially those who perform tasks that involve recording their voice for data generation are often ignorant of the fact that this activity serves to produce AI-based virtual assistants. The companies that post these tasks on platforms do not always explain their purposes, and our fieldwork indicates that even some experienced, assiduous workers miss this point. The remote listeners who transcribe and check conversations for verification purposes are more likely to know—or at least guess—the purpose of their work. However, as one interviewee told us, especially on platforms, workers are sometimes left alone to handle the personal information of users. This case occurred before GDPR legislation entered into force in Europe; nevertheless, it suggests that platforms shift the responsibility to protect the personal data they handle onto workers. The objectives of the work become fuzzy—is it about improving the technology or enabling massive intrusions into other people's lives?

A second psychosocial risk is loss of control over the quality of work. Especially on platforms, tasks may be rejected, but workers are not systematically given feedback or allowed to redo their assignments. Contact with support services is often difficult. Under these conditions, it becomes hard to define quality standards, and any rejection is perceived as an abuse. A third risk involves suffering and conflict at work. On platforms, demand for labor is highly volatile, and workers are exposed to broad competition. Even with BPO vendors that secure more predictable flows of tasks, job contracts are often short-lived. Hence, workers constantly feel that there is insufficient demand and that they have to fight against others for tasks. The fourth risk is isolation. Especially on platforms, work from home and anonymity may prevent communication and sharing with others. Some platforms do offer online forums to let workers get in touch with each other, but others do not, and a few actively limit communication in order to avoid any claims or protests (Casilli et al. 2019). In some cases, workers do not even manage to share their experience and concerns with their closest social group of family, partner, and friends. Many of our questionnaire respondents said they find it difficult to explain what they do on platforms, how, and why. Isolation may prevent the emergence of a common reflection on working conditions and on possible improvements. The individual has no control over his or her working environment.

Conclusion

The collection and disclosure of the personal data of very large numbers of people are needed for the development and commercialization of AI-driven assistants. Human voice, which as discussed constitutes personal data, must be gathered from the platform workers who execute data generation tasks and from those who use the product. Their recorded voices are necessarily disclosed to other people, whom we have referred to here as listeners: the workers who perform data enrichment tasks and those who check whether the AI has correctly understood users' utterances.

This is not to say that there are no efforts to design privacy-preserving algorithms. For example, recent research uses "federated learning" as a decentralized procedure that enables the training of a central model on the local data of many users, without the need to ever upload this data to a central server (Leroy et al. 2019). However, this alleviates the problem on the side of consumers without reducing that of the workers. What is at stake here is the privacy of both groups. In this respect, research in computer science is working toward solutions to design tasks that keep platform workers' identities more protected (see Duguépéroux and Allard 2020), but risks still remain high as of mid-2021.

Contrary to optimistic claims commonly heard in the industry, it appears that the need for human labor to support AI voice assistants is unlikely to be temporary. Even when a new voice-activated technology is sufficiently mature and no longer needs human impersonators, the need for workers to prepare datasets and, more importantly, to perform quality checks on outputs remains high. It can even be expected to grow as more and more applications of voice technologies emerge, from home automation to industrial production and even health services (where, for example, nurses can simultaneously provide care to patients and dictate notes about their condition).

Privacy risks for both consumers and workers and psychosocial risks for workers go together and stem from the very nature of production in these systems. The way voice-based AI is produced today, requiring massive amounts of data, generates the need for ever-larger masses of recordings at all stages of the production process, with potentially disclosive effects. The models of industrial organization that best serve these technologies, based on subcontracting and platformization, place workers in a position of disadvantage and expose them to the consequences of precarity and low pay. Every country in which a voice-activated device is sold needs an internal supply of workers for audio data production and verification—a need that is going to grow, rather than diminish, as these technologies spread worldwide. At the same time, whenever linguistic factors allow recruitment of workers in lower-income countries, the production chains extend across borders to (for example) Madagascar from France. In these cases, competition among workers from multiple sites brings remunerations further down, and deterritorialization disconnects workers from the very purposes of their activities. As data crosses national boundaries, working conditions deteriorate and risks of leakages increase. Thus, any solution must be dual—protecting workers to protect consumers.

References

Amazon. n.d. "Alexa and Alexa Device FAQs." Accessed September 10, 2021. https://www.amazon.com/gp/help/customer/display.html?nodeId=201602230.

Aytes, Ayhan. 2012. "Return of the Crowds: Mechanical Turk and Neoliberal States of Exception." In *Digital Labor: The Internet as Playground and Factory*, edited by Trebor Scholtz, 79–97. New York: Routledge.

Bayhan, Rabia. 2019. "Get Paid to Read Out Loud—Audio Recording Jobs." Clickworker, October 16. https://www.clickworker.com/2019/10/16/get-paid-to-read-out-loud-audio-recording-jobs/.

Carr, Austin, Matt Day, Sarah Frier, and Mark Gurman. 2019. "Silicon Valley Is Listening to Your Most Intimate Moments." *Bloomberg Businessweek*, December 11.

Casilli, Antonio A. 2017. "Digital Labor Studies Go Global: Toward a Digital Decolonial Turn." *International Journal of Communication* 11: 3934–3954. https://ijoc.org/index.php/ijoc/article/viewFile /6349/2149.

Casilli, Antonio A., and Julián Posada. 2019. "The Platformization of Labor and Society." In *Society and the Internet: How Networks of Information and Communication Are Changing Our Lives*, 2nd. ed., edited by Mark Graham and William H. Dutton, 293–306. Oxford: Oxford University Press.

Casilli, Antonio A., Paola Tubaro, Clément Le Ludec, Marion Coville, Maxime Besenval, Touhfat Mouhtare, and Elinor Wahal. 2019. *Le Micro-travail en France. Derrière l'automatisation, de nouvelles précarités au travail?* [Micro-work in France. Behind Automation, New Forms of Precarious Labor?]. Final Report of the DiPLab (Digital Platform Labor) Project. http://diplab.eu/wp-content/uploads /2019/05/Le-Micro-Travail-En-France_DiPLab-2019.pdf.

Chen, Brian X., and Cade Metz. 2019. "Google's Duplex Uses A.I. to Mimic Humans (Sometimes)." *New York Times*, May 22.

Coucke, Alice, Mohammed Chlieh, Thibault Gisselbrecht, David Leroy, Mathieu Poumeyrol, and Thibaut Lavril. 2019. "Efficient Keyword Spotting Using Dilated Convolutions and Gating." *ICASSP 2019—2019 IEEE International Conference on Acoustics, Speech, & Signal Processing*, 6351–6355. https://doi.org/10.1109/ICASSP.2019.8683474.

Couldry, Nick, and Ulises Ali Mejias. 2019. *The Costs of Connection: How Data Is Colonizing Human Life and Appropriating It for Capitalism*. Stanford, CA: Stanford University Press.

Cox, Joseph. 2019. "Revealed: Microsoft Contractors Are Listening to Some Skype Calls." *Vice*, August 7. https://www.vice.com/en/article/xweqbq/microsoft-contractors-listen-to-skype-calls.

Day, Matt, Giles Turner, and Natalia Drozdiak. 2019. "Amazon Workers Are Listening to What You Tell Alexa." *Bloomberg*, April 10.

Duguépéroux, Joris, and Tristan Allard. 2020. "From Task Tuning to Task Assignment in Privacy-Preserving Crowdsourcing Platforms." In *Transactions on Large-Scale Data- and Knowledge-Centered Systems XLIV*, edited by A. Hameurlain, A. M. Tjoa, P. Lamarre, and K. Zeitouni, 67–107. Berlin/ Heidelberg: Springer.

Ekbia, Hamid R., Bonnie Nardi, and Selma Šabanović. 2015. "On the Margins of the Machine: Hetcromation and Robotics." *iConference 2015 Proceedings*. https://www.ideals.illinois.edu/handle /2142/73678.

Frier, Sarah. 2019. "Facebook Paid Contractors to Transcribe Users' Audio Chats." *Bloomberg*, August 13.

Fuchs, Christian. 2016. "Digital Labor and Imperialism." *Monthly Review* 67 (8): 14–24. https:// monthlyreview.org/2016/01/01/digital-labor-and-imperialism/.

Graham, Mark, Isis Hjorth, and Vili Lehdonvirta. 2017. "Digital Labour and Development: Impacts of Global Digital Labour Platforms and the Gig Economy on Worker Livelihoods." *Transfer: European Review of Labour and Research* 23 (2): 135–162. https://doi.org/10.1177/1024258916687250.

Hern, Alex. 2019. "Apple Contractors 'Regularly Hear Confidential Details' on Siri Recordings." *The Guardian*, July 26. https://www.theguardian.com/technology/2019/jul/26/apple-contractors -regularly-hear-confidential-details-on-siri-recordings.

Irani, Lilly. 2015. "Difference and Dependence among Digital Workers: The Case of Amazon Mechanical Turk." *South Atlantic Quarterly* 114 (1): 225–234.

Kelley, J. F. 1983. "An Empirical Methodology for Writing User-Friendly Natural Language Computer Applications." In *CHI '83: Proceedings of the SIGCHI Conference on Human Factors in Computing Systems*, 193–196. New York: Association for Computing Machinery.

Leroy, David, Alice Coucke, Thibaut Lavril, Thibault Gisselbrecht, and Joseph Dureau. 2019. "Federated Learning for Keyword Spotting." *ICASSP 2019—2019 IEEE International Conference on Acoustics, Speech, & Signal Processing*, 6341–6345.

Martinez, Michael, and Lori Cameron. n.d. "Voice Technology: As Google Duplex Wows and Scares, a Post-screen World Emerges with Questions That the Smart Speakers Cannot Answer." IEEE Computer Society. Accessed September 10, 2021. https://www.computer.org/publications /tech-news/trends/voice-assistants-technology-smart-speakers.

Schmidt, Florian A. 2019. "Crowdsourced Production of AI Training Data: How Human Workers Teach Self-Driving Cars How to See." Working Paper Forschungsförderung no. 155, August. Düsseldorf: Hans-Böckler-Stiftung. https://www.boeckler.de/pdf/p_fofoe_WP_155_2019.pdf.

Tubaro, Paola, Antonio A. Casilli, and Marion Coville. 2020. "The Trainer, the Verifier, the Imitator: Three Ways in Which Human Platform Workers Support Artificial Intelligence." *Big Data & Society* 7(1). https://doi.org/10.1177/2053951720919776.

Verheyden, Tim, Denny Baert, Lente Van Hee, and Ruben Van Den Heuvel. 2019. "Hey Google, Are You Listening?" *VRT NWS*, July 10. https://www.vrt.be/vrtnws/en/2019/07/10/google-employees-are -eavesdropping-even-in-flemish-living-rooms/.

11   The Proletarianization of Data Science

James Steinhoff

Pick up any business-oriented publication today, and you are likely to find at least one article vaunting the economic potential of data science and artificial intelligence (AI). For instance, analysts from consulting firm PwC expect AI to increase global gross domestic product up to $15.7 trillion by 2030 and reckon it as the "biggest commercial opportunity in today's fast changing economy" (Rao and Verweij 2017). Big technology firms such as Google and Amazon, as well as a host of smaller companies, are aiming to seize this opportunity by producing AI commodities for consumers (e.g., smart speakers) and for businesses (e.g., face and object recognition software). The economic opportunity presented by AI is, however, contingent on the labor of data science workers who possess the relatively rare skills to develop said technology.

Data science workers are celebrated for their desirable working conditions and posh benefits. Data scientist has been touted as the "sexiest job of the 21st century" (Davenport and Patil 2012), and it was rated the best job in the world, based on wage, satisfaction, and number of openings, by employment site Glassdoor (Columbus 2019). Data science work is also cited as the planetary future of employment, projected to both revitalize the deindustrializing Global North and boost the Global South into the digital era (Microsoft 2018). As the bright future of the digital economy, it is contrasted both with submission to the algorithmic management of Uber-like platforms and tedious "ghost work," or digital piecework on platforms such as Amazon Mechanical Turk (Gray and Suri 2019).

This chapter shows that the data science labor force, while globally distributed, is predominantly tied to powerful firms concentrated in specific locales. In particular, I argue that the planetary data science labor force is increasingly created *by* and *for* powerful technology capital in the United States of America. The increasing efforts of large technology firms to produce their own bespoke labor force has implications for digital labor in general.

From the perspective of capital, data science labor power is a scarce commodity to be competed for. Around the world, efforts are thus being made to proletarianize data science labor power, to increase its supply and decrease its value, while capturing a competitive share of it. Even the sexiest kinds of work are, for capital, wage expenditures to be minimized. Wider distribution of the skills to perform currently rewarding and well-remunerated digital labor is often positioned as a way to close the economic gap between the Global North and South, but the distribution of such skills is accompanied by their simplification and consequent devaluation. While the proletarianization of data science labor power may make more data science jobs available outside the Global North, it will do so only insofar as it reduces labor costs for big technology firms. Rather than the elevation of less privileged laborers to the Silicon Valley stratum, the proletarianization of data science labor power suggests the coming degradation of a privileged type of labor to the status of precarious and poorly remunerated ghost work.

This chapter begins by introducing the concept of labor power. I then outline data science work in the context of the AI industry, which is concentrated foremost in the United States and China. Next, I discuss how governments around the world are attempting to increase local supplies of data science labor power by adopting national AI strategies. Then, I show that US tech firms, unsatisfied with national efforts, now operate their own private education programs in an effort to generate suitable stocks of labor power distributed across national boundaries. I also discuss efforts to automate data science work and show how firms are motivated to pursue such forms of automation by the shortage of data science labor power. I conclude by considering how the proletarianization of data science labor power could combine with the mediation of digital platforms to transform data science work into something resembling ghost work.

The Special Commodity of Labor Power

Capitalism is defined by the production of commodities: products and services intended for profitable sale. However, the production of commodities requires the prior purchase of other commodities, including materials, tools, and the ability of someone to work. Karl Marx ([1867] 1990, 270) referred to this ability to work as labor power and emphasized that it is a "special commodity." It is what is exchanged for when someone is paid for work. This exchange is unequal because labor power is unique among commodities insofar as it can produce more value than is paid for it. But Marx's theory of value is not of interest here. The relevant point is that capitalism depends on there being people who need to sell their labor power. Capitalism is incompatible with a society in which large portions of the population can meet their own survival needs autonomously. Capital thus has an impetus to make people dependent on earning a wage.

Marxists call the process of rendering people dependent on a wage proletarianization. Marx describes it as "when great masses of men are suddenly and forcibly torn from their means of subsistence, and hurled onto the labour market as free, unprotected and rightless proletarians" ([1867] 1990, 876). Examples of this include the enclosure of common land beginning in the thirteenth century in England and the appropriation of peasant lands in China since the 1990s (Zhang 2014). In both cases, stripped of the possibility of self-subsistence, great new chunks of the population were forced to sell their labor power for a wage.

Developed capitalist economies do not simply leave the availability of the special commodity labor power to chance: "Capital itself regulates [the] production of labor power, the production of the mass of men it intends to exploit in accordance with its own needs. Hence capital not only produces capital, it produces a growing mass of men, the material through which alone it can function as additional capital. . . . [C]apital produces on a steadily increasing scale the productive wage-labourers it requires" (Marx [1867] 1990, 1061). Proletarianization thus occurs wherever new markets emerge (McNally 1993, 31).

Capital can also create new proletarians by "extending its rule to sections of the population not previously subject to itself, such as women or children" (Marx [1867] 1990, 1061). Here capital does not create new proletarians by dispossessing those with access to the means of subsistence. Instead, women and children, who depend on the wage of an already proletarianized man, are compelled to sell their labor power as well. This hints at the diversity of ways in which capital can create new supplies of labor power. This chapter focuses on a scenario in which capital requires labor power possessing a rare, technical, and highly profitable skill set. These are data science workers. Their proletarianization proceeds by different means.

Data Science Work

Roles in the nascent field of data science have yet to settle into rigid categories. So rather than try to draw hard lines between data scientists, data engineers, and machine learning scientists, for example, I follow Muller et al. (2019, 126) and employ the general term *data science worker*.[1]

Data science work occupies a position near the apex of hype around the so-called "Fourth Industrial Revolution" (Schwab 2016). Data science draws on statistics, computer science, and mathematics to perform operations of "data collection, data engineering, data analytics and data architecture" (Getoor et al. 2016). Data science is usually, but not necessarily, associated with "big" data, defined in terms of high velocity, variety, and volume (Zikopoulos and Eaton 2011). One notable component of data science is machine learning, a subfield of AI based on statistical pattern recognition in large data-sets. Machine learning involves "extract[ing] patterns from data" (Kaplan 2016, 27) and automatically constructing an algorithm, called a model, from those patterns that can be used to analyze or make predictions on new data (Alpaydin 2014, 2–3). The automatic production of a model from data is the source of much excitement for machine learning and data science.

Data science work is appearing in all sectors of the economy as businesses strive to incorporate data-driven analysis and decision making into their operations. However, this chapter focuses specifically on the data science workers involved in the production of machine learning systems. As such, its context is the AI industry, a subset of the larger technology industry.

In 2017, both Google and Microsoft declared themselves "AI first," and the rest of the tech industry followed (Agrawal, Gans, and Goldfarb 2018). Today's AI industry is global, but it is concentrated in the Global North and China. One study of governmental AI "readiness" concludes that "countries in the Global North are better placed to take advantage of these gains [produced by AI] than those in the Global South" (Miller and Stirling 2019, 5). However, China is second only to the US in AI stature, and all of the biggest AI companies are from either the United States (Google, Apple, Microsoft, Amazon, Facebook, Intel, and IBM) or China (Baidu, Alibaba, and Tencent). Smaller AI companies are also concentrated in these two countries. The *China AI Development Report 2018* shows that the US leads the AI start-up tally at 2,028 companies, China takes second place with 1,011, and the United Kingdom and Canada come in third and fourth with 392 and 285 companies, respectively (CISTP 2018, 46).

One study, based on LinkedIn data, reports that in 2018 there were 36,524 "self-reported AI specialists" in the world, a 66 percent increase from the previous year (Gagne 2019). According to this data, the majority of AI specialists work in the United States (43 percent), the United Kingdom (9.8 percent), Canada (4.1 percent), France (3.9 percent), and Germany (3.7 percent). However, as the authors point out, LinkedIn is not used uniformly around the world (44 percent of Americans use it, compared to only 3 percent of Chinese), so these figures leave much to be desired. Another analysis (data source unspecified) is provided by the *China AI Development Report, which* puts the global AI talent pool at the end of 2017 at 204,575, with the majority concentrated in the United States (13.9 percent), China (8.9 percent), India (8.5 percent), Germany (4.6 percent), and the United Kingdom (3.9 percent) (CISTP 2018, 34).

The dominance of the United States and China is clear, but the picture becomes more nuanced when one looks at where data science workers are educated and where they end up finding employment. One analysis of "top-tier" AI researchers reports that while 29 percent received their undergraduate degree in China, 20 percent in the United States, 18 percent in Europe, 8 percent in India, 5 percent in Canada, and the rest in the United Kingdom, Iran, Israel and other countries, 59 percent end up working in the United States, 11 percent in China, 10 percent in Europe, 6 percent in Canada, and 4 percent in the United Kingdom (Banerjee and Sheehan 2020). While China is the largest producer of data science workers, the United States ultimately retains most of this labor power.

The lead held by the United States and China in AI is such that several analyses describe them as a duopoly of nearly uncontestable AI "superpowers" (see, for example, Lee 2018). Both countries benefit from large populations of users essential for generating the data necessary for training machine learning models, regulations amenable to business, and wide availability of venture capital. Some analyses argue that if other countries fail to invest aggressively in AI soon, they will fall irrevocably behind as exponential productivity gains, powered by AI, will boost the economies of China and the United States beyond all competition (Cummings et al. 2018, vi). Lee (2018, 169) speculates that not only will AI research remain out of reach for less developed countries, but they will also "lose the one competitive edge that their predecessors used to kick-start development: low-wage factory labor" because the AI superpowers will run automated factories at lower costs. According to such accounts, the current lead on AI research will evolve into a new global economic divide in which whole countries will be rendered surplus to the market. However, there are more optimistic appraisals of the current situation. Analysts from consulting firm PwC suggest that since AI is at a "very early stage of development overall . . . there are therefore opportunities for emerging markets to leapfrog more developed counterparts" (Rao and Verweij 2017, 3). Below, I will discuss how many governments are attempting to do just that.

By all accounts, the AI industry is growing rapidly. The global revenue of the AI industry was around $5 billion in 2015, and by 2019 it had increased to somewhere between $15 billion and $37 billion (Statista 2020). From 2010 to 2018, investment in AI start-ups increased from $1.3 billion to over $40.4 billion (Perrault et al. 2019, 6). The burgeoning number of AI companies creates a large demand for data science labor power, which continues to outpace supply. According to the AI Index (Shoham et al. 2017), AI jobs in the United States grew by 4.5 times between 2013 and 2017. Fresh graduates find themselves in a job seeker's market where companies compete to offer lucrative employment offers (Saphir 2018). A survey by Stack Overflow (2018) puts the global median salary for a data scientist at $60,000, and at $102,000 in the United

States. Salaries can reach into the millions for acclaimed experts (Metz 2018). In general, capital rewards data science workers much better than academia does, resulting in a "brain drain" to industry (Kunze 2019; Perrault et al. 2019, 6).

Despite the enormous demand for data science work, this sector is marked by a "diversity crisis" (Snow 2018; see also West, Whittaker, and Crawford 2019). Only 22 percent of AI professionals in the world are women (Duke 2018), and sexism is rampant in the industry (Vassallo et al. n.d.). Global data about the racial identities of data science workers has yet to be produced, but the demographics of the workforces of the largest US tech companies give an idea of the broader picture. In 2018, at Google, Facebook, Microsoft, and Apple, white people made up around 40–51 percent of the workforce and Asians between 35 and 52 percent, while Latinx, Black, and Native people represented only single digits (Harrison 2019).

Bucking a history of apoliticism (Hyde 2003), tech workers have recently begun mobilizing around issues of gender and race, as well as around the militarization of AI. In 2018, over 20,000 Google employees walked out after the company gave a $90-million severance package to a senior employee after he was fired for sexual assault (Canon 2018). The same year, Google employees forced their employer to drop a contract to develop drone vision technology for the Pentagon (Harwell 2018).

In sum, while their situations are not identical the world over, data science workers occupy a relatively privileged position in the digital economy. One might therefore reasonably describe data science workers, especially the white and Asian men working for large US firms, as a "labor aristocracy" or a group of workers who enjoy a relatively privileged position of power vis-à-vis capital (Fuchs 2014, 229–230). However, processes are underway that aim to undermine such aristocratic privilege, to proletarianize data science labor power by both reducing its scarcity and devaluing its content. The following sections show how this is occurring in three ways: through the deployment of national AI strategies aiming to create and retain skilled data science workers, through the creation of proprietary data science education programs by large tech companies, and through the automation of data science work.

National AI Strategies

Faced with the prospect of USA/China AI hegemony, nearly 20 countries have released national AI strategies since 2017 (Dutton, Barron, and Boskovic 2018). A central component of the global race for AI is data science labor power. While national AI strategies vary in their details, all involve increasing the national supply of data science labor power, along with other objectives such as boosting academic research output and speeding up the commercialization of AI. To achieve these goals, governments are establishing AI institutes in partnership with industry and academia. These institutes provide lucrative positions for experts in AI and data science, and some provide education and training to increase the supply of data science labor power. To take two examples, in 2017 the Canadian government established three AI institutes across the country (Finance Canada 2017), with founding sponsorship from Google, and in 2019 the Brazilian government announced the creation of eight AI research labs and an institute in partnership with IBM (Henriques 2020).

National AI plans also frequently include the allocation of funds to universities to increase their capacities to provide data science education as well as new regulations to streamline immigration processes and the dispensation of work visas. In connection with the 2017 Pan-Canadian Artificial Intelligence Strategy, Canada has adopted high-speed, uncapped pathways to citizenship for foreign students and workers with data science skills (Huang and Arnold 2020).

The proliferation of national AI strategies is significant because it is the "first time that governments around the world have almost simultaneously released national plans to develop the same technology" (Dutton, Barron, and Boskovic 2018, 4). This wave of investment is also distinguished from previous ones in that "AI is seen as strategic technology by many governments" (Walch 2020). This does not mean that AI is being sought solely for military capacities, although this is certainly of interest to some governments.[2] More broadly, the strategic interest in AI is economic.

Competing national AI strategies may aim to draw data science labor power away from US capital, but the US government also has its own plans.

The Trump administration sought to make it harder for highly skilled labor to enter the country. On June 22, 2020, President Trump released an executive order temporarily suspending the H-1B work visa widely used by high-tech workers coming from China, India, and Iran and by foreign students seeking to remain in the United States after completing their studies. The purported motive was to keep jobs for American citizens. The ban was lifted in April 2021, but at the time of writing in 2021, the Biden administration aims to replace the previous lottery system for the H-1B with a system giving preference to workers with the highest previous salaries (Anderson 2021). This will make it harder for students to stay in the country and presumably is intended to increase the supply of experienced, rather than novice, labor power.

However, most analyses argue that the United States is so far from domestically meeting demand for data science labor power that making it harder for foreign students to stay in the country can only undermine its industry (Zwetsloot et al. 2019; Hao 2020).

Proprietary Data Science Education Programs

Amid international AI strategizing, US technology capital is taking the problem of the shortage of data science labor power into its own hands. Big US tech firms are now establishing their own education programs to generate the skilled labor power that they need, without regard for national boundaries or the strictures of post-secondary education.

Amazon has developed AWS [Amazon Web Services] Educate, a free education service that provides "Cloud Career Pathways" in specializations including machine learning, data science, and cloud computing.[3] The service is available for people affiliated with educational institutions partnered with Amazon around the world. Salesforce similarly maintains Trailhead, a globally available gamified education platform for machine learning, coding, and business skills.[4] In mid-2020, Google announced the debut of "Google Career Certificates," for digital jobs including data analyst, UX designer, and IT [information technology] support specialist. These certificates cost a mere $39 per month and can be completed in less than six months of part-time study (Coursera n.d.). Positioning these certificates as a response to the COVID-19 pandemic, Google asserts that "we need new, accessible job-training solutions . . . to help America recover and rebuild" (Walker 2020). In their beneficence, Google also offers need-based scholarships and provides apprenticeship opportunities. The most striking aspect of these certificates is that Google will reportedly treat them as equivalent to a bachelor's degree (Bariso 2020). While currently there is no data science certificate available from Google, already there are a wealth of less prestigious options available on the Internet in the form of data science "boot camps" that typically last between two and six months.

The history of the AI industry contains a precedent for this situation. In the early 1980s, at the height of enthusiasm for expert systems, the first commercialized application of AI, Edward Feigenbaum, perhaps the first AI entrepreneur, developed an applied masters of science in artificial intelligence at Stanford University. The explicit goal of the degree was to "train students in enough AI to get them out pursuing practical applications, but not enough to make them career academics and researchers. It was one more attempt to get this new field out of the ivory tower and into the marketplace" (Roland and Shiman 2002, 196). Today, the AI industry is making a renewed push for this, which will take on a global scope.

Now that Internet access is more widely available across the Global South, US technology firms desire to outsource not only ghost work but also data science work there. Google, Facebook, and Amazon sponsored a Data Science Africa 2018 event in Abuja, Nigeria, where "building world-class capacity" was a central topic (Data Science Nigeria 2019, 25). A recent report on AI in Africa by policy-influencing firm Access Partnership, in conjunction with Microsoft, sums up the perspective of industry: "The private sector has a critical role to play in elevating the skills of African citizens" (Access Partnership 2019, 26). Such efforts frequently draw on the rhetoric of democratization.

Democratization and Automation of Data Science

Since 2017, big US technology firms have announced programs for the so-called democratization of AI and data science. Behind its political trappings and promises to allow "every person" to produce AI (Microsoft News Center 2016), the democratization of AI refers to the diffusion of basic data science skills combined with the proliferation of automated data science tools, such that data science functions can be performed by nonspecialists or "citizen data scientists" (O'Connell 2018).

The automation of work serves the interests of capital in several ways. I will discuss two. By increasing the speed of production and volume of output, automation increases the productivity of labor power. But automation also benefits capital by reducing the value of labor power. Automation allows the same products to be produced with less skill as machines take over certain tasks. In this respect, automation represents a culmination of the division of labor, in which complex labor processes are broken up into their constituent pieces. When a labor process can be "separated into elements some of which are simpler than others and each of which is simpler than the whole . . . the labor power capable of performing the process may be purchased more cheaply as dissociated elements than as a capacity integrated in a single worker" (Braverman 1998, 81). With automation, some pieces can be wholly given over to machines.

Perspectives on automation have changed in recent years. While historically it was assumed that manual labor was subject to automation while cognitive labor was less so, the sophistication of computing technology has led to a new distinction between automatable routine labor, whether manual or cognitive, and nonroutine labor, which is more difficult to automate (Autor, Levy, and Murnane 2003). Although celebratory discourse around data science work, as well as the scarcity of its requisite labor power, might lead one to believe that it is unautomatable, in fact the automation of data science work has been underway since around 2015. Efforts to automate programming, which contains large amounts of routine tasks, go back to the earliest days of computing (Chun 2011) and continue today, with boosted incentives from the shortage of skilled data science workers (Campbell 2020) and the COVID-19 pandemic (Salisbury 2020).

Data science work is a broad field, but if we consider machine learning in particular, we can schematize the labor process for its production as three stages (Dong 2017). The first stage, data processing, involves collecting, cleaning, labeling, and otherwise preparing data. In the second stage, model building, data is input into a learning algorithm, which produces a machine learning model (itself an algorithm) based on patterns in the data. The third stage is deployment, in which the model is integrated into a business environment. Typically, this is carried out by embedding it into a website or application through a cloud-based application programming interface (API).

Data science work is a new field. Since there is not yet a mature ecosystem, data science workers "generally manage their workflows in ad-hoc ways" (Toews 2020), and overall, there "isn't a codified set of strategies" for machine learning (Theuwissen 2015, 13). This leads some to describe it as an art (McClure 2018). The incipience of data science has not, however, prevented its automation. Parts of all three stages of the machine learning labor process are being automated with a technology called automated machine learning (AutoML).

AutoML tools being developed by tech giants include Google Cloud AutoML, Microsoft Azure Automated ML, and Amazon SageMaker. In general, AutoML works by recursively applying the capacity of machine learning for the extraction of patterns from large datasets to the production of machine learning models. For instance, deciding on the precise architecture for a neural network is a time-consuming task, which requires trial-and-error based adaptation to each particular case. AutoML can be used to automatically generate and compare thousands of candidate architectures and can produce outputs that exceed the performance of handcrafted architectures (Zoph et al. 2017). One review of AutoML techniques reports that a team of three data scientists worked for weeks to produce a machine learning model for a predictive maintenance application, but only months later, an AutoML tool was used to automatically produce, from the same dataset, a better performing model (Tuggener et al. 2019, 2). Another survey of AutoML techniques concludes that currently available options enable one to build "reasonably well performing ML pipelines without knowledge about ML or statistics" and enable skilled data scientists to "profit from the automation of tedious manual tasks," even if approaches that aim to automate not just one task but the whole process are "still very basic and are not able to beat human experts yet" (Zöller and Huber 2021, 448).

Regardless, AutoML presents the prospect of devaluing expensive data science labor power by making the ability to produce machine learning models available to novices. While prediction of the future is not the intent of this chapter, it seems safe to agree that if AutoML is "truly able to automate the data science workflow, [it] may be instrumental in bridging the gap between the high demand and low supply of data scientists" (Wang et al. 2019, 211).

Conclusion

A global competition for scarce data science labor power is underway. While many countries are deploying national plans to boost AI and data science capacities, they must face off with big technology firms in the United States, which have developed proprietary data science education programs and tools for the automation of data science work. I have argued that these phenomena can be interpreted as parts of a process of proletarianization whereby capital seeks to generate an abundant and cheap supply of the scarce but highly profitable commodity of data science labor power. Education programs will increase overall supply, while AutoML will lower skill requirements for some data science tasks. Both will contribute to the devaluation of data science labor power.

AutoML may also, by fragmenting the data science labor process into automatable and nonautomatable components, render data science work increasingly amenable to outsourcing via digital platforms such as Amazon Mechanical Turk. Today's data science jobs could be broken up into piecework tasks performed by workers wherever ghost work wages constitute sufficient incentive. This will likely provide jobs for the Global South but not only there. Substantial ghost work contributions come from India but also from the United States and Europe (Berg et al. 2018). Regardless, the aristocratic status of data science workers at large US tech firms will be diminished by the emergence of a globally distributed pool of devalued data science labor power.

In the wake of the 2020 COVID-19 pandemic and concurrent recession, the business incentive to economize on labor costs will be exacerbated (Blit 2020). High-skill jobs are not immune from transformation into something like ghost work, and techniques of digital proletarianization, outlined here in the context of data science work, are likely to play an important role in the future of work in the planetary market.

Notes

1. *Data science worker*, as I use the term here, does *not* refer to ghost workers, who do perform operations essential to data science, such as data labeling.

2. As Haner and Garcia (2019, 331) point out, autonomous weapons research is "advancing rapidly and without sufficient public debate or accountability."

3. See https://aws.amazon.com/education/awseducate/.

4. See https://trailhead.salesforce.com/.

References

Access Partnership. 2019. *Artificial Intelligence for Africa: An Opportunity for Growth, Development, and Democratisation*. Nairobi: Microsoft Policy Innovation Centre, Strathmore University. https://pic.strathmore.edu/wp-content/uploads/2019/03/PIC_AI_for_Africa_Whitepaper.pdf.

Agrawal, Ajay, Joshua Gans, and Avi Goldfarb. 2018. "Companies Are Suddenly Declaring Themselves 'AI First.' Why It's a Problem for Their Current Customers." LinkedIn *Weekend Essay*, April 27. https://www.linkedin.com/pulse/companies-suddenly-declaring-themselves-ai-first-why-its-joshua-gans/.

Alpaydin, Ethem. 2014. *Introduction to Machine Learning*. Cambridge, MA: MIT Press.

Anderson, Stuart. 2021. "Biden Administration Defends Trump H-1B Visa Rule." *Forbes*, July 27. https://www.forbes.com/sites/stuartanderson/2021/07/27/biden-administration-defends-trump-h-1b-visa-rule/?sh=2b72f1321602.

Autor, David H., Frank Levy, and Richard J. Murnane. 2003. "The Skill Content of Recent Technological Change: An Empirical Exploration." *Quarterly Journal of Economics* 118 (4): 1279–1333.

Banerjee, Ishan, and Matt Sheeran. 2020. "America's Got AI Talent: US' Big Lead in AI Research Is Built on Importing Researchers." *Macro Polo*, June 9. https://macropolo.org/americas-got-ai-talent-us-big-lead-in-ai-research-is-built-on-importing-researchers/?rp=m.

Bariso, Justin. 2020. "Google Has a Plan to Disrupt the College Degree." *Inc.*, August 19. https://www.inc.com/justin-bariso/google-plan-disrupt-college-degree-university-higher-education-certificate-project-management-data-analyst.html.

Berg, Janine, Marianne Furrer, Ellie Harmon, Uma Rani, and M. Six Silberman. 2018. *Digital Labour Platforms and the Future of Work: Towards Decent Work in the Online World*. Geneva: International Labour Organization. www.ilo.org/wcmsp5/groups/public/---dgreports/---dcomm/---publ/documents/publication/wcms_645337.pdf.

Blit, Joel. 2020. "Automation and Reallocation: Will COVID-19 Usher in the Future of Work?" *Canadian Public Policy* 46 (S2): S192–S202.

Braverman, Harry. 1998. *Labor and Monopoly Capital: The Degradation of Work in the Twentieth Century*. New York: New York University Press.

Campbell, Mark. 2020. "Automated Coding: The Quest to Develop Programs that Develop Programs." *Computer* 53 (2): 80–82.

Canon, Gabrielle. 2018. "Google Gave Top Executive $90m Payoff but Kept Sexual Misconduct Claim Quiet—Report." *The Guardian*, October 25. https://www.theguardian.com/technology/2018/oct/25/google-andy-rubin-android-creator-payoff-sexual-misconduct-report.

CISTP. 2018. *China AI Development Report 2018*. Beijing: China Institute for Science and Technology Policy at Tsinghua University. http://www.sppm.tsinghua.edu.cn/eWebEditor/UploadFile/China_AI_development_report_2018.pdf.

Chun, Wendy Hui Kyong. 2011. *Programmed Visions: Software and Memory.* Cambridge, MA: MIT Press.

Columbus, Louis. 2019. "Data Scientist Leads 50 Best Jobs in America for 2019, According to Glassdoor." *Forbes*, January 23. https://www.forbes.com/sites/louiscolumbus/2019/01/23/data-sci entist-leads-50-best-jobs-in-america-for-2019-according-to-glassdoor/#12abe5667474.

Coursera. n.d. "Google IT Support Professional Certificate." Accessed September 10, 2021. https:// www.coursera.org/professional-certificates/google-it-support?action=enroll.

Cummings, M. L., Heather M. Roff, Kenneth Cukier, Jacob Parakilas, and Hannah Bryce. 2018. *Artificial Intelligence and International Affairs: Disruption Anticipated.* London: Chatham House. https://www.chathamhouse.org/sites/default/files/publications/research/2018-06-14-artificial -intelligence-international-affairs-cummings-roff-cukier-parakilas-bryce.pdf.

Data Science Nigeria. 2019. *Annual Report July 2018–June 2019: Building One Million AI Talents in 10 Years.* Lagos: Data Science Nigeria. https://www.datasciencenigeria.org/wp-content/uploads /2019/08/annual-report-final.pdf.

Davenport, Thomas H., and D. J. Patil. 2012. "Data Scientist: The Sexiest Job of the 21st Century." *Harvard Business Review*, October. https://hbr.org/2012/10/data-scientist-the-sexiest-job-of -the-21st-century.

Dong, Catherine. 2017. "The Evolution of Machine Learning." *TechCrunch*, August 8. https:// techcrunch.com/2017/08/08/the-evolution-of-machine-learning/.

Duke, Sue. 2018. "Will AI Make the Gender Gap in the Workplace Harder to Close?" World Economic Forum (website), December 21. https://www.weforum.org/agenda/2018/12/artificial -intelligence-ai-gender-gap-workplace/.

Dutton, Tim, Brent Barron, and Gaga Boskovic. 2018. *Building an AI World: Report on National and Regional AI Strategies.* Toronto: CIFAR. https://cifar.ca/wp-content/uploads/2020/05/buildinganai world_eng.pdf.

Finance Canada. 2017. "Growing Canada's Advantage in Artificial Intelligence." Ottawa: Government of Canada. https://www.canada.ca/en/department-finance/news/2017/03/growing_canada_ sadvantageinartificialintelligence.html.

Fuchs, Christian. 2014. *Digital Labour and Karl Marx.* New York: Routledge.

Gagne, JF. 2019. *Global AI Talent Report 2019.* https://jfgagne.ai/talent-2019/.

Getoor, Lise, David Culler, Eric de Sturler, David Ebert, Mike Franklin, and H. V. Jagadish. 2016. "Computing Research and the Emerging Field of Data Science." *CRA Bulletin*, October 7. https:// cra.org/data-science/.

Gray, Mary L., and Siddharth Suri. 2019. *Ghost Work: How to Stop Silicon Valley from Building a New Global Underclass.* Boston: Houghton Mifflin Harcourt.

Haner, Justin, and Denise Garcia. 2019. "The Artificial Intelligence Arms Race: Trends and World Leaders in Autonomous Weapons Development." *Global Policy* 10 (3): 331–337.

Hao, Karen. 2020. "Trump's Freeze on New Visas Could Threaten US Dominance in AI." *MIT Technology Review*, June 28. https://www.technologyreview.com/2020/06/26/1004520/trump-executive-order-h1b-visa-threatens-us-ai/.

Harrison, Sara. 2019. "Five Years of Tech Diversity Reports—and Little Progress." *Wired*, October 1. https://www.wired.com/story/five-years-tech-diversity-reports-little-progress/.

Harwell, Drew. 2018. "Google to Drop Pentagon AI Contract after Employee Objections to the 'Business of War.'" *Washington Post*, June 1. https://www.washingtonpost.com/news/the-switch/wp/2018/06/01/google-to-drop-pentagon-ai-contract-after-employees-called-it-the-business-of-war/?utm_term=.f27036684980.

Henriques, Bruno. 2020. "Brazil Is Emerging as a World Class AI Innovation Hub." *Venture Beat*, January 12. https://venturebeat.com/2020/01/12/brazil-is-emerging-as-a-world-class-ai-innovation-hub/.

Huang, Tina, and Zachary Arnold. 2020. *Immigration Policy and the Global Competition for AI Talent*. Washington, DC: Center for Security and Emerging Technology. https://cset.georgetown.edu/publication/immigration-policy-and-the-global-competition-for-ai-talent/.

Hyde, Alan. 2003. *Working in Silicon Valley: Economic and Legal Analysis of a High-Velocity Labor Market*. Armonk, NY: ME Sharpe.

Kaplan, Jerry. 2016. *Artificial Intelligence: What Everyone Needs to Know*. Oxford: Oxford University Press.

Kunze, Lars. 2019. "Can We Stop the Academic AI Brain Drain?" *Künstlich Intelligenz* 33: 1–3.

Lee, Kai-Fu. 2018. *AI Superpowers: China, Silicon Valley, and the New World Order*. New York: Houghton Mifflin Harcourt.

Marx, Karl. (1867) 1990. *Capital Volume I*. New York: Penguin.

McClure, Sean. 2018. "GUI-fying the Machine Learning Workflow: Towards Rapid Discovery of Viable Pipelines." *Towards Data Science*, June 25. https://towardsdatascience.com/gui-fying-the-machine-learning-workflow-towards-rapid-discovery-of-viable-pipelines-cab2552c909f.

McNally, David. 1993. *Against the Market: Political Economy, Market Socialism and the Marxist Critique*. London: Verso.

Metz, Cade. 2018. "A.I. Researchers Are Making More than $1 Million, Even at a Nonprofit." *New York Times*, April 19. https://www.nytimes.com/2018/04/19/technology/artificial-intelligence-salaries-openai.html.

Microsoft. 2018. *The Future Computed: Artificial Intelligence and Its Role in Society*. Redmond, WA: Microsoft Corporation.

Microsoft News Center. 2016. "Democratizing AI: For Every Person and Every Organization." *Microsoft Features*, September 26. https://news.microsoft.com/features/democratizing-ai/.

Miller, Hannah, and Richard Stirling. 2019. *Government Artificial Intelligence Readiness Index 2019*. Malvern, UK: Oxford Insights.

Muller, Michael, Ingrid Lange, Dakuo Wang, David Piorkowski, Jason Tsay, Q. Vera Liao, Casey Dugan, and Thomas Erickson. 2019. "How Data Science Workers Work with Data: Discovery, Capture, Curation, Design, Creation." In *Proceedings of the 2019 CHI Conference on Human Factors in Computing Systems*, 1–15. New York: Association for Computing Machinery.

O'Connell, Michael. 2018. "Citizen Data Science and the Democratization of Analytics." *Information Week*, August 28. https://www.informationweek.com/big-data/ai-machine-learning/citizen -data-science-and-the-democratization-of-analytics/a/d-id/1332679.

Perrault, Raymond, Yoav Shoham, Erik Brynjolfsson, Jack Clark, John Etchemendy, Barbara Grosz, Terah Lyons, James Manyika, Saurabh Mishra, and Juan Carlos Niebles. 2019. *The AI Index 2019 Annual Report*. Human-Centered AI Institute. Stanford, CA: Stanford University.

Rao, Anand S., and Gerard Verweij. 2017. "Sizing the Prize: What's the Real Value of AI for Your Business and How Can You Capitalise?" PwC. https://www.pwc.com/gx/en/issues/analytics/assets /pwc-ai-analysis-sizing-the-prize-report.pdf.

Roland, Alex, and Philip Shiman. 2002. *Strategic Computing: DARPA and the Quest for Machine Intelligence, 1983–1993*. Cambridge, MA: MIT Press.

Salisbury, Allison Dulin. 2020. "COVID-19 May Become 'An Automation Forcing Event': Already Vulnerable Look to Reskilling for Path Forward." *Forbes*, May 7. https://www.forbes.com/sites /allisondulinsalisbury/2020/05/07/covid-19-may-become-an-automation-forcing-event-already -vulnerable-workers-look-to-reskilling-for-path-forward/.

Saphir, Ann. 2018. "As Companies Embrace AI, It's a Job-Seekers Market." Reuters, October 15. https://www.reuters.com/article/us-usa-economy-artificialintelligence/as-companies-embrace-ai -its-a-job-seekers-market-idUSKCN1MP10D.

Schwab, Klaus. 2016. *The Fourth Industrial Revolution*. New York: Crown Business.

Shoham, Yoav, Raymond Perrault, Erik Brynjolfsson, Jack Clark, and Calvin LeGassick. *The AI Index 2017 Annual Report*. Human-Centered AI Institute. Stanford, CA: Stanford University. https://hai.stanford.edu/ai-index-2017.

Snow, Jackie. 2018. "'We're in a Diversity Crisis': Cofounder of Black in AI on What's Poisoning Algorithms in Our Lives." *MIT Technology Review*, February 14. https://www.technologyreview .com/2018/02/14/145462/were-in-a-diversity-crisis-black-in-ais-founder-on-whats-poisoning-the -algorithms-in-our/.

Stack Overflow. 2018. *Developer Survey Results 2018*. London: Stack Overflow. https://insights .stackoverflow.com/survey/2018/#overview.

Statista. 2020. "Market Size and Revenue Comparison for Artificial Intelligence Worldwide from 2015 to 2025." Accessed November 30, 2020. https://www-statista-com.proxy1.lib.uwo.ca /statistics/941835/artificial-intelligence-market-size-revenue-comparisons/.

Theuwissen, Martijn. 2015. The Different Data Science Roles in the Industry. KDnuggets, November. https://www.kdnuggets.com/2015/11/different-data-science-roles-industry.html.

Toews, Rob. 2020. "A Massive Opportunity Exists to Build 'Picks and Shovels' for Machine Learning." *Forbes*, March 22. https://www.forbes.com/sites/robtoews/2020/03/22/a-massive-opportunity-exists-to-build-picks-and-shovels-for-machine-learning/#6b3f036a7ab3.

Tuggener, Lukas, Mohammadreza Amirian, Katharina Rombach, Stefan Lörwald, Anastasia Varlet, Christian Westermann, and Thilo Stadelmann. 2019. "Automated Machine Learning in Practice: State of the Art and Recent Results." In *Proceedings of the 2019 6th Swiss Conference on Data Science*, 31–36. Bern, Switzerland: IEEE.

Vassallo, Trae, Ellen Levy, Michele Madansky, Hillary Mickell, Bennett Porter, Monica Leas, and Julie Oberweis. n.d. "Elephant in the Valley." Accessed August 18, 2021. https://www.elephantinthevalley.com/.

Walch, Kathleen. 2020. "Why the Race for AI Dominance Is More Global Than You Think." *Forbes*, February 9. https://www.forbes.com/sites/cognitiveworld/2020/02/09/why-the-race-for-ai-dominance-is-more-global-than-you-think/.

Walker, Kent. 2020. "A Digital Jobs Program to Help with America's Economic Recovery." *Grow with Google* (blog), July 13. https://blog.google/outreach-initiatives/grow-with-google/digital-jobs-program-help-americas-economic-recovery/.

Wang, Dakuo, Justin D. Weisz, Michael Muller, Parikshit Ram, Werner Geyer, Casey Dugan, Yla Tausczik, Horst Samulowitz, and Alexander Gray. 2019. "Human-AI Collaboration in Data Science: Exploring Data Scientists' Perceptions of Automated AI." In *Proceedings of the ACM on Human-Computer Interaction* 3, Issue CSCW: 1–24.

West, Sarah Myers, Meredith Whittaker, and Kate Crawford. 2019. "Discriminating Systems: Gender, Race, and Power in AI." New York: AI Now Institute, New York University. https://ainowinstitute.org/discriminatingsystems.html.

Zhang, Yulin. 2015. "Land Grabs in Contemporary China." *Nao's Blog*, January 6. Translated by Pancho Sanchez. https://libcom.org/blog/china-land-grabs.

Zikopoulos, Paul, and Chris Eaton. 2011. *Understanding Big Data: Analytics for Enterprise Class Hadoop and Streaming Data*. New York: McGraw-Hill Osborne Media.

Zöller, Marc-André, and Marco F. Huber. 2021. "Benchmark and Survey of Automated Machine Learning Frameworks." *Journal of Artificial Intelligence Research* 70: 409–472. https://doi.org/10.1613/jair.1.11854.

Zoph, Barret, Vijay Vasudevan, Jonathon Shlens, and Quoc Le. 2017. "AutoML for Large Scale Image Classification and Object Detection." Google AI Blog, November 2. https://ai.googleblog.com/2017/11/automl-for-large-scale-image.html.

Zwetsloot, Remco, James Dunham, Zachary Arnold, and Tina Huang. 2019. *Keeping Top AI Talent in the United States: Findings and Policy Options for International Graduate Student Retention*. Washington, DC: Center for Security and Emerging Technology. https://cset.georgetown.edu/wp-content/uploads/Keeping-Top-AI-Talent-in-the-United-States.pdf.

III Dissecting Planetary Networks

12   Organizing in (and against) a New Cold War: The Case of 996.ICU

JS Tan and Moira Weigel

At least since John Perry Barlow (1996) published his famous "Declaration of the Independence of Cyberspace" from the meeting of the World Economic Forum at Davos in 1996, cyberutopians have celebrated the power of digital technologies to transcend national borders. From the PayPal founders, who claimed that fintech would free individuals from state currency controls (Jackson 2004), to Facebook and Twitter executives who touted the role of social media in precipitating the Arab Spring (see Reuters 2012; Roberts 2017), prominent figures within the US tech industry have for a long time articulated a vision in which globalization and digitization dovetail, freeing individuals anywhere and everywhere to create, communicate, and compete on their own terms. Now, many signs point away from such universalism—or imperialism—and toward a more bordered Internet. These include the theater of the escalating US-China trade war and new regulations and demands for data sovereignty in the EU, South Asia, and Latin America. Yet even amid pushes for "cybersovereignty" (*wangluo zhuquan*) and attendant calls for "decoupling" of national tech industries, both the labor and capital that drive those industries remain global. Western politicians pushing for sanctions against China have tended to focus on the globalization of manufacturing and physical supply chains. But software engineering and other forms of knowledge work that drive planetary-scale technology industries remain highly dispersed, and entangled, as well.

In recent years, a growing body of research has examined the globalization of such labor and the formation of entrepreneurial subjects outside the US (Pham 2015; Amrute 2016; Chumley 2016; Irani 2019; Lindtner 2020; Wang 2020), as well as the far-flung geographies of content moderation (Tufekci 2017; Roberts 2019) and of the "ghost work" that powers much of what is sold as artificial intelligence (Ekbia and Nardi 2017; Taylor 2018; Gray and Suri 2019). Much of this work either implicitly or explicitly critiques the concepts of "cognitive" or "immaterial labor" developed by Maurizio Lazzarato (1996, 2004), Bifo Berardi (2009), Michael Hardt and Antonio Negri (2001, 2005), Tiziana Terranova (2004), and others in the Italian autonomist tradition, as well as Gilles Deleuze (1992).

While these studies accept the premise that post-Fordist capitalism commodified communicative and symbolic activities in novel ways, they reject the idea that such activities are essentially different or indeed separable from manual labor. Furthermore, several of these authors directly contest the suggestion that knowledge work can be detached from the bodies of the people who perform it or the geographies where it takes place.[1]

In this chapter, we will take up a series of distinct but related questions.[2] If research has revealed that contemporary labor is structured in ways that belie imaginaries of post-racial and post-national equality, history also demonstrates that imaginaries of equality play an important role in bringing workers together around common causes. Can workers in global technology industries organize across racial differences and national boundaries? Can they do so in the absence of shared imaginaries? If so, how?

In order to explore these questions, we will focus on an unprecedented labor action initiated by programmers in China in 2019: the anti-996, or 996.ICU movement. While it was focused primarily on changing work culture at Chinese tech firms, as we shall discuss, the 996.ICU movement expanded to include communication and coordination with tech workers in the US as well. Readers of this volume may have encountered the activities of the Tech Workers Coalition (TWC), a group founded in the Bay Area in 2014 that now comprises a network of thousands of participants both in the US and in international chapters in India, the UK, the Netherlands, Ireland, Italy, Canada, and Germany. Volunteers with TWC came to support the 996.ICU movement, and we will return to the TWC origin story in what follows as a point of comparison. However, in addition to connections between the US-based tech worker movement and the 996.ICU movement, our analysis highlights significant *differences* in how participants in these two movements have described and organized themselves.

While both TWC and 996.ICU organizers make strong appeals to notions of worker identity, we find that they conceptualize that identity differently. TWC has elaborated an expansive, or universalizing, notion of the tech worker that includes anyone who works for a technology company. By contrast, the 996.ICU organizers address a specific, bounded class of professional programmers. This case study thus brings into focus how cooperation might take place even among movements that develop different understandings of, and approaches to organizing, tech sector work. Cooperation around 996.ICU was especially striking because it took place across the "Great Firewall,"[3] in the context of an increasingly belligerent "New Cold War" between China and the US in which politicians and business leaders alike often describe data-driven technologies as the single most important front. In this context, organizers were able to collaborate not because they shared a precise sense of their own identities but because they worked with a common set of tools. Specifically, they took advantage of a platform that remains essential to software development in both countries: GitHub.

996.ICU

In November 2018, in response to revelations of sexual harassment in the company, over 20,000 employees walked out of Google offices worldwide. Five months later, the largest-ever tech worker mobilization in terms of online engagement swept the Internet. Unlike the Google walkout, this viral mobilization, known as the 996.ICU campaign, took place in China. While these two events were apparently unconnected, both highlighted and protested more or less open secrets about the conditions of white-collar tech work. Named after the brutal system of working 9:00 a.m. to 9:00 p.m., six days a week (the 996 *gong-zuozhi*), the 996.ICU campaign opposed the 72-hour workweeks that many Chinese tech companies require and sparked a nationwide conversation about white-collar working conditions. The campaign's website explains the origin of the name: working 996 hours is a health risk and will put employees in the intensive care unit (ICU). Despite taking place among Chinese tech workers, the 996.ICU campaign was organized, built, and published entirely on popular US-based web services, most notably the Microsoft-owned code hosting and sharing platform GitHub (figure 12.1) and the team messaging service Slack.

The 996.ICU campaign was run by anonymous employees in the tech sector who hid their identities in fear of retaliation from their employers and the Chinese government. (In the past, Chinese labor organizers and civic activists have dealt with

Figure 12.1
Screenshot of 996.ICU channel on GitHub.
Source: 996icu 2019a.

retaliation at all scales—from having their social media accounts shut down to getting "disappeared" by Chinese authorities.) The campaign started when these employees created the 996.ICU project on GitHub, the largest and most popular code-sharing and collaboration platform in the world. GitHub gives coders a way to save their codebases, share them with collaborators, and provide feedback to each other. The platform also includes a social component, allowing its users to view which projects are currently trending. Today, most major tech companies use GitHub to share new open-source projects and to foster community engagement. In the spirit of open-source code, many projects on GitHub are hosted publicly, meaning that anyone (even those without GitHub accounts) can view the contents of a project.

The 996.ICU campaign used GitHub to showcase a few of its key parts (996icu 2019a). First was the crowdsourced creation of a blacklist of tech companies who forced their employees to work overtime and a whitelist of those who did not. The idea was to shame blacklisted companies into dropping their culture of overwork. Second was the promotion of a newly created "anti-996 software" license, which would bind companies who use anti-996 software to "laws, regulations, rules and standards of the jurisdiction relating to labor and employment" of the country where the company is located (996icu 2019b). In China, this would subject companies to adhere to Article 36 of China's labor law, which states: "Laborers shall work for no more than eight hours a day and no more than 44 hours a week on average" (NPC 1994). Third was a forum-like section (on the campaign's GitHub "Issues" page) where tech workers who supported the campaign discussed their work hours and shared workplace frustrations with each other.

This forum soon became an important space for Chinese tech workers to openly discuss their working conditions and collectively express frustration about the 996 schedule, which for a long time had been an accepted facet of working in the tech sector. A widely read post garnering over a thousand comments had previously appeared on Zhihu (a question-and-answer website similar to the US-based Quora) about Alibaba's DingTalk (*Dingding*), a tool employers could use to more closely monitor employee attendance in the office. One comment criticized DingTalk for allowing bosses to feel like "company emperors" (*gongsi huangdi*) (Yang 2018). Another comment ridiculed employers using DingTalk as "rubbish companies" (*laji gongsi*) for allowing bosses to surveil workers, the poster sarcastically adding that the only thing the software was missing was a direct way for bosses to eavesdrop on employees (Dugu 2017). However, the 996.ICU campaign's use of GitHub represents the first time that a tech worker campaign reached this scale and the first time that it did so on a global platform.

In addition to their work on GitHub, the 996.ICU campaign organizers also ran a Slack workspace for dedicated supporters to convene privately and, for the most part, anonymously. During the campaign, the workspace quickly grew to over 2,000 members, who created different channels to discuss various aspects of the public campaign, share legal resources, and plan other related actions. In contrast to the public GitHub project, which served primarily as the public location of the 996.ICU campaign to post resources and updates, the Slack workspace gave Chinese programmers a private space to congregate and strategize about how to push the campaign forward. In the span of a few weeks after it was created on March 26, 2019, the 996.ICU project on GitHub was bookmarked over 200,000 times, making it the second most bookmarked project ever to exist on the code-sharing platform (GitHub n.d.).

The campaign also saturated the Chinese microblogging site Weibo and was widely reported on by major media outlets in China, forcing a nationwide conversation about work-life balance (Anonymous 2020). The *People's Daily*, an official paper of the Chinese Communist Party, published several articles commenting on the campaign. One was titled "We Shouldn't Label Employees Who Are Anti-996 'Lazy.'" (Anonymous 2019). A post criticizing 996 working hours, made from the paper's official account on Weibo, attached another story that called for the Ministry of Labor Supervision to intervene (*People's Daily* 2019). Chinese tech executives were cornered into making a public response. Alibaba founder Jack Ma criticized the 996.ICU protesters, saying that working a 996 schedule was in fact a "huge blessing" (Gilchrist 2019). The CEO of Chinese e-commerce giant JD.com, Richard Liu, also denounced the campaign, declaring "slackers are not my brothers" (Horwitz and Goh 2019). According to the GitHub blacklist, Tencent, ByteDance, and Huawei are also among the tech companies in China that mandated a 996 schedule.

The use of GitHub to conduct this campaign was both strategically and symbolically important. One week after the 996.ICU campaign launched, Tencent, Xiaomi, and Alibaba blocked the 996.ICU GitHub project on the browsers they control, describing its contents as "containing illegal information" or "malicious" (Shen 2019). But despite these attempts, these Chinese companies did not have much success in blocking the GitHub-hosted project. To access the project, people could simply use other browsers, such as the Google-built Chrome browser, which has by far the largest market share in China. It turned out that nothing short of blocking GitHub entirely, in the same way that Twitter, Facebook, and Google services have been blocked, would have prevented tech workers from accessing the campaign. However, because GitHub is widely used as critical engineering infrastructure by Chinese tech companies, banning the website in China would have caused a major disruption in the productivity of the Chinese tech sector.

Since the early years of the twenty-first century, tech firms—both inside and outside of China—have reaped the benefits of a culture of open-source software, most of which lives on GitHub. The transfer of AI research in particular has relied on GitHub, with key libraries for developing AI models, such as Google's TensorFlow and Facebook's PyTorch, being open-sourced there. This in turn has created a culture where AI researchers will share their latest implementations of new models on GitHub as well. In other words, banning GitHub would have significantly hurt the Chinese tech industry, striking at an area that the government has identified as particularly important to the advancement of Chinese cybersovereignty, for instance in their "New Generation Artificial Intelligence Development Plan" (China State Council 2017).

Without compromising GitHub's value in China's tech industry, the only way to censor the campaign would have been to force Microsoft to remove the project from GitHub. As news of possible attempts to censor the anti-996 campaign spread internationally, Microsoft employees in the US grew concerned that their company, which has a history of succumbing to Chinese demands in order to access China's massive market,[4] was already being pressured to remove the campaign from GitHub. Preempting any attempt from Microsoft to pull the campaign, these employees created a "support.996.ICU" GitHub project (figure 12.2), demanding that the code-sharing platform remain "uncensored and available to everyone," and invited tech workers around the world to join them in a show of solidarity with the anti-996 struggle. In a matter of

Figure 12.2
Screenshot of support. 996.ICU channel on GitHub.
Source: MSWorkers 2019a.

days, the solidarity project was signed by hundreds of tech workers around the world, including in Spain, Turkey, Singapore, the UK, France, and the US (MSWorkers 2019a).

Seeing global support for their movement, anti-996 tech workers from China started to leave comments in the new support.996.ICU GitHub project, expressing gratitude to the Microsoft employees who created it. One of the original contributors to the anti-996 project collaborated with the Microsoft employees to translate the solidarity statement into Mandarin, which was posted alongside the English statement on the public page. A forum on the solidarity project was also used to discuss differences in tech work between the US and China. Recognizing the rare moment of cross-border solidarity in the tech industry, one Chinese contributor even posted lyrics to "The Internationale," the left-wing anthem first translated from French by the early Chinese Communist Party leader Qu Qiubai in 1923. This act of tech worker solidarity was covered in several English-language online media outlets, including Business Insider, Buzzfeed, and Vice, and the project remains available on GitHub to this day.

"Tech Workers" and "Code Farmers"

While the 996.ICU campaign built connections between Chinese tech workers and their counterparts in the US, a comparison of this movement and its US counterpart, the Tech Workers Coalition (TWC), reveals striking differences. In particular, participants in the 996.ICU movement placed far less emphasis than their TWC counterparts on the concept of the tech worker. Since the mid-2010s, the US tech worker movement has centered on an expansive concept of the tech worker identity. Indeed, the term has always been a provocation. Founded in 2014 by Rachel Melendes, a cafeteria worker who became an organizer of the North American labor union UNITE HERE, and engineer Matt Schaefer, the TWC formulated an argument: that whether they were high-salaried full-time employees (FTEs) or contractors, white collar or blue collar, all the people working at tech firms in the Bay Area had interests in common (Weigel 2017). This novel identity—that all workers at tech firms are by definition tech workers—and the form of solidarity that it attempted to realize, emerged from the exigencies of a particular moment and movement. Melendes cofounded TWC together with software engineer Matt Schaefer in San Francisco in 2014, partly in order to involve Bay Area engineers in a campaign that Melendes was helping to lead, the FairHotel Program. Through Melendes, that campaign enlisted engineers at several large tech firms to pressure their employers not to use hotels that mistreated their staff for industry conferences. The campaign coincided with a wider wave of unionization of blue-collar contract workers at tech campuses in the Bay Area, including at Intel, Cisco, NVIDIA, Agilent, and Yahoo (Weigel 2017).

The identity of the tech worker, as Melendes and TWC formulated it, was self-consciously aspirational. Grounded in a claim about the universality of labor, it attempted strategically to occlude or overcome the significant class differences among the actors involved. The gambit was premised on a fundamental irony: that by recognizing that they were workers like anybody else, the most privileged tech workers would become able to exercise their special power within their firms for common good. For a time, these contradictions remained manageable and generative. In order to manage the tensions within the identity of the tech worker, Melendes and other members of TWC originally appealed not only to the Marxist distinction between labor and capital but also to shared experiences of common locations. Conceptually, this meant stating that everyone working on a tech campus was a tech worker; practically, it involved encouraging in-person interactions between FTEs and contract workers in campus cafeterias or other social spaces nearby. In the wake of Trump's election in 2016, dozens of new members rapidly joined TWC in the Bay Area, and the group engaged in a series of new actions (Weigel 2017). Some of these were aimed at improving conditions of blue-collar labor at tech firms; for instance, volunteers with TWC cooperated with UNITE HERE in their successful effort to unionize Facebook's cafeteria workers. However, other initiatives, such as internal campaigns to pressure tech companies like Google and Microsoft to stop competing for Department of Defense contracts, focused on giving software engineers more say over the content and conditions of their own work (Tarnoff 2020).

This expansive concept of the tech worker did not come up in the 996.ICU movement. The 996.ICU campaign took place amid a longer tradition of worker struggle in China. Since the 2008 global financial crisis, the Chinese workers, primarily in factories in the Pearl River Delta, have protested for more pay, the payment of wage arrears, and better working conditions. Protests are often spontaneous; dozens of wildcat strikes happen each year. After President Xi came to power in 2013, organized labor and labor advocacy became the object of government crackdown. This culminated with the Jasic incident, a labor rights conflict that took place in Shenzhen over the summer of 2018, commencing with a series of public demonstrations and strikes by workers at Jasic, a factory that produces industrial equipment. It culminated with the arrest of the organizers, other workers, and student supporters. Researchers have debated the political significance of these actions—whether second generation migrant workers have more rights and class-consciousness or whether they represent, in Ching Kwan Lee's words, a form of "militancy without radicalization" (2017, 100). In any case, the 996.ICU campaign claims on its GitHub page that it is not a political movement. Even though the 996.ICU campaign sometimes identified employees as "laborers" (*laodongzhe*, which could also be translated as "workers"), participants more commonly referred to themselves as "programmers" or "developers" (*chengxuyuan*), a term that emphasizes technical proficiency and professionalism.

While TWC used the term tech worker malleably to unite employees across class and even professions, the 996.ICU movement remained focused on white-collar workers in the tech sector, even though employers in many other sectors in China force their employees to work overtime. There were good reasons for this narrower focus: both the dominant ideologies of tech work and the class structure of the tech industry in China differ significantly from their counterparts in the US. For decades, scholars have described and theorized a prevalent ideology within Silicon Valley that aligns tech company employees with their bosses and presents their work as essentially different from other forms of waged labor, if it can be seen as work at all (Hayes 1989; Saxenian 1994; Barbrook and Cameron 1996). Indeed, these attitudes have often been characterized as a feature of neoliberalism, broadly speaking (Tokumitsu 2015). This ideology is reflected in specific management practices within the tech industry. Even at big companies, smaller teams tend to conceptualize themselves as start-ups. Entry-level employees are encouraged to think of themselves as CEOs or CTOs of the project they are working on. The suggestion is that after a few years of work experience, employees will be equipped to start their own companies. The tech worker identity functioned as a provocation in the US context precisely because it helped redefine programmers, engineers, and other white-collar employees in the tech sector *as* workers, contesting the idea that they were simply entrepreneurs in waiting. This redefinition in turn made possible new forms of solidarity.

There are many reasons why this ideology has not manifested in the Chinese tech sector in the same form it has in the US. Broadly speaking, the idea that engineers are unlike "ordinary" workers and that their relations to their bosses should be friendly or familial has not exercised the same hold in China as it has in the US. Some engineers within the industry do espouse a strong belief in meritocracy. In a 2019 post titled "996 Should Be an Attitude, Not a Regime," the author—a young software engineer— defended the 996 schedule, saying that "the essence of 996 is about relentlessly improving one's own value and attitude towards learning" (Z. Li 2019). However, the ideology of "loving your work" is not nearly as prevalent in China as it is in Silicon Valley and throughout many sectors in the West. Even though the Chinese tech sector had a lot of entrepreneurial optimism in the early years of the new millennium, with many tech workers believing they had a shot at founding their own companies, this optimism was short-lived. By the mid-2010s, big Chinese tech companies had grown into monopolies, leaving no space for smaller ventures to flourish. As a result, Chinese tech workers were forced to put their entrepreneurial ambitions aside, opting instead to find steady work among the largest players (X. Li 2019).

Since then, Chinese software engineers have increasingly seen themselves as distinct from management and the tech entrepreneurial class. In a conversation about working a 996 schedule, a low-level manager at a Chinese gaming company told one of us: "Not everyone is a genius and can live off their innovation. Most people depend on technology and on working long hours." Some Chinese tech workers also jokingly refer to themselves as "code farmers" (*manong*), "code monkeys" (*chengxuyuan* [using a pun, 程序猿, which sounds identical to the standard term for programmer, 程序员]), or "physical laborers" (*banmagong*) in online forums like Zhihu. Although used jokingly, these self-deprecating labels are clear indicators that unlike their US counterparts, many software engineers in China feel like they have no agency in their workplace and exist in a distinctly lower tier than management.

We can also look at tech workers' relationship with their managers to get a sense of how workers conceptualize their own identities. In the US, managers at large tech companies are sometimes thought of as protecting the software engineers who report to them from unnecessary bureaucracy. They are also meant to manage the nontechnical aspects of a project, often considered less worthy of an engineer's time. In contrast, Chinese managers have a much more hierarchical relationship with their employees. Unlike US-based tech workers, who usually work on a project basis and have more control over their working hours, Chinese tech workers often have more rigid work schedules and are typically expected to stay at work for as long as their manager. This expectation to work rigid work hours and stay in the office for as long as their managers, even when there is nothing to do, has led to the popularization of the term "touching fish" (*moyu*), which means to slack off and kill time until permitted to go home.

These differences in ideology arise not only from broad cultural differences or differences in the trajectories of US versus Chinese neoliberalism but also from the way tech workers are compensated. In the US, software engineers at companies like Google and Microsoft have high entry salaries but on average can expect an annual raise of only 1.5–3 percent, unless they are promoted. In China, entry-level engineers have much lower salaries, even taking into account a lower cost of living, but can expect much higher raises depending on their performance. According to one report on Echowall, a collaborative platform for research on China, entry-level salaries for programmers can be as low as RMB 7,000, or around $1080, a month and can vary dramatically depending on the employee's level of education. As employees accumulate experience with a company, salaries can then increase sharply—sometimes by a factor of 25 over a decade (Wu 2020). However, because raises are not ubiquitous and are dependent on employee performance, many workers are left with limited prospects for career advancement. According to a 2017 blog post by a Huawei employee, low-performing employees who have been at the company for four or five years are not able to make a monthly salary of more than RMB 8,000/9,000, compared with a starting salary of RMB 10,000 for 2015 college hires (Anonymous 2017).

The large spread of incomes among Chinese software engineers has produced a class of high-end programmers and an underclass of low-paid ones, with many levels in between—an "IT pyramid," as the Echowall report calls it (Wu 2020). In contrast, US white-collar tech workers at large tech companies are split into two groups: FTEs and contract workers. Unlike the Chinese IT pyramid, this bifurcation of white-collar tech work in the US makes it extremely difficult for contract workers to be hired as FTEs; at most firms, no formal process for this exists. While many FTEs in the US tech sector start their careers earning six-figure salaries, Chinese tech workers—who begin their careers on meager wages but on average receive more significant salary raises than their US counterparts—are driven more directly by competition with their coworkers. This large spread in salaries has produced class stratification in the Chinese tech industry that is largely unfelt among US-based FTEs, showing that the ideological difference regarding tech work in China versus in the US also has a material basis. When it comes to employee resistance, these different circumstances also play an important role: participants of the 996.ICU campaign conceptualize their identities in a vastly different way from tech workers in the US—not only because of cultural differences but because of the more extreme incentive structure in the Chinese tech sector. Indeed, the competitive, raise-based system used by Chinese tech companies threatens to atomize workers and eliminate the chance for solidarity among Chinese tech workers, let alone solidarity with their US counterparts.

Solidarity beyond Identity

While the scholars of globalized, digitally mediated labor cited above have highlighted the ways that racialized, gendered, and national differences shape cognitive work, our case study foregrounds international variations in the self-understandings of workers or worker identity. Nonetheless, it also demonstrates how networks of solidarity can be built across such differences. Despite differences in their working conditions and conceptualization of tech worker identity, participants in the 996.ICU movement were able to establish ties with and build support among their counterparts in the US. They were able to build these transnational connections both because they belonged to overlapping networks of academics and organizers and because they used a common set of tools. The 996.ICU solidarity actions at Microsoft emerged from preexisting relationships between Chinese labor organizers, US-based Chinese academics, and Chinese immigrants working in the US tech sector. The 996.ICU movement first came to the attention of engineers at Microsoft in the US because a Microsoft engineer who volunteered with TWC attended a conference on the Jasic incident organized by academics at Cornell in the spring of 2019. The communications and translation work that followed was facilitated primarily by individuals who were either Chinese nationals working in the US or US-educated engineers who had returned to China. It was within this network that members of the Chinese diaspora practically and conceptually linked the 996.ICU movement to the US-based tech worker struggle.

However, alongside these relationships, GitHub also played a crucial role in making the transnational dimensions of anti-996 organizing possible. Not only did the platform make the 996.ICU campaign incredibly difficult to censor in China, but its global footprint—as a platform used by both Chinese and American workers—allowed the campaign to spread to Silicon Valley and other international tech hubs. Unlike many other Chinese social media services that require users to sign up with their official government-issued identification, GitHub—like most other Western online services—requires nothing more than an email address. This guarantees GitHub users a degree of anonymity and therefore safety. Other workplace tools have played a role in other tech worker movements. TWC has used Slack to facilitate conversation among members of far-flung chapters. Even though the TWC remains a leaderless and decentralized organization, the TWC Slack—with nearly 3,000 participants—acts as a centralized space for its members to collaborate on projects, share knowledge, and host events. Tech worker organizers have also cited the utility in their organizing of internal workplace tools like Google's Memegen (Tarnoff 2018). However, the role of GitHub in global software industries—its status as a site of important interdependencies and knowledge transfer—allowed it to play a unique role in connecting engineers and workers across national borders. In contrast to Slack or Memegen, GitHub was designed with the ethos of open source. While the platform is fundamentally collaborative and open to anyone with an Internet connection, interacting with GitHub projects is not intuitive and requires a skill set that is unique to software engineering. Most users use the platform by issuing commands in the terminal—an interface that would be incomprehensible to nonprogrammers and, crucially, to higher-up or nontechnical managers.

The choice of GitHub was strategic both because the state could not easily block it and because it spoke to a specific professional identity. Since higher-up managers and executives seldom work directly on GitHub, the platform facilitated communications among members of a specific class layer. The organizing approach that Chinese tech workers developed using this tool was vastly different from the kind of cross-class solidarity that TWC mobilized in its early days, when, for instance, the organization encouraged white-collar engineers to support cafeteria workers. In a sense, its close association with a particular professional layer narrowed the scope for solidarity with other classes of workers in the tech industry; however, it also opened up the possibility of new kinds of communication across space. During the 996.ICU movement, GitHub gave Chinese and US tech workers a transnational space to talk about their struggles for the first time. Since then, GitHub has played a role in several unrelated actions. Microsoft organizers have continued to use the platform for other campaigns (MSWorkers 2019b). Tech workers in New York flooded one of Palantir's GitHub projects with posts about Palantir's complicity in the US government's draconian immigration practices (Paul 2019). Iranian developers, whose GitHub project was taken down due to US sanctions, also took to GitHub to protest the removal of their work (1995parham 2019).

Even in the absence of a universalizing concept like the "tech worker," then, familiarity with GitHub has allowed workers in the tech sector to coordinate transnational action. In other words, this key tool facilitating the globalization of technologically mediated cognitive labor has also served as a site for organizing workers over the conditions of such labor. Of course, it is always challenging to measure the impact of worker actions on a firm, and the 996.ICU project is no exception. No proof ultimately emerged that Microsoft was under pressure from China to pull the 996.ICU project from GitHub. However, it is possible that pressure from US-based employees played a role in preventing censorship. Similarly, while GitHub allowed the 996.ICU movement to build international connections, it is unclear whether the solidarity it fostered can last. After a few weeks of exchange, discussions on the support.996.ICU GitHub project tapered off, and conversations between Chinese and American tech workers ceased. The domestic successes of 996.ICU remain modest. While the Slack channel that was created with the launch of the campaign remains somewhat active, organizing efforts around working conditions haven't progressed. Despite the virality of 996.ICU, most large tech companies in China continued to practice 996 working hours in the ensuing years.

Conclusion

We began this chapter by asking how the kinds of embodied and geographic differences that scholars of globalized labor have explored shape the self-understandings of cognitive workers and the possibilities for worker organizing in a planetary context. The case of China's 996.ICU movement and its connections with the US-based tech worker movement is illuminating in several respects. As we have described, 996.ICU provided an alternative to the dominant philosophy embraced by TWC in the US. The 996.ICU movement was not based on broad appeals to worker identity but rather focused on a particular subset of the professional class and spoke to them about their specific conditions. Our analysis reveals that this tactical difference corresponds to differences in the work culture between US and Chinese tech firms, and suggests that those differences themselves emerge from differences in the material organization of the industry in the two countries, including pay structures and management practices. However, our case study also shows that despite these differences in self-conception and strategy, workers in the 996.ICU movement were able to build ties with counterparts in the US by building on existing relationships in the academic and diasporic community and, crucially, activating the shared tools of their trade. By using GitHub, a platform that is crucial to software development in both countries, widely dispersed organizers drawn into tech worker movements by different interests found themselves able to communicate and coordinate. They did so despite ostensibly being on opposite sides of a "New Cold War."

There are many reasons to believe that political conflict between the US and China will continue to shape the conditions of activism and organizing in the tech industries of both countries in the years to come. In the US, tech firms have repeatedly raised fears of China in order to parry threats of government regulation—ironically deploying "tech nationalism" (Weigel 2020) to disarm the nation-state itself. In a speech that he made at Georgetown in 2019, Mark Zuckerberg discussed the rise of China as instigating a global battle of values. "If another nation's platform sets the rules, our nation's discourse could be defined by a completely different set of values," he said (Feuer 2019). In response to the prospect of government regulation of Facebook's new digital currency, Libra, Zuckerberg further argued that such regulation would endanger the spread of America's "democratic values and oversight around the world." Executives have used a similar language of nationalism and American exceptionalism to justify military contracts in the face of employee protests. In the Big Tech antitrust congressional hearing that took place on July 29, 2020, for example, Republican politicians pilloried Google CEO Sundar Pichai for letting employee activism force their company into dropping a contract with the US Department of Defense. Pichai responded by pronouncing renewed loyalty: "We're proud to support the US government. We recently signed a big project with the DoD where we are bringing our world class zero-trust based cybersecurity approach to help protect the Pentagon's network from cybersecurity attacks" (US Congress 2020).

At the same time, Chinese tech leaders have weaponized US aggression toward the Chinese tech sector, justifying the exploitation of their employees, and particularly required working hours, as a matter of national pride. In an interview by Christine Tan on CNBC, Huawei founder and CEO Ren Zhengfei discussed his company's response after being put on the US Entity List, which prohibits Huawei from using American technology. "We are not in peace time anymore," he remarked. "We must take this opportunity to prevent our employees from slacking off" (Zhengfei 2019). As the Chinese tech sector continues to challenge the global hegemony of the US tech industry in the coming years, it is likely that executives and politicians on both sides of the Pacific will continue to invoke their enmity in order to justify disciplining their workers.

While the New Cold War has been rhetorically useful to both politicians and executives, it is not only a matter of rhetoric. Any future transnational organizing efforts along the lines of 996.ICU will have to contend with the threat of a "splinternet"—a fracturing of the Internet along geopolitical lines. Adding to division based on cultural and language barriers, Internet platforms are increasingly localized and, in some cases, banned outright. In China, Gitee, a GitHub competitor backed by the Chinese government, is increasing its market share and making Chinese software engineers less reliant on Western-built services like GitHub. In the US, in 2020, the Trump administration issued an executive ban on the Chinese multipurpose app WeChat, used in the US chiefly by members of the Chinese diaspora, and the Chinese video-sharing app TikTok. As of late 2020, there are some signs that President-elect Joe Biden will attempt to reverse or reduce the aggressive measures that the Trump administration took against China. However, campaign videos that denounced Trump as "rolling over for China" and pictured Trump with Xi suggest the opposite (Biden 2020).

Decoupling does not mean that the US and Chinese tech industries are fully separated, however, or that their workers have nothing to gain from transnational organizing. The capital that finances tech firms in both the US and China is highly global; in this respect, the two systems remain closely entangled. While Chinese tech investment in US firms has plummeted dramatically since 2018 as a result of the escalating trade war between the two countries, Chinese investors had already pumped tens of billions of dollars into the US tech sector in the early-to-mid 2010s. In the ride-hailing sector, for example, US-based Uber is the second largest investor in its Chinese counterpart DiDi Chuxing, and DiDi Chuxing invested US$100 million in Uber's competitor, US-based Lyft (Buhr 2015; Levy 2021). Alibaba, which owns China's second largest food-delivery service, Ele.me, teamed up with US-based venture capital firm Andreessen Horowitz to invest $250 million in Lyft (Mishkin and Waters 2014). This status quo means that Uber or DiDi Chuxing drivers might benefit from coordinating globally in order to exact concessions from their respective companies. One could make similar points about the gaming industry, which saw organizing efforts by white-collar workers, led by the labor rights organization Game Workers Unite, in 2018 and 2019. The Chinese tech conglomerate Tencent (which was guilty of practicing 996) is one of the biggest investors in the US gaming industry. Tencent's portfolio includes Riot

Games (which they outright own), Epic Games, Ubisoft, and Activision Blizzard, all of which have seen employee activism in recent years. If game workers in the US and Europe were to unite with agitated Chinese tech workers to demand changes to their working conditions, the combined pressure they could put on Tencent might exceed anything that they could accomplish separately.

In the future, participants in 996.ICU hope that transnational solidarity between Chinese and American tech workers could be the basis for fighting against both exploitation and militaristic government contracts. The question of transnational organizing in a New Cold War is not an easy one. As we noted above, while the movement gained widespread attention around the world, its momentum subsided without changing the behavior of any of China's tech giants, and the connection made between tech workers in China and the US did not persist. This outcome highlights what Zeynep Tufekci has called the "power and fragility" of networked movements. First, movements restricted to online spaces can grow and garner public attention rapidly, but the connections they establish among workers remain relatively weak if little or no organizational capacity backs the movement (Tufekci 2017). Moreover, given the political pressures that favor the continued fragmentation of the Internet, and the decoupling of Chinese and US systems in particular, tech workers may not be able to count on global infrastructures like GitHub in the future. Yet the 996.ICU movement points toward pathways that will remain urgent to pursue—namely, identifying crucial, shared points in the global supply chains producing data-driven technologies and using them to coordinate mutually beneficial actions; and building affinities across difference rather than seeking universal identities that would suppress difference. Such opportunities for solidarity can vary and may involve other members of other class layers, such as logistic or gig workers. Indeed, the limitations of solidarity with the 996.ICU movement point to the need for future organizers to engage in a wide range of strategies. Conceptual and tactical innovations will only become more necessary as the COVID-19 pandemic and its fallout continue to push more and more cognitive workers toward working remotely, and firms toward developing new tools to manage them ever more closely, at a distance.

Notes

1. For instance, based on her ethnography of Indian IT workers on temporary work visas in Berlin, Amrute writes that "race and class are integral to producing differently valued bodies at work and to producing the communicative content of so-called immaterial goods"; these identity categories cannot be added as afterthoughts to analyses of contemporary capitalism "from the outside" (2016, 18). In her study of Asian fashion bloggers, Minh-ha T. Pham similarly "pushes against the assumptions of upward post-racial mobility that structure popular understandings

of the new Asian digital creative class" in order to "demonstrate that the roles race, gender, and class play in structuring work opportunities and constraints under informational capitalism are evolving, not diminishing" (Pham 2015, 9).

2. JS Tan is a former tech worker and organizer. Some of the details provided in this piece are drawn from his first-person experiences and participatory research.

3. The term "Great Firewall" (*fanghuo changcheng*) has its origins in a series of state initiatives that began in the late 1990s with the goal of giving the Communist Party control over the spread of information among Chinese citizens online and, some have alleged, protecting domestic technology companies. The Great Firewall Project encompassed both legislative actions and technical measures, for instance, blocking particular IP ranges or keywords. The term is now widely used to refer to the division that separates Internet users located in the People's Republic of China from those in the rest of the world.

4. In China, Microsoft's search engine Bing filters out results relating to controversial subjects, such as political dissidents or Taiwan. Similarly, LinkedIn continues to operate in China by complying with the censorship rules through a local joint venture.

References

1995parham. 2019. "Github Do Not Ban Us." [GitHub repository]. https://github.com/1995parham /github-do-not-ban-us.

996icu. 2019a. "996.ICU." [GitHub repository]. https://github.com/996icu/996.ICU.

996icu. 2019b. "996.ICU LICENSE." https://github.com/996icu/996.ICU/blob/master/LICENSE.

Amrute, Sareeta. 2016. *Encoding Race, Encoding Class: Indian IT Workers in Berlin*. Durham, NC: Duke University Press.

Anonymous. 2017. "一位在华为工作2年员工的心路历程" [My first two years working at Huawei]. Blog post on *Techug*, February 8. https://www.techug.com/post/first-two-years-i-work-in-huawei.html.

Anonymous. 2019. "不能给反对996的员工贴"混日子"标签" [We shouldn't label employees who are anti-1996 'lazy']. *People's Daily* (人民日报), April 14. https://finance.sina.com.cn/roll/2019-04-14 /doc ihvhiewr5682764.shtml.

Anonymous. 2020. "[青年就业]社畜们的故事: 逃离、互助、反抗与救赎" [(Youth employment) The story of society's livestock: escape, mutual aid, resistance and redemption]. 多数派 [*Masses*], August 14. http://www.masseshere.com/【青年就业】社畜们的故事: 逃离、互助、反抗与救赎.

Barbrook, Richard, and Andy Cameron. 1996. "The Californian Ideology." *Science as Culture* 6 (1): 44–72. http://www.imaginaryfutures.net/2007/04/17/the-californian-ideology-2/.

Barlow, John Perry. 1996. "Declaration of the Independence of Cyberspace." *Electronic Frontier Foundation*, February 8. https://www.eff.org/cyberspace-independence.

Berardi, Franco "Bifo." 2009. *The Soul at Work: From Alienation to Autonomy*. Los Angeles: Semiotext(e).

Biden, Joe. 2020. "Joe Biden for President: 'Unprepared.' | Campaign 2020." Campaign video, 1:50. April 18. https://www.washingtonpost.com/video/politics/joe-biden-for-president-unprepared--campaign-2020/2020/05/14/ec602523-306c-4fe6-8340-311ea381d7f7_video.html.

Buhr, Sarah. 2015. "China's Didi Kuaidi Put $100M into Lyft, Inks Ridesharing Alliance to Rival Uber." *TechCrunch*, September 16. https://techcrunch.com/2015/09/16/ubers-rivals-didi-kuadi-and-lyft-form-international-ridesharing-partnership/.

China State Council (国务院). 2017. "新一代人工智能发展规划的通知" [New generation AI development plan]. July 8. http://www.gov.cn/zhengce/content/2017-07/20/content_5211996.htm.

Chumley, Lily. 2016. *Creativity Class: Art School and Culture Work in Postsocialist China*. Princeton, NJ: Princeton University Press.

Deleuze, Gilles. 1992. "Postscript on Societies of Control." *October* 59: 3–7.

Dugu, Yi (独孤义). 2017. "在公司被迫使用 钉钉 是怎样的一种体验?" [An Answer To: What Is It Like Being Forced to Use DingDing at Work?]. Zhihu, December 24. https://www.zhihu.com/question/38377585/answer/282273375.

Ekbia, Hamid R., and Bonnie A. Nardi. 2017. *Heteromation, and Other Stories of Computing and Capitalism*. Cambridge, MA: MIT Press.

Feuer, Will. 2019. "Watch Mark Zuckerberg Deliver a Speech on Free Expression at Georgetown University." CNBC, October 17. https://www.cnbc.com/2019/10/17/facebook-ceo-mark-zuckerberg-georgetown-speech-on-free-expression.html.

Gilchrist, Karen. 2019. "Alibaba Founder Jack Ma Says Working Overtime Is a 'Huge Blessing.'" CNBC, April 15. https://www.cnbc.com/2019/04/15/alibabas-jack-ma-working-overtime-is-a-huge-blessing.html.

GitHub. n.d. 996icu/996.ICU. Accessed September 10, 2021. https://github.com/search?q=stars:%3E1&s=stars&type=Repositories.

Gray, Mary L., and Siddharth Suri. 2019. *Ghost Work: How to Stop Silicon Valley from Building a New Global Underclass*. Boston: Houghton Mifflin Harcourt.

Hardt, Michael, and Antonio Negri. 2001. *Empire*. Cambridge, MA: Harvard University Press.

Hardt, Michael, and Antonio Negri. 2005. *Multitude: War and Democracy in the Age of Empire*. New York: Penguin Press.

Hayes, Dennis. 1989. *Behind the Silicon Curtain: The Seductions of Work in a Lonely Era*. Boston: South End Press.

Horwitz, Josh, and Brenda Goh. 2019. "RPT-China's JD.com Boss Criticizes 'Slackers' as the Company Makes Cuts." Reuters, April 13. https://www.reuters.com/article/jdcom-labour/rpt-chinas-jd-com-boss-criticises-slackers-as-company-makes-cuts-idUSL3N21W00U.

Irani, Lilly. 2019. *Chasing Innovation: Making Entrepreneurial Citizens in Modern India*. Princeton, NJ: Princeton University Press.

Jackson, Eric M. 2004. *The PayPal Wars: Battles with eBay, the Media, the Mafia, and the Rest of Planet Earth*. Chicago: WND Books.

Lazzarato, Maurizio. 1996. "Immaterial Labor." In *Radical Thought in Italy: A Potential Politics*, edited by Paolo Virno and Michael Hardt, 133–148. Minneapolis: University of Minnesota Press.

Lazzarato, Maurizio. 2004. "From Capital-Labour to Capital-Life." *Ephemera* 4 (3): 187–208.

Lee, Ching Kwan. 2017. "After the Miracle: Labor Politics under China's New Normal." *Catalyst* 1 (3): 93–115.

Levy, Ari. 2021. "Uber's Stake in Didi Shrank by $2 Billion This Week amid China Crackdown on U.S. Listings." CNBC, July 23. https://www.cnbc.com/2021/07/23/uber-lost-2-billion-in-didi -stake-this-week-on-china-crackdown-threat.html.

Li, Xiaotian. 2019. "The 996.ICU Movement in China." *Made in China Journal*, June 18. https:// madeinchinajournal.com/2019/06/18/the-996-icu-movement-in-china-changing-employment -relations-and-labour-agency-in-the-tech-industry/.

Li, Zonghang. 2019. "996 该是态度，而非制度" [996 should be an attitude, not a system]. GitHub post, April 22. https://lizonghang.github.io/2019/04/22/996-An-Attitude-For-Work-And-Life.

Lindtner, Silvia M. 2020. *Prototype Nation: China and the Contested Promise of Innovation*. Princeton, NJ: Princeton University Press.

Mishkin, Sarah, and Richard Waters. 2014. "Alibaba Invests in Ride-Sharing App Lyft." *Financial Times*, April 2. https://www.ft.com/content/85597f12-ba81-11e3-8b15-00144feabdc0.

MSWorkers. 2019a. "Support 996.ICU." [GitHub repository] https://github.com/MSWorkers /support.996.ICU.

MSWorkers. 2019b. "Microsoft Workers for Climate Justice." GitHub README, September 18. https://github.com/MSworkers/for.ClimateAction.

NPC. 1994. "Labour Law of the People's Republic of China." National People's Congress of the People's Republic of China. http://www.npc.gov.cn/zgrdw/englishnpc/Law/2007-12/12/content _1383754.htm.

Paul, Kari. 2019. "Tech Workers Protest Data Mining Firm Palantir for Role in Immigrant Arrests." *Guardian*, May 14. https://www.theguardian.com/us-news/2019/may/13/tech-workers-palantir-immi gration-protest-github.

People's Daily (人民日报) Official Account. 2019. "工作996生病ICU，劳动监察部门应积极介入)" [996 working hours will send you to the ICU, the Labor Inspection Department should intervene]. Weibo post, April 5. https://m.weibo.cn/status/4357697258275940.

Pham, Minh-ha T. 2015. *Asians Wear Clothes on the Internet: Race, Gender, and the Work of Personal Style Blogging*. Durham, NC: Duke University Press.

Reuters. 2012. "Zuckerberg's Letter to Investors." Reuters, February 1. https://www.reuters.com /article/us-facebook-letter/zuckerbergs-letter-to-investors-idUSTRE8102MT20120201.

Roberts, John Jeff. 2017. "Twitter's CEO Says It's Having an 'Arab Spring' Moment in the US." *Fortune*, February 5. https://fortune.com/2017/02/15/twitter-jack-dorsey-arab-spring/.

Roberts, Sarah T. 2019. *Behind the Screen: Content Moderation in the Shadows of Social Media*. New Haven, CT: Yale University Press.

Saxenian, AnnaLee. 1994. *Regional Advantage: Culture and Competition in Silicon Valley and Route 128*. Cambridge, MA: Harvard University Press.

Shen, Xinmei. 2019. "Chinese Browsers Block Protest against China's 996 Overtime Work Culture." *South China Morning Post*, April 3. https://www.scmp.com/abacus/culture/article/3029260/chinese-browsers-block-protest-against-chinas-996-overtime-work.

Tarnoff, Ben. 2018. "Tech Workers versus the Pentagon: An Interview with Kim." *Jacobin*, June 6. https://jacobinmag.com/2018/06/google-project-maven-military-tech-workers.

Tarnoff, Ben. 2020. "The Making of the Tech Worker Movement." *Logic*, May 4. https://logicmag.io/the-making-of-the-tech-worker-movement/full-text/.

Taylor, Astra. 2018. "The Automation Charade." *Logic* 5: 149–163. https://logicmag.io/failure/the-automation-charade/.

Terranova, Tiziana. 2004. *Network Culture: Politics for the Information Age*. London: Pluto Press. https://compthink.files.wordpress.com/2011/04/terranova-network-culture.pdf.

Tokumitsu, Miya. 2015. *Do What You Love, and Other Lies about Success and Happiness*. New York: Regan Arts.

Tufekci, Zeynep. 2017. *Twitter and Teargas: The Power and Fragility of Networked Protest*. New Haven, CT: Yale University Press.

U.S. Congress. House Subcommittee on Antitrust, Commercial, and Administrative Law. 2020. *Hearing on Online Platforms and Market Power, Part 6: Examining the Dominance of Amazon, Apple, Facebook, and Google*. 116th Congress, 1st session, July 29. https://judiciary.house.gov/calendar/eventsingle.aspx?EventID=3113.

Wang, Xiaowei. 2020. *Blockchain Chicken Farm, and Other Stories of Tech in China's Countryside*. New York: FSG Originals × Logic.

Weigel, Moira. 2017. "Coders of the World Unite." *Guardian Long Read*, October 31, 25–27.

Weigel, Moira. 2020. "Palantir Goes to the Frankfurt School." *b2o*, July 10. https://www.boundary2.org/2020/07/moira-weigel-palantir-goes-to-the-frankfurt-school/.

Wu, Jing. 2020. "Working 996." *Echowall*, February 18. https://www.echo-wall.eu/chinese-whispers/working-996.

Yang, Su (杨苏). 2018. "在公司被迫使用 钉钉 是怎样的一种体验?" [An answer to: What is it like being forced to use DingTalk at work?]. Zhihu, May 4. https://www.zhihu.com/question/38377585/answer/359758889.

Zhengfei, Ren. 2019. CNBC Transcript: Ren Zhengfei, Founder & CEO, Huawei. CNBC, October 4. https://www.cnbc.com/2019/10/04/cnbc-transcript-ren-zhengfei-founder-ceo-huawei.html.

13 Planetary Potemkin AI: The Humans Hidden inside Mechanical Minds

Jathan Sadowski

In 1770, the Hungarian inventor Wolfgang von Kempelen unveiled the Mechanical Turk, a chess-playing contraption that "consisted of a wooden cabinet behind which was seated a life-size figure of a man, made of carved wood, wearing an ermine-trimmed robe, loose trousers and a turban—the traditional costume of an Oriental sorcerer" (Standage 2002, 22). The chess-playing robot was toured around Europe and America, and exhibition matches were staged with such famous opponents as Napoleon Bonaparte. All the while, Kempelen maintained that the automaton operated by its own accord.

To prove there was no trickery, he opened the cabinet before every exhibition and showed spectators the dense tangle of gears, wheels, and levers. The sheer mechanical complexity on display convinced observers that advanced technology—beyond what they could comprehend—was powering the system. But Kempelen had actually created an elaborate illusion, not a robot. Inside was a human chess master who used magnets and levers to operate the Mechanical Turk; he simply hid behind the fake machinery when Kempelen opened the cabinet. In other words, the complex mechanical system that Kempelen showed people was meant to distract their attention from how the automaton really worked: human labor. Kempelen sold the idea of an intelligent machine, but what people witnessed was just human effort disguised by clever engineering.

In the 1730s, a French inventor named Jacques de Vaucanson constructed a copper-plated cyborg called *le Canard Digérateur*, or the Digesting Duck. It was the size of a duck, walked like a duck, and quacked like a duck. But its real trick, which amazed and baffled audiences, was that it could poop like a duck. The automaton "ate food out of the exhibitor's hand, swallowed it, digested it, and excreted it, all before an audience" (Wood 2002).

Vaucanson claimed that he had built a "chemical laboratory" in the duck's stomach to decompose the food before expelling it from the mechanical butt. While Vaucanson was an expert engineer—the duck was an intricate piece of machinery—like a good magician, he did not reveal how the duck worked. After his death, the secret was uncovered: there was no innovative chemical technology inside the duck; rather, there were just two containers, one for the food and one for preloaded excrement. (Strangely, the Digesting Duck and the Mechanical Turk were both destroyed by museum fires around the same time in the mid-nineteenth century.)

Kempelen and Vaucanson would fit very well into Silicon Valley today. They could spend their days making mysterious machines and uttering wondrous proclamations about their supposed abilities, while attracting major venture capital investment. Perhaps Vaucanson—who literally snuck duck excrement into his technological system and called it innovation—would create the next biotech darling built on deception (à la Theranos). Whereas Kempelen's Mechanical Turk was a forerunner of current systems of artificial intelligence (AI) not because it managed to play a game well, like IBM's Deep Blue or Google's AlphaGo, but because many AI systems are, in large part, also technical illusions designed to fool the public. Whether it's content moderation for social media (Gray and Suri 2019) or image recognition for police surveillance (Mozur 2018), claims abound about the effectiveness of AI-powered analytics, when in reality the cognitive labor may very well come from an office building full of (low-waged) workers in outsourcing destinations such as the Philippines or India (Roberts 2019). This is not to say that the only options are a binary divide of either 100 percent machine power or 100 percent human power. Rather, the reality is a hybrid relationship where workers use technology to create value, managers use technology to discipline labor, and entrepreneurs use technology to erase the existence of the other two groups.

I call this way of building and presenting such systems—whether analog automatons or digital software—"Potemkin AI." Potemkin refers to a façade designed to hide the reality of a situation. The term functions as an analytical label meant to help us understand the actual, existing practices and promises of the technology sector, as well as the conditions of workers that make these systems function. It also functions as a theoretical concept meant to reveal the expanded networks of labor, capital, production, and information that are hidden inside so many supposedly AI systems. Much as the theory of technopolitics shows that embedded within any given technology is a tangle of values, interests, and priorities (Winner 1978; Sadowski 2020), Potemkin AI opens the black box of digital labor in the planetary market. In other words, Potemkin AI is, at once, a way to demystify the real operations of these technological systems and the real relations of this political economic system.

This type of technology is the inverse of decision-making systems that seem to have humans-in-the-loop but actually do not, what Brennan-Marquez, Levy, and Susser (2019) term "skeuomorphic humanity." Digital assistants and robocallers, for example, have been programmed to mimic the qualities and characteristics of humans—even including vocal tics designed to make us feel like we are interacting with a person.

When it comes to Potemkin AI, however, there is a long list of services that purport to be powered by sophisticated software but actually rely on hidden humans acting like robots (Solon 2018; Taylor 2018; Altenried 2020). Autonomous vehicles commonly use remote driving and human drivers disguised as seats to hide their Potemkin AI.[1] App developers for email-based services like personalized ads, price comparisons, and automated travel-itinerary planners use humans to read private emails (MacMillan 2018). A service that converted voicemails into text, SpinVox, was accused of using humans and not machines to transcribe audio (Cellan-Jones 2009). Facebook's much-vaunted personal assistant, M, relied on humans to answer questions—until Facebook shut down the service to focus on other AI projects (Newton 2018). The *Wall Street Journal* has called the pervasive use of human eyes marketed as AI "tech's 'dirty secret'" (MacMillan 2018).

The list of Potemkin AI continues to grow with every cycle of venture capital investment. The structural obfuscation of human labor is critical to the functioning of the financial system that props up the technology sector, pushing forward the constant development of so-called innovation. It is a system built on speculation, or the production of expectations that certain things will materialize and value will be realized (Pollock and Williams 2010); it is a system where the accumulation of data capital and the technology needed to generate and process data is treated as the overriding imperative (Sadowski 2019), and where the interests of massive institutions, like SoftBank's Vision Fund 2 (a proposed $108 billion investment fund for AI companies), dictate the very trajectory of technological development (van Doorn and Badger 2020). If the machinery of real AI is not advanced enough to fulfill the wild promises and infinite desires of finance, then we should expect Potemkin AI to continue propagating as financiers and technologists sell the next best thing. Rather than the old marketing slogan "Accept no imitations," Potemkin AI is an ideological project to convince the public that they should "accept only imitations."

This chapter fleshes out the political economy of Potemkin AI. The first section situates this argument in recent work on digital labor, particularly regarding the emerging geographies of what Graham and Anwar (2019) have analyzed as a "planetary labor market" for gig work on digital platforms. These networks of (data) capital and (digital) labor are a crucial component of the "artificial artificial intelligence" that is now behind so much of what is sold as innovation. Following this, we will further unpack the psychopolitics of these black-boxed labor machines. For it is the *illusion* of being powered by AI that grants these systems efficacy. It's not only that their operations are hidden but that their proponents mistake an ideology for a technology, that they believe—or at least act as if—human labor has been replaced by mechanical minds. The chapter then concludes by exploring a simple yet critical question: Why go to the trouble of creating Potemkin AI?

Global Potemkin Village

The term *Potemkin* derives from the name of a Russian minister who in 1787 built temporary, fake villages to impress Empress Catherine II and disguise the true state of her empire. Potemkin technology, then, constructs a facade that not only hides what is actually going on but deceives potential users, investors, and the general public alike. In place of the Wizard of Oz telling us to pay no attention to the man behind the curtain, we have entrepreneurs telling us to pay no attention to the people behind the platform.

Importantly, the predecessors to Potemkin AI were constrained in space and time. The chess master sat inside the Mechanical Turk, manipulating the machinery in response to his opponent. The village facades stood in particular places and only had to be propped up long enough for the empress to pass through. When it comes to Potemkin AI, the homunculi are not inside the system per se; rather, their labor is transmitted into it over space and time. "Digital technologies extend and intensify working activity, rendering the boundaries of the workplace emergent" (Richardson 2018, 244). For instance, the cognitive labor of African workers today may power the American autonomous vehicles of the future (Anwar and Graham 2020). Or the "human computation" done by Indian workers in the past may support the valuation of a European start-up now (Irani 2015). In short, Potemkin AI is propped up by planetary networks of (data) capital and (digital) labor.

As Graham and Anwar (2019) explain in their geographical study of online outsourcing work mediated by platforms, by embedding digital work in "stretched-out networks of production" and information, the planetary labor market "facilitates a confluence that can transcend the spatial boundaries that constrained the convergence of employers and workers but remained shaped and characterized by multi-scalar and asymmetrical technological, political, social, cultural, and institutional factors." It's no coincidence that these geographies of (data) capital and (digital) labor tend to be organized along familiar colonialist political-economic relations wherein the "margins" are made to serve the "core," providing it with sources of value that can be exploited to power the machine of growth and progress (Couldry and Mejias 2019; Sadowski 2019). The dominant "imaginaries of the digital economy" marshal the language of development and inclusion to justify deeply asymmetrical power-geometries (Wahome and Graham 2020). The fact that many citizens in wealthy nations also earn precarious wages through piecemeal digital work—producing datasets, training AI systems, serving platforms—says more about how the periphery is also nestled unevenly inside the imperial core of innovation (Gregory and Maldonado 2020).

Peeking behind the Curtain

When the inner workings of a technology are obscured, it is often labeled a "black box"—a term derived from engineering diagrams where you can see a system's inputs and outputs but not what happens in between. An algorithm, for example, might effectively be black-boxed because the technical details are described using dense jargon decipherable by only a small group of experts. Or, with more advanced machine learning systems, even these experts might be epistemically shut out from understanding their automated decision-making processes (Burrell 2016). Accusations of willful obscurantism are often reserved for postmodernism, but as a paper on "troubling trends in machine learning scholarship" points out, research and applications in this field are rife with ambiguous details, shaky claims, and deceptive obfuscation (Lipton and Steinhardt 2018). Being baffled by abstruse critical theory is one thing, but not being able to discern, say, how an AI application makes medical diagnoses or assesses insurance risk is much more consequential (Prince and Schwarcz 2020).

Algorithms might also be black-boxed through the force of law by the tech companies who claim them as trade secrets. In *The Black Box Society*, Frank Pasquale (2015) details how many of the algorithms that govern information and finance—the circulation of data and dollars—are shrouded in opacity. Algorithms are often described as a type of recipe. Just as Coca Cola keeps their formula a tightly guarded secret, so too do tech companies fiercely protect their "secret sauce." In this case, analysts and regulators are institutionally shut out from inspecting the ingredients and probing the processes of these technologies. Again, it's one thing to enjoy a beverage we cannot reverse engineer but quite another to take on faith proprietary software that makes sentencing decisions in criminal cases (Angwin et al. 2016).

Potemkin AI is related to black boxing, but it pushes obfuscation into deception. The Mechanical Turk, like many of the much-discussed AI systems today, was not just a black box that hid its inner workings from prying eyes. After all, Kempelen opened his automaton's cabinet and explained the workings of what looked to be a complex machine. Except that he was lying. Similarly, marketing about AI systems deploys technical buzzwords that work like a magician's incantations: Smart! Intelligent! Automated! Cognitive computing! Deep learning! Abracadabra! Alakazam!

Weaving the right spell can endow an AI system with seeming powers of objectivity, neutrality, authority, efficiency, and other desirable attributes and outcomes. As with any good trick, it matters less if the system actually works that way than if people believe it does and act accordingly. This power operates somewhat differently from a purely panoptical gaze wherein you are always potentially being observed by an unseen watcher. Disciplinary power is certainly part of Potemkin AI's purpose, though, as the example of policing in the next section shows. Byung-Chul Han's (2017) work on psychopolitics helps tell a different story of Potemkin AI as a manifestation of what he calls smart power: "Power that is smart and friendly does not operate frontally—i.e., against the will of those who are subject to it. Instead, it guides their will to its own benefit. . . . It leads astray instead of erecting obstacles. . . . Smart power cosies up to the psyche, rather than disciplining through coercion" (Han 2017, 14). In other words, this is the power of coaxing and cajoling, of implanting beliefs and inducing action.

There's an undeniably seductive quality to AI. For consumers, it offers new heights of convenience, responsiveness, and personalization. We're not supposed to say out loud that we want a clever companion whose only purpose is to serve us, but most people would likely gladly accept their very own robot—from *robota*, the old Slavic word for "servitude" or "forced labor"—or at least get used to owning one pretty quickly. For capital, the prospect of possessing and controlling workers who "lack nothing but a soul," as the Czech playwright who coined the word *robot* described them (Intagliata 2011), has always been the dream. But in most applications AI is still an unsatisfying reality, if not a total fantasy. Potemkin AI is role-play. It's people masquerading as soulless systems. There's nothing wrong with this game per se, so long as everybody is aware and honest about who is actually serving whom. Yet as I've explained, Potemkin AI is seduction based on deception.

Psychopolitics reveals Potemkin AI to be more of an ideology than a technology. But that's not to say there is no material substrate to the ideology or that it's all just ephemeral relations. This is an ideology supported by planetary systems of control and capital (Bratton 2016; Sadowski 2020). After all, there is still labor to manage, data to administer, value to extract. How like capitalism to construct complex tangles of transnational networks for circulating money, information, and commodities, all to perpetuate a fetish for dehumanization! Exercising power is not just about effectively achieving particular outcomes or doing what works; it's also about deciding the parameters for how those ideas and goals will be defined. It's about preserving certain interests over others and reasserting the value of certain people over others. The desire for AI in some places supplants the rights of humans in other places.

Fake It till You Make It

Why go to the trouble of creating Potemkin AI? What's at stake for those propping up the façade? Broadly, we can point to two ancient reasons: profit and power. If an AI application relies heavily on human labor rather than machine learning, that doesn't make for a good sales pitch to venture capitalists and customers, nor does it convince the public of the technology's capabilities. There are, of course, other motivations like fame and recognition, but I think we can safely label them as secondary to profit and power.

I illustrate these main motivations through the following two examples of Potemkin AI. The first is Amazon's Mechanical Turk platform (or MTurk), which enables mass exploitation of "microwork" distributed across global networks. The second is the advanced surveillance systems being deployed by the Chinese state. In the former, a dehumanized labor platform provides cheap "intelligence," while buying time for innovation to finally arrive. In the latter, a dehumanized monitoring apparatus creates the illusion of inescapable control.

MTurk allows employers to post discrete, often routine tasks like completing surveys or tagging pictures. Workers who complete these microjobs are then paid microwages: one study calculated the median wage at around $2 an hour (Hara et al. 2018). As the *Financial Times* notes, MTurk is sometimes described by its creators in terms of "humans-as-a-service," or the "human cloud," or even "artificial artificial intelligence" (Hook 2016). These labels capture MTurk's approach of organizing a legion of human workers—hundreds of thousands of people—scattered across the world and hiding them behind a digital platform. Many companies rely on this pool of cheap labor that is ready to click and submit, allowing them to quickly scale up by completing tasks that they hope will one day be accomplished by AI software. Through this microwork, these workers are crucial to the development of AI, whether by producing and verifying datasets used to train AI systems or by simply impersonating the AI (Tubaro, Casilli, and Coville 2020). Yet their contributions to these technologies are belittled—that is, if their very existence is even acknowledged. Undervaluing the work of these people, while profiting off their labor, is all too common in a tech industry heavily biased with gendered, racialized, and classist notions of what entrepreneurs look like, who does innovation, and where venture capital is best invested.

Given that the name "Mechanical Turk" explicitly references the eighteenth-century hoax, it appears that there is no intention to deceive users about the flesh-and-blood foundations of the system. MTurk is indeed up-front about how work is outsourced to real live humans. However, whereas the original Mechanical Turk's inventor overtly claimed that his machine was autonomous, MTurk uses clever design to induce that impression in an audience eager to believe in the platform's Potemkin trick. As Lilly Irani describes, MTurk masks the MTurkers by making them appear to be just another soulless system. "By rendering the requisition of labor technical and infrastructural," she writes, MTurk "limits the visibility of workers, rendering them as a tool to be employed by the intentional and expressive hand of the programmer" (Irani 2015, 730). The platform and its interfaces allow employers to command people as though operating a mindless machine. In this case, Potemkin AI provides a convenient way to rationalize exploitation—often of precarious workers in places with a large reserve army of disempowered labor—while calling it progress. "The result is that workers can lose a sense of any collective organization and feel replaceable, while clients exploit this lack of associational power of workers to exert their demands on workers" (Graham and Anwar 2019).

Irani (2015, 723) explains how, in addition to outsourcing tasks treated as "menial" (another way to devalue this type of work and the people doing it), Potemkin AI—such as MTurk—has helped compensate, both technically and ideologically, for the shortcomings of actual AI in completing cognitive tasks "by simulating AI's promise of computational intelligence with actual people." Even clickwork that seems brainless and dull is often still too advanced for "smart" machines. This simple fact does not bode well for funding of AI research and development, especially when investors eventually expect real results and profitable products. Contrary to their cheery marketing copy, investors and corporations don't funnel their money into AI simply because they are interested in innovation for its own sake. AI promises to solve the problems of capital by unlocking exponential growth, eliminating labor costs, optimizing efficiency, and manifesting a slew of other expected outcomes. But the AI solution will only come about if the systems eventually actually work as promised.

There is a looming fear among those in the tech industry that once reality catches up with the hype, another "AI winter" will arrive, freezing all funding and interest in AI. The first cycle of hype for AI began building in the 1950s and grew until the mid-1970s, when enthusiasm was replaced by disillusionment. The ensuing AI winter lasted until the latter years of the first decade of the twenty-first century, when the combination of big data, processing power, and digital platforms opened up new advances in machine learning research.

As the hype began warming up and AI attracted more attention again, it became a label that start-ups could use as a shorthand for calling their service innovative, disruptive, and all-around superior to that of their dumb competitors. The inflated claims of what AI can achieve feed an expectation economy sustained by a circular logic: investment leads to promises, which leads to branding and more investment . . . and so on until yet another tech bubble bursts. Arguably, right now the most fully actualized product of AI systems is the sociotechnical imaginaries of a smarter planet (Sadowski and Bendor 2019).

Some of the most hyped, most cutting-edge applications of AI are supported by this sort of propaganda. A prime case is the extensive surveillance system being deployed in China. With millions of cameras deployed throughout Chinese cities, the state is looking to upgrade analysis of these feeds via AI and facial recognition that can automatically identify people and even punish criminals (Anderson 2020). For example, a camera at a busy intersection can now witness jaywalkers in action, shame them by displaying their personal information on a screen, and send them a text message with a fine (Mozur 2018). It is questionable, however, just how accurate and automatic this name-and-shame system actually is right now. Buried at the bottom of a *New York Times* article about China's totalitarian tech is a revealing tidbit that highlights how the AI involved in this system is currently more hype than real:

> The system remains more of a digital patchwork than an all-seeing technological network. Many files still aren't digitized, and others are on mismatched spreadsheets that can't be easily reconciled. Systems that police hope will someday be powered by AI are currently run by teams of people sorting through photos and data the old-fashioned way. . . . Still, Chinese authorities who are generally mum about security have embarked on a campaign to persuade the country's people that the high-tech security state is already in place. (Mozur 2018)

Potemkin AI is an effective way of constructing a panopticon. The disciplining power is much greater if people believe that an inhuman force is tirelessly processing feeds from the ubiquitous cameras, rather than groups of human analysts who take time, get fatigued, and make mistakes. Persuading people that the police are using AI is a way to normalize the idea that AI should be and, perhaps more importantly, already is ceaselessly monitoring society. Again, for the purposes of power and discipline, it matters less if the AI is real or fake—what matters is if people believe in the Potemkin deceit and behave accordingly.

It's easy to say that of course the Chinese government would employ propaganda to deceive the public about its power. But it's simply using a tried-and-true tactic of Silicon Valley: fake it till you make it. There is a long history of hiding the dead ends and delays in the process of technological development. This makes the process appear to be linear (no divergences), deterministic (no stopping), and progressive (no worries), while at the same time it suppresses any skepticism and convinces the public that resistance is futile because the tech is so effective and so much better than any alternatives. You can't argue with an algorithm, and the AI in the sky is always watching.

To varying degrees, many applications of AI are more like simulations of AI. This isn't to say that all research and development on artificial intelligence is an elaborate plot to erect a facade of efficacy. Plenty of researchers out there are working to advance the science bit by bit and devise practical applications without falling into the traps of obfuscation and overpromising. Yet at the same time, Potemkin AI is not just limited to a few bad actors, or a few bad apps, in an otherwise healthy industry. It's a core pillar of the political economic structure propping up this sector.

The problem with the industry isn't necessarily with AI not yet working, but rather with the cultural hype, ideological goals, and financial speculation that drive the development of AI. These technologies are not merely corrupted by global capitalism, they are created out of it. They are presented as standalone self-sufficient systems, yet they are deeply dependent on a planetary network of production and information—not that we would ever know it without critically analyzing the real operations and real relations that their creators work so hard to hide. Too much of the attention and funding for AI is garnered by those who are looking to maximize their profits and/or secure their power. We see so many attempts to use AI as a tool for replacing human decisions, exploiting human labor, and administering human life that it becomes easy to believe these are simply the best, even natural, applications. But AI is an alibi, a way to rationalize these applications. Potemkin AI is a placeholder, a way to normalize this attitude in advance, that only works if we don't look beyond the facade.

Acknowledgments

This chapter is an expanded version of a 2018 essay originally published in *Real Life Magazine* as "Potemkin AI" (reallifemag.com/potemkin-ai/). I thank Mark Graham and Fabian Ferrari for their invitation and feedback on this chapter. And I especially thank Rob Horning for invaluable editorial guidance on the original essay, which really helped refine my thinking on the subject.

Note

1. Companies and researchers doing field tests with autonomous vehicles have used "ghost drivers"—human operators wearing a full body hood meant to make the car look driverless—to test how other drivers and pedestrians react to autonomous vehicles on the street (Lefkowitz 2020).

References

Altenried, Moritz. 2020. "The Platform as Factory: Crowdwork and the Hidden Labour behind Artificial Intelligence." *Capital & Class* 44 (2): 145–158.

Anderson, Ross. 2020. "The Panopticon Is Already Here." *The Atlantic*, September. https://www.theatlantic.com/magazine/archive/2020/09/china-ai-surveillance/614197/.

Angwin, Julia, Jeff Larson, Surya Mattu, and Lauren Kirchner. 2016. "Machine Bias." *ProPublica*, May 23. https://www.propublica.org/article/machine-bias-risk-assessments-in-criminal-sentencing.

Anwar, Mohammad Amir, and Mark Graham. 2020. "Digital Labour at Economic Margins: African Workers and the Global Information Economy." *Review of African Political Economy* 47 (163): 95–105.

Bratton, Benjamin H. 2016. *The Stack: On Software and Sovereignty*. Cambridge, MA: MIT Press.

Brennan-Marquez, Kiel, Karen Levy, and Daniel Susser. 2019. "Strange Loops: Apparent versus Actual Human Involvement in Automated Decision Making." *Berkeley Technology Law Journal* 34 (3): 745–772.

Burrell, Jenna. 2016. "How the Machine 'Thinks': Understanding Opacity in Machine Learning Algorithms." *Big Data & Society* 3 (1): 1–12. https://doi.org/10.1177/2053951715622512.

Cellan-Jones, Rory. 2009. "Voice Technology Firm under Fire." *BBC*, July 23. http://news.bbc.co .uk/2/hi/technology/8163511.stm.

Couldry, Nick, and Ulises A. Mejias. 2019. "Data Colonialism: Rethinking Big Data's Relation to the Contemporary Subject." *Television & New Media* 20 (4): 336–349.

Graham, Mark, and Mohammad Amir Anwar. 2019. "The Global Gig Economy: Towards a Planetary Labour Market?" *First Monday* 24 (4), April 1. https://doi.org/10.5210/fm.v24i4.9913.

Gray, Mary L., and Siddharth Suri. 2019. *Ghost Work: How to Stop Silicon Valley from Building a New Global Underclass*. Boston: Houghton Mifflin Harcourt.

Gregory, Karen, and Miguel Paredes Maldonado. 2020. "Delivering Edinburgh: Uncovering the Digital Geography of Platform Labour in the City." *Information, Communication & Society* 23 (8): 1187–1202.

Han, Byung-Chul. 2017. *Psychopolitics: Neoliberalism and New Technologies of Power*. Translated by Erik Butler. London: Verso.

Hara, Kotaro, Abigail Adams, Kristy Milland, Saiph Savage, Chris Callison-Burch, and Jeffrey P. Bigham. 2018. "A Data-Driven Analysis of Workers' Earnings on Amazon Mechanical Turk." In *Proceedings of the 2018 CHI Conference on Human Factors in Computing Systems (CHI '18)*, Paper 449, 1–14. New York: ACM Press.

Hook, Leslie. 2016. "The Humans behind Mechanical Turk's Artificial Intelligence." *Financial Times*, October 26.

Intagliata, Christopher. 2011. "The Origin of the Word 'Robot.'" *Science Friday*, April 22. https:// www.sciencefriday.com/segments/the-origin-of-the-word-robot/.

Irani, Lilly. 2015. "The Cultural Work of Microwork." *New Media & Society* 17 (5): 720–739.

Lefkowitz, Melanie. 2020. "'Ghostdrivers' Test Cultural Reactions to Autonomous Cars." *Cornell Chronicle*, April 22. news.cornell.edu/stories/2020/04/ghostdrivers-test-cultural-reactions-autonomous -cars.

Lipton, Zachary C., and Jacob Steinhardt. 2018. "Troubling Trends in Machine Learning Scholarship." *Queue* 17 (1): 45–77. https://doi.org/10.1145/3317287.3328534.

MacMillan, Douglas. 2018. "Tech's 'Dirty Secret': The App Developers Sifting through Your Gmail." *Wall Street Journal*, July 2. https://www.wsj.com/articles/techs-dirty-secret-the-app-developers-sifting -through-your-gmail-1530544442.

Mozur, Paul. 2018. "Inside China's Dystopian Dreams: A.I., Shame and Lots of Cameras." *New York Times*, July 8. https://www.nytimes.com/2018/07/08/business/china-surveillance-technology.html.

Newton, Casey. 2018. "Facebook Is Shutting Down M, Its Personal Assistant Service That Combined Humans and AI." *The Verge*, January 8. https://www.theverge.com/2018/1/8/16856654 /facebook-m-shutdown-bots-ai.

Pasquale, Frank. 2015. *The Black Box Society: The Secret Algorithms That Control Money and Information.* Cambridge, MA: Harvard University Press.

Pollock, Neil, and Robin Williams. 2010. "The Business of Expectations: How Promissory Organizations Shape Technology and Innovation." *Social Studies of Science* 40 (4): 525–548.

Prince, Anya E. R., and Daniel Schwarcz. 2020. "Proxy Discrimination in the Age of Artificial Intelligence and Big Data." *Iowa Law Review* 105: 1257–1318. https://ilr.law.uiowa.edu/assets/Uploads/ILR-105-3-Prince-Schwarcz-6.pdf

Richardson, Lizzie. 2018. "Feminist Geographies of Digital Work." *Progress in Human Geography* 42 (2): 244–263.

Roberts, Sarah T. 2019. *Behind the Screen: Content Moderation in the Shadows of Social Media.* New Haven, CT: Yale University Press.

Sadowski, Jathan. 2019. "When Data Is Capital: Datafication, Accumulation, and Extraction." *Big Data & Society* 6 (1): 1–12. https://doi.org/10.1177/2053951718820549.

Sadowski, Jathan. 2020. *Too Smart: How Digital Capitalism Is Extracting Data, Controlling Our Lives, and Taking Over the World.* Cambridge, MA: MIT Press.

Sadowski, Jathan, and Roy Bendor. 2019. "Selling Smartness: Corporate Narratives and the Smart City as a Sociotechnical Imaginary." *Science, Technology, & Human Values* 44 (3): 540–563.

Solon, Olivia. 2018. "The Rise of 'Pseudo-AI': How Tech Firms Quietly Use Humans to Do Bots' Work." *Guardian*, July 6. https://www.theguardian.com/technology/2018/jul/06/artificial-intelligence-ai-humans-bots-tech-companies.

Standage, Tom. 2002. *The Turk: The Life and Times of the Famous Eighteenth-Century Chess-Playing Machine.* New York: Walker.

Taylor, Astra. 2018. "The Automation Charade." *Logic*, August 1. https://logicmag.io/failure/the-automation-charade/.

Tubaro, Paola, Antonio A. Casilli, and Marion Coville. 2020. "The Trainer, the Verifier, the Imitator: Three Ways in Which Human Platform Workers Support Artificial Intelligence." *Big Data & Society* 7 (1): 1–12. https://doi.org/10.1177/2053951720919776.

van Doorn, Niels, and Adam Badger. 2020. "Platform Capitalism's Hidden Abode: Producing Data Assets in the Gig Economy." *Antipode* 52 (5): 1475–1495. https://doi.org/10.1111/anti.12641.

Wahome, Michel, and Mark Graham. 2020. "Spatially Shaped Imaginaries of the Digital Economy." *Information, Communication & Society* 23 (8): 1123–1138.

Wood, Gaby. 2002. "Living Dolls: A Magical History of the Quest for Mechanical Life by Gaby Wood." *Guardian*, February 16. https://www.theguardian.com/books/2002/feb/16/extract.gabywood.

Winner, Langdon. 1977. *Autonomous Technology: Technics-Out-of-Control as a Theme in Political Thought.* Cambridge, MA: MIT Press.

14   Data, Compute, Labor

Nick Srnicek

Pivotal to the future of the political economy of artificial intelligence (AI)[1]—and indeed, the future of current technology giants—is the question of whether AI is a centralizing technology. When we turn to the existing research on AI's impact on the economy, however, nearly all the attention has been on what we might call the automation/productivity channel, with discussion centered around whether, when, and how the spread of machine learning will automate and/or augment existing jobs (Royal Society and British Academy 2018; Frank et al. 2019; Acemoglu and Restrepo 2020). In this reading, AI is simply another labor-saving/-augmenting technology in a long line of such technologies. Much less attention has been given to how the nature of AI today may facilitate the centralization and concentration of capital, but this neglect has important consequences. For instance, one of the common arguments made by the defenders of today's technology giants is that their monopoly power is more precarious than it appears because of the ever-present threat of a disruptive innovation (Evans 2017; Christensen 2016; Pleatsikas and Teece 2001): IBM's mainframe monopoly lost out to personal computers; Microsoft's personal computing powerhouse lost out to mobile; and today's monopolies will eventually see similar disruption. Yet if the nature of the next major technologies is, for example, capital-intensive, and they have high barriers to entry, then we have good reason to believe disruption is unlikely. An understanding of the political economy of AI is therefore essential for understanding the stability of the current balance of power—and also for determining how the tech giants are consolidating power and acting strategically today. This knowledge is also crucial to our understanding of how the centralization of capital will play out across the planetary economy as American and Chinese platforms expand across the planet. In response to this gap in the literature, this chapter will examine the question of AI centralization in light of three key inputs: data, compute, and labor. Each of these inputs offers important insights into the global political economy of AI and its future trajectories.

The chapter will first examine the industry structure of AI. Far too often, the focus lies on the firms that *use* AI as opposed to the firms that *provide* AI. The latter, I will argue, are more important to understanding the nature of AI's political economy. The second section will show that most research on AI monopolies has been on data as an input into the production process, but in the third section, I will set out a schematic model of the AI production process that shows data is only one small part of a larger set of inputs and tasks.[2] The remainder of the chapter will then look at three key inputs—data, compute, and labor—discussing in turn why data is becoming less competitively important, and why compute and labor are becoming more significant. In the conclusion, I will attempt to draw out some initial geo-economic consequences of this new perspective on AI and monopolies.

Industry Structure

Within the last few years, each of the world's top technology companies (all based out of the US and China) has begun focusing on AI. Google, for instance, now declares itself to be an "AI-first company" and in May 2018 renamed Google Research as Google AI (Howard 2018). In March 2018, Microsoft reorganized its entire business and placed AI and the cloud together in their own unit (Nadella 2018). Baidu believes that its "strategic future relies on AI" (Clark 2017). And even more traditional companies like Apple and IBM are rapidly shifting to try to become AI-first companies. In contrast to the era of mutually exclusive fiefdoms, with platform giants dominating over their own particular areas, this new era presents an increasing convergence of the major platforms. The result is that companies—particularly Alibaba, Amazon, Baidu, Facebook, Google, Microsoft, and Tencent—are more frequently bumping up against each other. They are no longer just monopolists over particular industries and services, but active oligopolists fighting over an emerging AI and cloud computing sector.

Why are these companies moving into this field? Simply put, the belief (importantly, it remains a belief) is that AI provision will be an immensely lucrative and profitable field that will underpin the future of the global economy. In Marxist terms, AI is on its way to becoming a "general condition of production" (Dyer-Witheford, Kjosen, and Steinhoff 2019, 46–49)—or what mainstream economists call a general-purpose technology (Bresnahan and Trajtenberg 1995; Jovanovic and Rousseau 2005; Trajtenberg 2018). These are technologies that are not limited to particular sectors of the economy but instead have major impacts on production processes across the economy. Already we see signs of this, with a number of tasks increasingly being taken up by machine learning—from medical diagnoses to fraud detection, recommendation systems to translation services, demand forecasting to logistics optimization, and many more. Many of the tasks achievable by contemporary AI are common across businesses, and therefore the providers of AI services have large potential markets to tap into. Control over AI provision therefore means control over a new, and possibly immense, global economy–spanning technology worth perhaps trillions of dollars (Rao and Verweij 2017; Bughin et al. 2018).

It is not just the largest tech platforms that are getting involved in the AI industry, though. Billions of dollars are already being invested in AI research and deployment by venture capital, private equity, tech companies, and nontech companies (Bughin and Hazan 2017). Numerous countries have launched AI strategy documents with the aim of supporting and investing in nascent AI firms (Niklas and Dencik 2020), and venture capital investment and start-ups have been growing rapidly over the past decade (Furman and Seamans 2018, 5–6). Crunchbase, the database of start-ups, lists over 20,000 companies involved in AI as of August 2021.[3] We can bring some clarity to this rapid proliferation of activity by modeling the AI industry as comprising three distinct actors: AI providers, AI start-ups, and AI consumers.

AI providers involve the ownership and provision of the means of production for AI. This is currently the preserve and focus of the major platforms, with many of them adopting a cloud computing approach, or what is sometimes called "AI as a service." These companies (Alibaba, Amazon, Google, Microsoft, and Tencent, most notably) supply hardware, software, and even data for other companies to use. Rather than building their own internal AI models, the vast majority of companies are instead relying on this handful of AI providers to create, host, and maintain their AI models for them. The AI providers now offer increasingly industrialized versions of AI: standardized, off-the-shelf, and widely applicable models for tasks like image recognition, voice recognition, and natural language processing (Varian 2018, 7; Evans 2019; Clark 2020). In cases where AI models need more customization—for example, idiosyncratic data that the system needs to be trained on—these AI providers again offer the tools and computing power other companies need to perform these tasks. The result is that AI is effectively becoming like a utility, whether in the form of preexisting systems and services or in the form of the tools necessary to build their own, that firms can pay a fee (per inference or even per second) to access.

On a second level, there are the AI start-ups: companies that are creating new, artisanal AI services—often pitched at more niche markets than those the generic AI providers pitch to and often reliant on proprietary data. These companies are typically focused on specific problems that the big platforms are not in a position to recognize (e.g., automating the intricacies of a particular production process), and they tend to create specialized machine learning–based applications to provide solutions. These start-ups disprove the idea that the major platforms have "all the data," as they are often built on collecting data that others have ignored (Evans 2018). Google, for instance, may have a lot of search data, but it does not (yet) have telemetry data from wind turbines. But the AI start-ups that might collect such data still usually remain dependent on the AI providers: the storage capacity, the hardware, the database back ends, and the pretrained AI models that can then be customized are all rented from the major platforms. Yet these services are often quite expensive, with model training costing potentially US$100,000+ and with retraining often being necessary because of "data drift" (Casado and Bornstein 2020). The result is that the AI providers are routinely skimming around a quarter of the revenues of the AI start-ups, leaving the latter with small margins (Casado and Bornstein 2020).

Lastly, there is that group of firms that could be considered AI consumers: those who purchase and use AI services from others. This group includes, at its upper limits, the rest of the economy. As competitive pressures drive the adoption of machine learning across the economy, ever more firms will become AI consumers dependent upon a handful of AI providers (with some mediation by AI start-ups). Research on this group has been the primary focus of management literature on AI, as businesses seek to capture more value through the use of the technology (Agrawal, Gans, and Goldfarb 2018b; Davenport 2019).

Data and Monopoly

As I noted earlier, few scholars have to date examined the monopolization aspects of AI. Yet this monopolization tendency is particularly important insofar as all of the top AI companies are based out of the US or China. Even Europe remains far behind in terms of amounts invested, data collected, start-up successes, intellectual properties patented, and labor available. With this vast global disparity between the two leading countries and everyone else, the value created economy-wide by AI is more likely than not to be captured predominantly by the monopolists.

Among those who have looked at the potential for AI to create monopolization tendencies, two core arguments have emerged. First, there are those who have focused on the ways in which the *use* of AI will lead a handful of AI consumers to capture larger and larger market shares. The McKinsey Global Institute, for instance, argues that those who more rapidly adopt AI will gain significantly in the coming decades, while those who do not will fall further and further behind (Bughin et al. 2018, 39–41). These early adopters tend to already be highly digitized and large-scale, and therefore primed to take advantage of the benefits that AI might offer (Bughin and Manyika

2018). Research in management studies comes to similar conclusions: late adopters of AI will struggle because it takes a lot of time and effort to collect data and adapt AI systems to local conditions and requirements (Mahidhar and Davenport 2018). Those who get a head start on this process are deemed likely to pull away from their competitors (Mahidhar and Davenport 2018). More elaborate accounts have focused on how algorithms across a number of firms may interact in such a way as to unintentionally create collusion and an oligopolistic market structure (Ezrachi and Stucke 2016, 2015).

If this first series of arguments has applied to the firms that use AI (consumers), a second set of arguments applies to both the consumers and providers. Here, attention has centered on the role of data in the process of training AI models. This is particularly the case for deep learning, which relies upon massive amounts of data, and for which research has repeatedly found that more data makes for better AI (Sun et al. 2017). Given that the extraction of data is already concentrated in the hands of a few major platforms, it is hardly a leap to expect that a technology that relies on that data will be similarly concentrated. We might therefore expect the technological requirements of contemporary AI to induce a strong tendency toward centralization and concentration of capital. Yet the debate so far has been divided.

On the one hand, there are those who are largely skeptical about the possibility of machine learning increasing monopolization of providers. Hal Varian, a well-paid employee of Google, is the clearest articulator of this position. In his account, AI is unlikely to involve increasing returns to scale on the supply side, as the cost of supplying AI software does not significantly decrease after the creation of the software. Whereas traditional software could replicate and sell innumerable copies at decreasing marginal cost, today's AI systems instead require updates and other continual improvements that mean costs continue (Varian 2018, 16). Neither is AI likely to have demand-side increasing returns to scale, as Varian believes network effects will not operate here—and in the cases where they might (e.g., firms choosing an AI provider because it is well-known), these are no different than what happens in any other industry. Lock-in, or path dependency, is deemed not to be a major issue either, as developments like containerization[4] enable firms to shift from one AI provider to another (Varian 2018, 19). And lastly, data is argued to have decreasing returns to scale, in that while more data may mean more accurate predictions from models, it increasingly takes more and more data to eke out smaller and smaller predictive gains (Agrawal, Gans, and Goldfarb 2018a, 20–21).

Similar arguments against data's role in facilitating monopolization come from the venture capital firm Andreessen Horowitz. As they note, after a certain point, getting the data needed to improve an AI system can become systematically more difficult even as the benefit to the predictive accuracy becomes increasingly marginal (Casado and

Lauten 2019). New data often overlaps with existing data, the relevant data needed can be difficult to find and can involve edge cases, and since it involves edge cases, the number of times the data will be relevant can be minimal. The former chair of Barack Obama's Council of Economic Advisors likewise finds in a review of the literature that there is "limited evidence of increasing returns to scale for data" (Furman and Seamans 2018, 19).

On the other hand, there are those who argue that, at least under certain conditions, data does generate a virtuous cycle that can lead to a handful of firms dominating. Agrawal, Gans, and Goldfarb (2018a, 21), for instance, agree with Varian that more data may not have increasing returns for technical value but counter that it often does have increasing returns for economic value. For example, in many image recognition applications, marginally better accuracy may not matter. But in some circumstances (e.g., medical diagnoses), an algorithm that is accurate 99 percent of the time will be vastly more useful than one that is accurate only 95 percent of the time. In such cases, the decreasing returns of data still manifest significant economic advantages. Monopolization can emerge here, as more data will lead to better-quality services, which leads to more customers, which leads to more data—and so on (Casado and Lauten 2019). And perhaps the boldest version of the argument comes from another venture capitalist, Kai-Fu Lee, who is one of the few to also draw out the geopolitical implications of this tendency (Lee 2018). As he writes,

> First, most of the money being made from artificial intelligence will go to the United States and China. A.I. is an industry in which strength begets strength: The more data you have, the better your product; the better your product, the more data you can collect; the more data you can collect, the more talent you can attract; the more talent you can attract, the better your product. It's a virtuous circle, and the United States and China have already amassed the talent, market share and data to set it in motion. (Lee 2017)

Here we see that not only is data a facilitator of monopolization, but it will also facilitate a planetary concentration of AI's value in the hands of two beneficiary countries. All others, in Lee's account, will become dependent on the US and China for AI services.

These latter arguments about the significance of data and its potential to create virtuous cycles appear far more plausible than the denial of this trajectory. Regulators appear to have agreed, with much of the discussion around how to regulate AI companies (with respect to their political economy rather than their ethical applications) hinging upon proposals for data sharing. A recent European Commission report, for instance, suggests that "where specific circumstances so dictate, access to data should be made compulsory, where appropriate under fair, transparent, reasonable, proportionate and/or nondiscriminatory conditions" (European Commission 2020, 13). Similar policy proposals have been put forward in Germany as well (Nahles 2018).

AI Production Process

While the focus of existing research on monopolization and AI has been on who dominates in data collection, the AI production process involves several other stages. Broadly speaking, we can distinguish between four different stages (Dong 2017): data collection, data processing, model production, and model deployment/monitoring/retraining. The first of these, data collection, is the finding of data to feed into and train machine learning models.

The second stage is data processing, involving the cleaning up and (often) labeling of data. In terms of concrete labor time, this is the most involved part of the entire process; it typically requires scores of workers to accomplish. One study, for instance, found that this work took around 80 percent of the labor time needed to build an AI system (Cognilytica 2019). A raft of new companies has emerged to offer data labeling services, often relying on marginalized populations within countries (e.g., prison labor or refugees; see also chapter 9) or marginalized populations globally (e.g., low-wage workers in Africa, Asia, and Latin America) (Batha 2018; Cadell 2019; Chen 2019; Gray and Suri 2019; Metz 2019; Murgia 2019b; Anwar and Graham 2020; see also chapter 6). There is an emerging global inequality here, with some businesses in the Global North offering more specialized data processing services—and charging higher fees as a result. The production of properly labeled data for sensitive issues (e.g., legal classification, driverless car data, or medical imagery) requires people familiar with the subject area (Peng 2019). And even apparently low-level data labeling—such as facial key-point labeling—increasingly demands extraordinary skills: "The task was much simpler a few years ago, when labellers only had to put several dots on a human face. Now, facial key-point labelling can involve up to 206 dots—8+ on each eyebrow, 20+ on the lips, 17+ along the jawline, and so on" (Peng 2019). The need for high-quality labeling is leading to the emergence of an industry to provide it, while lower-quality labeling is outsourced to the margins of the planetary economy. The growth of the AI economy is following well-worn paths already set out by existing global hierarchies.

Once the data has been collected and labeled, the third stage of the AI production process is model production: the process of selecting an AI model and feeding the data into it in order to train it. This stage often requires highly skilled labor—to tune algorithms and other tasks—though it is much less labor-intensive than earlier stages. It is, however, computationally intensive—a point to which I will return later. Lastly, there is the deployment and monitoring stage. This involves seeing whether the model works in practice (e.g., does it produce significant bias problems?), as well as updating and retraining old models. The latter is particularly important, as models typically degrade over time due to the fundamental limitation that they are trained on a finite dataset (Abrahamson 2019). As the world changes, so too do the patterns that the model is aiming to mirror, and therefore this final stage of the AI process is often a matter of continually retraining models to reflect new data.

With this expanded image of the AI production process in hand, the argument I want to make in the remainder of this chapter is that the first two stages are decreasing sources of competitive advantage (and decreasing monopolistic footholds), while the latter two are becoming the real battleground for who will control AI.[5] Yet as we saw in the review of the existing literature, the latter two stages are largely ignored in favor of a focus on data alone.

Data

Let us deal with a first question that might come to mind. Despite all the attention paid to the importance of data and its being lauded as the new oil, why is data losing significance as a competitive advantage? The first reason is the general spread of the platform business model and its unique capacities to collect data (Srnicek 2016). Whereas a decade ago relatively few companies had platforms and systems in place to monitor and record data, today the data-centric business model has become increasingly widespread. Whether legacy companies or start-ups, everyone is trying to collect their own proprietary data. There are, of course, still significant disparities in the amount of data being collected by various firms. But the gap in the amount of data being collected between the companies collecting vast amounts and the companies collecting none is arguably decreasing.

A second reason why data is losing some of its competitive advantage is the explosive growth of open datasets. For instance, Google subsidiary Waymo's Open Dataset for training driverless vehicles contains nearly 17 hours of video, with labeling for 22 million 2D objects and 25 million 3D objects (Peng 2019). Google's Open Images Dataset contains 9.2 million photos, with over 30 million labels for almost 20,000 concepts (Kuznetsova et al. 2020). And data is available for even the most niche of interests. Clemson University and the University of Essex, for example, released a database of 4.5 million transcriptions of speeches given in the Irish parliament between 1919 and 2013 (Herzog and Mikhaylov 2017). As ever more vast and labeled datasets are being made available, new companies will have less need to go out and find their own data. The problem of how to bootstrap from no data is, simply put, increasingly less of a problem. To be sure, none of this is to say that the open datasets are equivalent in value to proprietary ones—but they do go some way toward lessening the competitive advantages of the latter and reducing the problems of bootstrapping training from nothing.

The final, and potentially most significant, reason for data's relative decline is the emergence of synthetic data. Rather than relying on getting data from the real world, a growing number of companies is synthetically creating new data and synthetically augmenting low-quality and sparse data. The perhaps best-known examples of this involve generative adversarial networks (GANs) creating realistic-looking photos of individuals. But others have used GANs to generate videos that algorithms can then be trained on. And other researchers have taken small datasets (of plants in this case) and used GANs to create more images. After comparing systems trained on the two datasets, the researchers found that the larger (part synthetic) dataset ended up having less overfitting and slightly more accuracy (Giuffrida, Scharr, and Tsaftaris 2017). Other approaches to synthetic data involve artificial environments—often artificial worlds created with videogame engines—that AI agents interact with and learn from. The explosion of videogame-playing AI, often based on reinforcement learning, is one expression of this. Artificial environments offer several advantages—if real-world experiments with AI-driven robots take significant time, running the same experiments in simulations can be vastly quicker (and safer). In this vein, even well-known videogames like the Grand Theft Auto series are being deployed as environments to train driverless cars (Li et al. 2017). These environments are also becoming industrialized and open-source, with OpenAI Universe including over 1,000 environments and Facebook releasing the TorchCraft environment for researchers to use.

These processes of creating data from nothing are allowing a number of start-ups lacking their own data to get past the initial hurdles (Simonite 2018) and have led some to argue that synthetic data will lead to the end of any competitive advantage in the area of data for the tech giants (Nisselson 2018). But incumbent firms are also using these methods, with, for example, Amazon using GANs to create e-commerce data, Facebook generating synthetic users to test out its platform, and Google creating synthetic skin lesion images to train healthcare AI (Kumar, Biswas, and Sanyal 2018; Ahlgren et al. 2020; Kohlberger and Liu 2020). The result of all this may be AI companies moving from "data competition" to "environment competition" (Clark 2018a). As these new approaches to AI continue to gain traction, it is more likely that data will become less of a competitive advantage.

Compute

If data collection and labeling are becoming less significant, the other stages of the production process are increasingly where AI monopolies and moats are being built. This is for two reasons in particular: the concentrated ownership of immense computing resources (compute) and the systems and lures built for attracting the small supply of high-skill workers.[6]

With respect to the former, increases in computing power have been driving advances in AI—not only during its most recent deep learning incarnation but for many decades now (Sutton 2019). In the past decade, we have seen AI models getting larger as well, with more parameters than ever before. In 2019, for example, NVIDIA released a model with 8.3 billion parameters, while Google released a model with over 50 billion parameters (Bapna and Firat 2019; Toole 2019). To meet the immense challenges of training these models, AI hardware has been scaling up to data centers and supercomputers. More attention is also being given to how to network hundreds and even thousands of graphics processing units (GPUs) together in order to train these massive models (Hazelwood et al. 2018; Laanait et al. 2019). The result of all this has been a significant leap forward in the computing power being used to train the largest AI systems. Between 1959 and 2012, the use of compute for training AI systems increased at broadly the same rate as Moore's Law—doubling every 24 months (Amodei and Hernandez 2018). Yet between 2012 and 2018, there was a 300,000× increase in the amount of compute used to train the largest models—a doubling every 3.4 months. This rapid increase has been fostered by better chips and, more significantly, by an increase in the ability to use parallel processing (Amodei and Hernandez 2018). Beyond the production stage of models, the deployment stage is also ramping up in terms of compute requirements, making some of the largest models increasingly unwieldy (Kaiser 2020).

It is, unsurprisingly, the AI providers who are positioned to be able to use and deploy the sorts of compute needed for cutting-edge AI. The shift to cloud computing is an expression of this, as it is data center–scale computing that is required—and providers can use GPUs at one point to further their own research and at another point as a rental for a small AI start-up. Computing resources are, in turn, an expression of financial resources. For example, it cost an estimated $35 million to train AlphaGo Zero, the groundbreaking self-taught AI program for playing the game of Go (note that this does not include the cost of researchers or anything that went into initially building the project) (Huang 2018). Data centers are immensely expensive propositions for any company. And while detailed figures on the amounts being spent on this infrastructure are not available publicly, the financial statements of the big cloud companies all reveal tens of billions of dollars being poured annually into fixed capital. Amazon, Microsoft, and Google, for example, collectively had $73.5 billion in capital expenditures in 2019 (Fitzgerald 2020). Far from being immaterial companies, these are significantly embodied companies. And as these companies turn to designing their own specialized computer chips to gain more speed and power, the entry fees to compete with them are growing. Nearly all the major tech companies are investing in their own designs (e.g., Google's Tensor Processing Units) or buying up smaller chip start-ups (e.g., Amazon's purchase of Annapurna Labs). The economics of all this again favor the largest tech companies with the capital to invest in new chip design, buy the chips in data center quantities, and deploy them for their own benefit. The capital expenditure required for this scale of computing creates extremely high barriers to entry, the result being that AI provision is ultimately a market in which only a handful of companies globally stand a chance.

This scale of compute lends itself to further benefits for these companies. First, AI systems tend to perform better when they have more compute. As one review of the impact of compute notes, "There is a close tie from compute operation rate (e.g., floating point operations, or 'FLOPs') to model accuracy improvements" (Hestness et al. 2017, 13). And while there are diminishing returns to the value of increasing available compute, as we saw earlier, significant economic value can still be extracted from even marginal increases in accuracy.

More compute also enables companies to train and retrain models much more quickly than their competitors. As AI remains an empirical science, it involves running a number of experiments to see what works best—tuning hyperparameters, testing on data from outside the training set, debugging any problems, and so on. The more rapidly a firm can do this, the more rapidly it can deploy models to users. Moreover, as the world changes, models degrade and need updating. Again, the more rapidly one can retrain models, the better they will perform and the more users they are likely to attract. The differentials in speed between an average firm and a major platform can be immense. For example, in 2012, to train a model on the ImageNet dataset to a 75 percent degree of accuracy took 7–14 days with a single GPU. By 2019, one Chinese company had managed to train a model on the same dataset, to the same degree of accuracy, in 75 seconds with 2048 GPUs—a time reduction of 99.9 percent (Clark 2019). These sorts of advantages can be massive in a rapidly changing world.

Lastly, more computing power enables better research. It allows researchers to try ideas at scales that are unavailable to smaller firms. Innovations, as a result, are more likely to come from the larger AI providers. These innovations may eventually filter down to smaller firms as improvements and efficiencies make them more readily available. But as one investor puts it, "Having a really, really big computer is kind of like a time warp, in that you can do things that aren't economical now but will be economically [feasible] maybe a decade from now" (Levy 2017). More computing power also lets researchers explore the boundaries and limits of different approaches in much more thorough ways—determining, in one example, whether reinforcement learning or evolutionary learning is better for a particular problem set (Clark 2018b). In another instance, Facebook researchers used large-scale training to find faster ways to do machine translation (Edunov, Auli, and Ott 2018). Additionally, the rapidity of training lets these researchers determine what are unfruitful ventures and what might be productive avenues far more quickly than those who must limit themselves to testing on smaller systems that may not scale up (Clark 2018c). More compute, in the end, allows the big AI providers to more rapidly and effectively research AI possibilities and gain even more ground on their competitors.

Labor

To make effective use of compute resources, though, requires workers with the skills to put these systems together in the first place. The task of scaling from one GPU to 1,000 is highly technical and challenging, and workers capable of doing it remain in short supply. This leads us to the third key element of monopolization in the AI world: labor.

On the first level, the short supply of these workers means they can often command very large salaries. Average salaries for data scientists now range into six figures in America. DeepMind, arguably the world's leading AI center, spent nearly £400 million on "staff and related costs" in 2018.[7] This means that companies with the cash to spend on the best talent are the ones who tend to be winning the race for AI talent. Academia has been one of the big losers, with a major brain drain of AI researchers from universities to companies. Large salaries and access to unprecedented amounts of compute are drawing these researchers into the arms of the top AI companies (Murgia 2019a).

Yet beneath the flashy salaries lies a series of much subtler ways in which the AI providers are channeling talent their way. In particular, the seemingly noncapitalist practice of releasing their AI software for free in fact obscures a significant capitalist battle between the major companies. These open-source frameworks offer a range of premade tools, libraries, and interfaces for others to build their AI models with—often based on the same tools that companies are using internally. At present, Google's TensorFlow is the most popular in the industry, though others have more niche markets, and Facebook's PyTorch is coming to dominate the research sector (He 2019; Kaggle 2019, 19). Why would these companies give away such potentially valuable software, though? First, these projects invoke what Paolo Virno once called the "communism of capital" (Virno 2004, 110).[8] Such open-source projects foster and support communities of labor that provide inputs back into the software—all for free. The more widely a framework is used, the more likely it is that the community will find bugs, add features, and generally innovate and develop the software in useful ways. And the easiest way to ensure widespread usage is through lowering the cost barrier by open-sourcing these projects.

In addition, a successful framework builds up a community of developers who know how to work within a particular company. Graduate students, for instance, who have trained with these tools are primed to slide into a corporate position when they leave university looking for a career. Frameworks become feeder networks for the emerging generations of talent. Such is the importance of these frameworks that other major companies have begun working together in an attempt to compete against Google's TensorFlow. Apple and Amazon, for instance, have teamed up to enable applications written in Amazon's MXNet framework to be easily translated into Apple's Core ML framework (Menant and Gupta 2017). Microsoft and Facebook, meanwhile, created the Open Neural Network Exchange (ONNX) format, which makes their own frameworks (CNTK, PyTorch, and Caffe2) interoperable (Boyd 2017). Each of these strategic capitalist alliances is an effort to overthrow the current dominance of TensorFlow and the advantages that it lends Google. In any case, though, with the channeling of labor away from lower-tier companies that the communism of capital entails, all the frameworks are increasingly controlled by the top-tier AI companies. The powerful grow stronger.

Conclusion

The argument I have tried to set out here is that contemporary AI is a monopolizing technology but that the often-assumed driver of this tendency—data—is less significant than believed. Instead, contemporary AI is increasingly driven by the inputs of compute and labor, and these are forming the real competitive advantages for the largest AI providers as they continue to pull away from any possible challengers. Far from being a disruptive threat to existing technology giants, AI appears set to further consolidate their power. In this conclusion, I will briefly examine some of the important implications that this analysis might have for uneven planetary economic development.

If data, for instance, were the only key input to the AI production process, one could imagine something like a national data commons being sufficient to chart a path for digital sovereignty. Take control over data, and you would have taken control of the key resource that gives the AI providers their power. This belief, as we saw earlier, seems to motivate a number of the policy proposals currently being put forth across Europe. However, if compute and labor are also key aspects, it is hard to avoid the conclusion that the biggest cloud AI companies, centered solely in the US and China, will continue to pull away from the rest regardless of data policies. Other countries and other companies have not shown an ability to invest the same amount into fixed capital as the top American AI firms, nor do they have much capacity to retain talent when a company like Google is willing to pay enormous salaries and give luxurious amounts of research freedom to data scientists and other skilled workers.

These companies, moreover, are rapidly stretching their tentacles across the remainder of the world. Kai-Fu Lee (2017), for example, paints a plausible picture of US companies carving up the developed world while Chinese platforms expand across the developing world. In this possible future, it seems likely that much of the world, developed or otherwise, will remain relatively low in the AI value chain (Weber 2017). Low-waged data labeling is already spread across the peripheries, reliant on hyperexploited and marginalized workers. There is an unevenness here as well, as we saw earlier, with high-skill labeling being brought into the metropole of the AI world. In the world of AI consumers, other countries and the US will continue to be able to grab a part of the AI value chain. Start-ups can find novel uses of machine learning and apply them to new products. Yet they will remain tenants on the clouds provided by the biggest AI companies, dutifully paying their rents to these American and Chinese companies. Meanwhile, start-ups that appear promising are all too likely to be swallowed up by the tech giants. Activity in mergers and acquisitions related to AI, for instance, increased by 500 percent between 2013 and 2017. Between 2010 and 2019, Apple made over 20 AI acquisitions, Google made 14, and Microsoft made 10.[9] By comparison, the vast majority of the companies that purchased an AI company in that decade only bought a single company.[10] The largest companies continue to pull away, and the market for AI provision continues to consolidate.

This means that in thinking about digital development in the Global South, a focus on start-ups is insufficient to overcome existing imbalances. Moreover, the impacts on broader ideas of economic development are likely to be significant. Not only is the profit of the emerging global value chains for AI being captured by a handful of companies, but the secondary effects of that value capture—the conglomeration effects and other spillovers from AI growth—are also likely to be concentrated in a handful of countries (Weber 2017, 412). To put it starkly, it may turn out that while workers in Kampala are spending their poorly paid time labeling images of faces, wealth and talent are creating virtuous cycles of local growth in Silicon Valley and Shenzhen. Developing countries—and many developed countries—look likely to remain trapped in positions of relative digital underdevelopment. The emerging planetary value chain of AI is a profoundly unequal one.

Let me conclude with three points. First, as I have argued here, the monopolization tendency is not just—or even primarily—a data issue. Monopolization is driven more by the barriers to entry posed by fixed capital and the virtuous cycles that compute and labor are generating for the AI providers. The academic literature has, to date, largely neglected to examine these elements. Second, a consequence of the preceding argument is that open-source software is not an alternative so much as a strategic tool for these AI platforms. Existing arguments about how large tech companies freely build their proprietary empires on top of open-source software must be supplemented with attention to the ways in which free—and waged—labor is brought into the companies' ambit via things like open-source frameworks. Lastly, another notable consequence is that policy in response to AI development must go beyond the fascination with data. If, as I argue, hardware and labor are important inputs too, then opening up data is an ineffective idea at best and a counterproductive one at worst. It could simply mean that the tech giants get access to even more free data—while everyone else trains their open data on Amazon's servers. If we want to take back control over big tech, we need to pay attention to more than just data.

Notes

1. By "artificial intelligence," I specifically mean the constellation of machine learning models and techniques that have emerged in the wake of the 2012 deep learning revival inspired by the ImageNet success of Krizhevsky, Sutskever, and Hinton (2012).

2. A recent paper by Mucha and Seppälä (2020) has made clear just how narrow most research on the economics of AI currently is.

3. See https://www.crunchbase.com/search/organization.companies/6fc9f338b99a553e2633171 8a9377efc.

4. Containerization is a recent development that enables applications to run more easily in any cloud environment rather than being built for and able to run in only specific ones.

5. Thanks to Jack Clark's *Import AI* newsletter for initially bringing my attention to the significance of other aspects in contemporary AI development and competition. This chapter attempts to build on and systematize some of the arguments he has made in his newsletter.

6. *Compute* here is a term commonly used in the cloud computing and AI industries to refer to computing resources (as opposed to, say, network resources or memory resources).

7. See https://beta.companieshouse.gov.uk/company/07386350/filing-history.

8. Thanks to Nick Dyer-Witheford, Atle Mikkola Kjolsen, and James Steinhoff for reminding me of this reference.

9. We have not focused on Apple in this piece because their AI strategy is focused more on devices than on cloud platforms. While the focus on devices remains lucrative for Apple at the moment, AI companies based on cloud platforms appear to be far more significant in their implications.

10. See https://interactives.cbinsights.com/artificial-intelligence-acquisitions-by-famga/.

References

Abrahamson, Joseph. 2019. "Model Performance Often Degrades over Time." Simplicial, April 22.

Acemoglu, Daron, and Pascual Restrepo. 2020. "The Wrong Kind of AI? Artificial Intelligence and the Future of Labour Demand." *Cambridge Journal of Regions, Economy and Society* 13 (1): 25–35.

Agrawal, Ajay, Joshua Gans, and Avi Goldfarb. 2018a. "Economic Policy for Artificial Intelligence." Working Paper 24690. Cambridge, MA: National Bureau of Economic Research.

Agrawal, Ajay, Joshua Gans, and Avi Goldfarb. 2018b. *Prediction Machines: The Simple Economics of Artificial Intelligence*. Boston: Harvard Business Review Press.

Ahlgren, John, Maria Eugenia Berezin, Kinga Bojarczuk, Elena Dulskyte, Inna Dvortsova, Johann George, Natalija Gucevska, Mark Harman, Ralf Lämmel, Erik Meijer, Silvia Sapora, and Justin Spahr-Summers. 2020. "WES: Agent-Based User Interaction Simulation on Real Infrastructure." Facebook Research. https://research.fb.com/publications/wes-agent-based-user-interaction-simulation-on-real -infrastructure/.

Amodei, Dario, and Danny Hernandez. 2018. "AI and Compute." *OpenAI*, May 16. https://openai .com/blog/ai-and-compute/.

Anwar, Mohammad Amir, and Mark Graham. 2020. "Digital Labour at Economic Margins: African Workers and the Global Information Economy." *Review of African Political Economy* 47 (163): 95–105.

Bapna, Ankur, and Orhan Firat. 2019. "Exploring Massively Multilingual, Massive Neural Machine Translation." Google AI Blog, October 11.

Batha, Emma. 2018. "Mobile App Pays Refugees to Boost Artificial Intelligence." Reuters, November 15. https://www.reuters.com/article/us-refugees-conference-tech-jobs-idUSKCN1NK2SR.

Boyd, Eric. 2017. "Microsoft and Facebook Create Open Ecosystem for AI Model Interoperability." *Microsoft Azure* (blog), September 7. https://azure.microsoft.com/en-us/blog/microsoft-and -facebook-create-open-ecosystem-for-ai-model-interoperability/.

Bresnahan, Timothy F., and M. Trajtenberg. 1995. "General Purpose Technologies: 'Engines of Growth'?" *Journal of Econometrics* 65 (1): 83–108.

Bughin, Jacques, and Eric Hazan. 2017. "The New Spring of Artificial Intelligence: A Few Early Economies." *VoxEU*, August 21. https://voxeu.org/article/new-spring-artificial-intelligence-few-early -economics.

Bughin, Jacques, and James Manyika. 2018. "Technology Convergence and AI Divides: A Simulation Appraisal." *VoxEU*, September 7. https://voxeu.org/article/technology-convergence-and-ai-divides.

Bughin, Jacques, Jeongmin Seong, James Manyika, Michael Chui, and Raoul Joshi. 2018. "Notes from the AI Frontier: Modeling the Global Economic Impact of AI." Washington, DC: McKinsey Global Institute. https://www.mckinsey.com/featured-insights/artificial-intelligence/notes-from -the-ai-frontier-modeling-the-impact-of-ai-on-the-world-economy.

Cadell, Cate. 2019. "Faces for Cookware: Data Collection Industry Flourishes as China Pursues AI Ambitions." Reuters, June 27. https://www.reuters.com/article/us-china-ai-data-insight-idUSKCN1TS3EA.

Casado, Martin, and Matt Bornstein. 2020. "The New Business of AI (and How It's Different from Traditional Software)." Andreessen Horowitz, February 16. https://a16z.com/2020/02/16/the-new-business-of-ai-and-how-its-different-from-traditional-software/.

Casado, Martin, and Peter Lauten. 2019. "The Empty Promise of Data Moats." Andreessen Horowitz, May 9. https://a16z.com/2019/05/09/data-network-effects-moats/.

Chen, Angela. 2019. "Inmates in Finland Are Training AI as Part of Prison Labor." *The Verge*, March 28. https://www.theverge.com/2019/3/28/18285572/prison-labor-finland-artificial-intelligence-data-tagging-vainu.

Christensen, Clayton M. 2016. *The Innovator's Dilemma: When New Technologies Cause Great Firms to Fail*. Boston: Harvard Business Review Press.

Clark, Jack. 2017. "The AI Data Grab, the Value of Simplicity, and a Technique for Automated Gardening." *Import AI* no. 41, May 8. https://jack-clark.net/2017/05/08/.

Clark, Jack. 2018a. "Virtual Beijing with ParallelEye, NVIDIA Tweaks GPU Licensing, and Saving Money by Getting AI to Help Humans Label Data Generated by AI." *Import AI* no. 75, January 1. https://jack-clark.net/2018/01/01/.

Clark, Jack. 2018b. "Trading Cryptocurrency with Deep Learning; Google Shows Why Evolutionary Methods Beat RL (for Now); and Using Iwatch Telemetry for AI Health Diagnosis." *Import AI* no. 81, February 12. https://jack-clark.net/2018/02/12/.

Clark, Jack. 2018c. "Sony Researchers Make Ultra-Fast ImageNet Training Breakthrough; Berkeley Researchers Tackle StarCraft II with Modular RL System; and Germany Adds €3bn for AI Research." *Import AI* no. 121, November 19. https://jack-clark.net/2018/11/19/.

Clark, Jack. 2019. "AIs Play Doom at Thousands of Frames per Second; NeurIPS Wants Reproducible Research; and Google Creates & Scraps AI Ethics Council." *Import AI* no. 141, April 8. https://jack-clark.net/2019/04/08/.

Clark, Jack. 2020. "The Industrialization of AI, BERT Goes Dutch, plus, AI Metrics Consolidation." *Import AI* no. 182, January 27. https://jack-clark.net/2020/01/27/.

Cognilytica. 2019. "Data Engineering, Preparation, and Labeling for AI 2019." *Cognilytica Research*, January 31.

Davenport, Thomas. 2019. *The AI Advantage: How to Put the Artificial Intelligence Revolution to Work*. Cambridge, MA: MIT Press.

Dong, Catherine. 2017. "The Evolution of Machine Learning." *TechCrunch*, August 8. http://social.techcrunch.com/2017/08/08/the-evolution-of-machine-learning/.

Dyer-Witheford, Nick, Atle Mikkola Kjosen, and James Steinhoff. 2019. *Inhuman Power: Artificial Intelligence and the Future of Capitalism.* London: Pluto Press.

Edunov, Sergey, Michael Auli, and Myle Ott. 2018. "Scaling Neural Machine Translation to Bigger Data Sets with Faster Training and Inference." Facebook Engineering, September 7. https://engineering.fb.com/ai-research/scaling-neural-machine-translation-to-bigger-data-sets-with-faster-training-and-inference/.

European Commission. 2020. "A European Strategy for Data." Brussels: European Commission. https://ec.europa.eu/info/sites/info/files/communication-european-strategy-data-19feb2020_en.pdf.

Evans, Benedict. 2018. "Does AI Make Strong Tech Companies Stronger?" *Benedict Evans* (blog), December 20. https://www.ben-evans.com/benedictevans/2018/12/19/does-ai-make-strong-tech-companies-stronger.

Evans, Benedict. 2019. "The Deployment Phase of Machine Learning." *Benedict Evans* (blog), October 4. https://www.ben-evans.com/benedictevans/2019/10/4/machine-learning-deployment.

Evans, David S. 2017. "Why the Dynamics of Competition for Online Platforms Leads to Sleepless Nights but Not Sleepy Monopolies." *SSRN*, August 3. https://ssrn.com/abstract=3009438.

Ezrachi, Ariel, and Maurice E. Stucke. 2015. "Artificial Intelligence & Collusion: When Computers Inhibit Competition." *SSRN*, April 9. https://ssrn.com/abstract=2591874.

Ezrachi, Ariel, and Maurice E. Stucke. 2016. *Virtual Competition: The Promise and Perils of the Algorithm-Driven Economy.* Cambridge, MA: Harvard University Press.

Fitzgerald, Charles. 2020. "Follow the CAPEX: Cloud Table Stakes 2019 Edition." *Platformonomics* (blog), February 11. https://www.platformonomics.com/2020/02/follow-the-capex-cloud-table-stakes-2019-edition/.

Frank, Morgan R., David Autor, James E. Bessen, Erik Brynjolfsson, Manuel Cebrian, David J. Deming, Maryann Feldman, Matthew Groh, José Lobo, Esteban Moro, Dashun Wang, Hyejin Youn, and Iyad Rahwan. 2019. "Toward Understanding the Impact of Artificial Intelligence on Labor." *Proceedings of the National Academy of Sciences* 116 (14): 6531–6539.

Furman, Jason, and Robert Seamans. 2018. "AI and the Economy." Working Paper 24689. Cambridge, MA: National Bureau of Economic Research.

Giuffrida, Mario Valerio, Hanno Scharr, and Sotirios A. Tsaftaris. 2017. "ARIGAN: Synthetic Arabidopsis Plants Using Generative Adversarial Network." Preprint, submitted September 4. http://arxiv.org/abs/1709.00938.

Gray, Mary L., and Siddharth Suri. 2019. *Ghost Work: How to Stop Silicon Valley from Building a New Global Underclass.* Boston: Houghton Mifflin Harcourt.

Hazelwood, Kim, Sarah Bird, David Brooks, Soumith Chintala, Utku Diril, Dmytro Dzhulgakov, Mohamed Fawzy, Bill Jia, Yangqing Jia, Aditya Kalro, James Law, Kevin Lee, Jason Lu, Pieter Noordhuis, Misha Smelyanskiy, Liang Xiong, and Xiaodong Wang. 2018. "Applied Machine Learning at Facebook: A Datacenter Infrastructure Perspective." In *2018 IEEE International Symposium on High*

Performance Computer Architecture (HPCA), 620–629. https://research.fb.com/wp-content/uploads/2017/12/hpca-2018-facebook.pdf.

He, Horace. 2019. "The State of Machine Learning Frameworks in 2019." *The Gradient*, October 10. https://thegradient.pub/state-of-ml-frameworks-2019-pytorch-dominates-research-tensorflow-dominates-industry/.

Herzog, Alexander, and Slava J. Mikhaylov. 2017. "Database of Parliamentary Speeches in Ireland, 1919–2013." *2017 International Conference on the Frontiers and Advances in Data Science (FADS)*, 29–34. https://doi.org/10.1109/FADS.2017.8253189.

Hestness, Joel, Sharan Narang, Newsha Ardalani, Gregory Diamos, Heewoo Jun, Hassan Kianinejad, Md. Mostofa Ali Patwary, Yang Yang, and Yanqi Zhou. 2017. "Deep Learning Scaling Is Predictable, Empirically." Preprint, submitted December 1. http://arxiv.org/abs/1712.00409.

Howard, Christian. 2018. "Introducing Google AI." Google AI Blog, May 7. http://ai.googleblog.com/2018/05/introducing-google-ai.html.

Huang, Dan. 2018. "How Much Did AlphaGo Zero Cost?" *Dansplaining* (blog), March. https://www.yuzeh.com/data/agz-cost.html.

Jovanovic, Boyan, and Peter L. Rousseau. 2005. "General Purpose Technologies." Working Paper. Cambridge, MA: National Bureau of Economic Research.

Kaggle. 2019. "State of Data Science and Machine Learning 2019." Kaggle. https://www.kaggle.com/kaggle-survey-2019.

Kaiser, Caleb. 2020. "Too Big to Deploy: How GPT-2 Is Breaking Production." *Medium*, February 2. https://explainjay.wordpress.com/2020/02/02/too-big-to-deploy-how-gpt-2-is-breaking-production/.

Kohlberger, Timo, and Yuan Liu. 2020. "Generating Diverse Synthetic Medical Image Data for Training Machine Learning Models." Google AI Blog, February 19. http://ai.googleblog.com/2020/02/generating-diverse-synthetic-medical.html.

Krizhevsky, Alex, Ilya Sutskever, and Geoffrey Hinton. 2012. "ImageNet Classification with Deep Convolutional Neural Networks." In *Proceedings of the 25th International Conference on Neural Information Processing Systems* 1: 1097–1105. Red Hook, NY: Curran Associates Inc.

Kumar, Ashutosh, Arijit Biswas, and Subhajit Sanyal. 2018. "eCommerceGAN: A Generative Adversarial Network for E-Commerce." Preprint, submitted January 10. http://arxiv.org/abs/1801.03244.

Kuznetsova, Alina, Hassan Rom, Neil Alldrin, Jasper Uijlings, Ivan Krasin, Jordi Pont-Tuset, Shahab Kamali, Stefan Popov, Matteo Malloci, Alexander Kolesnikov, Tom Duerig, and Vittorio Ferrari. 2020. "The Open Images Dataset V4: Unified Image Classification, Object Detection, and Visual Relationship Detection at Scale." *International Journal of Computer Vision* 128: 1956–1981. https://doi.org/10.1007/s11263-020-01316-z.

Laanait, Nouamane, Joshua Romero, Junqi Yin, M. Todd Young, Sean Treichler, Vitalii Starchenko, Albina Borisevich, Alex Sergeev, and Michael Matheson. 2019. "Exascale Deep Learning for Scientific Inverse Problems." Preprint, submitted September 24. http://arxiv.org/abs/1909.11150.

Lee, Kai-Fu. 2017. "The Real Threat of Artificial Intelligence." *New York Times*, June 24. https://www.nytimes.com/2017/06/24/opinion/sunday/artificial-intelligence-economic-inequality.html.

Lee, Kai-Fu. 2018. *AI Superpowers: China, Silicon Valley, and the New World Order*. Boston: Houghton Mifflin Harcourt.

Levy, Steven. 2017. "Bill Joy Finds the Jesus Battery." *Wired*, August 16. https://www.wired.com/story/bill-joy-finds-the-jesus-battery/.

Li, Xuan, Kunfeng Wang, Yonglin Tian, Lan Yan, and Fei-Yue Wang. 2017. "The ParallelEye Dataset: Constructing Large-Scale Artificial Scenes for Traffic Vision Research." Preprint, submitted December 22. http://arxiv.org/abs/1712.08394.

Mahidhar, Vikram, and Thomas H. Davenport. 2018. "Why Companies That Wait to Adopt AI May Never Catch Up." *Harvard Business Review*, December 6. https://hbr.org/2018/12/why-companies-that-wait-to-adopt-ai-may-never-catch-up.

Menant, Sebastien, and Pracheer Gupta. 2017. "Bring Machine Learning to iOS Apps Using Apache MXNet and Apple Core ML." *Amazon Web Services* (blog), September 6. https://aws.amazon.com/blogs/machine-learning/bring-machine-learning-to-ios-apps-using-apache-mxnet-and-apple-core-ml/.

Metz, Cade. 2019. "A.I. Is Learning from Humans. Many Humans." *New York Times*, August 16. https://www.nytimes.com/2019/08/16/technology/ai-humans.html.

Mucha, Tomasz, and Timo Seppälä. 2020. "Artificial Intelligence Platforms: A New Research Agenda for Digital Platform Economy." ETLA Working Paper no. 76. Helsinki: Elinkeinoelämän Tutkimuslaitos. https://www.etla.fi/wp-content/uploads/ETLA-Working-Papers-76.pdf.

Murgia, Madhumita. 2019a. "AI Academics under Pressure to Do Commercial Research." *Financial Times*, March 13.

Murgia, Madhumita. 2019b. "AI's New Workforce: The Data-Labelling Industry Spreads Globally." *Financial Times*, July 24. https://www.ft.com/content/56dde36c-aa40-11e9-984c-fac8325aaa04.

Nadella, Satya. 2018. "Embracing Our Future: Intelligent Cloud and Intelligent Edge." Microsoft News Center, March 29. https://news.microsoft.com/2018/03/29/satya-nadella-email-to-employees-embracing-our-future-intelligent-cloud-and-intelligent-edge/.

Nahles, Andrea. 2018. "Die Tech-Riesen des Silicon Valleys gefährden den fairen Wettbewerb" [The Tech Giants of Silicon Valley Endanger Fair Competition]. *Handelsblatt*, August 13. https://www.handelsblatt.com/meinung/gastbeitraege/gastkommentar-die-tech-riesen-des-silicon-valleys-gefaehrden-den-fairen-wettbewerb/22900656.html.

Niklas, Jędrzej, and Lina Dencik. 2020. "European Artificial Intelligence Policy: Mapping the Institutional Landscape." Working Paper. Cardiff: Data Justice Lab. https://datajusticeproject.net/wp-content/uploads/sites/30/2020/07/WP_AI-Policy-in-Europe.pdf.

Nisselson, Evan. 2018. "Deep Learning with Synthetic Data Will Democratize the Tech Industry." *TechCrunch*, May 11. http://social.techcrunch.com/2018/05/11/deep-learning-with-synthetic-data-will-democratize-the-tech-industry/.

Peng, Tony. 2019. "Data Annotation: The Billion Dollar Business behind AI Breakthroughs." *Synced*, August 28. https://medium.com/syncedreview/data-annotation-the-billion-dollar-business-behind-ai -breakthroughs-d929b0a50d23.

Pleatsikas, Christopher, and David Teece. 2001. "The Analysis of Market Definition and Market Power in the Context of Rapid Innovation." *International Journal of Industrial Organization* 19 (5): 665–693.

Rao, Anand S., and Gerard Verweij. 2017. "Sizing the Prize: What's the Real Value of AI for Your Business and How Can You Capitalise?" New York: PwC. https://www.pwc.com/gx/en/issues /analytics/assets/pwc-ai-analysis-sizing-the-prize-report.pdf.

Royal Society and British Academy. 2018. *The Impact of Artificial Intelligence on Work*. London: Royal Society and British Academy. https://royalsociety.org/-/media/policy/projects/ai-and-work /evidence-synthesis-the-impact-of-AI-on-work.PDF.

Simonite, Tom. 2018. "Some Startups Use Fake Data to Train AI." *Wired*, April 25. https://www .wired.com/story/some-startups-use-fake-data-to-train-ai/.

Srnicek, Nick. 2016. *Platform Capitalism*. Cambridge: Polity Press.

Sun, Chen, Abhinav Shrivastava, Saurabh Singh, and Abhinav Gupta. 2017. "Revisiting Unrea-sonable Effectiveness of Data in Deep Learning Era." *2017 IEEE International Conference on Com-puter Vision (ICCV)*, 843–852. https://doi.org/10.1109/ICCV.2017.97.

Sutton, Richard. 2019. "The Bitter Lesson." *Incomplete Ideas* (blog), March 13. http://www .incompleteideas.net/IncIdeas/BitterLesson.html.

Toole, Jameson. 2019. "Deep Learning Has a Size Problem." *Heartbeat*, November 5. https:// heartbeat.fritz.ai/deep-learning-has-a-size-problem-ea601304cd8.

Trajtenberg, Manuel. 2018. "AI as the Next GPT: A Political-Economy Perspective." Working Paper 24245. Cambridge, MA: National Bureau of Economic Research.

Varian, Hal. 2018. "Artificial Intelligence, Economics, and Industrial Organization." Working Paper 24839. Cambridge, MA: National Bureau of Economic Research.

Virno, Paolo. 2004. *A Grammar of the Multitude*. Los Angeles: Semiotext(e).

Weber, Steven. 2017. "Data, Development, and Growth." *Business and Politics* 19 (3): 397–423.

15 Cellular Capitalism: Life and Labor at the End of the Digital Supply Chain

Matthew Hockenberry

On one end of the line, a consumer touches the smooth glass surface of their mobile phone. On the other, a new kind of logistical laborer enters the correspondingly smooth landscape this device claims to deliver. In the function of their phone, they find an interface of operation that partitions the world into nodes of logistical time and space—the segmented structure of the data center sutured to the mundane materiality of supply. As the lines of this new network spread from the streets of New York to Mumbai, London to Beijing, the movement of trucks, bikes, feet, and hands are abstracted onto objects, encoded into emerging algorithms of assembly. The workers captured alongside them become the vanguard of virtualization.

This chapter considers the place of the mobile phone in contemporary logistical networks, taking last-mile logistical service Amazon Flex as a case study for theorizing the phone as an interface to the ends of the global supply chain. As the world's largest digital retailer, Amazon has access to a phenomenal amount of aggregate data from user transactions and order fulfillment. As the corporation turns toward total integration of their supply chain, the Amazon Store—with its tailored product suggestions—finds a counterpart in the Taylorization of apps for their digital delivery, routing Fresh and Prime orders through algorithmic predictions of customer demand, traffic patterns, and stock availability. As the cloud's calculations average out any remaining human traces from the world below, it is not only global sites of assembly that become accessible as operationalized objects in the software systems of planetary production. The local sites of distribution—along with the lives and labor that remain there—necessarily do so as well. Here, all supply chains are digital supply chains.

The economic structures of the gig economy, I argue, have emerged in response to the integration of the interfaces common to the mobile phone. For consumers, a logistical service like Uber, Postmates, or Amazon Flex offers a convenience. But for delivery drivers (both of human and nonhuman cargo), the regimented control of the app, which integrates the networked requests of passengers with an awareness of the driver's precise position, defines the totality of labor. The coordination of connectivity—of Internet access, image processing, and global positioning—within the confines of the cellular phone is what renders every part of the operation operationalizable, distributed into the smallest tasks requiring the least possible skill. Every pickup, every turn, is now governed by the app. This is also what allows these new labor platforms to present themselves to drivers as turnkey solutions for turning time into money. It is cell phone as assembly line.

Logistics is the management of flow, the elimination of friction in pursuit of a smooth and seamless world of efficient operation. Everywhere and always, companies like Amazon work to secure supply chains absent the rough edges that define contemporary commerce—to remove the tired drivers, porch pirates, and fraudulent orders that break the continuity of consumption. A digital supply chain, then, may seem to be a contradiction. This, after all, is the domain of the discrete. It is the logic of the network, of lines and nodes. But this abstraction is crucial to contemporary logistics: the operative appearance of a continuous process overlaying a materially discontinuous one. Or perhaps it is the other way around. In either case, this uncertain processual appearance is, I argue, what the cell phone has come to offer global capital.

To examine this offer, this chapter begins by introducing the idea of mobility—and, more significantly, cellularity—as cultural conceptions critical to the operational control afforded by the mobile phone. Situating this control in the functions of Amazon Flex, I explore how the mobile phone enables the ordered divisions necessary for Flex's gig economy work by allowing workers to operate in digital representations of physical space, from geolocated directions to the structured images of two-dimensional barcodes. I conclude with the suggestion that, in constructing an actor capable of acting digitally on the analog world, the mobile phone enables at a planetary scale a future where all work, inevitably, will become digital work.

Cordless Confines

There is a conventional understanding that the mobile phone was a modification of an already established technology. But this perception neglects the fundamental distinctions essential to its history. The telephone connected places, after all, not people. Installed in a subscriber's home or office, it tamed the vast geographies of the world with wire and cable, indexing distant sites into directories made answerable at the point of call. Loosened from the limitations set out by the landline telephone's fixed inhabitance in space and time, however, the mobile phone constituted a radical reconfiguration of the nature of telecommunication—one that media scholars still grapple with (see Ito, Matsuda, and Okabe 2005; Katz 2008; Ling and Donner 2010). Misa Matsuda (2005, 20–21), for example, points out that in Japanese, the name for the mobile phone is the combination of *denwa* (telephone) and *keitai* (portable). But when *keitai*, rather than the conventional portmanteau of *kei-den*, became the standard term, it was as if the telephone was eliminated. All that remained was portability.

Americans, in contrast to most English-speaking callers, are more likely to reach for a *cellular* telephone than for a *mobile* one. At first this distinction seems meaningful only insofar as, while mobility is a cultural concept, a meaning attached to technology by its use and value in society, *cellular* is a technical description—both more specific and more recent—that references an underlying technological system and infrastructure. But *cellularity*, I argue, *is* a cultural concept, one that inspires allusions to Foucault's "cellular prison," its "regular chronologies, forced labor, and authorities of surveillance and registration" (1977, 227–228). This understanding is what is present when the phone is deployed as a tool for control rather than communication, when it enables not just a multiplicity of mobility but a multiplication of management. The mobile phone brings with it a promise of flexibility, of both geographic independence and economic opportunity. But in buying into the mobile phone, we get the cellular one as well.

The history of cellular networks is, after all, a logistical history. As the car became increasingly critical to the expanding suburban landscape in the United States, so did the idea of connecting the mobility afforded by the automobile with the more closely coupled communication of the telephone system. The challenge was in scaling this connection within the finite constraints of the radio spectrum. In 1947, Bell Labs engineers Douglas Ring and William Rae Young proposed a mechanism for frequency reuse that could efficiently employ the radio bands they had available. By dividing the coverage area into an (effectively) hexagonal grid, their approach allowed frequency repetition in nonadjacent cells so long as they were spaced sufficiently far apart (Ring 1947). While this system would not be implemented until decades later, the implication was that—unlike a traditional telephone, which had (at least at the local level) to provide a static point of contact tied to an individual subscriber—the "cellular network" need only provide a *space* for connection.

To speak of cells is to speak not only of wireless communication but also of prisons, monasteries, biology, and batteries. The Latin *cella* is also the root for the word *cellar*, and it was indeed used in the ancient world to mean a chamber or storeroom. In this etymology, we find structures like the *cella olearia* containing olive oil and the *cella vinaria*, which stored wine. But this type of storage was not limited to the organization of large numbers of objects; it could also serve to render "accessible to a multitude the inspection of a small number" (Foucault 1977, 216). And so, in the temple's cella, we find the image or figure representing the deity, a sacred sense of storage partly echoed by the chambers found in medieval monasteries centuries later. Over time, the divisions formed by these clustered rooms came to resemble nothing so much as "the cells of a honeycomb," such that Virgil could describe the secretions of bees in the same language his contemporaries used for the dormitories of slaves, the sleeping quarters of the public house, and the workrooms of the brothel. All were *cellae* (Smith 1890, 391). Common to these confines was their lack of connection to an individual inhabitant. They were spaces in want of an occupant. And this, I will argue, is what connects them to the defining function of the mobile phone in the labor regime of contemporary capitalism. As a means for imposing cellularity, it constructs a simultaneously connected and disconnected space of operation—one filled by an actor who can be redistributed and reconfigured according to demand.

Flexible Labor

New media technologies have always brought with them the potential for new techniques of social and material organization. The productive power of the assembly line, for example, was possible only because the ruled "blanks" of paper forms had altered the organization of the shop to enable this demanding division (Yates 1993). The introduction of the telephone itself brought a new means of managerial access—one that precipitated many of the patterns of remote operation and outsourcing that now define the global economy (Hockenberry 2021). Indeed, the early history of the gig economy can be traced, in part, to the ways in which freelance websites like Elance (now Upwork) provided opportunities for outsourcing on the back of the global telecommunication network (Florzak 2002). But while its predecessor may have had some raw capability for disassembling tasks, it was the mobile phone—through start-ups like Uber—that demonstrated how this logic could be so effectively distributed.

Amazon Flex (see figure 15.1) is a digital platform for fulfilling Amazon's on-demand delivery efforts. Launched in 2015 as a last-mile logistical program for paying gig economy workers to deliver certain kinds of Amazon orders, it is one of several options the company has developed for putting packages from the company's Prime Now, Amazon Fresh, and Amazon Restaurants offerings into the hands of its increasingly insatiable consumers (though only Amazon Fresh remains active). Operating worldwide in countries like the United States, Germany, Australia, the UK, Spain, and India, Flex promises workers the opportunity to "be your own boss, set your own schedule, and have more time to pursue your goals and dreams." All with "the power of Amazon" behind them (Amazon 2019b;

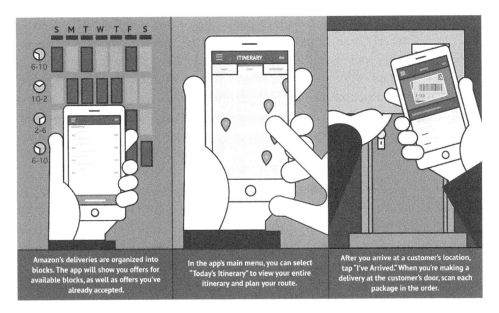

Amazon's deliveries are organized into blocks. The app will show you offers for available blocks, as well as offers you've already accepted.

In the app's main menu, you can select "Today's Itinerary" to view your entire itinerary and plan your route.

After you arrive at a customer's location, tap "I've Arrived." When you're making a delivery at the customer's door, scan each package in the order.

Figure 15.1
Screenshots from Amazon Flex (2018) training videos.

Yin 2019). But despite the otherwise unique invitation to "deliver smiles with Amazon" (Amazon 2019b), Flex is only one instance of an emerging platform economy (Kenney and Zysman 2016) specializing in last-mile logistics. Almost ubiquitously branded as "technology platforms," rather than delivery companies, this constantly shifting landscape includes (at the time of this writing) firms such as: Postmates, Shipt (now owned by Target), Walmart's Spark (powered by the cloud-based fulfillment service Bringg), Deliv (also acquired by Target), Senpex, Xpedigo, and Cargomatic in North America; CitySprint, Hermes, Stuart, and Yodel in Europe and the UK; Dunzo and Ekart in India; Rappi in Latin America; and Blu Couriers in Australia and New Zealand. Operating in a range of contexts, some of these firms are specifically oriented toward the delivery of food (Uber Eats, Seamless, Foodora, Deliveroo, DoorDash, Glovo, Ocado, Wolt, and Instacart, for example) while others are heavily tied to particular retailers (like Flex, Shipt, and Spark). And while Flex brings to bear only *some* of the labor patterns that can be distributed through the mobile phone, the fact that it was developed by a company like Amazon underlines the critical importance of the gig economy for increasing the density of contemporary logistical networks. Of course, given Amazon's fraught labor history, it also represents a particularly problematic entry into an already precarious field (see Scholz 2016, 9; Hill 2020).

Like more publicly recognizable examples such as Uber, Seamless, and Postmates, Amazon *is* a delivery company. Indeed, over the past decade it has become one of the largest logistical operations in the world, not just a retailer, but a company managing inventory and point of sale for thousands of third-party vendors (and, in some markets, directly selling logistics the way it sells digital offerings like its Amazon Web Services). But while its customers may still largely prefer one-click delivery to one-click streaming, Amazon—unlike its gig economy competitors—has an advantage in marketing digital as well as physical goods. The edge Amazon finds in services like Kindle, Audible, and Prime Video is not just in the low cost to store and distribute these digital materials, but in the unprecedented control the firm exercises over this distribution process. The business model of the marketplace for "odd jobs" favors a distributed workforce largely removed from the social relations and economic attachments that had governed earlier forms of capitalistic exploitation. But while Uber remains dependent on allegedly independent contractors to drive cars, and Seamless requires restaurants willing to interface with its order system, Amazon's digital offerings (and their corresponding labor platforms) are provided by the company's own web services—often delivered to devices they have designed. This has not been the case for their more conventional commerce.

While the boxes may have been branded with Amazon's smile logo, their delivery had traditionally depended on logistical networks largely outside the company's control. The trucks they were carried in belonged to companies like FedEx and DHL, or to local postal services. And the firm's relationship with these entities has been fraught—both economically and logistically. The solution, Amazon has decided, is in a more complete control of distribution—one arguably analogous to a digitization of delivery. Indeed, while e-commerce may have begun as an uncertain proposition, with Amazon's first store little more than a catalog for transactions completed by phone or fax, the supply chain leading to the firm's fulfillment centers has now been almost entirely digitized. All that remained were those few miles between purchase and package. The company once claimed that "connecting your mouse to your front door was our moon landing," but more regular trips have required the company to launch what has amounted to a sort of shadow postal network (Amazon 2012; Cheng 2019). And while successful, with many deliveries now completed by Amazon's own delivery service partners, Flex has brought a more flexible—and more digital—response (see Amazon 2019a).

"The first step to delivering for Amazon Flex," the company explains, is to "download the app" (Amazon 2019b). Indeed, the platform has only a few requirements for its newly minted logistical laborers—mainly that they can navigate through the unpredictable space of the material world and that they have a phone. After a worker has downloaded the app and consented to the requisite notifications, location tracking, and camera access (the invasiveness of which previously required that they "sideload" the app onto their device outside the auspices of the official app stores), they provide a driver's license and a bank account. They then undergo a background check and complete the mandatory training. This is not a driving test or an interview (after all, Amazon has confirmed that the worker is licensed to drive and eligible to be paid) but a program consisting entirely of viewing several three- to four-minute instructional videos. Alana Semuels (2018) describes watching 19 videos followed by quizzes, but when I completed my training, I watched only 8—with no quizzes (see also figure 15.1). Now armed with a not-at-all-comprehensive understanding of how they fit into Amazon's logistical empire, the worker need only schedule their availability and wait for a final approval.

The freedom these videos promise a worker may suggest the kind of adaptability of life and labor to which we have long aspired. But though they may give the impression that Amazon is a benevolent employer, it is neither particularly benevolent nor are these workers really employees. Regardless of a worker's preferred shift calendar, work—and, consequently, pay—is dependent on getting what Amazon refers to as "offers." These offers represent a batch of customer deliveries, and accepting one commits the worker to a "block" of time—essentially a two- or three-hour shift during which a worker will be responsible for making all of the deliveries aggregated for that offer. There are a few different kinds of blocks. The regular sort appear on the system either the day of delivery or (at most) the day before, typically remaining visible for only a second or two before a worker commits to them. The company also provides "reserved blocks." These are shifts set aside for a particular worker before they are opened up to others. These can be given out as often as once a week, but they usually appear with a less reliable frequency. Indeed, their availability, as well as their value, has been one of the most frequent topics of discussion in the many online forums—such as Amazon Flex Drivers (Reddit 2020) and a number of private Facebook groups—where workers congregate (and where Amazon, apparently, observes them; see Gurley 2020).

Questions abound about what reserved blocks are, why they are offered, or why they might have gone away. Details change constantly, with seemingly minute adjustments in the operational particulars of the Flex platform sometimes developing into long-term structural changes. What's more, with several tiers of logistical labor at Amazon's disposal, increased demand does not always translate to increased work. Even as the company has (at the time of this writing) introduced a "Flex Rewards" program with preferential scheduling to mitigate some of these concerns (with increased time to accept blocks and special "Rewards reserved offers"; see Amazon 2020), some workers have resorted to a black market in shift scraping scripts and autoswipe devices—complete with exorbitant prices and the risk of "cancellation" if they are detected

(Palmer 2020). Still, the primary position for the majority is to wait, swiping to refresh their phones in the hope that an offer will appear. Even when a reserved block is available, workers may have as little as 15 seconds to respond. Swipe to accept.

The frustrating friction of securing an offer stands in stark contrast to the smooth structure in place to work the delivery once it is accepted. When a block actually begins, all a worker needs is a delivery vehicle and a phone (and insurance, though Amazon's commercial insurance usually covers workers during shifts). The app takes care of everything else. It tells the worker where to pick up packages, where to drop them off, and what route to take. For migrant workers, it can even speak another language. Bringing with it all of the inhuman sensibilities afforded by the mobile phone, it can determine location with incredible precision. It can see and scan packages with no opportunity for error. It remembers it all for you, storing records in a system designed for precise timing and technique. All it asks in exchange is a human body capable of the messy and mundane business of moving. The app cannot climb stairs (though it can tell if you have), nor can it navigate congested streets or decide when to double park. For this, it still requires a human host. But as every driver knows, the Faustian bargain will persist only so long as these technologies require human coordination (Scott 2019). For a workforce severed from the promises of Fordist security that once defined postwar capitalism, the cellular phone seems a valuable prosthesis, but it is only a temporary one.

The nature of this prosthesis, and the key to its cellular logic, is in the phone's capacity to provide logistical control, enabling ever-more-digital representations of physical space. Indeed, to call these devices mobile is not just to privilege a particular social and technical character, or even to enroll them within a particular class of media technology, but to signify their place as, first and foremost, a *logistical* media technology. "Harnessing and mobilizing, incarcerating and accelerating things and people," the cellularity of the phone is not Foucault's prison but—fitting for a form frequently coupled to the car—Paul Virilio's racetrack (Virilio 2006, 69–70). The purpose it serves for the digital systems of delivery is to translate "strategic space" into the "logistical time" required for routing the movement of workers into lanes of material flow. As "cities, partitions, trading circuits, satellites, and software" pull back to a crystalline landscape of competing forces of "surveillance, fortification, and movement," Benjamin Bratton argues, everything from architecture to computation has come to constitute successive iterations of the media necessary for capital's "mobilization and its administration" (2006, 7–9). The phone is only the most recent example.

Logistical mobility is not about speed in the raw sense. It is about the *control* of movement, who can produce it, when, and under what circumstances. "In every revolution," Virilio explains, there is always the "paradoxical presence of circulation," with the revolutionary contingent attaining its ideal form "not in the place of production"—that is to say, the factory—but rather "in the street." It is only here that the worker "stops being a cog in the technical machine" and, "becomes a motor." This is where they can become a "producer of speed" (Virilio 2006, 29–30). But despite the promises of economic agency handed over to workers through these devices, they can only ever serve counter to those aims. Like other logistical techniques, cellularity brings both "integration and disintegration," producing divisions it assembles under standards it defines (Bratton 2006, 8). Exemplary prompts for Flex drivers are: "Proceed to pick-up point" and "Wait for customer order to be completed." With the same illusory smoothness of time as the Amazon Store itself, this leaves the app as the sole "motor," the phone as the only regulator of movement. Coordinating communication from one newly divided cell to another, the prosthetic potential of the phone surrenders control to the abstract and structured space of the network (Cuppini et al. 2013). As it consolidates territory into logistical fields organized on the basis of "abstract calculation over omni-directional spaces," we find here the sort of operation that Bratton argues now orders the vast reaches of the "open oceans" and the grids of "shared spreadsheets" alike (Bratton 2006, 8).

It is in this way that apps like Amazon Flex construct a digital interchange universalizing access to what critical logistics scholars such as Deborah Cowen have termed "logistical space." But while earlier technologies like the cargo container may have replaced the inefficiencies of material exchange with inputs and outputs measured by the standard size of the 20-foot equivalent unit, platforms like Flex standardize the exchange of *services* (Cowen 2014, 40–44). Here, the "algorithmic management" of equivalent labor allows for the substitution of direct managerial control over workers (Altenried 2019, 124). As Alexander Klose explains, the container once suggested a "smooth, lossless," "almost immaterial" image of transportation, so much so that it was easily forgotten that it was the result of tens of thousands of workers laboring amid a gigantic system "of steel and silicon" (Klose 2015, 26). So too is it easy to miss how structures like Flex's blocks are not interface elements but a new order of logistical space-time (and perhaps *the annihilation of space by time*). They are literal building blocks for a representation of the material world built entirely for the cellular logic of the phone.

Age of the World, Pictured

Given this representational reconstruction, it is not surprising that images are fundamental to the Flex platform. After workers swipe "I've arrived" at the initial pickup station, the Flex app (and usually another human) will direct workers to the set of shelves containing the boxes and bags they will deliver. Deciding how to fit three hours' worth of deliveries (usually 30 to 50 packages—though sometimes more) into consumer cars is no easy task, and here drivers generally take some time to sort their items for delivery: determining what goes in the backseat or the trunk; making sure items to be delivered at the same stop are grouped together; and packing their initial deliveries to be more accessible than their later ones. But from Amazon's perspective, all that matters is that each item is recorded. In the platform's early days, the two-dimensional barcodes attached to each package would need to be scanned individually. Now it is more common for workers to receive a single code that aggregates all of the items associated with a block (though this varies by location; some workers will still scan individual packages at cart-scan sites to avoid the possibility they were missorted; see Reddit 2020). Scanning the symbols on the barcode preloads a list of addresses—with a delivery radius that can average around 30 to 40 miles in less dense areas—all to be mapped out by the mobile phone app.

Despite Amazon's designs for automated operation, forums overflow with tips for getting blocks and strategies for delivering them (along with calls to unionize and complaints about Flex's increasingly onerous terms of service; see again Reddit 2020). Driving is a skill, of course, but so is knowing how to park, avoid tickets, and overcome the obstacles the system either fails to capture or does not care about. The workarounds Flex requires, and the folk knowledge it demands, speak to the difficulties that still remain in this last leg of logistical operation (see Soper 2020). While the app builds its own routes after a block's packages have been scanned, many workers suggest that it doesn't take traffic or related challenges into account—and they find they can often complete shifts faster through their own navigation. Individual judgment is likewise needed to determine how to access particular buildings, how to predict customer preferences, and how to decide when an item can be left and when it should be returned. "Undeliverables" occur when workers return packages for customers who are not home to receive them or when they are unable—or unwilling—to deliver them. But too many can produce negative weekly summaries. These can, in turn, result in canceled blocks, limited offers, or "deactivation"—an appropriately mechanical term for the sort of logistical cyborg imagined to be performing this labor. While Amazon acknowledges that deliveries sometimes go awry, and that accidents— vehicular or otherwise—happen, the company is vague about the exact consequences. The rating system for assessing a worker's standing is notoriously opaque, with a sluggish response to appeals. And given Flex's contingent nature, there is no guarantee of work and no protections (or overtime) when a delivery proves troublesome. When faced with an insecure delivery, then: "you gotta use your judgment, you gotta see who's around, who's looking, who's watching, you know [make sure] people don't steal that stuff and it's gonna cost you your job." As one worker concludes: "I'd rather be safe and bring it back to the warehouse" (Reality of Andy 2017; see also Flexing with Flex 2018).

When a driver indicates they have arrived at a destination, the app is supposed to provide all the protocols for delivery: Does the recipient need to be present, do they require an access code, and is there a preferred drop-off location? Workers verify they have delivered packages by recording an image to their phone. For customers, these porch pictures confirm that their items have been delivered. For Amazon, it ensures compliance from the driver. It may seem surprising that these are the only real images taken during the entire process. But the purpose of the other pictures is to scan two-dimensional barcodes, not to record the objects they are attached to. Flex's operations are heavily mediated even at the moment of delivery. After all, completing an order is not about interacting with the customer. When, for example, a bike delivery driver arrives at their destination and puts down their (usually waterproof) duffel bag, they are directed only to look for the printed sticker containing the delivery's optical machine code and its short (human-readable) four-character identifier (see figure 15.2). With Flex recalling for them how many items are to be delivered, it is just a matter of assembling and scanning the correct number of matching codes. As the system does not intend for the consumer to see the worker, the worker need not see the consumer. It is the camera—the system—that sees.

Figure 15.2
Barcode stickers from a Prime Now order delivered via Amazon Flex.

The era of the camera phone was remarkably brief, wedged in between the novel opening of the mobile phone and the attribution of the previously human quality of *smartness* to these freshly fitted attachments. But to neglect the importance of the camera in the history of these devices is to neglect the fact that the smartphone is smart only because of its confluence with other media technologies—*because* of the active accumulation of these rich and versatile sensory capabilities into a singular mobile prosthesis (for such an alternate genealogy, see Huhtamo 2011, 23–38). The smartphone's geospatial awareness of position, sensitivity to radio waves, and perception of acceleration rivaling even the most well-tuned ear, not only suggest that this newfound intelligence is an entirely nonhuman one, it further distinguishes these devices from the lineage of electric speech that began with the telephone. In some sense, the history of all media is a history of mobility, of new mechanisms for the movement of thoughts, sounds, and images. But in substituting the sharing of "structured" images—either interfaces of operation or optical codes processed by machines—for auditory exchange, the mobile phone distributed the telephone's network of signal processing out into the world, to segmented symbols providing a link not just between the physical and the digital but between the human and nonhuman (with the same sense of "structure" described in Heidegger 1977). Moving in the world, the mobile camera-phone constructed a world that could itself be made mobile.

Cellular Structures

While the camera on a driver's phone is the one featured in Flex's training videos, it is not the only camera on which the system depends. Less obvious are the orbiting imagers responsible for delivering satellite views routing drivers to their destinations. Like the structured images of the barcode, these are not pictures produced to join the world together. They serve only to take it apart. A view from everywhere and nowhere, these stitched tiles of pixels separate the planet into a grid that covers every hill, valley, ocean, and island. Brought into a singular frame, it is captured in the confines of an objectivity that demands a particular kind of object.

Logistics is a "matrix of rationality," and the grid is one of its most fundamental structures (Cuppini 2018). Fred Moten and Stefano Harney trace this relationship to the carefully ordered architectures of the slave ship (Harney and Moten 2013; see also Cuppini and Frapporti 2018), while Bernhard Siegert (2015, 98) describes how Le Corbusier's cellular architectures, hundreds of years later, proposed extending "forms of standardization" to the entirety of existence—reconfiguring the "dwelling, the office, the workshop, the factory" in the extruded shape of the skyscraper. The grid, Siegert writes, is the "medium that operationalizes deixis," linking "deictic procedures with chains of symbolic operations that have effects"—sometimes quite profound ones—"in the real" (2015, 98).

As a structure, the grid accomplishes two critical things. First, it normalizes—to various degrees—the geography over which it is laid. This is not to say that it makes the features of that geography identical, but rather that it *permits* difference by presupposing identicality in their *function* in the cells. In describing the role of the Seven Ranges Survey in "designing" the western United States, Siegert (2015, 114–118) notes that the survey grid was based on repeatability. Its "projective nature" is what allowed territory to be divided up, sight unseen. As a "cultural technique aimed at dominating space," the grid could be "cast across the land," opening the West for operationalization by the East. Settlements were no longer "centers that may undergo centrifugal expansion," but "cells in a homogeneous grid covering the entire territory." As a result of this "Ptolemaic grid" of latitudes and longitudes, Siegert argues, the "transformation of America into one nationwide suburb was preprogrammed."

The second function of the grid is to index and (as a consequence) to provide a function of location. Writing of the Bauhaus architect Ernst Neufert, Siegert (2015, 115–116) recalls that he "outlined a method for the complete standardization and totalization of the grid on all scales." Anticipating "the linkup of matrix screen and global coordinate system," Neufert's grid enabled (on a planetary scale) the ability to index the exact location of individual buildings and (on a smaller one) the size and position of each object within them. With each index so defined, the objects that filled the space were standardized such that what constituted a building had *become* what would fit into the grid. As a result, it was axiomatic that "any new building would fit as seamlessly into any new settlement as any door into any door frame or any piano into any drawing room" (116). Once the grid has been laid, once its cells have been indexed, the expected value of their contents become defined—regardless of whether the space is yet occupied. The ordered structures that descend from these comparatively primitive forms cascade into an expanding polygonal fractal of possibilities for the range of their connective movement (see Krejewski 2011; Rossiter 2016). But while their cells approach perceptual smoothness, closer inspection shows only an asymptotic array of well-defined, standardized edges. They are revealed as just the latest iteration of the "totalizing, frequently fantasmatic standardization projects" that have sought to rationalize the twentieth century (Siegert 2015, 116).

It is in this way that cellularity prefigures the digital. Indeed, Alexander Galloway (2014, 68–69) notes that while the analog is "the universe of proportion, of continuous variability," the digital "is the universe of separation, alienation, distinction, division, and making discrete." In the "flat digitality" of grid screens like the "montage of closed-circuit security camera feeds," "video compression codes," or "computer desktop with its multiple parallel and overlapping windows" we find structures that are "no longer images." They are merely "aggregations of cells that combine and coordinate to create some kind of whole." Opposite this, he argues, stands the "deep digitality" formed by a "reduplicative multiplexing of the *subject*." While in flat digitality the object is cellular, in deep digitality it is the subject who is cellular. Initiatives like Amazon's Mechanical Turk attempted to distribute labor *out* onto cellular objects, objects that had been carved into "thousands of bits" for Turk's "human intelligence tasks" (see Rossiter 2016, 130–131; Scholz 2016, 8). In producing a cellular *subject*, Flex operates in the reverse. It constructs an actor who is capable of acting digitally on what are otherwise analog objects—one who can indeed be redistributed or reconfigured on demand. It is indeed the case that the cellular prison "arranges things in such a way that the exercise of power is not added on from the outside, like a rigid, heavy constraint . . . but is so subtly present in them as to increase their efficiency by itself" (Foucault 1977, 206).

As far as Amazon is concerned, it is the production of this cellular subject that serves to "make digital" the material flows of an analog world. In the history of logistics, the "intermodalism" of the standard cargo container allowed distribution to be seen as an integrated system because the container was not just a vehicle for the efficient movement of materials but one that could itself be more efficiently moved (Cowen 2014, 40–44). Benjamin Bratton (2015) has argued that one of the critical characteristics of the accidental megastructure he calls "the stack" is the way in which it orders components for assembly into "higher order systems" (45, 81). Here, a device like the mobile phone is not only a vehicle for the movement of materials but one that can be upgraded. It provides mechanisms for standards-compliant interfacing to the various subsystems of the stack by (among other things) making labor more accessible to the Amazon Store's software systems, with a cellular subject linked not just to radio waves but to an infrastructure designed to ensure compliance with neoliberal demands for a flexible, mobile, networked worker. The result is that for a company already efficient in digital design, there need be no difference between delivering bits for Prime Video and bins filled with Digital Video Discs. Amazon does not need to deal with the world, only with the "world in miniature." Dematerialized and discontinuous, the "geography of the screen" replaces the analog landscape with a digital network that surfaces only those necessary points of contact (Dodge 1999, 7). Like links in a chain conditioned for contingency, this brings a kind of generalized departure that mirrors Virilio's "generalized arrival" (1997, 16). The real is replaced by the virtual. Everything seems to have left without having to arrive. Logistics becomes just another software problem.

Conclusion: Cellular Futures

In the last decades of the twentieth century, management formalized a model through which global capital came to direct an unprecedented scale of productive assembly. The result was a singular and total unit of managerial analysis—the supply chain. While the elements that the supply chain operated on were not in themselves new, the changes brought by "supply chain capitalism" lay in the infrastructural and managerial requirements it set out. Contemporary production was no longer composed of siloed sites of assembly. It was a "networked enterprise," tightly coupling suppliers and distributors to maximize the efficiency of every productive process. It defined an order of operation with associations formed by arrangements of subcontracting and outsourcing; a new mobility of labor; and an overriding logic of flexibility and interchange. As Anna Tsing (2009, 148–176) suggests, these sorts of changes have provided capital with "a model for thinking simultaneously about global integration, on the one hand, and the formation of diverse niches, on the other"—standardization and connection, and only at the cost of "growing gaps between rich and poor, across lines of color and culture, and between North and South."

To speak of the cellular is to speak of cells, of divisions and isolation, the discrete and the digital. Cellular capitalism comes with the introduction of a device that renders supply as nodes in the network as easily as it does pixels on a screen. Replacing the messy materiality of the real with the controlled computation of the virtual, it is the outward manifestation of a structure with the inevitable aim of coordinating the worldwide activity of every single connection. The value digital work offers global capital is that it supposedly permits the extraction of value outside of the traditional confines of geography. Proximity, this volume argues, is no longer needed between workers and the objects and subjects of their work. But cellular capitalism extends this logic of efficient immateriality to work that could otherwise be nothing but local, nothing but material. In extending the planetary system of digital production and distribution to the closest connections of the supply chain, it is not just that which is far away that is rendered invisible, but that which has, until quite recently, remained very near.

References

Altenried, Moritz. 2019. "On the Last Mile: Logistical Urbanism and the Transformation of Labour." *Work Organisation, Labour & Globalisation* 13 (1): 114–129.

Amazon. 2012. "Amazon New Kindle TV Commercial." YouTube video, 1:00. September 5. https://www.youtube.com/watch?v=2EQ0e7dYuaI.

Amazon. 2019a. "Amazon Logistics." Amazon. Accessed February 1, 2020. https://logistics.amazon.com/.

Amazon. 2019b. "What Is Amazon Flex?" Amazon. Accessed February 1, 2020. https://flex.amazon.com/.

Amazon. 2020. "Amazon Flex Rewards." Amazon. Accessed February 1, 2020. https://flex.amazon.com/amazonflexrewards/.

Bratton, Benjamin. 2006. "Introduction: Logistics of Habitable Circulation." In *Speed and Politics*, edited by Paul Virilio, 7–26. Los Angeles: Semiotext(e).

Bratton, Benjamin. 2015. *The Stack: On Software and Sovereignty*. Cambridge, MA: MIT Press.

Cheng, Andria. 2019. "Amazon Ships 2.5 Billion Packages a Year, with Billions More Coming." *Forbes*, December 12.

Cowen, Deborah. 2014. *The Deadly Life of Logistics*. Minneapolis: University of Minnesota Press.

Cuppini, Niccolò. 2018. "Platform Urbanism: 'Traditional' Logistics, Amazon and the Food-Delivery Platforms." Paper presented at Supply and Command Conference, New York, April 19–20.

Cuppini, Niccolò, and Mattia Frapporti. 2018. "Logistics Genealogies. A Dialogue with Stefano Harney." *Social Text* 36 (3): 95–110.

Cuppini, Niccolò, Mattia Frapporti, Floriano Milesi, Luca Padova, and Maurilio Pirone. 2013. "Logistics and Crisis: The Supply Chain System in the Po Valley Region." Paper produced during the *Teaching the Crisis—Geographies, Methodologies, Perspectives* Summer School, Humboldt-Universität zu Berlin. http://teachingthecrisis.net/wp-content/uploads/2014/03/Italy_Logistics_and_Crisis.pdf.

Dodge, Martin. 1999. "Finding the Source of the Amazon.com: Examining the Truth behind the Hype of the 'Earth's Biggest Bookstore.'" Paper presented at E*Space 5 Conference, Cape Town, July 10–15.

Flexing with Flex. 2018. "Amazon Flex: Getting Access and Reducing Undeliverables." YouTube video, 16:07. July 29. https://www.youtube.com/watch?v=hOuOu_ncnV0.

Florzak, Doug. 2002. "Are You Ready for the E-lance Economy?" *Technical Communication* 49 (2): 162–170.

Foucault, Michel, 1977. *Discipline and Punish: The Birth of the Prison*. New York: Random House.

Galloway, Alexander. 2014. *Laruelle: Against the Digital*. Minneapolis: University of Minnesota Press.

Gurley, Lauren Kaori. 2020. "Amazon Is Spying on Its Workers in Closed Facebook Groups, Internal Reports Show." *Motherboard*, September 1.

Harney, Stefano, and Fred Moten. 2013. *The Undercommons: Fugitive Planning & Black Study*. New York: Minor Compositions.

Heidegger, Martin. 1977. "The Age of the World Picture." In *Science and the Quest for Reality*, edited by Alfred Tauber, 70–88. London: Palgrave Macmillan.

Hill, David W. 2020. "The Injuries of Platform Logistics." *Media, Culture & Society* 42 (4): 521–536.

Hockenberry, Matthew. 2021. "'Every Man within Earshot': Auditory Efficiency in the Time of the Telephone." In *Assembly Codes: The Logistics of Media*, edited by Matthew Hockenberry, Nicole Starosielski, and Susan Zieger. Durham, NC: Duke University Press.

Huhtamo, Erkki. 2011. "Pockets of Plenty. An Archaeology of Mobile Media." In *The Mobile Audience: Media Art and Mobile Technologies*, edited by Martin Rieser, 23–38. Amsterdam/New York: Rodopi.

Ito, Mizuko, Misa Matsuda, and Daisuke Okabe, eds. 2005. *Personal, Portable, Pedestrian: Mobile Phones in Japanese Life*. Cambridge, MA: MIT Press.

Katz, James E., ed. 2008. *Handbook of Mobile Communication Studies*. Cambridge, MA: MIT Press.

Kenney, Martin, and John Zysman. 2016. "The Rise of the Platform Economy." *Issues in Science and Technology* 32 (3): 61–69.

Klose, Alexander. 2015. *The Container Principle: How a Box Changes the Way We Think*. Cambridge, MA: MIT Press.

Krejewski, Markus. 2011. *Paper Machines: About Cards & Catalogs, 1548–1929*. Cambridge, MA: MIT Press.

Ling, Rich, and Jonathan Donner. 2010. *Mobile Communication*. Cambridge: Polity Press.

Matsuda, Misa. 2005. "Discourses of Keitai in Japan." In *Personal, Portable, Pedestrian: Mobile Phones in Japanese Life*, edited by Mizuko Ito, Misa Matsuda, and Daisuke Okabe, 19–40. Cambridge, MA: MIT Press.

Palmer, Annie. 2020. "Amazon Flex Drivers Are Using Bots to Cheat Their Way to Getting More Work." *CNBC*, February 9. https://www.cnbc.com/2020/02/09/amazon-flex-drivers-use-bots-to -get-more-work.html.

Reality of Andy. 2017. "Step by Step Amazon Flex Driver Tutorial." YouTube video, 13:15. November 1. https://www.youtube.com/watch?v=h4FDr9KlgeA.

Reddit. 2020. Amazon Flex Driver. Accessed May 7, 2020. https://www.reddit.com/r/AmazonFlex-Drivers/.

Ring, Douglas. 1947. "Mobile Telephony—Wide Area Coverage." *Bell Telephone Laboratories Technical Memorandum*, December 11.

Rossiter, Ned. 2016. *Software, Infrastructure, Labor: A Media Theory of Logistical Nightmares*. London: Routledge.

Scholz, Trebor. 2016. *Platform Cooperativism: Challenging the Corporate Sharing Economy*. New York: Rosa Luxemburg Stiftung.

Scott, Sean. 2019. "Meet Scout: Field Testing a New Delivery System with Amazon Scout." Amazon, January 23. https://www.aboutamazon.com/news/transportation/meet-scout.

Semuels, Alana. 2018. "The Day I Drove for Amazon." *Atlantic*, June 25.

Siegert, Bernhard. 2015. *Cultural Techniques: Grids, Filters, Doors, and Other Articulations of the Real*. New York: Fordham University Press.

Smith, William. 1890. *A Dictionary of Greek and Roman Antiquities*. London: John Murray.

Soper, Spencer. 2020. "Amazon Drivers Are Hanging Smartphones in Trees to Get More Work." *Bloomberg*, September 1.

Tsing, Anna. 2009. "Supply Chains and the Human Condition." *Rethinking Marxism: A Journal of Economics, Culture & Society* 21 (2): 148–176.

Virilio, Paul. 1997. *Open Sky*. London: Verso.

Virilio, Paul. 2006. *Speed and Politics*. Los Angeles: Semiotext(e).

Yates, JoAnne. 1993. *Control through Communication*. Baltimore: Johns Hopkins University Press.

Yin, Katrina. 2019. "Amazon Flex." Landscapes of Fulfillment. https://landscapes-of-fulfillment.org/Amazon-Flex.

IV Reimagining Planetary Networks

16   An International Governance System for Digital Work in the Planetary Market

Janine Berg

"The failure of any nation to adopt humane conditions of labour is an obstacle in the way of other nations which desire to improve the conditions in their own countries." This statement from the preamble to the constitution of the International Labour Organization (ILO) reflects concerns shared by delegates at the founding of the ILO in 1919 over the potential for countries to gain an unfair advantage in international trade based on poor working conditions. Founding members of the ILO expressed their concern that without a commitment by countries to respect working conditions, social justice—and the peace that it ensures—would forever be wanting.

Thus, the ILO was conceived as a system of international labor regulation that would guide and prompt member States to uphold labor rights. Each year, the ILO's International Labour Conference, comprising government, worker, and employer representatives from the organization's 187 member States, meets to discuss key social and labor questions of concern. In most years, the conference also establishes and adopts international labor standards—conventions, which are binding on member States when ratified, and recommendations—that member States should implement, covering most areas of labor law and a vast array of supportive labor market policies. By encouraging member States to incorporate these standards into national laws and policies, the organization seeks to realize its mission of promoting greater justice and fairer international trade.

The establishment of the ILO, at the end of the First World War, followed the first period of globalization, dating from roughly 1870 until 1914. During this period, the steamship and railroad led to an unprecedented economic integration, based primarily on the trading of raw materials, but also on that of finished goods. Following the First World War, global trade declined and remained stagnant until after the Second World War, when it resumed slowly, as countries upheld trade barriers in an effort to protect their infant industries. It was not until the 1980s and 1990s that trade barriers throughout the world were dismantled. In 1989, world trade accounted for 14 percent of world GDP, the same level as 1914, but then climbed, steadily and swiftly, to reach 60 percent of world GDP by 2018.

As in the first globalization period, important technological developments propelled much of this expansion, particularly the introduction of container shipping but also breakthroughs in information and communication technologies (ICTs). Political shifts supported globalization, as witnessed by the establishment of the World Trade Organization (WTO) in 1995 as well as the signing of numerous national and regional trade agreements throughout the world.

But trade in this current age is vastly different from that in the past. To begin with, today's trade is of intermediate goods, with workers from around the world contributing to the production of components that are part of complex global supply chains. Countries no longer trade wine for cloth, as elucidated in David Ricardo's (1817) treatise on political economy, but rather produce parts for the Barbie doll, the iPhone, and most other consumer products (Tempest 1996; Barboza 2010). Global trade is also increasingly in services. Advances in ICTs have led to a similar slicing of service production, with the offshoring of customer service and back office jobs to lower-cost locations throughout the world. Sometimes the offshoring is to the subsidiaries of lead firms in lower-cost countries, but as in manufacturing, it is more often to independent suppliers competing for the contract from different sides of the planet.

Among Organisation for Economic Co-operation and Development (OECD) countries, trade in intermediate goods and services made up more than half of overall goods trade and nearly three-quarters of trade in services in 2005 (Miroudot, Lanz, and Ragoussis 2009). Because procurement drives the decision of where and whom to source from, intermediate goods and services trade is highly price sensitive in comparison with final goods trade, which is about access to markets. Suppliers are highly dependent on lead firms, sometimes accepting orders at or below costs in an attempt to secure future work.[1]

Digital platform work is the latest manifestation in the outsourcing of production across the planet. Since its advent in the early years of the twenty-first century, digital labor platforms offer lead firms the possibility of outsourcing directly to individuals located anywhere in the world. Individuals who have signed up to work on digital labor platforms compete for tasks posted and, if they are lucky enough to be assigned the task, then complete and deliver the service from their home in exchange for remuneration. These digital supply chains can involve short "microtasks" that are essential for the smooth operation of e-commerce or the training of AI systems, or they can involve "macrotasks" performed on freelancing platforms. On these platforms, individual workers offer their services as programmers, graphic designers, statisticians, and translators, among other professions, with platforms matching freelancers with clients for a fee.

An International Labor Governance System That Has Not Kept Up

The labor governance model put in place at the ILO's founding was designed for the first wave of globalization, when countries exchanged raw materials and finished goods. National labor legislation was meant to mirror the principles and guidance embodied in ILO standards so as to avoid unfair advantages from child labor, low minimum wages, lack of worker voice, or lax health and safety standards. At least that was the founding vision. But in a globalized world organized around multinational firms outsourcing different parts of production, whether in manufacturing or digital services, to low-cost labor spread across the world, the motivation among nations to protect against unfair advantage in global trade is diminished. While it would be unfair to dismiss the ILO's work—its guidance on the design and application of labor laws has been instrumental in upgrading working conditions for workers throughout the world—it is clear that restricting labor governance to the nation-state has reached its limits. A new form of labor governance is needed—one that can tackle the challenges of a planetary labor market.

Recognizing the importance of global supply chains, a few countries and regional bodies have passed legislation with a view to holding lead firms operating in their jurisdictions accountable for activities in their supply chains, even if occurring extraterritorially. With few exceptions, these initiatives have been limited to human trafficking, corruption, or trading in minerals originating from conflict zones.[2] For the most part, the laws require disclosure and due diligence on the part of the lead firm, though the requirements are typically limited to company subsidiaries or first-tier suppliers. Furthermore, the legislation that concerns labor issues is usually limited to the most egregious labor violation—human trafficking—as opposed to less nefarious but nonetheless critical issues such as lack of compliance with minimum wages, unpaid overtime, anti-union practices, and unsafe working conditions.

Although these supply chain regulations are an advance in that they recognize and attempt to address the responsibility of multinational firms in fragmented, global production, they are not designed for the planetary digital labor market that is the subject of this book. With digital labor markets, businesses can bypass suppliers and engage workers directly at the click of a button. The relationship may be mediated by a platform, or a platform may serve as a conduit for identifying suitable workers, but the work is performed as a bilateral, cross-border, virtual working arrangement, in some instances akin to that of a regular employee who would be teleworking. Except these relationships are not classified as an employment relationship, and as they span multiple jurisdictions, the worker is left unprotected should matters go awry.

In an ILO study of 1,000 platform workers in Ukraine, one-third of respondents reported that they had worked directly with a client, bypassing the platform through which an initial contract was established. Focus groups with platform workers in Ukraine also revealed the incidence of what they describe as "closed" platforms that could only be accessed by invitation and following several interview stages. Once admitted, workers would receive a steady stream of work and be requested to be available for work at regular times, in exchange for biweekly transfers to their bank account or payments via a third-party payment system (Aleksynska, Bastrakova, and Kharchenko 2018). In another ILO study, of 300 online, home-based workers in the Philippines, 14 percent reported working directly for clients, often as virtual assistants. Most of these virtual assistants had signed written agreements with their clients, with provisions pertaining to the worker's tasks and payment terms (pay rate, frequency, and manner of payment), followed by the number of working hours and a specification that the worker is an independent contractor. Fifteen percent of the workers reported that their clients used only verbal agreements (King-Dejardin, 2021). Workers in both countries reported their clients' practice of requesting that they download specialized software that would track their working hours and online activity, record keystrokes, and take random screenshots of their computer screen—in essence, an employment relationship in which the bosses exercise their managerial prerogative, but the workers do not benefit from the rights that would normally be accorded to them in such a relationship.

International Labor Governance for the Digital Age: Possible Ways Forward

The technological advances that allow a company to use a virtual assistant in the Philippines, a programmer in Ukraine, a graphic designer in Italy, and a copywriter in India—within the course of the same day and perhaps for the production of a single project—reveal the limits of geographically based labor regulation.

In 2019, to mark its centenary, the ILO convened an independent Global Commission on the Future of Work to produce a report on how to achieve a future of work that provides decent and sustainable work opportunities for all. The commission recognized that the rise of cross-border digital work had resulted in regulatory gaps that required specific interventions at the global level. It recommended the "development of an international governance system for digital labor platforms that sets and requires platforms (and their clients) to respect certain minimum rights and protections" (ILO 2019, 44). It noted furthermore that the ILO's Maritime Labour Convention, 2006 (MLC) was an important precedent of supranational regulation, as the MLC establishes and applies a global labor code for seafarers. Like work on digital platforms, the maritime industry involves multiple parties operating across different jurisdictions.

In maritime employment, the workers—along with the goods or passengers being transported—move from one country to another, often passing through other nations' waters. The first attempts at regulating the maritime industry date to 1897, when the International Maritime Committee began advocating for greater unification of maritime law and adopted regulations and protocols to further harmonization.[3] Prior to this, the dominant international law regulating the seas was the centuries-old concept of freedom of the seas—*mare liberum*. But in the nineteenth century, a seafarer's life was a difficult one, with few if any safeguards against wage theft, safety hazards, or poor working conditions. In extreme situations, workers could find themselves abandoned at foreign ports with wages unpaid, no passage to return home, and no legal recourse in the foreign country's courts (Link 2015).

While digital platform workers do not fear being abandoned at port, many of the other risks associated with seafaring are present in contemporary platform work. Unpaid wages are common, and legal recourse is difficult, as the client and the platform are often located in different jurisdictions. Another concern is that, over time, nations will likely begin passing regulations on the platform economy, but because these regulations will not be harmonized, parties will choose to file a legal action in the jurisdiction where the laws are most favorable to them (e.g., the country where the worker resides or works, the country where the platform has its headquarters, or the country where the client is located). Platforms will likely include choice of law or choice of forum clauses in their online terms of service—what in legal circles is known as "forum shopping" thereby heightening the risk of involving inconsistent and sometimes conflicting frameworks that create additional problems for all parties (Berg, Cherry, and Rani 2019). In addition, regulations protecting workers pertain primarily to employment contracts and may fall short of protecting workers who have been classified as self-employed by the platform.

Under the MLC, port authorities can check for compliance and impound cargo in the event of labor violations; with platform work, various host, server, or entry points could be monitored for compliance. Because the workers using the platforms are largely invisible, such regulatory checks might involve the sharing of data between platform operators, regulatory authorities, and the workers themselves. Giving workers access and rights to their data could also enable them to contest rankings or ratings that they believe are erroneous, as well as give them and the labor authority a record of time worked that could facilitate compliance with a minimum wage. Workers could also transfer their worker histories and other relevant data across platforms, or to their trade union representatives. Measures such as these would substantially improve workers' rights, regardless of their place of residence.

Conclusion

Technological advances have transformed the world of work and exposed the limits of labor regulation bounded by physical jurisdictions and conceived for the production of tangible products. Jobs such as administrative assistant that were once considered "nontradable" and thus protected from global competition have now become tradable, readily available through a digital platform at a competitive price. The weakness of the state-based regulatory structure was already apparent with global supply chains, but platform work and other forms of cross-border digital employment relationships have compounded this weakness.

In the nineteenth century, maritime work seemed impossible to regulate, but such regulation was achieved. In today's increasingly digitized world, with services moving invisibly across borders, the need for such international regulation of platform work grows greater by the minute. Devising a governance system that can respond to the special characteristics and requirements of virtual, cross-border platform work is achievable, but international cooperation is needed. Such cooperation would mark an important step in ensuring that the aspirations of the ILO, as set out at the Paris Peace Conference in 1919, are achieved.

Disclaimer

The views expressed in this article are the author's own and do not necessarily represent the views of the International Labour Organization.

Notes

1. A 2016 ILO–Ethical Trading Initiative survey of nearly 1,500 suppliers, located in 87 countries and covering a range of economic sectors, found that a quarter of them depended on one firm for more than half of their production. The lower the income of the country, the greater was their degree of dependence. In addition, 39 percent of the suppliers reported having accepted orders at a price that did not allow them to cover their production costs, usually in an attempt to secure future orders (ILO 2016).

2. Examples include the California Transparency in Supply Chains Act of 2010 (slavery and human trafficking), the UK Modern Slavery Act 2015, the Australian Modern Slavery Act 2018, and the EU's so-called Conflict Minerals Regulation of 2017. The EU Non-Financial Reporting Directive 2014 is wider in scope, covering environmental protection, social responsibility and treatment of employees, respect for human rights, anti-corruption and -bribery, and diversity on company boards. However, companies only need to publish reports on the policies they implement "in the way they consider most useful," and it applies only to companies with 500 or more employees. More far-reaching is the French "loi de vigilance" (Loi no. 2017–399), which obligates French companies with more than 5,000 employees to establish, publish, comply with, and evaluate a Vigilance Plan that identifies risks so as to prevent serious violations of human rights and fundamental freedoms, human health and safety, and the environment, taking into consideration the parent company's sphere of influence, subsidiaries, and subcontractors.

3. See https://comitemaritime.org/about-us/history/.

References

Aleksynska, Mariya Anastasia Bastrakova, and Natalia Kharchenko. 2018. *Work on Digital Labour Platforms in Ukraine: Issues and Policy Perspectives*. Geneva: International Labour Organization.

Barboza, David. 2010. "Supply Chain for iPhone Highlights Costs in China." *New York Times*, July 5. https://www.nytimes.com/2010/07/06/technology/06iphone.html.

Berg, Janine, Miriam Cherry, and Uma Rani. 2019. "Digital Labour Platforms: A Need for International Regulation?" *Revista de Economía Laboral* [Spanish Journal of Labor Economics] 16 (2): 104–128.

ILO. 1919. "Constitution of the International Labour Organization." Geneva: International Labour Organization. https://www.ilo.org/dyn/normlex/en/f?p=1000:62:0::NO:62:P62_LIST_ENTRIE_ID :2453907:NO.

ILO. 2016. "Purchasing Practices and Working Conditions in Global Supply Chains: Global Survey Results." INWORK Issue Brief no. 10. Geneva: International Labour Organization.

ILO. 2019. *Work for a Brighter Future*. Geneva: International Labour Organization.

King-Dejardin, Amelita. 2021. "Homeworking in the Philippines: Bad Job? Good Job." ILO Working Paper no. 25. Geneva: International Labour Organization. https://www.ilo.org/global /publications/working-papers/WCMS_775013/lang--en/index.htm.

Link, Peter. 2015. "One Small Step for the United States, May Be One Giant Leap for Seafarer's Rights." *Hofstra Labor and Employment Law Journal* 33 (1): 167–205.

Miroudot, Sébastien, Rainer Lanz, and Alexandros Ragoussis. 2009. "Trade in Intermediate Goods and Services." OECD Trade Policy Working Papers. Paris: OECD Trade Directorate.

Ricardo, David, 1817. *On the Principles of Political Economy and Taxation*. London: John Murray.

Tempest, Rone. 1996. "Barbie and the World Economy." *Los Angeles Times*, September 22. https:// www.latimes.com/archives/la-xpm-1996-09-22-mn-46610-story.html.

17   Righting the Wrong: Putting Workers' Data Rights Firmly on the Table

Christina J. Colclough

Workers across the world are increasingly becoming commodified—turned into numerous data points that can be used for statistical inferencing and, more invasively, for predictive analysis. From "gig" workers to warehouse workers, from those working from home due to COVID-19 to well-paid tech experts, numerous inferences are being drawn as workers work: the speed of their typing, the routes they take, their earnings, their ratings, what websites they visit, how their eyes move on video calls, the tone of their voice, and so much more. These systems for worker surveillance are often obscure, hidden under the hood, observing what you do, predicting what you will do, deciding what you should do, and affecting what opportunities will be available to you. Algorithms are shaping the opportunities available to workers as citizens. Is a worker investable? Will job advertisements be withheld from them by an algorithm that has deemed them unfit or unsuitable for the job? Job candidates can be screened, sourced, assessed, interviewed, and vetted by artificial intelligence (AI) systems (Raju 2020). Will they be fired or promoted?

What must be remembered is that all of these profiles and predictions about an individual do not just affect that person. Indeed, people who are similar to that person can be affected by the profiles that are built up about the person. In the data world, all workers and citizens are connected. These algorithmically calculated predictions are robbing workers of their fundamental right to form and shape their lives as best they can—essentially their right to be human.

At the same time, work itself is being chopped up into piecemeal tasks that can be assigned to workers across the world, and the rising individualization of work is going hand in hand with a growth in precarious contracts (ILO 2016). These workers are left to bear the risk of the market on their shoulders yet are stripped of most, if not all, of their social rights (Tan et al. 2020). Former colleagues are now competitors in a globally distributed labor market, fighting for piecemeal and often underpaid tasks. National industrial relations systems are inadequate to meet the needs of this distributed work-force, whose bargaining power is not space-bound. In addition, many of these workers are invisible, in Mary L. Gray's words, "ghost workers" (Chen 2019), making it hard for traditional unions to find them, let alone organize them.

In the words of Shoshana Zuboff, we are living in the world of "surveillance capitalism"—an economic system that is distinguished by the commodification of personal data with the core purpose of profit making. Dependent on the Internet, this net-worked and global economy extracts and claims "private human experience as free raw material for translation into behavioral data" (Laidler 2019). This economy transcends geographies and is void of time restraints, yet it has simultaneously highly spatial and temporal characteristics. Spatially, the digital divides that split the world between those with (affordable) Internet and those without are deepening. Temporally, the current expansion of surveillance capitalism has been able to manifest itself because of inadequate national and global regulatory responses.

Indeed, we are heading down a very destructive path that must be reversed through the development of stronger rights frameworks, better institutional capacities, and global enforcement systems. In the labor market, trade unions need to urgently revamp their strategies and find ways to cooperate across borders to organize this distributed workforce and ensure that all workers, in all forms of work, have the same social and fundamental rights.

One key policy area in need of immediate attention is the lack of workers' collective data rights. For all workers up and down corporate value chains, trade unions need to negotiate what I call the "data life cycle at work." These rights will be key in reversing the commodification of workers discussed above.

While better data rights for workers are an immediate concern, ideally, and echoing the strong voice of Shoshana Zuboff, the trading of algorithmic inferences should be made illegal: "I want to say that human futures markets [predictive analytics] need to be criminalized. They need to be made illegal. They cannot stand. Human futures markets have predictably antidemocratic consequences. Those consequences are already clear. The economic imperatives of surveillance capitalism are a direct result of the financial incentives in those markets" (Access Now 2020).

By outlawing the multibillion-dollar trading of the many inferences (profiles) that are constantly extracted from us based on our actions and nonactions, we will remove one of the greatest threats to our fundamental rights. This could be actualized by revising the United Nations' Universal Declaration of Human Rights so that it specifically includes articles on the right to be human (i.e., the right to be free from data manipulations that form and shape a human's life opportunities).

While we hold the vision of forbidding markets in human futures as a top priority, in this chapter I focus on the actions that need to be taken here and now in workplaces and in defense of workers. I start by describing the data life cycle at work and the various elements unions, on behalf of all workers, should be negotiating. I then move on to why these improved rights will benefit workers and prevent the commodification of workers that is currently taking place. The chapter ends with some reflections on why and how unions could become guardians of good data stewardship and empower workers through responsible data use.

Negotiating the Data Life Cycle at Work

What data rights should be covered by collective agreements and/or law? Figure 17.1 depicts the data life cycle at work. My claim is that unions should negotiate across the entire data life cycle, for both conventional workers and distributed workers in the platform economy and otherwise. Work is work, and rights are rights, irrespective of contract form.

Let's look at the phases of the data life cycle at work one at a time and unpack the potentials. While some of the demands are already fulfilled for workers who are covered by Europe's General Data Protection Regulation (GDPR), far from all are. For workers in most other jurisdictions across the world, these rights will be new, as workers are

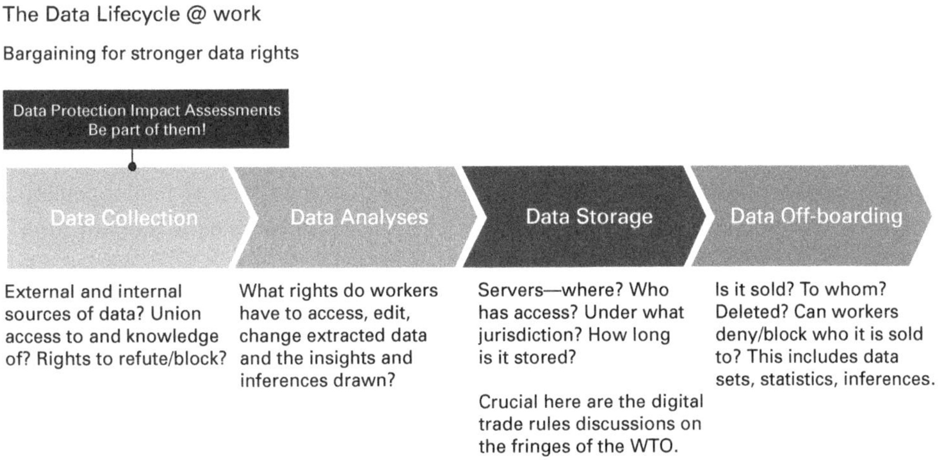
The Data Lifecycle @ work
Bargaining for stronger data rights
Data Protection Impact Assessments Be part of them!
Data Collection
Data Analyses
Data Storage
Data Off-boarding
External and internal sources of data? Union access to and knowledge of? Rights to refute/block?
What rights do workers have to access, edit, change extracted data and the insights and inferences drawn?
Servers—where? Who has access? Under what jurisdiction? How long is it stored?
Crucial here are the digital trade rules discussions on the fringes of the WTO.
Is it sold? To whom? Deleted? Can workers deny/block who it is sold to? This includes data sets, statistics, inferences.

Figure 17.1
The data life cycle at work.
Source: Author.

explicitly exempt from national data protection regulations (for example, in Australia and Thailand).

The *data collection phase* refers to data that is extracted and/or generated by digital systems that are either internal or external to the company/workplace. Here shop stewards (i.e., labor union officials or union representatives) and workers must be informed about the tools, and negotiate for the right to refute or block (parts of) this data extraction and generation. Recalling that much data extraction takes place under the hood, hidden from the worker or citizen, these points are extremely important. Management should be held accountable for their responses.

Importantly, in my conversations with union officials and management, many union officials say they are unaware of the algorithmic systems in place in their companies. But just as importantly, management indicates that they too are unaware of the systems' details and, according to many, simply do not understand the risks, challenges, or potentials of using them. Interestingly, in the GDPR zone, companies are obliged to conduct data protection impact assessments (DPIAs) on the introduction of new technology that is likely to involve a high risk to people's information (European Commission 2016). They are also obliged to consult the workers (European Commission 2017). However, very few of the unions I have spoken with have been involved in, have access to, or even know about these DPIAs.

In the *data analysis phase*, until trading in human futures is banned, unions must cover the gaps identified by Wachter and Mittelstadt (2019)—namely, the lack of rights with regard to the inferences made by algorithmic systems, which can even be used to predict behavior based on emotional data derived from video or audio recordings and/or activity data. Here workers should have greater insight into, access to, and rights to rectify, block, or even delete the inferences. They should also have the right to ban the selling of datasets and inferences that include personal information and personally identifiable information (i.e., any data that can be used to identify a particular person). This could be a social security number, a driver's license number, a bank account number, a passport number, or an email address.

Because such inferences can be used to determine scheduling and wages (if linked to performance metrics), or, in human resources, to decide whom to hire, promote, or fire, unions should demand that shop stewards, on behalf of a worker or group of workers, can gain access to the data/datasets and inferences that workers are subject to. Access to the inferences is key to the empowerment of workers and indeed to our human rights. Without these access rights, there will de facto be few checks and balances on management's legitimate, or ethical, use of algorithmic systems. Nor will there be any check or balance on data-generated discrimination and bias.

The *data storage phase* has to do with jurisdiction under which the data generated and extracted at work is stored. Current digital trade rules proposals within and on the fringes of the World Trade Organization are pushing for rules specifying that it is the laws of the country in which the data is stored that should determine who has access to the data, whom it can be sold to, and what it can be used for (James 2020). The majority of data centers are currently in the United States.[1] The digital trade proposals want data to flow freely across borders, unhindered by any national laws or regulations on data flows such as the GDPR, which has strict regulations on the flow of personal data. If adopted, these new digital trade rules will allow data to be used, sold, rebundled, and sold again, unlimited by national law. Although the 2020 Court of Justice of the European Union ruling (CJEU 2020), which invalidates the EU-US Privacy Shield,[2] can be seen as a slap in the face of proponents of unrestricted data flows, the demand is nonetheless still on the table. To prevent data from ending up in areas of the world with as little data protection as possible, two things must happen simultaneously. First, trade unions across all jurisdictions need to negotiate the data life cycle at work to obtain much improved data rights; and second, these digital trade negotiations must be stopped.

Lastly, the *data off-boarding phase* is also one where unions must be vigilant. Off-boarding refers both to the deletion of personal data or personally identifiable data extracted at the workplace and to the selling or passing on of these data/inferences/profiles/datasets to third parties. Unions should negotiate for much better rights regarding (1) knowing what data/inferences/profiles/datasets are off-boarded and to whom (e.g., an intelligence agency or data broker) and (2) objecting to and even blocking off-boarding to third parties. I cannot stress enough the importance of negotiating these rights, especially in light of the push in digital trade negotiations for an unrestricted global free flow of data that includes data generated on and extracted from workers.

Benefiting Workers

While the above negotiations across the data life cycle at work will require a coordinated and dedicated effort from unions across the world, promising first steps are already being taken. The Financial Services Union in Ireland has, in one of their agreements (Financial Services Union 2020), negotiated two key articles—namely, (1) an anticommodification clause stipulating that Ulster Bank/RBS commits that it will not turn employee data into a commodity for sale or trade (this relates directly to the data off-boarding phase above) and (2) a commitment to the Universal Declaration of Human Rights and the International Labour Organization's (ILO's) code of practice on the protection of workers' data (ILO 1997). In professional sports, "the NFL

Players' Association signed a deal with WHOOP [a fitness wearable company] to make it the Officially Licensed Recovery Wearable of the NFLPA and allow players to commoditize their own data. In their new [collective bargaining agreement], the NBA and NBA Players' Association agreed to terms protecting the right of individual players to decline the use of wearables at any time" (Chung 2017). UNI Global Union (2019), a global trade union federation for the skills and services sectors, has signed a global framework agreement with the global bank Crédit Agricole that includes reference to UNI Global Union's "Top 10 Principles for Workers' Data Privacy and Protection" (UNI Global Union 2017). This global framework agreement covers all of the bank's 140,000 employees across the world and gives the workers a string of rights in relation to the worker-related data collected by the company. For example, the workers and their union representatives have the right to access, influence, edit, and delete data that is collected on them and via their work processes (this relates to the data collection and data analysis phases in the data life cycle at work). Although these examples are promising, much more must be done.

Beyond successfully negotiating the data life cycle at work, what additional actions need to be taken and which new regulations are needed? First, we must move toward collective rights in a datafied world with a planetary labor market rather than the individual rights stipulated in current national/regional data protection laws. If workers have these rights over their data, they will also have the right to decide what to do with them—share them, pool them, for example, into workers' data collectives (Colclough 2020). The ILO could beneficially develop their nonbinding 1997 code of practice "Protection of Workers' Personal Data" (ILO 1997) into a new convention to establish these collective rights across the world.

Second, although companies covered by the GDPR must conduct DPIAs prior to, and periodically after, using algorithmic systems, many other data protection regulations, such as the California Consumer Privacy Act (CCPA), do not include this obligation. Unions and/or the ILO should be the ones demanding that the processing of workers' data cannot take place before a DPIA has been made *together* with the workers.

Third, workers and/or their union representatives must have a seat at the table regarding the periodic governance of data usage and algorithmic systems. This should be enshrined in a new global convention by the ILO.

Fourth, many data protection regulations across the world, even those aimed exclusively at consumers, are relatively weak and offer far fewer protections than, for example, the GDPR. To prevent the race to the bottom predicted if the digital trade rules proposed by the tech giants and supportive governments are adopted, workers and citizens up and down value and supply chains need sound data rights and protection.

Workers must fight for a digital ethos that is responsible and puts their rights above profit. In the world of work, unions must be the guardians of this alternative ethos.

Finally, power asymmetries between management and workers will only continue to expand if workers and their unions do not build capacity in the fields of data, algorithmic systems, and the governance of these. This implies digital awareness campaigns designed around workers' interests. But also a resource-demanding transformation in union strategies, policies, and operations. Funding is urgently needed to ensure that all unions across the world have the possibility to engage in these change processes.

The suggested ILO conventions will be crucial for the globalization of workers' digital rights and the extension of them to all workers in all forms of work. However, the ILO's supervisory system/mechanism (ILO n.d.) needs to be expanded to true enforcement rights so that breaches of, or failure to comply with, the conventions can be effectively addressed.

Realizing the above will be no simple task, resistance in relation to agreeing on and later ratifying the proposed ILO conventions is to be expected. Yet ILOs relevance in the digital age might well depend on the organization's very ability to unify around these rights-based demands. Already today, COVID-19 has led to a massive rise in the demand for, and supply of, worker surveillance technologies (Graziosi 2020; Jones 2020; Rees 2020). Little indicates that this will change unless global regulations are put in place.

Commitments within and between unions on a national, regional, and global scale are also called for to ensure that no workers are left behind. Unions' baseline understanding of digital technologies and their impact on workers' rights could be supplemented by a more advanced toolkit of model clauses, standard questions to ask management on the use of digital technologies, and model language and articles to be addressed in the ongoing assessment of these technologies. Given the complexity of the issues at hand, unions could consider training specialized "digital shop stewards." The union movement has the structures to do this and, if any of the above rings true, also the reasons to.

Unions must also unite to find ways to juxtapose the hegemonic narratives around digital technologies. This can be done by finding responsible ways to gather data about working conditions, and using these data in union campaigns, organizing efforts, and storytelling. It is to this we now turn.

Responsible Tech for Unions

One responsible and privacy-preserving way for unions to utilize tech for good and get information about their members' working conditions is by using the new open-source app WeClock (figure 17.2). WeClock functions as a self-tracking tool where the data

Figure 17.2
WeClock, the app for workers by workers.
Source: https://weclock.it.

generated is held exclusively by the worker until they decide to share it. Unions could use WeClock to support campaigns and prove to the world the realities facing workers. For example, via location, data workers can track their working time and time between shifts. Warehouse workers can log the exact distance they cover during a working day and whether they get any breaks. Home care workers can measure distance traveled and compare that to fixed-mileage fuel coverage. Gig workers can track their routes and idle time, and compare them to their earnings.

Another example of empowering workers through data is Driver's Seat (figure 17.3), a delivery and ride-share driver cooperative that, via an app, pools the data from drivers, analyzes it, and shares helpful insights with the drivers or sells the data to city and transportation agencies. For example, Driver's Seat can tell the drivers where the customers are and in what part of town the highest earnings can be made, and help calculate the odds of earning bonuses depending on the ride-sharing company (e.g., Uber, Lyft, or other local options). Proceeds from data selling to transport or city agencies are shared as dividends.

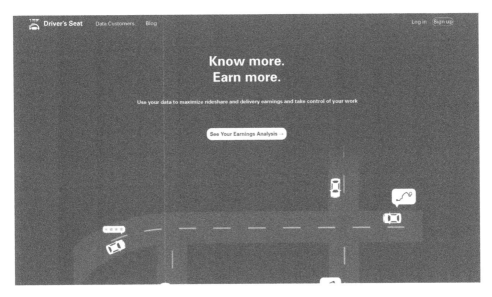

Figure 17.3
Screenshot from the website of the driver cooperative Driver's Seat.
Source: https://www.driversseat.co.

Lastly, unions must themselves become stewards of good data governance. In the Young Workers' Lab I was running, in which we produced WeClock, we developed an online, privacy-preserving guide to help unions with their own data governance. The tool is called Lighthouse (figure 17.4). Lighthouse takes the form of a guide or quiz where you work through a series of questions to rate your workplace's methods and practices along a range of topics—namely, writing a plan, building a community, handling data, assigning responsibility, writing rules, and managing risk.

These three examples of digital tools exemplify how unions, if they adopt an organization-wide strategy, can begin to battle back and address the commodification of workers taking place through the currently unfettered digitalization of work.

Concluding Reflections

We are at a critical moment in history, spurred by the COVID-19 pandemic and its dire economic, social, and humanitarian affects. Digital technologies are boundaryless, which is why a worker-led response needs to be globally coordinated and locally embedded. The damaging digital inferences that can affect not only individuals' life and work opportunities but also groups of citizens and workers that are statistically

Lighthouse: a guide to good data stewardship for trade unions

Welcome to Lighthouse, a purpose-made digital governance maturity test for trade unions.

This is a tool to help your union become more responsible stewards of data. You'll find a mix of guidance and quiz questions to help you better protect, manage, and harness data.

You can use Lighthouse to help evaluate a data or technology project that your union is currently running. (Although we've written Lighthouse to focus on projects, you could also use it to review your union's overall data practices.)

Take the quiz!

Lighthouse is a collaboration of Prospect, Digital Public, Duke Center on Law and Technology, and small scale.

prospect

Digital Public

Figure 17.4
Landing page of Lighthouse website.
Source: http://lighthouse.prospect.org.uk/.

similar to one another must be banned. In the meantime, workers, their unions, and the ILO should take immediate action to bridge regulatory gaps and ensure that workers benefit from much stronger collective data rights. No worker should be left without these rights. For the many workers in areas of the world that have no Internet access as yet, a globally established and enforceable set of rights will make sure that they too will be protected. Capacity building is required for all of this to happen. In 1919, as part of the Treaty of Versailles, the international community recognized that "labour is not a commodity"

(ILO 1920, art. 427). It is time to recommit to that treaty and stop the commodification of workers that we are currently witnessing through the datafication of work.

Notes

1. See https://www.datacenters.com/.

2. The EU-US Privacy Shield was a framework for regulating transatlantic exchanges of personal data for commercial purposes between the European Union and the United States. One of its purposes was to enable US companies to receive personal data more easily from EU entities under EU privacy laws meant to protect European Union citizens. The European Court of Justice declared the EU-US Privacy Shield invalid on July 16, 2020.

References

Access Now. 2020. "Real Corporate Accountability for Surveillance Capitalism with Shoshana Zuboff and Chris Gilliard." YouTube video, 59:39. July 28. https://youtu.be/FX2g6xPeftA.

Chen, Angela. 2019. "How Silicon Valley's Successes Are Fueled by an Underclass of 'Ghost Workers.'" *The Verge*, May 13. https://www.theverge.com/2019/5/13/18563284/mary-gray-ghost-work-microwork-labor-silicon-valley-automation-employment-interview.

Chung, Jason. 2017. "Who Owns Your FitBit Data? Biometric Data Privacy Problems." The Health Care Blog, November 25. https://thehealthcareblog.com/blog/2017/11/25/who-owns-your-fitbit-data-biometric-data-privacy-problems/.

CJEU. 2020. Data Protection Commissioner v. Facebook Ireland Limited, Maximillian Schrems. Case C-311/18. Luxembourg City: Court of Justice of the European Union. http://curia.europa.eu/juris/document/document.jsf;jsessionid=CF8C3306269B9356ADF861B57785FDEE?text=&docid=228677&pageIndex=0&doclang=EN&mode=req&dir=&occ=first&part=1&cid=9812784.

Colclough, Christina. 2020. "Towards Workers' Data Collectives." Bangalore: IT for Change. https://itforchange.net/digital-new-deal/2020/10/22/towards-workers-data-collectives/.

European Commission. 2016. "Data Protection Impact Assessment." General Data Protection Regulation 2016/679, art. 35. https://gdpr.eu/article-35-impact-assessment/.

European Commission. 2017. "Opinion 2/2017 on Data Processing at Work - wp249." https://ec.europa.eu/newsroom/article29/items/610169.

Financial Services Union. 2020. "FSU Achieves Employee Data Protection Commitments." Financial Services Union, January 29. Accessed September 20, 2020. https://www.fsunion.org/updates/2020/01/29/fsu-achieves-employee-data-protection-commitments/.

Graziosi, Graig. 2020. "Amazon Uses Worker Surveillance to Boost Performance and Stop Staff Joining Unions, Study Says." *Independent*, September 1. https://www.independent.co.uk/news/world/americas/amazon-surveillance-unions-report-a9697861.html.

ILO. n.d. "ILO Supervisory System/Mechanism." Geneva: International Labour Organization. Accessed August 31, 2021. https://www.ilo.org/global/about-the-ilo/how-the-ilo-works/ilo-supervisory-system -mechanism/lang--en/index.htm.

ILO. 1920. "The Labour Provisions of the Peace Treaties." Geneva: International Labour Office. https://www.ilo.org/public/libdoc/ilo/1920/20B09_18_engl.pdf.

ILO. 1997. "Protection of Workers' Personal Data." Code of practice. Geneva: International Labour Organization. https://www.ilo.org/safework/info/standards-and-instruments/codes/WCMS_107797 /lang--en/index.htm.

ILO. 2016. *Non-standard Employment around the World: Understanding Challenges, Shaping Prospects.* Report. Geneva: International Labour Organization. https://www.ilo.org/global/publications /books/WCMS_534326/lang--en/index.htm.

James, Deborah. 2020. *Digital Trade Rules: A Disastrous New Constitution for the Global Economy, by and for Big Tech.* Brussels: Rosa Luxemburg Stiftung. https://www.rosalux.eu/kontext/controllers /document.php?528.5/c/01b5be.pdf.

Jones, Lora. 2020. "'I Monitor My Staff with Software That Takes Screenshots.'" *BBC News*, September 29. https://www.bbc.com/news/business-54289152.

Laidler, John. 2019. "High Tech Is Watching You." *Harvard Gazette*, March 4. https://news.harvard.edu /gazette/story/2019/03/harvard-professor-says-surveillance-capitalism-is-undermining-democracy/.

Raju, Vishwanadh. 2020. "30 AI-Driven Tools to Optimize Your Talent Acquisition Process." https:// www.digitalhrtech.com/artificial-intelligence-talent-acquisition/#5.

Rees, Glenn. 2020. "Employee-Monitoring Technology: Productivity vs Privacy." *In the Black*, September 1. https://www.intheblack.com/articles/2020/09/01/employee-monitoring-technology -productivity-privacy.

Tan, Zhi Ming, Nikita Aggarwal, Josh Cowls, Jessica Morley, Mariarosaria Taddeo, and Luciano Floridi. 2020. "The Ethical Debate about the Gig Economy: A Review and Critical Analysis." *SSRN*, September 22. https://ssrn.com/abstract=3669216.

UNI Global Union. 2017. "Top 10 Principles for Workers' Data Privacy and Protection." Nyon, Switzerland: UNI Global Union. http://www.thefutureworldofwork.org/media/35421/uni_workers_data_ protection.pdf.

UNI Global Union. 2019. "Crédit Agricole Committed to Trade Union Rights and Freedoms in New International Agreement Signed Today with UNI Global." UNI Global Union, July 31. https:// www.uniglobalunion.org/news/credit-agricole-committed-trade-union-rights-and-freedoms-new -international-agreement-signed.

Wachter, Sandra, and Brent Mittelstadt. 2019. "A Right to Reasonable Inferences: Re-Thinking Data Protection Law in the Age of Big Data and AI." *Columbia Business Law Review* 2019 (2): 494–620. https://doi.org/10.7916/cblr.v2019i2.3424.

18   Fair Work, Feminist Design, and Women's Labor Collectives

Payal Arora and Usha Raman

The complexity of global supply chains has led to a lack of the transparency and monitoring practices meant to ensure fair working conditions (Arora and Thompson 2019). Factories producing goods for an international market often operate in developing countries where labor is cheap and regulations are weak or challenging to enforce. Some industries, like the garment business, handicrafts, sanitation, and salon services, are female-intensive, with women often constituting much of their workforce (Huq 2019). In such a global and gendered labor operation, communication between workers, employers, nongovernmental organizations, and other vested intermediaries remains a challenge, given the multiplicity of cultural, social, and political contexts spanned by such value chains. The many layers of disconnection and alienation between those who work at the bottom of the value chains—often informal labor—and these various intermediaries render invisible the complexities of lived experiences and situational dynamics that structure inequality into the workplace.

Negotiating fair work conditions and communicating needs become particularly challenging for women in these contexts, given the way globalized markets add a layer of precarity[1] over existing gender-related inequalities. Hazardous working conditions are a marker of the global sweatshop regime (Selwyn 2016). Complicating this, women are more vulnerable due to gender and traditional hierarchical structures, often facing harassment and violence—whether verbal or physical—and extreme pressure to increase their productivity. For instance, according to a 2019 report by the Centre for Policy Dialogue in Bangladesh (Moazzem and Radia 2018), 70–80 percent of female garment workers either experience or witness abuse at work. They are often subjected to sexual harassment, molestation or assault, and extreme verbal abuse within their working environments. Due to the dearth of bargaining agencies or worker unions (only around 10 percent of factories are unionized) and the fear of further harassment or losing their jobs, most of these workers avoid disclosing these incidents and openly collectivizing.

In recent years, extraordinarily cheap data plans and mobile phones in low-income countries have paved the way for the "next billion users"—that is, first-time consumers of digital platforms[2]—to express and organize themselves (Arora 2019). Crowdsourcing platforms, social media, and mobile technology are creating novel opportunities for dialogue in which laborers can access information on rights and share grievances about their working contexts. Corporations and labor rights organizations can gain insight from these collective digital engagements to monitor working conditions and create more supply chain transparency. Moreover, novel digital storytelling campaigns have reenergized these dialogues, leveraging the creative collectivities and imaginaries of everyday people to mobilize and institute change (Hull and Katz 2006; Jiang and Esarey 2018). Not only have digital platforms become important sites for social activism and lateral communication within labor communities, but they also serve as novel match-makers between laborers and employers, with a promise to professionalize otherwise informal services.

While these are encouraging developments, stringent sociocultural norms in domi-nantly patriarchal systems continue to act as barriers to women's ability to empower themselves through such digital infrastructures. According to the GSM Association 2020 report *Connected Women*, women in low-income contexts are 20 percent less likely than men to use mobile Internet (GSMA 2020). The reality among many of the women workers in these precarious working conditions is that they have limited access to mobile phones and the Internet; often have to share their phones with their family members; are mandated to request permission from their husbands, fathers, and broth-ers to use basic social media platforms; and can pay a high price for openly expressing themselves on the Internet, as their actions are closely tied to family and community honor (Arora and Scheiber 2017; Barboni et al. 2018).

For the Internet to become a critical humanizing and empowering tool for women workers as they seek fair work, it is essential to adopt a feminist approach to global development and design—one that would by default consider the lived experiences and contexts of a diverse range of users. Such an approach would inform both techno-logical and social aspects of infrastructure in a manner that not only includes women and other marginalized identities but also the possibility of encouraging the formation of productive collectives. This chapter proposes a feminist approach to labor collectives and platform design by decentering the discourse and practice around global value chains and labor movements in ways that pay heed to the concerns, grievances, aspira-tions, tactics, and strategies of women workers in low-income contexts and precarious conditions and industries. We offer a conceptual roadmap for makers and implement-ers of communication technologies that imagines how design can be informed by the voices of female workers at the bottom of supply chains. Such technologies could afford (digital) collectivization, amplification, and redress, and thus become tools that redesign the planetary market as humane, ethical, and responsible sociotechnical infrastructures of care.

To make the argument for such an approach to design, we first provide an overview of the gendered nature of global value chains and the precarities that result, including those that emerge from new ways of accounting for and recognizing labor, and then proceed to discuss the possibilities of collectivization opened up by networked digital tools, leading into feminist approaches to technology design, particularly in the context of emerging economies. We then offer a roadmap for a new approach to the design of communicative interfaces that draws on an understanding of the lived experiences of women workers at the margins. This roadmap envisages a pathway to change driven by (1) insights from feminist perspectives, (2) a focus on engagement of the most marginalized, and (3) principles of feminist design.

Gendered Dimensions of Global Value Chains

While the most recent wave of globalization has had far-reaching impacts on ways of life and work, it is only in the past decade or so that the gendered nature of inequality stemming from transnational flows of labor, capital, and goods—as well as from processes of automation and mechanization—has been systematically documented (Bassett, Kember, and O'Riordan 2019). Decades of research on global supply chains has revealed that while global development and innovation have long rested on the linkup of local suppliers with transnational firms, these linkups have become "global poverty chains" (Selwyn 2016). Revelations include "how workers in these chains are systematically paid less than their subsistence costs, how transnational corporations use their global monopoly power to capture the lion's share of value created within these chains, and how these relations generate processes of immiserating growth" (Selwyn 2016, 6).

It is no secret that global capitalism has lost much of its legitimacy as a system that can be relied on to provide equal opportunities that enable self-mobility to improve human welfare and enhance livelihoods. The myth of the free-market system is realized through the hypermonopolization of industries, leaving behind many more people and widening income and opportunity gaps. For instance, global brands in the garment sector in South Asia have increasingly pushed wages below subsistence levels. The high-tech company Apple has come under fire for turning a blind eye to the military-style labor regime deployed by their partner in Taiwan, Foxconn—including the draconian monitoring of workers' movements, few to no toilet breaks, and intensification of the workday with little overtime compensation—which has led to suicides and a wave of public protests (Chan, Selden, and Pun 2020). This comes through viscerally in the numerous worker blogs that document their experiences at Foxconn for the world to see and feel their plight: "To die is the only way to testify that we ever lived. Perhaps for the Foxconn employees and employees like us, the use of death is to testify that we were ever alive at all, and that while we lived, we had only despair" (Chan, Selden, and Pun 2020, 3).

Multinational corporations are thus under pressure to rethink their strategies of disaggregation and reconstituting of human value. Advocacy from activists and humanitarian organizations has forced some companies to recognize that they cannot simply externalize their moral responsibility nor easily dehumanize and devalue their workforces, especially in this age of digital activism.

Despite an abundance of research in this area, there continues to be a significant gap in our understanding of how gender shapes the experience of work life, including but not limited to concerns around security, freedom from the threat of gender-based harassment, and child and elder care, all of which need to be factored into the workings of global value chains and the fashioning of labor conditions and rights (Maertens and Swinnen 2012; LeBaron and Gore 2020). This lacuna is surprising, given the fact that women serve as the backbone to several global industries in developing countries, from the food supply chain in Africa to the apparel industry in Bangladesh. The few studies done in this area have found that women's status of informality and systemic exclusion from contractual work has misrepresented the extent of their contribution and participation in global supply chains (Maertens and Swinnen 2012; ILO 2018; LeBaron and Gore 2020). Recent surveys of the informal labor market by the International Labour Organization (ILO) and other multilateral agencies have brought to the fore the deeply gendered nature of disadvantage, particularly in the informal labor sector, which in the emergent economy is made up mostly of women (ILO 2018).

Forced labor is widely acknowledged to be an endemic feature of the contemporary global economy, and women are particularly vulnerable and disproportionately impacted by this (LeBaron and Gore 2020). For instance, in the cocoa supply chain in Ghana, LeBaron and Gore (2020) found that women experience nonpayment, underpayment, withholding of payment, physical violence and verbal abuse, threats of dismissal, deception, nonphysical coercion (especially food deprivation), and sexual violence. The authors discovered that "women workers tend to experience more severe forms of labor exploitation within the cocoa industry than men, and that business models are configured to profit from women's unequal position within the industry and society more broadly." (1097). They argue that the way to dismantle such gendered regimes lies in restructuring labor norms, division of labor, payment practices, and income; increasing women's land access and ownership; providing clear avenues of redress and access to justice; and enhancing women's status within the household and family environment.

Surveys done on the gender dimensions of labor conditions in the agro-food supply chain in sub-Saharan Africa have revealed that women's labor is not formalized. This is due to patriarchal sociocultural norms dictating that they cannot work outside the home and family farm. Many women are thereby not registered and do not have a bank account, and are often not allowed to claim their personal income. Widespread illiteracy among the women further deters them from seeking contractual agreements (Maertens and Swinnen 2012). This finding builds on prior studies that point to occupational segregation as an issue (Anker 1997; Kabeer, Stark, and Magnus 2008), with men usually being given permanent positions and higher-skilled jobs while women get low-skilled and casual or seasonal jobs, resulting in indirect wage discrimination. However, compared to other forms of traditional employment for women, jobs within the global supply chain were nevertheless found by Maertens and Swinnen (2012) to be less discriminatory. With strategic interventions of upskilling, contractual assistance, and control over finances, there remains the promise of a pathway toward formalization and dignity of labor conditions.

With the rise of the gig economy and digital intermediation of labor, there is a question of whether gender inequities travel over to the digital space or are being reconfigured in the design of these platforms. Certainly, reinvention coexists with the pressure to maintain the status quo. Recent studies on gender differences within the platform economy reveal that the gender wage gap persists, as women desire more flexibility because of their higher domestic responsibilities than men, impacting their level of participation and hourly wages (Foong et al. 2018; Hunt and Samman 2019). Moreover, gender inequalities in pay and workplace evaluation in the broader labor market often persist in digital labor marketplaces.

For example, in marketplaces with platform-determined rates, women tend to earn less due to behavioral differences (e.g., how fast they drive, in the case of ride-sharing apps). On cloud platforms with varied rates that depend on reviews, women tend to receive fewer and less favorable reviews than men (Foong et al. 2018), impacting their position in search rankings and thereby their employability. Also, men tend to overestimate their value compared to women in their profiles and self-descriptions (Foong et al. 2018). At the same time, it is difficult to deny that these platforms allow an increased participation of women in the labor force through their remote work opportunities, and they also serve as an entry into diverse industries with the possibility of advancing and professionalizing one's services—more so than traditional work options.

But what seems to be emerging is that even as opportunities are created, there remain significant gaps in access to fair work conditions and sensitivity to the lifeworlds that women must negotiate. If technology is the force that creates such opportunity, we argue, it can also become the tool that helps recreate the space of work.

Organizing Digitally and Formalizing Labor Solidarity

Digital information and communication technologies offer the potential to pioneer scalable solutions, where workers—both informal and formal labor pools—are included in information loops and can gain visibility and voice. A recent study analyzing three crowdsourcing tools designed for employer and worker dialogue in the garment industry argues for new forms of digital unionization to create systemic change in the labor movement of the twenty-first century (Arora and Thompson 2018). The authors recommend four elements that could strengthen monitoring systems for mitigation of labor exploitation: (1) the platform and its specific affordances; (2) design, which needs to be accessible, user-friendly, and based on workers' digital literacy skills; (3) marketing and engagement efforts through leveraging already-popular usage behavior such as Facebook use in addition to local radio advertisements; and (4) well-researched and dynamic content that covers the most important issues for workers to learn about and to report on, and that can be regularly updated to ensure user interest and motivation.

These elements can open up the possibility for workers to receive information on their rights, factory standards, and other issues meaningful to them. A platform's design should allow workers to share grievances anonymously through open-ended messages or surveys. The collected and computed data can thus create transparency down the supply chain, which can hold corporations to account for their insufficient monitoring practices. This can be a scalable and less costly monitoring practice than traditional audits and a potentially more effective way to detect exploitation. However, these tools are not stand-alone mechanisms, and they operate within a regulatory environment that can either disincentivize or encourage their use. Therefore, enforcement mechanisms such as local labor laws and regulations both directly and indirectly affect workers' empowerment (Arora and Thompson 2018, 2326).

Even as technologies that encourage bottom-up reporting, collectivization, and administrative transparency promise social transformation,[3] there are questions about their use on the ground and their actual impact. The design of these platforms can strongly affect the ways in which they enable empowerment and outreach for social change. While digital tools can contribute to breaking the silence and help support expression of unfair treatment and human rights violations, systemic change can best occur when there is stakeholder buy-in to incorporate these changes into the material conditions (Graham and Woodcock 2018). Civic social and digital collectivities of volunteerism, while showcasing the virtues of solidarity, also reveal the designs of institutional practice that give rise to and even perpetuate such inequality. As Tolentino (2020) argues in the *New Yorker*, "We can be so moved by the way people come together to overcome hardship that we lose sight of the fact that many of these hardships should not exist at all." The recognition of structural inequalities thus begs reform at a much more fundamental level, in a manner driven by a different value system—one characterized by care and empathy rather than dominated by concern about efficiency and productivity.

Drawing on Feminist Thinking

The Asia Floor Wage Alliance (AFWA), a global coalition of trade unions and human rights organizations, reports that while women are the dominant work group in the textile and export industry, increasing and structural violations are risking their well-being; this demands a more feminist approach to reporting these matters (AFWA 2019). Global Labour Justice, in their reports to the ILO, have revealed that women factory workers in global supply chains are often forced to meet unrealistic productivity targets, and failure to do so results in verbal, sexual, and physical abuse (Rahim 2020). Moreover, gendered exploitation often intersects with caste- and religion-based discrimination. Human Rights Watch reports that there is a lack of meaningful implementation of laws and guidelines against sexual harassment in these settings, and that company audits rarely mention incidents of abuse despite evidence to the contrary (Huq 2019).

Women workers face specific vulnerabilities, such as the possibility of miscarriages due to long working hours, no access to sanitary pads, and sexual harassment. However, this limited, instrumental view does not recognize the deep sociopolitical and gendered values behind the physical, digital, and legal infrastructures in place for female workers (Prentice et al. 2018). It is therefore important to take a more holistic and multistakeholder approach to the context of work and measures of productivity to promote the well-being of female precarious workers.

We propose that, given the rich history of women's movements in diverse marginalized contexts (Shiva 2016; Badri and Tripp 2017), it is important to explore how women workers could use digital tools that enable lateral communication and administrative transparency to organize themselves and strengthen their positions at work. While the history of women's movements has been closely tied to issues of land, labor, and utility-driven justice, it would be instructive to understand how recent digital affordances could intervene and broaden these paradigms to allow aspirational justice of self-actualization and increased personal freedoms via stable, secure, and soul-fulfilling employment. In the next section, we describe how a feminist approach could help inform development and design in a way that accounts for the specific experiences of women in informal labor, particularly in conditions of precarity.

Applying the Feminist Lens to Development and Platform Design

At its core, feminist thinking seeks to redress equations of power to acknowledge the differential experiences of those at the margins. In the context of labor relations, questions of concern might include the following: How can female workers gain more direct access to information on rights and working conditions? How can platforms be designed to protect women workers in the gig economy from vulnerabilities associated with gender hierarchies and skewed sociocultural norms? Can precarious laborers trust crowdsourcing tools and social media groups so that they will share their plight and report on work-related injustices? Can cloud work and gig economy platforms be used to mitigate gender-based discrimination and create more equitable labor markets and supply chains?

A feminist-informed approach to gender-related issues, including harassment and gender-skewed workplace affordances, requires looking at the context and culture of work, and the ways in which intermediaries—technologies, infrastructures, legal and regulatory systems—are planned and implemented, to gain insight into the gendered interactions between the human and nonhuman actors in a sociotechnical system. Undergirding such an approach is the recognition that technologies are inscribed with values (after Haraway 2013), including that of gender and that to build (rather than rebuild) structures and tools would require us to work from behind the interfaces and beneath the systems (Raman and Komarraju 2017). Proceeding from Sandra Harding's (1986) understanding of gender as an organizing principle that moderates—even creates—meaning, prefigures social relations, and structures identity, such a project of construction decenters technology while emphasizing the interactional and meaning-making processes that it affords.

Studies have shown that not only are existing technologies—platforms and social media tools in this instance—used differently across genders, but the social and cultural systems in which they are embedded privilege the male user (Wajcman 2007). This may be addressed in part by including women and other minority genders at the design and development stage (Faulkner 2001), but perhaps more effectively by including the perspectives and the lived experiences of women who use or could use such technologies. One would have to begin by understanding ownership and control of digital devices and access to networks, as well as modes and meanings of usage, before one could explore opportunities for participation and organization using such technologies. Ott (2018, 94) noted that "the technologies embedded in social media platforms contribute . . . to the formation of our networks," and the "presumed democratic environment" they offer is rarely realized, as users have limited opportunities and capabilities to participate in it.

The challenge, then, is how to apply feminist design principles (fostering openness, participation, and community) in building technology within a patriarchal system, with the affordances that will allow users without privilege to participate and gain from it. Exploring this in the context of Bangladesh, Sultana et al. (2018) found that designing technology for underprivileged women forced negotiations between the (absence of) feminist ideas in the community and the goals of the feminist design project. Women in such contexts, they noted, fearing possible backlash from their families, were reluctant to or simply could not make use of tools even when they were made accessible. Feminist principles have in recent times permeated the field of human-computer interaction, where a push to examine understudied cultures and geographies has led to the application of ideas such as Chandra Mohanty's feminist solidarity to technology design (Kumar et al. 2019). Key to this approach, which builds on commonalities while attending to the particular, is the incorporation of such values at every stage of technology design and deployment, a recursive process that imagines the user in context.

A feminist framework put forward persuasively by Anita Gurumurthy and Nandini Chami (2017) of the Bangalore-based IT for Change places the right to communicate at the center of a reconfiguration of the network economy, arguing that this can guide a more ethical, empathetic approach to thinking about digital technologies, development, and gender in a planetary economy. While research in the information and communication technology for development field has acknowledged the potential for digital technologies and networked media, including mobile phones and social media, to help share and amplify voice for women workers, there is a parallel recognition that given the commercial nature of these platforms, there is the distinct possibility of reproducing existing power hierarchies and maintaining the status quo at the macro level (Cummings and O'Neill 2015). As a result, even as research tells us that women participate in organically formed kinship and neighborhood communities, that they share communal and caregiving tasks, and that they have historically collectivized and accumulated power in numbers, platforms rarely afford such mobilization through their interfaces. This speaks to an urgent need to rethink the very structures of communication technologies—including their design and deployment—as intrinsic to challenging such patriarchally determined structures of power and to making voice amplification meaningful.

A feminist approach has at its foundation a sensitivity to the local, disparate, lived realities of women and identifies and nurtures opportunities for collectivization that challenge the paternalistic, patriarchal structures of domination—in both mediated and proximate contexts. It is predicated on listening and allowing models of negotiation to emerge from the bottom up, and aims to build affordances into technologies that are responsive to women's needs, while allowing for a new imaginary of change.

Gender Bias in Data Governance

To understand and disrupt the gendered dimensions of algorithmic injustice (where computer code predetermines relationships of power), it is important to attend to how women are represented and computed on the Internet, not just as individuals but as a group. Discriminatory practices on the Internet often stem from the continued sharing of stereotypes and traditional framings of women that become the data feed, fueling such reproductions. Hence, we need to critically attend to these meaning-making processes and allow for a more flexible imaginary of digital belonging as part of feminist design.

It matters how women are conceptualized as a group, as a category, and as a cluster in today's algorithmic age, as data collectives enable the amplifying of a narrative, an audience, and even policymaking. Take for instance the gender-based policies that the Peruvian and Panamanian governments instituted at the onset of the COVID-19 pandemic to regulate the number of people out in public. They passed a policy that allowed only men or only women to travel on alternate days (Woskie and Wenham 2021). It turned out that this measure forced women to gather in large groups on their given days, as domestic work such as household shopping was relegated to them. Moreover, there was backlash from LGBTQ+ activists because transgender and nonbinary people faced increased street harassment by police. Within a few weeks, both governments were compelled to get rid of this policy, recognizing its uneven impact.

Glorifying women hardly works either. When Barack Obama, in solidarity with and support for women, announced that women are better leaders than men (Asher 2019), he inadvertently tapped into the long-standing, unreasonable expectations women have faced to "doing it all" and being the "superwoman"—as hard workers, good savers, moral guardians of society, the virtuous gender, bearing the burden of all that is best and pure of a community (Ross 2017). When they fail, they often receive severe social punishment in the form of loss of their job, loss of their reputation, loss of status, and even loss of life to preserve the community's honor.

Other forms of misrepresentation pervade the masculinization of certain work sectors. A typical image of a farmer or a construction worker is male. The pervasive media narrative builds empathy for the male worker struggling to put food on the table for his family. The reality, however, is that women constitute a dominant or at least a substantial part of the construction and agricultural sectors across the Global South (Williams, Devika, and Aandahl 2015). For instance, half of India's 30 million construction workers are women. Women hold the key to food production in most parts of the world, including Africa, where women grow 70 percent of the food (Agarwal 2018). According to the UN Food and Agriculture Organization, women account for an estimated two-thirds of the world's 600 million poor livestock keepers.[4] These misrepresentations of sectors such as construction, agriculture, and livestock as being male dominated have added consequences during COVID-19 times, as national bailouts are often tied to formalized arrangements of labor and mediated through the datafication of welfare systems.

When work is feminized—such as in the increasingly recognized "care economy," where healthcare and education take precedence—we often find a devaluation of women's labor, reflected, for instance, in pay gaps between women and men and lower-status jobs (Dengler and Strunk 2018). This stands as a remarkable irony, given that the rise of automation in work already signals that such caregiving is hard to automate and will become more desirable and in demand as economies adapt to this technological future.

The fact is that any simplistic dichotomy prompted by concepts such as the gender divide and the digital divide is problematic, as it denies the fact that being human is essentially a contradiction of roles, statuses, and interests, reflecting the complexity of social life. It is simplistic to believe that access to technology, upskilling, or bridging the pay gap alone can achieve gender equity. Gender equity is very much a "wicked problem," where the solution of one problem, for example increasing women's participation in the workforce, can—especially in patriarchal societies—create other issues, such as the rise of violence against women due to spousal jealousy and the imposition of other regressive gender norms. In our approach to designing feminist systems, both socioeconomic and digital, we need to first demystify the framing of women groups/clusters and allow them the chance of being diverse, and even—dare we say it—ordinary.

Roadmap for Feminist Development and Design

Networks of labor—both formal and informal—are intricately linked to the myriad webs of power and consumption that fuel the planetary system. The digital and data infrastructures that drive the world economy, and shape and funnel information flows, also affect the lives of workers far removed from Wall Street and Silicon Valley. As socioeconomic and financial systems become digital in the Global South, we need to ask who and what determines how women workers are represented and reproduced on the Internet, how communities are formed and sustained, and whether and what kinds of change are possible.

Feminist design has at the heart of its objective the reordering of the social and political world, a refashioning of the tools we use to see, explain, and interact with it. At a more fundamental level, designing communication infrastructures that realize such a vision would draw directly from the lives of women and other marginalized groups that occupy the peripheral regions of the network. Shifting the conversation and the action to an inclusive approach to technology development would require the active participation and reeducation of multiple actors across the value chain, from policymakers to corporations to developers. This roadmap would possess the following three characteristics:

1. Insight driven Feminist design recognizes the complex and layered realities of the most disadvantaged workers in global value chains—women—and understands how communication technologies could both empower and complicate their lives. For instance, among the poor, mobile phones are often a shared resource, with the woman having the least right of access and little privacy or control over use. Carving out time and acquiring the capacity for meaningful and productive use of technology would necessitate advocating for contextual change. In other words, design would need to account for the social and cultural dimensions of use while imagining the consequences of shifting power dynamics within the home, in workspaces, among peer groups, and in relation to the state.

2. Engagement driven Based on a deep understanding of vocabulary and affect, how might we cocreate a narrative of change with marginalized women? Can visual and aural forms be used to include these women in setting terms with and demanding responsibility from employers? Can such vocabularies then become elements of technological interfaces that engage rather than alienate? Action research and digital storytelling can be powerful tools to aid in this process. Audiovisual and immersive storytelling plays an important role in building collaboration by highlighting key messages from the marginalized majority (Arora 2019), showcasing different points of view and signposting blind spots that can otherwise be left out of purely textual formats. We can take a page from Kolb's (2014) five steps of design—empathize, define the problem, ideate, prototype, and test—to translate insights into outreach for change.

3. Design driven Traditional design assumes a thinking-from-above mindset, an approach that architects change from above. However, feminist design is about bottom-up thinking. It begins with the imagination of social justice as it may be experienced, not conceptualized. In practical terms, for women in the informal labor force, it is prompted by questions of fairness, equity, and care, and the infrastructures that would have to be put in place that realize these values. This addresses specific issues, from making visible the cultures of servitude that limit professionalization (such as in the domestic work sector in Southeast Asia), to working through the oppressions of family, to broader questions of privacy, data gaps, and algorithmic control.

Women workers at the bottom of global value chains are in fact the most crucial links in the global poverty chain. Creative use of technology that is thoughtfully designed and sensitively implemented can go a long way in building women's capacity to create nurturing work communities. Such collectives can advocate for changes that are collaboratively agreed upon and can build toward a more just, equitable future.

Acknowledgment

This chapter draws from our FemLab.Co project, a seed-funded initiative by Canada's International Development Research Centre (IDRC) as part of their Future of Work series. The proposal is titled "Organizing Digitally: Opportunities for Collectivization for Female Workers in South Asia" (IDRC Project 109331-001).

Notes

1. The 2013 collapse in the Dhaka District of Bangladesh of the multistory Rana Plaza garment factory, which supplied multinational companies like JCPenney and Walmart, has become emblematic of the precarious work conditions occupied by many women workers at the bottom of global supply chains.

2. In this chapter, we use *platforms* to mean the wide range of communication interfaces now available on mobile devices, ranging from social media such as Facebook to messaging services like WhatsApp, as well as more narrowly focused tools developed for business-to-consumer or business-to-business communication and exchange.

3. Some examples of bottom-up digital tools for collectivization include Ushahidi, a crowdsourcing platform initially developed in 2008 for people to report violence during the elections in Kenya but now used for other grassroots initiatives; LaborVoices and Quizrr, nonprofit companies that launched platforms among factory workers to gather insights about their working experiences to inform brands and pressure them to improve work conditions; and Kamako Chhnoeum (Outstanding Worker), a crowdsourcing project run by the nonprofit organization Better Factories Cambodia, part of the International Labour Organization.

4. See http://www.fao.org/reduce-rural-poverty/resources/resources-detail/en/c/468431/.

References

AFWA. 2019. "Asia Floor Wage Alliance's Step-by-Step Approach to Prevent Gender Based Violence at Production Lines in Garment Supplier Factories in Asia." https://asia.floorwage.org/wp-content/uploads/2021/01/AFWA-Step-by-Step-approach-to-Prevent-GBV-compressed.pdf.

Agarwal, Bina. 2018. "Gender Equality, Food Security and the Sustainable Development Goals." *Current Opinion in Environmental Sustainability* 34: 26–32.

Anker, Richard. 1997. "Theories of Occupational Segregation by Sex: An Overview." *International Labour Review* 136 (3): 315–339.

Arora, Payal. 2019. *The Next Billion Users: Digital Life beyond the West.* Cambridge, MA: Harvard University Press.

Arora, Payal, and Laura Scheiber. 2017. "Slumdog Romance: Facebook Love and Digital Privacy at the Margins." *Media, Culture & Society* 39 (3): 408–422. https://doi.org/10.1177/0163443717691225.

Arora, Payal, and Linnea Holter Thompson. 2019. "Crowdsourcing as a Platform for Digital Labor Unions." *International Journal of Communication* 12: 2314–2332. http://irawan.lecture.ub.ac.id/files/2017/12/crowdsourcing-labor-ijoc.pdf.

Asher, Saira. 2019. "Barack Obama: Women Are Better Leaders Than Men." *BBC*, December 16. https://www.bbc.com/news/world-asia-50805822.

Badri, Balghis, and Aili Mari Tripp. 2017. *Women's Activism in Africa: Struggles for Rights and Representation.* London: Zed Books.

Barboni, Georgia, Erica Field, Rohini Pande, Natalia Rigol, Simone Schaner, and Charity Troyer Moore. 2018. *A Tough Call: Understanding Barriers to and Impacts of Women's Mobile Phone Adoption in India.* Cambridge, MA: Harvard Kennedy School.

Bassett, Caroline, Sarah Kember, and Kate O'Riordan. 2019. *Furious: Technological Feminism and Digital Futures.* London: Pluto Press.

Chan, Jenny, Mark Selden, and Ngai Pun. 2020. *Dying for an iPhone: Apple, Foxconn, and the Lives of China's Workers.* Chicago: Haymarket Books.

Cummings, Clare, and Tam O'Neill. 2015. *Do Digital Information and Communications Technologies Increase the Voice and Influence of Women and Girls? A Rapid Review of the Evidence.* ODI Literature Review. London: Overseas Development Institute.

Dengler, Corinna, and Birte Strunk. 2018. "The Monetized Economy versus Care and the Environment: Degrowth Perspectives on Reconciling an Antagonism." *Feminist Economics* 24 (3): 160–183.

Faulkner, Wendy. 2001. "The Technology Question in Feminism: A View from Feminist Technology Studies." *Women's Studies International Forum* 24 (1): 79–95.

Foong, Eureka, Nicholas Vincent, Brent Hecht, and Elizabeth M. Gerber. 2018. "Women (Still) Ask for Less: Gender Differences in Hourly Rate in an Online Labor Marketplace." In *Proceedings of the ACM on Human-Computer Interaction* 2 (CSCW): 1–21. New York: Association for Computing Machinery.

Graham, Mark, and Jamie Woodcock. 2018. "Towards a Fairer Platform Economy: Introducing the Fairwork Foundation." *Alternate Routes* 29: 242–253.

GSMA. 2020. *Connected Women: The Mobile Gender Gap Report 2020*. London: GSM Association. https://www.gsma.com/mobilefordevelopment/wp-content/uploads/2020/05/GSMA-The-Mobile -Gender-Gap-Report-2020.pdf.

Gurumurthy, Anita, and Nandini Chami. 2017. "A Feminist Action Framework on Development and Digital Technologies." APC Issue Papers. Melville, South Africa: Association for Progressive Communications. https://www.apc.org/sites/default/files/FeministActionFrameworkOnDevelopment AndDigitalTechnologies.pdf.

Haraway, Donna. 2013. *Simians, Cyborgs, and Women: The Reinvention of Nature*. New York: Routledge.

Harding, Sandra G. 1986. *The Science Question in Feminism*. Ithaca, NY: Cornell University Press.

Hull, Glynda A., and Mira-Lisa Katz. 2006. "Crafting an Agentive Self: Case Studies of Digital Storytelling." *Research in the Teaching of English* 41 (1): 43–81. http://www.lchc.ucsd.edu/uclinks .org/reference/research/hull_katz.pdf.

Hunt, Abigail, and Emma Samman. 2019. "Gender and the Gig Economy." ODI Working Paper 546. London: Overseas Development Institute. https://www.odi.org/publications/11272-gender -and-gig-economy-critical-steps-evidence-based-policy.

Huq, Chaumtoli. 2019. "Women's 'Empowerment' in the Bangladesh Garment Industry through Labor Organizing." *Wagadu: A Journal of Transnational Women's & Gender Studies* 20: 130–154.

ILO. 2018. *Women and Men in the Informal Economy: A Statistical Picture*, 3rd ed. Geneva: International Labour Organization. https://www.ilo.org/wcmsp5/groups/public/---dgreports/---dcomm /documents/publication/wcms_626831.pdf.

Jiang, Min, and Ashley Esarey. 2018. "Uncivil Society in Digital China: Incivility, Fragmentation, and Political Stability—Introduction." *International Journal of Communication* 12 (2018): 1928–1944. https://ijoc.org/index.php/ijoc/article/view/9478.

Kabeer, Naila, Agneta Stark, and Edda Magnus, eds. 2008. *Global Perspectives on Gender Equality: Reversing the Gaze*. London: Routledge.

Kolb, David A. 2014. *Experiential Learning: Experience as the Source of Learning and Development*. Upper Saddle River, NJ: Pearson FT Press.

Kumar, Neha, Naveena Karusala, Azra Ismail, Marisol Wong-Villacres, and Aditya Vishwanath. 2019. "Engaging Feminist Solidarity for Comparative Research, Design, and Practice." In *Proceedings of the ACM on Human-Computer Interaction* 3 (CSCW): 1–24. New York: Association for Computing Machinery.

LeBaron, Genevieve, and Ellie Gore. 2020. "Gender and Forced Labour: Understanding the Links in Global Cocoa Supply Chains." *Journal of Development Studies* 56 (6): 1095–1117. https://doi.org /10.1080/00220388.2019.1657570.

Maertens, Miet, and Johan F. M. Swinnen. 2012. "Gender and Modern Supply Chains in Developing Countries." *Journal of Development Studies* 48 (10): 1412–1430.

Moazzem, Khondaker Golam, and Marzuka Ahmad Radia. 2018. "'Data Universe' of Bangladesh's RMG Enterprises: Key Features and Limitations." CPD Working Paper 123. Dhaka: Centre for Policy Dialogue. https://cpd.org.bd/cpd-working-paper-123-data-universe-of-bangladeshs-rmg-enterprises/.

Ott, Kate. 2018. "Social Media and Feminist Values: Aligned or Maligned?" *Frontiers: A Journal of Women Studies* 39 (1): 93–111.

Prentice, Rebecca, Geert De Neve, Alessandra Mezzadri, and Kanchana N. Ruwanpura. 2018. "Health and Safety in Garment Workers' Lives: Setting a New Research Agenda." *Geoforum* 88: 157–160.

Rahim, Mia Mahmudur. 2020. "Humanising the Global Supply Chain: Building a Decent Work Environment in the Readymade Garments Supply Industry in Bangladesh." In *Research Handbook on Human Rights and Business*, edited by Surya Deva and David Birchall, 130–150. Northampton: Edward Elgar.

Raman, Usha, and Sai Amulya Komarraju. 2017. "Researching Online Worlds through a Feminist Lens: Text, Context and Assemblages." In *Re-presenting Feminist Methodologies: Interdisciplinary Explorations*, edited by Kalpana Kannabiran and Padmini Swaminathan, 131–157. London: Routledge.

Ross, Loretta J. 2017. "Reproductive Justice as Intersectional Feminist Activism." *Souls* 19 (3): 286–314.

Selwyn, Benjamin. 2016. "Global Value Chains or Global Poverty Chains? A New Research Agenda." CGPE Working Paper no. 10. Brighton, UK: Centre for Global Political Economy, University of Sussex. https://www.sussex.ac.uk/webteam/gateway/file.php?name=selwyn-global-chains-2016-w-imprint.pdf&site=359.

Shiva, Vandana. 2016. *Staying Alive: Women, Ecology, and Development*. Berkeley: North Atlantic Books.

Sultana, Sharifa, François Guimbretière, Phoebe Sengers, and Nicola Dell. 2018. "Design within a Patriarchal Society: Opportunities and Challenges in Designing for Rural Women in Bangladesh." In *Proceedings of the 2018 CHI Conference on Human Factors in Computing Systems*, 1–13. New York: Association for Computing Machinery.

Tolentino, Jia. 2020. "What Mutual Aid Can Do during a Pandemic." *New Yorker*, May 11. https://www.newyorker.com/magazine/2020/05/18/what-mutual-aid-can-do-during-a-pandemic.

Wajcman, Judy. 2007. "From Women and Technology to Gendered Technoscience." *Information, Community and Society* 10 (3): 287–298.

Williams, Glyn, J. Devika, and Guro Aandahl. 2015. "Making Space for Women in Urban Governance? Leadership and Claims-Making in a Kerala Slum." *Environment and Planning A: Economy and Space* 47 (5): 1113–1131. https://doi.org/10.1177/0308518X15592312.

Woskie, Liana R., and Clare Wenham. 2021. "Do Men and Women 'Lockdown' Differently? An Examination of Panama's COVID-19 Sex-Segregated Social Distancing Policy." *Feminist Economics* 27 (1–2): 327–344.

19   Tilt the Scroll to Repair: Efficient Inhuman Workforce at Global Chains of Care

Joana Moll and Jara Rocha

High quanta of energy degrade social relations just as inevitably as they destroy the physical milieu.
—Ivan Illich (1974)

[We] must rethink the question of "reproduction" in a planetary perspective. Reflecting on the activities which reproduce our life dispels, in fact, the illusion that the automation of production may create the material conditions for a non-exploitative society, showing that the obstacle to "revolution" is not the lack of technological know-how, but the divisions which capitalist development reproduces.
—Silvia Federici (2009)

The numerous user interfaces encountered in everyday life play an essential role in obscuring and diluting the material realities of the global chains of production and reproduction that structure the world around us. This is especially true when it comes to the many tangible and intangible workforces that are triggered by our mundane on-screen clicking and scrolling behavior. In this chapter, we claim that user interfaces act as a well-engineered capitalist machine that disconnects users from the material complexities of global chains of commodity and data production—and also social reproduction—with the aim of increasing economic profit. Thus, we believe, it is necessary to trace the connections that exist between things—as well as the workload involved in the basic maintenance of those connections—if the user is to fully understand the systems they operate within in order to balance and repair the profoundly asymmetrical distribution of agency, energy, labor, time, care, and resources within these planetary networks. In this chapter, we will draw on feminist economics (Waring 1999; Federici 2012; Pérez Orozco 2014) and historical efficiency criticism (Jevons 1865; Illich 1973) to shine a light on the complexity that sits at the heart of platform capitalism (Srnicek 2016; McAfee and Brynjolfsson 2017; Weatherby 2018).

On June 17, 2019, in Utrecht, artist Joana Moll[1] (n.d.) purchased *The Life, Lessons & Rules for Success: The Journey, the Teachable Moments & 10 Rules for Success Cultivated from the Life & Wisdom of Jeff Bezos* from the Amazon website. The web browser used to buy the book was Firefox Quantum 67.0.4, installed on a Dell XPS 13 computer that used the operating system Ubuntu 18.04.2. In order to place the order, the customer was forced by the Amazon website to go through 12 different interfaces composed of large amounts of computer code—normally hidden from view. This code executes various operations, such as composing the site's content, supporting interactivity, and tracking the user's activity—that is, their clicks and scrolls. Overall, Moll saved 1,307 different requests to all sorts of scripts and documents, totaling 8,724 A4 pages' worth of printed code, adding up to 87.33 MB of information per hour. The amount of energy needed to load each of the 12 web interfaces, along with each one's endless fragments of code, was approximately 30 watt-hours.

Infamously, Amazon's business model is based on "obsessive customer focus," entailing "constantly listening to customers to enhance and improve the customer experience" (Premack 2018). In other words, their business relies on continuous monitoring and recording of their customers' behavior and activity to improve the monetization of each user, thereby increasing Amazon's revenue. These processes are carried out by cookies and other supporting technologies embedded on websites, apps, videos, and other digital media formats. When a user visits a website, tracking software will automatically trigger the collection of user data, which is now owned by the company that executes the tracking (e.g., Amazon, Google, Facebook)—and which it has a legal right to exploit.

The act of buying (for example, a book on Amazon) has thus been turned into a tracking and monetization device, with the aim of adding layers to the already-complex setting of power relations online—including user profiling, social sorting, task assignment, energy use and waste, and smoothening of liberal logi(sti)cs. Put differently, the 8,724 pages of code that track and personalize a user's behavior and shopping experience on the website—and that were involuntarily loaded by the customer through the browser—are evidence of Amazon's core money-making machinery at work. This machinery that sustains the patriarchal-colonial regime that determines how power is distributed along hands, territories, and whole modes of existence at large. Moreover, this distributive operation implies that all the energy needed to load this relatively large amount of information was effectively demanded from the user, who ultimately assumed not just part of the economic cost of Amazon's hidden monetization processes but also a portion of its environmental footprint.

The Hidden Life of an Amazon User

All these aspects are drawn on in *The Hidden Life of an Amazon User,*[2] an interactive artwork that details the intricate labyrinth of interfaces, code, and energy that make possible the purchase of Jeff Bezos's book—with the aim of casting light on Amazon's often unacknowledged but aggressive exploitation of their users, which is embedded at the heart of the company's business strategies. Such strategies would not work on apparently neutral, personalized user experiences afforded by convenient user interfaces. These interfaces conceal the sophisticated business models embedded in endless pages of indecipherable code, all of which are set in motion by the user's labor—again, clicking and scrolling—and hence based on a hidden mode of delegation. In turn, these strategies incur a significant energy cost, part of which is involuntarily assumed by the user. To put it bluntly, not only is the user exploited by means of their free labor, which allows these companies to collect and trade in massive amounts of user data, but the user is also forced to assume part of the energy costs of such exploitation (see figure 19.1).

Figure 19.1
The Hidden Life of an Amazon User at BIG D@T@! BIG MON€Y! Exhibition, curated and produced by HALLE 14 (HALLE 14, Leipzig | Walther Le Kon, 2020). The artwork integrates the following contents: a large-scale wall projection displaying a 14-minute video that scrolls down the 12 different interfaces and the 87 MB of code needed to purchase the Jeff Bezos book; the almost 9,000 printed pages of code; and Jeff Bezos' *Life and Lessons for Success.*
Source: Joana Moll.

In response, Moll's artwork accumulates, organizes, and inscribes the accountability of these energies in the form of a very specific device: the scrolling screen. The device of the scroll takes on the task of transmitting, carrying, and containing the evidence of *practices of mattering* in danger of irreversible erasure. Such mattering propagate along global chains of delegation of responsibility in diversified forms—waste, maintenance, and decision-making being some of the most outsourced. As the user interacts with the scrolling screen, and as the Amazon pages flow downward through their thick mass of code, the mundane gesture of scrolling invokes an urgent consideration of which geometries of relation configure the regime where *The Hidden Life of an Amazon User* takes place. A simple, repetitive praxis—the page scroll—activates a frictional rendering of the measurements of vectors that intersect (through the simple act of browsing an Amazon page) with the so-called life of a so-called user. During the continuous process of the scroll, three vectors are braided together—information load noted in megabytes (MB), energy rate given in kilowatt-hours (Wh), and caloric value estimated in kcal (Rocha n.d.).

Through Amazon's process of userizing—that is, turning customers into users—a form of subjective enclosure takes off from the already exclusive liberal subject to land in a flow of "nonlife" (i.e., isolated from the possibility of actively participating in how the material conditions of one's life are arranged). An agency cut takes place once the user emerges as a downgraded but translocal subjectivity: one devoid of options beyond going up and down the consumption line. The user is hence reduced to simply clicking and scrolling, in an activity that grabs energy and matter in a distributed manner across the globe. Kathryn Yusoff (2018, 2) puts it this way: "The human and its subcategory, the inhuman, are historically relational to a discourse of settler-colonial rights and the material practices of extraction, which is to say that the categorization of matter is a spatial execution, of place, land, and person cut from relation through geographic displacement."

Once personal agency is cut, the global division of labor is much easier to execute. And in this execution, what used to be called "life" is now technically turned into a (very productive) amalgam of inhuman, distributed workforces. All that matters now is energy, time, and capital relationalities. In being userized, the former human, the former customer, enters the realm of nonlife, becomes yet another disposable link in the global chain of industrial computing maintenance. The fungible user is now ready to welcome the outsourced costs and wastes of energy used by the platform: the user is ready to become a straightforward resource for the wider apparatus. In userizing us, Amazon has managed to produce its own set of inhuman workforces.

In this efficiently designed flow of nonlife, Amazon users merge with microtaskers—that is, those who spend their time occupied with care tasks such as cleaning tags, weeding features, or arranging annotations (Barriuso and Torralba 2012): all at high speed, all of course at their own energetic cost. Erasure in the quest for accumulation has historically been the main operation executed against bodies, lands, and cultural forms. The erasure of the vibrant, energetic life of all those who have been rendered invisible—and ultimately rendered inhuman—in the name of modern, universalized extractive progress, is precisely the erasure that resonates most with the scrolling gesture at the heart of Joana Moll's piece.

Hence, the act of scrolling sets in motion a visualization of the sophisticated, opaque, transnational machinery that exploits planetary resources in needing vast amounts of energy and labor to operate. As Amaia Pérez Orozco (2016) has put it in conversation with Cristina Vega, "Understanding how care is being globalized allows us to analyze the ways in which care systems are interconnected on a global scale. It also allows us to identify the co-existence of different social conceptions of care." Thus, a complexifying analysis of agencies of use, waste, occlusion, and platform-catalyzed damage is needed for public debate, sensibilization, and transformation. An analytic remains to be done: one that examines the distribution of power, presence, and response-abilities in the computational establishment (Ali 2016), of which the GAFAM and BATX apparatuses[3] are the main drivers.

Ivan Illich's lucid essay *Energy and Equity*, first published in 1973, identifies the critical impact of our ever-increasing energy demands on the environment, the individual, and society at large. He particularly reflects on the unbalanced distribution and use of energy and time: "Beyond a certain speed, motorized vehicles create remoteness which they alone can shrink. They create distances for all and shrink them for only a few" (Illich 1974, 25). This observation can be very well applied to the contemporary act of purchasing a book on Amazon—where the five minutes and trivial human power and external energy that it took the artist to purchase Jeff Bezos's book through the website was counterbalanced by the amalgam of labor, hardware, software, time, and energy that lies beyond the interface: a million employees,[4] more than 175 warehouses worldwide, more than 150 million square feet of space, a vast international network of transportation, and a countless microtasker/computer/algorithmic workforce. Yet even though the Amazon user is the primary trigger of a huge chain reaction of events, they are blind to the material reality that lies beyond the interface, and this is particularly true for most people using (or rather *used by*) any Internet-based service. In that sense, the ease of use of these interfaces, whose ultimate goal is to smoothen the accumulation of revenue, acts as a well-designed smokescreen to conceal complexity and material waste—or, in other words, the negative externalities of capitalist means of production.

Attentive Interface Politics

Moll's work urges us to reconsider the semiotic and material conditions that render online monetized experience possible (or not) and that cast users as complicit in a whole operation of multilayered damage—in terms of distribution of labor, resource extraction, and established narratives of progress and development. Indeed, we could argue that the political fiction of efficiency is resurfacing with a vengeance. In industrial terms, efficiency has been a core driver of technological progress and economic development. In essence, the value of efficiency applied to productivity translates into producing desired results with little, or no, wasting of time and material. Yet this historical quest for efficient productivity has broken the weak and precious balance that exists in all ecosystems. In his book *The Coal Question*, the English economist William Stanley Jevons (1865) described a paradox of efficiency, now commonly known as the Jevons Paradox. He observed that, contrary to common intuition, the technological progress that improved efficiency could not be relied upon to reduce fuel consumption (Jevons 1865). He argued that efficiency lowers the amount of resources and money needed to carry out a particular activity, however, this reduction in costs increases the rate of demand of the resources that were initially economized. Even though history has proven the Jevons Paradox right, it is still generally assumed that efficiency gains will lower the consumption of resources (Alcott et al. 2008). How is it possible that such an important premise, especially under a situation of climate emergency, has been erased from the social imagination?

The narrative of efficiency is deeply rooted and actively enacted in almost every aspect of our daily lives, but its paradox is not. The invention of the steam engine in 1712 came to be embraced by the scientific community as a metaphor to explain how things work; in other words, it allows us to understand the world as machine. Far from abandoning such a metaphor in the digital age, we have an increasing tendency to see the world as a well-engineered machine capable of producing increasingly smaller, lighter, and faster products and services. Thanks to the reductionist narrative of efficiency and the capitalist idea of progress, this is acknowledged in the culture of development seen as something good—while the material reality that allows these products and services to exist is ignored. Recognizing the Jevons Paradox would inevitably mean embracing complexity and including the fallacy of efficiency in the analytics of computerized relationalities—even when we do something as mundane as purchasing a book. In the contemporary planetary-scale networked society, where every tiny action activates a vast and uncontrollable number of interconnected but geographically displaced agents, acknowledging and embracing such complexity would mean reducing productivity and revenue, identifying damage along the multitudinous chains of supply and maintenance, and ultimately redistributing political and economic power. In that sense, collectively embracing the Jevons Paradox could potentially become a powerful political stance—a public commitment to balance and repair the profoundly asymmetrical distribution of energy, labor, and resources within global supply chains.

What we should also remember is that chains of production are always entwined with what Amaia Orozco (2007, 2) has described as "global chains of care." These are "chains of transnational dimensions that are formed with the objective of sustaining life on a daily basis, and in which households transfer care work from one to another based on axes of power, including gender, ethnicity, social class, and place of origin" (2). In the current landscape of environmental and social reproduction crisis, these chains of care are certainly thickened by, for example, the millions of micro-tasks involved in the maintenance of online platforms, and by the constant weeding, cleaning, and ordering of digital minutiae required for others to have a smooth online experience.

In the specific realm fabricated by Amazon, Moll's scroll aligns temporarily with Jevons to demand an attentive interface politics—in other words, a political engagement with the interface that continues to emerge for at least 14 minutes suspends the regime of efficiency. Something as simple as a page scroll invites attention to temporalities, technicalities, subjections, and discursive entanglements. The three vectors of Moll's artwork that inscribe the data of diverse powers (Mb, Wh, kcal) at the same time (conceptually) tilt the axis of the scroll obliquely, problematizing its linear ups and downs. The scroll works both as a logistic operation and as an active displacer of logics, unrolling the roughness of the 12 interfaces of a commercial exchange. Their transparent layers, which are cultural strata to sustain ongoing experience, become aesthetically opaque and ethically wrinkled.

The linearity of the scroll in Moll's work claims to be crooked, rotated, flipped, interlaced. In its coded disorientation, it asks: What transactions lie beneath, beyond, or behind the monumental source code of our banal shopping experiences? How many instances of capitalist turbouniversalism and technocolonialism are carried by this scrolling gesture? What are the nuances of totalitarian innovation (or what Donna Haraway[5] [1985] might refer to as the informatics of domination) brought about by this simple act? How can a tilted scroll—one that is oblique, nonobvious—provide us with an intersectional analytics of the multiple and hypercomputerized global chains of care, maintenance, extraction, and exploitation involved in the most mundane aspects of daily exchanges?

Conclusion

In *The Hidden Life of an Amazon User*, Moll underscores the need to add more friction (Tsing 2005) and density to the current technopolitical imagination, embodied in everyday relationships with technological devices and portrayed through simple performative gestures. such as the scroll, that activate digital services. Tilting the axis of the scroll implies considering how a "counterpolitical" scroll would operate. And for such a task, it is fundamental to challenge the GAFAM regime from a perspective of anticolonial and transfeminist intersectional analytics. The crisis of presence at the global chains of exploitation is already mundane: by user power wasted—or washed away—by a capitalist patriarchal-colonial matrix of woven and wefted infrastructures; by an infrastructure of damage arranged around supply chain events such as the domesticated labor production of microtaskers (or "Turkers"),[6] the offshore labor production of hardware assemblers; by the shipping routes that routinely trace the colonial scheme; by the waste around smelters and refiners erasing life all around; by the care workforce that shoulders all this productive weight. In sum, by a convergence of powers entwined in the project of massive extraction, growth, and control.

To continue with the urge for a denser and more complex technopolitical imagination, those global chains of care need to be scrolled up and down, sideways, and underneath. Scroll the chains away from the userized nonlife flows hidden by Amazon. Scroll the chains through to show their damage. Scroll the chains along to tilt forces and erase GAFAM & Co.'s efficient machinery. Scroll off the chains, and partially repair them through other computational geometries of relation (Snelting 2019).

Notes

1. One of this chapter's authors.

2. See https://www.janavirgin.com/AMZ.

3. Acronyms for the five biggest tech companies in the US (GAFAM: Google, Amazon, Facebook, Apple, Microsoft) and the four biggest in China (BATX: Baidu, Alibaba, Tencent, Xiaomi).

4. See https://www.aboutamazon.com/amazon-fulfillment/our-fulfillment-centers.

5. *Informatics of domination* is a term coined by Donna Haraway in "A Manifesto for Cyborgs" to refer to an emerging technosocial world order due to the transformation of power forms (Haraway 1985).

6. Mechanical Turk, as presented by Amazon, is "a crowdsourcing marketplace that makes it easier for individuals and businesses to outsource their processes and jobs to a distributed workforce who can perform these tasks virtually." Its motto is "Access a global, on-demand, 24×7 workforce." See https://www.mturk.com/.

References

Alcott, Blake, Mario Giampietro, Kozo Mayumi, and John Polimeni. 2008. *The Jevons Paradox and the Myth of Resource Efficiency Improvements*. London: Routledge.

Ali, Syed Mustafa. 2016. "A Brief Introduction to Decolonial Computing." *XRDS: Crossroads, the ACM Magazine for Students* 22 (4): 16–21.

Barriuso, Adela, and Antonio Torralba. 2012. "Notes on Image Annotation." Cornell University, October 12. https://arxiv.org/abs/1210.3448.

Federici, Silvia. 2009. "The Reproduction of Labour-Power in the Global Economy, Marxist Theory and the Unfinished Feminist Revolution." Presented at UC Santa Cruz seminar "The Crisis of Social Reproduction and Feminist Struggle," January 27. https://caringlabor.wordpress.com/2010/10/25/silvia-federici-the-reproduction-of-labour-power-in-the-global-economy-marxist-theory-and-the-unfinished-feminist-revolution/.

Federici, Silvia. 2012. *Revolution at Point Zero: Housework, Reproduction, and Feminist Struggle*. Oakland, CA: PM Press.

Haraway, Donna. 1985. "A Manifesto for Cyborgs: Science, Technology, and Socialist Feminism in the 1980s." *Socialist Review* 15 (80): 65–107.

Illich, Ivan. 1973. *Tools for Conviviality*. London: Calder and Boyars.

Illich, Ivan. 1974. *Energy and Equity*. London: Marion Boyars.

Jevons, William Stanley. 1865. *The Coal Question; An Inquiry Concerning the Progress of the Nation, and the Probable Exhaustion of Our Coal Mines*. London: Macmillan.

McAfee, Andrew, and Erik Brynjolfsson. 2017. *Machine, Platform, Crowd: Harnessing Our Digital Future*. New York: W. W. Norton.

Moll, Joana. n.d. *The Hidden Life of an Amazon User*. Joana Moll (website). Accessed January 22, 2020. https://www.janavirgin.com/AMZ/.

Orozco, Amaia. 2007. *Cadenas globales de cuidado* [Global chains of care]. Santo Domingo: Instituto Internacional de Investigaciones y Capacitación de las Naciones Unidas para la Promoción de la Mujer (INSTRAW). https://metgesdecatalunya.cat/uploaded/File/Documentacio/Cadenas_de_cuidado.pdf.

Pérez Orozco, Amaia. 2014. *Subversión feminista de la economía: aportes para un debate sobre el conflicto capital-vida* [Feminist subversion of the economy: Contributions to a debate on the capital-life conflict]. Madrid: Traficantes de Sueños.

Pérez Orozco, Amaia. 2016. "Global Care Chains: Reshaping the Hidden Foundations of an Unsustainable Development Model." In *Women Migrant Workers: Ethical, Political and Legal Problems*, edited by Zahra Meghani, 101–129. London: Routledge.

Premack, Rachel. 2018. "Jeff Bezos Said the 'Secret Sauce' to Amazon's Success Is an 'Obsessive Compulsive Focus' on Customer over Competitor." *Insider*, September 15. https://www.insider.com/amazon-jeff-bezos-success-customer-obsession-2018-9.

Rocha, Jara. n.d. "The Courier Bag Praxis of Friction." Joana Moll (website). Accessed May 22, 2020. https://www.janavirgin.com/AMZ/rocha.html.

Snelting, Femke. 2019. "Other Geometries." *Transmediale* (3). https://transmediale.de/content /other-geometries.

Srnicek, Nick. 2016. *Platform Capitalism*. Cambridge: Polity Press.

Tsing, Anna Lowenhaupt. 2005. *Friction: An Ethnography of Global Connection*. Princeton, NJ: Princeton University Press.

Waring, Marilyn. 1999. *Counting for Nothing: What Men Value and What Women Are Worth*. Toronto: University of Toronto Press.

Weatherby, Leif. 2018. "Delete Your Account: On the Theory of Platform Capitalism." *Los Angeles Review of Books*, October 24.

Yusoff, Kathryn. 2018. *A Billion Black Anthropocenes or None*. Minneapolis: University of Minnesota Press.

Contributors

Sana Ahmad, WZB Berlin Social Science Center, Weizenbaum Institute, Free University Berlin

Payal Arora, Erasmus University Rotterdam

Janine Berg, International Labour Organization (ILO)

Antonio A. Casilli, Télécom Paris

Julie Chen, University of Toronto

Christina J. Colclough, the Why Not Lab

Fabian Ferrari, University of Oxford

Mark Graham, University of Oxford and the Alan Turing Institute

Andreas Hackl, University of Edinburgh

Matthew Hockenberry, Fordham University

Hannah Johnston, Northeastern University

Martin Krzywdzinski, WZB Berlin Social Science Center, Weizenbaum Institute, Helmut Schmidt University

Johan Lindquist, Stockholm University

Joana Moll, Independent Artist and Researcher

Brett Neilson, Western Sydney University

Usha Raman, University of Hyderabad

Jara Rocha, Independent Researcher and Artist

Jathan Sadowski, Monash University

Florian A. Schmidt, University of Applied Sciences HTW Dresden

Cheryll Ruth Soriano, De La Salle University

Nick Srnicek, King's College London

James Steinhoff, University of Washington

JS Tan, Massachusetts Institute of Technology

Paola Tubaro, National Center for Scientific Research (CNRS)

Moira Weigel, Northeastern University

Lin Zhang, University of New Hampshire

Index

Note: Figures and tables are indicated by "f" and "t" respectively, following page numbers.

China (cont.)
  modernization in, 9
  nationalism in, 196–197
  Philippines and, 14–15, 41–42, 45–46, 49–55,
    51t
  platform economy in, 43–45
  politics in, 27–31, 33
  research from, 92n11
  ride-hailing market in, 50–51
  rural culture in, 39n3
  Rwanda and, 127
  Shanzhai for, 31–34, 35f, 36–37
  social media in, 84–85
  taxi industry in, 70
  tech workers in, 212–213
  TVEs in, 27–28, 39n6
  for TWC, 210
  US and, 7, 12, 131–132, 192, 210, 215–219,
    222–224
Chumley, Lily, 32
Clark, Jack, 255n5
Class politics, 221–222
Clickworker, 180
Clients, 46–48
Clouds
  for Alibaba, 121–124
  for Amazon, 198
  for APIs, 200
  compute for, 255n6
  containerization for, 255n4
  for cyberspace, 8
  for freelancers, 157–158, 169–170
  for geography, 17n3
  for storage, 244
Clustering, 10–11
Code farmers, 215–219
Cognitive human labor, 10, 14
Colonialism, 122–123
Commodification, 11–13
Commodities, 192–193
Communication, 3
Communism, 33–34
Communities of practice, 49–53, 51t

Competition
  in globalization, 13–15, 291–292
  for Google, 250–251
  for platforms, 30–31
  portfolios for, 46–47
  for Silicon Valley, 31–32
Compute, 241–242, 249–255, 255n6
Conjunctural geographies, 8–9
Consumers
  of digital platforms, 304, 320
  privacy for, 185–187, 296
  of technology, 244–245
  of Uber, 263
Containerization, 255n4
Content moderation
  agency in, 88–90
  GVCs for, 80–81
  history of, 78–79
  in India, 77–78, 83–85, 91–92
  labor process approach for, 79–81, 80f, 85–88
  news for, 87–88
  psychology of, 87–88
  research on, 81–83
  suppliers, 84, 92n9
  training for, 93n13
Content operators, 83
Content writing, 67
Copyright/patent systems, 28
Cottage industries, 69–70
COVID-19 pandemic, 198
  for culture, 299–300
  economy during, 201
  for globalization, 224
  for government, 312
  for ILO, 297
  labor markets during, 199
  poverty with, 313
  for refugees, 100, 102–103
  for work culture, 291
Cowen, Deborah, 271
Crime, 151–152
CrowdFlower, 143
Crowd Guru, 139, 149